400 Years:

Anglican/Episcopal Mission
Among American Indians

400 YEARS:
Anglican/Episcopal Mission Among American Indians

OWANAH ANDERSON

Forward Movement Publications
Cincinnati, Ohio

Cover Photos

Front cover—Bishop Theodore P. Thurston, Oklahoma's
bishop from 1919-1927 with Cheyenne mother and child.
Courtesy, St. Paul's Episcopal Church, Minneapolis.

Back cover—Christ Church, Anvik, the first mission in Alaska.
Courtesy, Archives of the Diocese of Alaska.

Author Owanah Anderson (Choctaw).

Forward Movement Publications
412 Sycamore Street
Cincinnati, Ohio 45202

To the memory of a serene and beautiful woman

Samantha Jones,
my mother

CONTENTS

Foreword vii

Preface ix

1 – Colonial Efforts to Introduce Anglican "Christian Civility" 1

2 – The Anglican/Episcopal Church and
the Great Iroquois Confederacy 17

3 – Minnesota: Well-Spring of Work in the West 45

4 – Niobrara: The Great Sioux Nation 81

5 – The North Dakota Mission 129

6 – Oklahoma: Too Late with Too Little! 145

7 – The Episcopal Church in Navajoland 171

8 – Episcopal Work in the Mountains and Desert 223

9 – The Episcopal Church's First 100 Years in Alaska 249

10 – Indians in the Cities 283

11 – Twentieth Century Southern Revival 301

12 – From Survival to Self-Determination:
The Last Half of the 20th Century 311

Appendix A
Chronology of Anglican/Episcopal Mission to
Native Americans in the United States 345

Appendix B
A Survey of Native American Episcopal Ministry: 1997 355

Appendix C
Episcopal Council of Indian Ministries 361

Appendix D
    Statement of Self-Determination 365

Selected Bibliography 367

About the Author 381

Index 383

FOREWORD

Dr. Owanah Anderson's original work, *Jamestown Commitment,* is something of a small classic for those interested in the historical relationship between America's indigenous people and the Episcopal Church. It is one of the clearest, most concise studies ever done on this long neglected subject.

Now, with her new work, *400 Years: Anglican/Episcopal Mission among American Indians*, Dr. Anderson improves on the original with fresh research and insights. With her wonderful story-telling style, she traces the complex history of the American Indian/Native Alaskan communities as they encountered the Anglican Communion over many generations across the North American continent.

Here are historical facts brought to life with the every human nuance that Dr. Anderson captures on almost every page. This is not the dry stuff of purely academic history, but the personal story of a cross-cultural dialogue that has gone on for centuries. The people, places, and emotions of a Christian community coming into being and changing the world around it are all intimate parts of *400 Years: Anglican/Episcopal Mission among American Indians*. This work helps us to understand the true nature of evangelism that is of such vital importance to the contemporary church. Looking back over the experience of American Indian/Native Alaskan people, we learn both what has served the church well, and what we ought to avoid in future mission exchanges with those of different cultures.

Perhaps in the years to come others may try to tell this story. If they do, they will have a firm foundation on which to build with Dr. Anderson's pioneering work. She has given us all a gift. It is the gift of revealing our past so that we might more fully comprehend our future. Few scholars have done more.

+Steven Charleston
Former Bishop of Alaska

PREFACE

Episcopal native peoples from 26 dioceses assembled in the season of Epiphany 1995 for the seventh annual Winter Talk in the Seminole Nation of Oklahoma and proclaimed their God-given right to determine their own destiny, under guidance of the Holy Spirit, as free and equal members of the Episcopal Church and the Anglican Communion.

Additionally, the assembled from 22 tribes affixed their signatures to a "Statement of Self-Determination" affirming native religious practices by proclaiming, "We respect the spiritual traditions, values and customs of our many peoples, and we incorporate them as we celebrate the Gospel of Jesus Christ." Such a statement would have been denounced as unlawful, if not heretical, as recently as the early 1900s.

From the legacy of "ecclesial colonialism"—during which missionaries denounced all aspects of native spirituality, and then denied converted native communities the freedom to shape their own churches in response to the Gospel—to a declaration of self-determination has indeed been an arduous journey covering 400 years.

This book undertakes the awesome task of telling the story of those 400 years. I seek to share the stories that I have unearthed in the brittle fading pages of old journals which bespeak the Anglican/Episcopal impact on the lives of the indigenous peoples of present-day United States.

Further, I seek, as a Choctaw Episcopalian, to call the Episcopal Church to its inherited commitment, a commitment set in motion by monarchs of England 400 years ago when Elizabeth I deemed it probable that God reserved indigenous people "to be introduced into Christian civility by the English nation." As both the old millennium and the tenure of a responsive Primate come to a close, the Church is challenged to take cognizance of the fact that indigenous people globally are demanding a true and equal partnership within the Christian churches.

In 1987 I published a small book entitled *Jamestown Commitment*, a sparse survey of Anglican/Episcopal mission among American Indians. Unprecedented changes in Indian ministry happened since the summer of 1987. Three new Indian bishops—a Navajo, a Choctaw, and a Dakota—have entered the House of Bishops. New training models have been launched; new networks have been established, including the Anglican Indigenous Network, banding together native peoples of Australia, Canada, Aotearoa (New Zealand) and Hawaii with American Indians. New annual consultations have blossomed, including Winter Talk, Paths Crossing and an urban coalition. New leaders have surfaced; new worshiping communities have sprung up.

The major transformation in Indian ministry had been the birth, in 1989, of a new national native ministry configuration: Episcopal Council of Indian Ministry (ECIM), which placed Indian leadership at the helm to allocate national church funding for native work within dioceses and to design programs to meet our needs—needs as we define them. The umbrella, predominantly Indian organization with far-reaching responsibilities, was designed by a predominantly Indian task force, adopted by Executive Council in 1989 and affirmed at the 70th General Convention in 1991, only to be targeted for demise in sweeping budget cuts in 1994. A sorely weakened ECIM managed to survive the Indianapolis General Convention, but Indian leaders pondered their potential as prey at the Philadelphia Convention in the summer of 1997.

In addition to the updating factor, this work fills in many gaps left untended by *Jamestown Commitment*. While a substantial amount of material in this work was included in the previous story of the Episcopal Church's mission among us, much new material has been gathered, often out of the generosity of individuals such as the retired Alaskan priest, Norman Elliott, esteemed scholar and venerable wit, who bundled up fading papers from years of research and mailed them to me in New York. A retired Canadian priest volunteered the answer to what happened to the communion silver that Queen Anne sent to the Mohawks in 1712. Others have come forward with generous gifts of stories. The Rev. Mark MacDonald shared a real treasure which by happenstance came into his possession. It was a 1954 manuscript, *The Good Shepherd Mission to the Navajo,* written by Archdeacon J. Rockwood Jenkins (retired, Arizona), who served as interim vicar at Good Shepherd in the summer of 1929. The archdeacon was 85 when he completed the manuscript, tediously typed in all capitals, elite-face and single-spaced.

Much of our story is yet missing. American Indians were not writing the chronicles during the westward movement. Records of ministry among Indians have generally been ill-kept and poorly chronicled in the obvious places such as archives and libraries. Stories of Indians in the role of significant evangelization of other Indians have been virtually hidden away. The scant materials available were unthinkably condescending. In one official Episcopal publication I discovered the Cheyenne saint, David Oakerhater, described as a boy when he was at least 35 years old, and I observed that Enmegahbowh, the first Indian priest, was dismissed with a scant mention. Reports in the old Episcopal periodical, *The Spirit of Missions,* were written in a perspective loathsome to a contemporary Indian person. In tedious research through 124 volumes of the passé periodical, dating from 1836 to 1959, I found it necessary at times to close the crumbling pages and walk away, questioning my own commitment to an institution whose history, as reflected in the language of its old publications, was so brazenly disparaging and patronizing. Then I would remind myself of lines of Herman Melville asserting that "Missionary undertaking—however blessed in Heaven—is in itself but human, and subject like everything else to frailty and abuse." So, I resumed research.

It has never been my purpose to recite a litany of old grievances on Indian/white relations over the centuries; other Indian writers have ably addressed this protest. While I did not set out to unmask the myths surrounding Church heroes such as William Hobart Hare or Henry Benjamin Whipple, my views simply do not parallel the views of non-native chroniclers of the past. Thus, in sketching our church's missionizing history among my people, I cannot with integrity avoid at times a confrontational posture. Racism and neglect have endured. Paternalism was indeed a burden.

John Steinbeck wrote fifty years ago, "The Indian survived our intention of wiping them out, and since the tide turned they have even weathered our good intentions toward them, which can be much more deadly."

In the last seven years of intermittent research, I made one surprising discovery, a discovery which my Indian activist contemporaries have overlooked as they have censured Christian churches for having robbed us of our traditional religions. With astonishing frequency missionaries were invited by tribal leaders to "come you, come and teach." Those were the exact words of Enmegahbowh, the Ottawa, pleading for an Episcopal missionary to come to Minnesota Territory. Then there was the persistent Chippewa, Rising Sun, who pounded on Episcopal doors for 15 years petitioning for a missionary. Among my own people, the Choctaw, it appears that there was an early recognition that the white man's education was essential to survival, and missionaries were welcomed, not so much for salvation of the soul, but for literacy in the language of the people who were infringing upon our homeland in a never-ending flow.

I extend very special appreciation to several authors for permission to quote most liberally from their publications: Virginia Driving Hawk Sneve for *That They May Have Life: The Episcopal Church in South Dakota, 1859-1976*, and for the Alaska section, my appreciation to Tay Thomas for *Cry in the Wilderness* and *An Angel on His Wing*. My appreciation as well to the Rev. Sidney H. Bird for material shared on Wounded Knee of 1890; to General George Pierce, Church Army (retired), for on-site insight on Wounded Knee II; to Joan Liebler for sharing materials and memory of Father H. Baxter Liebler; to Vine Deloria Jr., for sharing treasured photographs; to Betty Clark Rosenthal, now of Santa Fe, who shared her experiences of the 1960s and family memories of generations in Episcopal Indian ministry; and to a colleague, Jim Solheim, for editing assistance.

I acknowledge with much appreciation members of ECIM and the many other Indians and non-Indians who encouraged and championed, challenged and cajoled me toward completing this work and especially to Steve Charleston, Ginny Doctor, Mark MacDonald, Howard Anderson, Bill Wantland and Helen Peterson, my mentor. And, lastly, my deep appreciation goes to Edmond Browning who championed our right to try our wings.

Owanah Anderson, Choctaw
New York City
Epiphany 1997

1

COLONIAL EFFORTS TO INTRODUCE ANGLICAN "CHRISTIAN CIVILITY"

Manteo, a well-traveled chieftain from Roanoke Island, was the first aboriginal convert into the Church of England. It is recorded that "Manteo was on the 13th of August, 1587, admitted to Christ's Church by Holy Baptism."

Four hundred years ago, as the 16th century drew to a close, Elizabeth I was securely on the throne, the spirit of adventure in England was rife, and the zeal for evangelization of the heathen beyond the sea animated the English Church and realm. The queen herself propelled the Church of England's first evangelism effort when she dispatched the first would-be settlers off to the new world with a regal admonition:

> ... the honor of God and his compassion for the poor infidels, it seeming probable that God hath reserved these Gentiles to be introduced into Christian civility by the English nation.

Manteo had first encountered Englishmen three years previously when he met with a band of English explorers sent out by Sir Walter Raleigh to scout out a suitable location for a permanent English colony. The explorers described the area at the entrance of Albermarle Sound as flourishing with ". . . the most plentiful, sweet, fruitful, and wholesome of all the world; unspoiled natives such as live after the manner of the golden age . . ."

Manteo and a companion, Wanchese, were kidnapped by the scouting party and transported back to England. Spurred by the favorable reports of the exploring party, the following year, 107 men, women and children sailed from Plymouth on Good Friday, 1585. Sir

Walter, the queen's then-favorite courtier, waved the settlers off as they transported his gift of 100 pounds sterling to be applied in planting the Christian religion, and advancing the same. Thus, it was Sir Walter Raleigh who provided the first Anglican gift of record for evangelizing the American shores.

The ill-fated settlers landed on Roanoke, a swampy inhospitable island on present-day North Carolina's Outer Banks. History is silent on the immediate fate of Manteo after he was whisked away to London. He is next glimpsed two years later back on Roanoke Island on the occasion of his baptism, after which he was honored with the resounding title of Lord of Roanoke and Dasmonguepeuk. This first ecclesiastical act of record was followed one week later with the christening of Virginia Dare, the first English child born in America.

Having claim to being the first English missionary to the Indians is Thomas Heriot, the mathematician, who spent a year at the Roanoke settlement. He is best remembered, however, as inventor of the system of notation used in modern algebra. While at Roanoke, Heriot roamed the vicinity making careful notes on vegetation, including the potato and the "many and rare virtues" of the tobacco plant. His notes, preserved by the Rev. Richard Hakluyt, prebendary of Westminster, tell of Heriot's travels to Indian villages where he told the natives as best he could of the doctrine of salvation through Christ.

Manteo is again briefly sighted a few years later, hitching a ride with the old seadog, Sir Francis Drake, who stopped by Roanoke after one of his raids in the Spanish West Indies. Wanchese, the second native hostage, displayed everlasting hostility toward the colonists and registered no interest in their religion.

The ill-fated Roanoke Colony, established at the height of the reign of Elizabeth, was abandoned for three years while England faced the Spanish Armada. When the supply ships finally returned, the settlement had vanished. The single clue, carved on a tree, was the word "Croatoan," the Indian name for the nearby island on which Cape Hatteras is located and the place where Manteo was born. A century later, Hatteras Indians of the Croatoan area were "wont to tell that several of their ancestors were white people, and the truth of which may be affirmed by gray eyes being frequently found among these Indians." Forty thousand Lumbee Indians, today living in rural North Carolina, allude to descent from the Lost Colony settlers.

Thomas Heriot was not the first Englishmen to preach to the native peoples of the Americas. Under the unlikely auspices of Sir Francis Drake, the "freebooter," native peoples of the western hemisphere in 1579—on or about St. John the Baptist's Day—first heard the gospel preached by clergy of the Church of England. It occurred not along the eastern seaboard, so closely identified with Anglican influence, but at a "fir and good ba" on the mist-shrouded coast of Northern California. Drake's chaplain, the Rev. Francis Fletcher, held services for the ship's crew, and history provides a fleeting glimpse of "a large company of Indians gathered to see the newcomers."

William Stevens Perry, Bishop of Iowa, in 1885 produced a two-volume work, *The History of the American Episcopal Church: 1587-1882*. He described the Drake encounter:

> In the presence of the aborigines of this distant land, these rough sailors, who scrupled not to plunder or murder every Spaniard they met, lifted their eyes and hands to heaven, to indicate by these symbolic gestures that God is over all; and then, following their chaplain's lead, they besought their God, in the Church's prayers, to reveal himself to these idolaters and to open their blinded eyes to the knowledge of Him and of Jesus Christ, the salvation of the Gentiles.

Spain's Incursion

When European explorers, adventurers and missionaries arrived on the shores of what would become the continental United States of America there were at least 300 different functioning societies of native peoples, each speaking distinctively different languages and each with different cultures, histories and relationships with a Creator. Scholars disagree widely on estimates on the pre-Columbian total population, but the figure more recently accepted has been 112 million in the hemisphere with 18 million in the northern hemisphere. By 1892, four hundred years later, only a quarter of a million American Indians had survived in the contiguous states.

Though European sovereigns stoutly stated intentions "to gather millions of wandering heathen souls into the fold of Christ," for 45 years after the "discovery" of America theological debate raged across Europe as to whether Indians were indeed human. It was questioned whether, if Indians were unknown to biblical and classical authorities, they were part of the human race at all. It was not until 1537 that Pope Paul III issued a papal bull declaring that Indians were indeed "true men."

Timing of the "age of discovery" could not have been worse from the vantage point of native peoples of the western world. Political strife colored the whole of Europe and conflicts depleted royal treasuries. Protestants were leaving the Roman Church in large numbers. Spain, upon at last throwing off the yoke of Moorish domination after almost eight centuries, speedily embarked into the odious era of inquisition, and anyone who did not readily profess catholicism was automatically considered to be less than human.

Conversion of the natives was declared to be the prime objective of the second voyage of Christopher Columbus. Six priests were sent along to accomplish it. However, the second voyage, in 1494, also established a colony on the island of Hispaniola, and within two short decades enslaved Indians were working the Spanish mines and plantations and dying by the thousands. They were the same people who had so innocently welcomed Columbus in 1492.

Spanish evangelization tactics have been widely recorded. One case study, however, demands repeating. Hatuay, a *cacique* (ruler) on the island of Hispaniola, fled his homeland in 1511 to escape Spanish enslavement. He and his family were successful in reaching Cuba, but the Spanish soon captured him and sentenced him to be burned alive at the stake for the crime of "refusing to convert to Christianity." As Hatuay stood bound to the stake, a Franciscan friar described the eternal torment of hell and offered Hatuay one last opportunity for everlasting bliss. Hatuay inquired if there were Spaniards in heaven. After receiving an answer in the affirmative, Hatuay chose the stake, saying, "I will not go to a place where I may meet with one of that accursed race!"

By 1515 the native population on the fertile island of Hispaniola had shrunk from an estimated quarter of a million to around 14,000, and in a few more years, the native population would be extinct.

It was a wealthy Dominican friar who was among the first to accept as a religious duty influencing the Spanish government to amend its cruel and inhuman treatment of the native peoples. He was Bartholomew de las Casas, born in Seville. He journeyed to America in 1502 and took holy orders in 1510 to become the first Roman Catholic priest to be ordained in the new world. He was appalled by the exploitation of the Indians and labored through his long life to ameliorate the situation. He was also a historian and left behind insightful observations:

> God created these simple people without evil and without guile. They are most submissive, patient, peaceful and virtuous. Nor are they quarrelsome, rancorous, querulous, or vengeful. Moreover they are more delicate than princes and die easily from work or illness. They neither possess nor desire to possess worldly wealth. Surely these people

would be the most blessed in the world if only they worshiped the true God.

By the early 1600s Spain was engaged in planting Christianity among the Pueblo Indians of the present-day southwest United States. In generations to come other European nations, while seeking to reap the riches of the New World, would simultaneously seek to implant the gospel of Christ. Holland spread limited numbers of Dutch Reformed native converts through southern New England, while Swedish missionaries founded Lutheran Indian settlements outward from Delaware Bay after 1638. Much later, Russian fur expeditions sprinkled Orthodox missions along the west coast during the Russian imperial expansion.

Early French colonizing efforts were sporadic; missionizing efforts were primarily among the nations of the powerful Iroquois Confederacy in the present state of New York. There had been in 1562 an unsuccessful effort to establish a colony of French Huguenots along the coast of South Carolina, but previous encounters with the Spanish made the Indians afraid and unaccepting. The French influence among the Iroquois left a tangled skein to be dealt with in several ensuing colonial wars. It has been said that had not the Iroquois sided with the British crown, we all might be speaking French today.

Jamestown Settlement

In April, 1607, the month of white dogwood blossoms in the luxuriant forests along the Chesapeake Bay of present-day Virginia, three sailing ships anchored at the mouth of the James River and Englishmen waded onto a marshy malarial swamp to establish the first permanent English settlement on the North American continent. These Englishmen—104 colonists—carried with them a royal decree signed and sealed by King James I of England expressly stipulating:

> . . . the true word of God be preached, planted and used not only in the colonies, but also as much as might be, among the savages bordering upon them, and this according to the rites and doctrines of the Church of England.

The Jamestown party, accompanied by Robert Hunt, a clergyman and one of the original petitioners for the charter, celebrated the first Eucharist on the soil of Virginia on the day of landing. The first report sent back to England described flowers of diverse colors and fine and beautiful strawberries "four times bigger and better than ours in England." A report dated Whitsunday, May 24, informs of "kindly intercourse with the savages at a banquet to which their chieftain, Powhatan, had been an invited guest." A description of the people in this very early account attests to a fleeting recognition of the Indians' spirituality:

> ... I find they account after death to goe into another world, pointing eastward ... To conclude, they are a very witty and ingenious people, apt both to understand and speake our language. So that I hope in God, as he hath miraculously preserved us from all daungers both of sea and land and their fury, so he will make us authors of his holy will in converting them to our true Christian faith.

The best remembered convert of the Jamestown settlement was the chieftain's daughter, Pocahontas. The romanticized story of her interceding on behalf of Captain John Smith needs no retelling. Powhatan was chief of a strong confederacy of the James River tribes and only by the grace of the Indians did the colony survive. Neglecting corn-planting the first season, the English would have starved had it not been for the support of the Indians. During those first crucial years, Powhatan, at any chosen time, could have wiped away the English settlement. Afterward, more English arrived and seized more land, giving rise to friction, and the Indians decided too late to sweep away the white intruders.

The "Princess" Pocahontas—the English penchant for superimposing trappings of European nobility surfaced early—was being held hostage aboard an English ship at anchor in the James River at the time she was admitted to Holy Baptism. "Foure honest and learned Ministers," among them Alexander Whitaker, had arrived in the colony in May, 1611. According to Bishop Perry's research, Whitaker, accorded the title of "Apostle of Virginia," prepared Pocahontas for Holy Baptism, whereupon she took the name of Rebecca:

> Detained, with a view to secure from her father the return of men and stores which he had in possession, Pocahontas learned to love her captors ... [she] renounced publickly her countrey Idolatry [and] was as she desired baptized.

Her marriage to the widower John Rolfe, who originated the tobacco industry, was solemnized in the little church at Jamestown. Members of her family present included two brothers and an uncle. The date of her marriage, April 1, 1613, has puzzled scholars, considering the church's aversion to weddings during Lent. The first day of April in 1613 was Maundy Thursday. Three years later, Pocahontas accompanied her husband to England where she was received, under the name of Lady

Rebecca, in pomp and state, by King James, his queen, and the Bishop of London. As she prepared to return to Virginia with her husband and infant son, she died of smallpox at age 21. The poignant Pocahontas ". . . came to Grauesend, to her end and graue."

While the Pocahontas-Rolfe union is among the best remembered events of the Jamestown Settlement, it is interesting to note that one William Symonds in a sermon delivered in 1609 at St. Savior's, Southwark, threatened the wrath of God upon any Englishman who might take an Indian maid as his wife.

The Symonds sermon, along with several pontifical discourses of other clergy back in England, has been preserved in tracts circulated for the purpose of gaining financial support for the colony. These tracts, rife with anti-Roman bias, underscore a mission to establish a protestant "bulwark against the Papists." There is assertion that "the eyes of all Europe are looking upon our endeavors to spread the Gospel among the heathen people of Virginia."

This mission, however, seems propelled more by greed than grace. Robert Gray voiced a position that the settlers should consider it their divine right to "caste out the Canaanites." God gave the Englishmen Virginia; let them take it. Gray did, however, reason that it was better to convert the heathen than put him to the sword, "if the land can then be taken peaceably."

In 1619 the first legislative assembly of American colonists met in the "Quire of the Church in James City" and set forth a brief declaration of purpose to include "Conversion of the Savages." Out of this assembly came specific directions for establishment of a "University and College" for the sons of settlers and for the education of Indian children. Sir Edwyn Sandys, treasurer for the Virginia Company, was instrumental in setting aside a vast land grant for Henrico College for the "education of the children of the Barbarian." A fund-raising drive was mounted in England; the Bishop of London collected a thousand pounds toward Henrico College. However, by 1622, a new trend would emerge which precluded further efforts toward either education or conversion of the aborigines. The year 1622 brought the Indian "uprising." Thenceforth, Indian policy of the Virginians would be extermination. Bishop Perry's account of the 1622 event contains this interesting addendum:

> . . . the Massacre would have been complete had it not been for a Christian Indian named Chanco. Solicited the night before the outbreak by his own brother to engage in the fiendish plot, the faithful convert found means to acquaint his master with the impending danger.

So, the University of Henrico was never to be built and the clergy and colonists in Virginia "lost heart with respect to the advancement of Christian education, or the bringing of the natives to the faith and Church of Christ." Years would elapse before any attempt would be renewed.

Three men came upon the scene whose endeavors would influence relations between the Anglican Church and American Indians. They were James Blair, a Scotsman by birth, who was instrumental in founding the College of William and Mary (1693) and served as its first president; Thomas Boyle, an Irish philanthropist and scientist who displayed a lifelong interest in the conversion of the American aborigines and left a legacy for instruction of Indians at the college; and Thomas Bray, who in 1701 founded the Society for the Propagation of the Gospel in Foreign Parts (SPG), which would have a major role in missionizing American Indians during the colonial period.

In 1710 Robert Hicks and John Evans were sent as agents of Boyle's legacy, to try to obtain nine or ten children for instruction. The agents were instructed to assure the Indians that the children would be clothed and well treated, and that their parents might visit them whenever they wished. It was further suggested that the "students should also have an Indian man with them, to wait upon them and talk with them in Indian, so they would not forget the language of their people while they were at the College." These provisions show a more intelligent approach to the Indian problem than was generally made by colonial officials, but it cannot be said that the Indians received the offer with enthusiasm. Their family feeling was strong, they were suspicious of the English, and they were not particularly hospitable to English culture.

Alexander Spottswood was appointed Governor of Virginia in 1706 and demonstrated an uncommon interest in conversion of the Indians, personally visiting both nearby and certain remote tribes, seeking to persuade them to send children to the college. In 1712 he reported there were 14 Indians attending and that he expected six more from neighboring tribes. He also established a preparatory school for them at his own expense. In 1716 the governor sent the Rev. Charles Griffin to the frontier, chiefly to work among the Indians. In only a short time Griffin had opened a school and assembled 70 pupils. He reported they had learned "the Creed, the Lord's Prayer, the Ten Commandments, the existence of but one God." He further reported that his pupils "behaved reverently at prayers and were able to make responses."

This report marked the high point in the history of Virginia's Indian missionizing effort.

One illustrative story out of the Colonial period, which today's Indian scholars relish telling, concerns a generous bequest left to William and Mary College by a wealthy member of the Virginia gentry for the purpose of educating Indians. The William and Mary trustees set out recruiting; the distant Seneca of the North were contacted and offered a William and Mary education for six of their young men. The Seneca chiefs replied with a masterful, yet-quoted message which underscores yet-relevant cultural values:

> We know that you highly esteem the kind of learning taught in those colleges. But, you who are wise must know that the different nations have different conceptions of things; and you will not, therefore, take it amiss if our ideas of this kind of education happen not to be the same with yours.
>
> Several of our young men were formerly brought up at the colleges of the Northern provinces; they were instructed in all your sciences; but when they came back to us they were bad runners, ignorant of every means of living in the woods, unable to bear either cold or hunger, knew neither how to build a cabin, take a deer or kill an enemy; spoke our language imperfectly—they were, therefore, neither fit for hunters, warriors nor counselors. They were totally good for nothing.
>
> We are, therefore, not the less obliged by your kind offer, though we decline the accepting of it; and, to show our grateful sense of it, if the gentlemen of Virginia will send us a dozen of their sons, we will take care to their education, instruct them in all that we know, and make men of them.

Other Anglican Colonial Missionizing Efforts

In 1724, the Bishop of London, Edmund Gibbon, asked a question which paralleled the question that the Presiding Bishop of the Episcopal Church, Edmond Browning, asked 267 years later at the 70th General Convention of the Episcopal Church. The question dealt with racism.

The Bishop of London, who by custom held jurisdiction over the American colonies, asked of his colonial ministers: How many infidels, bond and free, are there in your parish? Responses to this, the first racism audit, were disconcerting indeed.

The colonial Anglican Church—with the decided exception of New

York—for the most part was indifferent to conversion of people of color, either of Indians who were found upon the continent or of the Negroes who were brought in bondage to it. A bland admission to the lack of response to the Great Command is found in *Indian Tribes and Missions: A Handbook of Early Missionary Efforts,* published in 1925 by Church Missions Publishing Company, Hartford, Connecticut. Though the prevailing obdurate tone of the work is unacceptable to 20th century American Indians, this Episcopal publication confesses the sin of omission thusly:

> As a rule, the Indian was left to be the prey of the trader and adventurer, and to learn the vices, and not the virtues, of the race which drove him further and further into the wilderness, and took possession of his lands, sometimes by purchase and more often by conquest.

Paying certain heed to the charter establishing the colony, Virginia had made some early efforts but by 1724 interest in Indians, except as potential enemies, died with Governor Spottswood's retirement. Scant more is reported on Indians at William and Mary College; by then Europeans were no longer a minority along the eastern seaboard. The college prospered through educating sons of planters who disdained associating on terms of equality with the aborigines.

In South Carolina there was considerable talk about sharing the gospel with Indians but little done about it. The Spaniards had earlier attempted to christianize the Yamassee Indians and later, in 1662, French Huguenots attempted to bring a mission. But when the SPG sent Samuel Thomas to minister to the Yamassee he reported they "were reverting to heathenism." Governor Johnson then ordered Thomas to go to Goose Creek Parish to instruct slaves. Thomas' successor at the Yamassee station, the devoted Francis Le Jau, was a man generations ahead of his time in attitude toward Indians. He endeavored conscientiously to understand and appreciate their ideas and standards, writing:

> They do make us ashamed by their life, conversation, and sense of religion quite different from ours. Ours consists in words and appearances; theirs in reality . . .

Le Jau, who later did more than any minister of the colonies toward conversion of black slaves, stated that he believed that the chief obstacle to conversion of Indians was the manner in which the Indian trade was carried on, as it consisted chiefly in fomenting wars among them for the purpose of getting slaves.

In 1714 a resident of the South Carolina colony wrote to a friend of the Society that "he had a son whom he designed for the ministry and that he proposed sending him among a neighboring tribe of Yamassees to learn the language and instruct them in Christianity." Nothing more is reported on the project. In 1715 the Yamassees revolted against English authority and the colony was exposed to terrors of an Indian war.

However, in 1723 Francis Varnod, the missionary at Dorchester, South Carolina, wrote to the SPG secretary that he thought conversion of the Indians a practicable object and suggested sending a discreet young man in deacon's orders to live among them. Like Le Jau, he had formed a good opinion of the Indian character:

> I find that these poor pagans are endued with very good natural parts, of a temper very sedate and tranquil . . .

Again, however, the matter ended in mere suggestion.

North Carolina in 1714 had Giles Rainsford, one of the SPG missionaries spend a few months among the Indians there and obtain some knowledge of their language. He then offered himself as minister at an Indian settlement but plans never matured and Rainsford sought employment elsewhere. By 1722, a North Carolina missionary reported that the Indians of the colony had been reduced to 300 fighting men.

In Maryland, in response to Bishop Gibson's questions, nothing was done for the Indians because "their language was unintelligible, and they were hostile to Christianity anyway."

In Georgia a missionary, Thomas Bosomworth, in 1747 married one of the most colorful women of the time—a Creek woman known as "Creek Mary," influential with her tribesmen to such an extraordinary extent that it was claimed that only she could keep the peace between the colonists and the Creeks. She would eventually become the largest single landholder in Georgia. As a child, Mary had been sent to live among the whites in present-day Charleston, South Carolina, and attended an English school and was baptized in an Anglican church. Before Bosomworth, Mary had been twice widowed and had learned skills as a trader as well as a peace-keeper. Soon after marrying the missionary, Mary and her new husband challenged the British Crown over Mary's land claim of thousands of square miles along the Savannah River, conveyed to her by her Creek kin. The claim, based on the traditional Creek matrilineage which bestowed property rights to women as opposed to the English presumption of male authority, dragged on for a dozen years, eventually being adjudicated in London. However when Mary died her land holdings passed not to her female relatives under Creek traditional practice, but to her white husband under British law. The missionary's demeanor won no Creek converts.

Shortly before the American Revolution Samuel Frink, the minister at Augusta, made some effort to convert the Chickasaw Indians but without success. He subsequently observed that he thought it desirable to reclaim the white people of the colony first as he found them "almost as destitute of any sense of religion as the Indians themselves."

The story was the same further up the coast: in Pennsylvania, the only attempt of the Anglican Church to convert the Indians seems to have been that made by Thomas Barton on his first coming into the western countries. He had hopes of succeeding in the endeavor, but they were dashed in the French and Indian wars which alienated the Indians from the English.

New England Obstinacy

Charters for establishment of the New England colonies of the Separatists (Pilgrims and Puritans) were virtual replicas of the Jamestown Charter, specifying evangelization of the Indian as a principal purpose. A difference, however, was that the New England colonies would shortly set out with zeal and fervor to bring the gospel, and they determined early the pattern and policy by which the gospel would be brought.

Ethnocentrism was crystallized in the efforts of the Puritan, John Eliot, who came to be known as the "Apostle to the Indians." The Roxbury minister brought the conviction that it was essential to "civilize" as well as to "evangelize" the Indian. Superiority of white religion, economy and culture was promulgated early in New England which, consequently, provided a convenient rationale for destruction and exploitation of Indians. Conditions were placed upon Indians as a prerequisite to conversion; they must desert their cultures, their social structures, their people and all vestiges of their traditional religion and, in fact, speak, act, and dress like the Western European in order to "walk the Jesus road."

Cultural imperialism was decreed by law in 1644 when a Massachusetts governing body prohibited Indians—on threat of death—from "paw-pawing" or performing worship to false gods. The same governing body also decreed the death penalty for any Indian who blasphemed God or the Christian religion. The New England Puritans initiated a cultural clampdown that smoldered for over 200 years, flaming ominously in 1883 when a circular was issued by the Bureau of Indian Affairs which declared all Indian traditional

ceremonies—sun dance, "giveaways," medicine men's curing rites—
to be crimes punishable by imprisonment.

New England missionaries exemplified ecclesiastical colonialism
when they extracted the Indian from his tribal life and established
him in mission towns. From the outset, in Indian and white relationships, the land was at stake. The mission towns of Christian or
"praying" Indians would effectively reduce land use by the native
people while at the same time serving as an agent to "civilize" the
Indian. This pattern would later evolve into the reservation system, a
policy favored two centuries later by another churchman known as
"Apostle to the Indians."

Though the Connecticut colony appeared more concerned about
compelling the Indians to keep the Sabbath than anything else, the
rest of New England took seriously the command of the King of England to serve as "instruments of spreading the Gospel of Christ among
the heathen Nationes."

Other ministers would toil in the mission field—Roger Williams
among the Narraganset, the Mayhew father and son among the
Wampanoag on Martha's Vineyard and Nantucket, Richard Bourne
among the Mashpee on Cape Cod—but it was John Eliot who is best
remembered.

Beginning his Indian work in 1649, Eliot continued until his
death in 1695. He learned the Algonquin language and began to preach.
He translated the Bible and had it printed at the Indian college he
established in Harvard Yard. One of the students at the college was
the youngest son of Massasoit, the Wampanoag who welcomed the
Pilgrims. Eliot in 1650 acquired 6,000 acres and settled Indian converts at Natick, located 17 miles southwest of Boston. The Natick
settlement was known as a Praying Town and by 1674 there were 14
such towns with a population of 4,000.

Eliot spearheaded efforts to establish seminaries to train Indians as teachers and preachers and by the year 1700, at a point of
decline after "King Philip's War," there were 37 Indian preachers in
the field working along with seven or eight English ministers. This
ratio has never again been attained.

The Puritans did not readily bestow full church membership on
their converts. Instead, the Indians were under heavy scrutiny for
years before being received into the religious congregation as fully
baptized members and it was not until 1759 that they were granted
church membership.

Metacom or Philip—dubbed King Philip by the Englishmen—
was a son of Massasoit, the Wampanoag chief who had come with 90
men to celebrate the first Thanksgiving with the Pilgrims. Philip is

recorded to have stated to an Englishman:

> But little remains of my ancestors' domain; I am resolved not to see the day when I have no country . . . The English are so eager to sell the Indians liquor that most of them spend all in drunkenness.

In an ill-fated frenzy to protect the remains of his ancestors' domain from the Englishmen's further encroachment, Philip in the summer of 1675 rallied tribes of the vicinity to join in a summer war dance, and thence move out to attack English settlements. Philip was joined by the Narragansetts and most of the smaller tribes. Town after town was put to flame, from Connecticut to the outskirts of Boston. Casualties of the so-called King Philip's War numbered 207 colonial militia and 1,000 Indians, including Philip. Hundreds of Indian captives, including many who had been promised protection on surrender, were sold into slavery in the West Indies.

Despite the pleading of John Eliot, Philip's wife and nine-year-old son were sold into slavery to Bermuda. Philip's head rotted on a pike high on a hill overlooking Plymouth Colony, over which today a statue of Massasoit, his father, imposingly stands. Warfare ended the Praying Towns and the Christian converts were simply abandoned. By the end of the war, many had died of starvation.

Generation after generation of American school children in less-than-authentic Indian costumes have commemorated Thanksgiving, fleetingly noting the role of Massasoit but not remembering his son, Philip, who a scant half century after that first Thanksgiving died in an effort to save his ancestors' domain.

Both before and after the King Philip episode, the rigid New Englanders created a legacy which would long linger and tinge Indian-white relations: the theory, spoken and written, which equated native peoples with forces of evil—children-of-darkness, children-of-satan. This theory would be used with artful cunning to justify dispossession of native peoples of their lands and cultures. Smallpox—a European import—became "the evident hand of Heaven . . . extinguishing whole nations of the savage" to prove God intended America for the Englishman. Native American scholars of the 20th century are hard pressed to forget Cotton Mather's description of Indians as "doleful creatures . . . the veriest ruines of mankind . . . abominable, slothful and perfidious wretches."

The first bona fide Anglican parish in New England was not organized until 1686 when King's Chapel in Boston was founded. The Indians expressed the desire for a missionary, but they were not supplied with one. An assistant at King's Chapel, Stephen Roe, accompanied the governor of Massachusetts to Maine in 1742 to make a treaty with the Indians. Roe reported that French missionaries had been among the Maine tribes and that he found many Indians wearing crucifixes, whereupon Roe "took occasion to warn them against the sinfulness of 'image worship and prayers to saints and angels.'"

In 1727 a Narraganset sachem, Charles Augustus Ninaagret, was baptized by Anglican clergy but when Ninaagret petitioned the Society for the Propagation of the Gospel to send a missionary, none was forthcoming. In Connecticut, the Mahican Indians asked the SPG for a share in the services of the missionary at Norwich; it possibly happened. In Rhode Island, at the outbreak of the Revolution, the Commissioner for Indian Affairs in New England was employing a minister of the church for Indians in Bristol County. Jacob Bailey, the devoted missionary on the Kennebec, found that the ravages of war by 1765 had left only 50 Indians, the remnant of the once powerful Norridgewolk tribe in the region. Like Roe he also found they had been under French influence. Other literature of the colonial period provides a preface to subsequent acculturation processes and policies of the new Republic of the United States designed to mold the Indian into a brown replica of the European conqueror. A history of Connecticut, published in 1781, included:

> They seized without scruple on the lands preserved by the Indians, voting themselves to be the children of God, and that the wilderness to the utmost part of the earth was given to them, and it is calculated that upwards of 180,000 of the aboriginal inhabitants were slaughtered by them in Massachusetts Bay and in Connecticut alone.

The Church of New England left another legacy with which 20th century stewardship committees must yet deal. The climate of dependency of Christian Indians on the bountiful largess of the Church can be traced back to the pages of 17th century Massachusetts legal documents. In 1644 measures were set out for purposes of "civilizing and evangelizing" and ministers were designated to instruct Indians. Provisions were thereto made for "gifts for Indians willing to receive instructions."

While John Eliot is credited—by Cotton Mather, in fact—with "blessed labor which bore much fruit" in his 46 years of mission and ministry among American Indians, the most consequential of Eliot's achievements would be his role in establishing the first and oldest missionary society of the Anglican Church. Of larger magnitude, perhaps, than his getting the first Bible printed in America was Eliot's getting his tracts published back in England. These tracts cemented the foundation of the Society for the Propagation of the Gospel in Foreign Parts (SPG). Initiated in the reign of Charles I, supported by Cromwell (under whose direction £12,000 were raised in England and Wales), SPG was reinforced by Charles II at the Restoration and became a major tool of good Queen Anne at the dawn of the 18th century in sharing the gospel with American Indians.

2

THE ANGLICAN/EPISCOPAL CHURCH AND THE GREAT IROQUOIS CONFEDERACY

High on a ridge, commanding a vast panorama of the rolling rural eastern Wisconsin countryside, stands the Church of the Holy Apostles on the Oneida Reservation. Into its unusual history are woven ardent Anglican missionaries, stalwart tribal leaders and a colorful clergyman—likely Mohawk—who claimed to be the lost dauphin of France. This imposing grey limestone gothic church building is monument to almost 300 years of Anglican endeavor to share the gospel with the peoples of the Iroquois Confederacy.

The quest began in 1704 when the six nations of the powerful Confederacy resided in present-day New York and English missionaries were sent among the Iroquois peoples to baptize and build small chapels and schools while, at the same time, bolstering a buffer against covetous French interests. Then came the American Revolution; the Anglican mission abruptly ceased; the magnificent league of six powerful Indian nations, fused for the sake of peace, was forever put asunder.

The young Episcopal Church in 1816 revived Anglican tradition among the Iroquois with a mission to the Oneida, a member nation of the Confederacy, then residing in their ancestral homeland in the valley of the Mohawk River, near present-day Utica, New York. The Oneida endeavor has the distinction of being the first "foreign" mission of the Episcopal Church. Not until 1830 did the Domestic and Foreign Missionary Society send out a team of missionaries elsewhere in the world.

Several centuries before white contact the Iroquois had established a representative form of government. In addition to the Oneida, original member nations were the Mohawk, Onondaga, Cayuga and Seneca. Early in the 18th century the Tuscarora of North Carolina joined as the sixth nation of the league. Each nation retained its identity, but the union bound them together.

As the flame for the American Revolution was kindled, Benjamin Franklin looked to the Iroquois Confederacy for a model to form a union which would provide both individual freedom and corporate strength. Franklin reminded his fellow colonists that "It would be a strange thing if Six Nations of ignorant savages could be capable of forming a scheme for such an union . . . and yet that a like union should be impracticable for ten or a dozen English colonies . . ." The framers of the American nation then borrowed the Iroquois model as the political structure of the United States; yet, it was the War of the American Revolution which broke forever the power of the great Iroquois Confederacy.

Early day Dutch settlers of New Amsterdam made an effort, albeit feeble, to share the gospel with the Iroquois. From their stronghold on Manhattan Island, the Dutch inched up the Hudson River into the ancestral domain of the Mohawk. The Dutch Reformed pastors succeeded in completing certain Bible translations into the Mohawk language.

In 1664 the English took New Amsterdam and named it New York. With the English settlers came the English Church. Early on the English made half-hearted efforts to send missionaries to the Iroquois, in part, no doubt at first to detach them from French interests. By the mid-1600s the Roman Catholic Church, brought by the French, had founded missions among all five of the Iroquois nations with 2,000 converts, the best known being Kateri Tekakwitha, the Lily of the Mohawks, who is the first American Indian Roman Catholic candidate for canonization.

In 1703 the colony's Indian agent, Robert Livingston, warning that Jesuits were becoming active among the Iroquois, submitted a plan for converting the Iroquois. He recommended using the Dutch ministers already in Albany and sending a missionary to each of the six nations, further suggesting that each missionary learn the languages and act as interpreter. His final advice was that the missionary bring a good supply of presents to win over the Indians.

In 1704 the Church of England sent to the Mohawks Thoroughgood Moore, the first missionary to the Indians funded by the Society for the Propagation of the Gospel in Foreign Parts. The society was founded under the resolution: ". . . propagating the Gospel in foreign parts does chiefly and principally relate to the conversion of heathens and infidels." The first SPG funding, however, for mission among Indians would prove both niggardly and sporadic, and within a year Moore departed. By 1709, Thomas Barclay was sent to Albany to minister both to the whites and the Indians. Barclay found 30 Indians around Albany who were communicants of the Dutch Church and moved to bring them into the Church of England. It was three years before he ventured up the river to visit the nearest Mohawk village, Fort Hunter, and his report informs only that he rebuked the Indians for profaning the old Dutch chapel there. The Mohawks were using it for a slaughterhouse.

A group of Iroquois chiefs, in 1710, was taken to London and had an audience with Queen Anne. Among the chiefs was the Mohawk Sagayeathquapiethtow, said to have been a grandfather of Thayendanegea who would be known as Joseph Brant and loom prominently in politics of church and state before the end of the century. The chiefs were presented in formal ceremony at St. James' Palace, where on cue, they expressed their distrust of the French, against whom they were preparing war, and reminded the queen of an earlier promise to send them military assistance. Through their interpreter they also conveyed:

> Since we were in Covenant with our Great Queen's Children, we have had some knowledge of the Saviour of the World, and have often been opportuned by the French Priests and Presents, but ever esteemed them as men of Falsehood, but if our Great Queen would send some to Instruct us, they should find a most hearty Welcome.

Not unmindful of an ever-present potential for French encroachment on her New York colony, the queen made haste to help her children of the Iroquois Confederacy. Her first mission work was principally among the Mohawk, and by 1712 the Queen Anne Chapel was built at Fort Hunter at the confluence of the Schoharie Creek and the Mohawk River near present-day Amsterdam. Queen Anne designated this little chapel as a Royal Chapel and toward furnishing the Mohawk chapel the queen sent linen and altar plate, which were a replica of the communion silver used in the queen's own coronation. The Archbishop of Canterbury sent 12 large Bibles and a table.

Late in the autumn of 1712 the missionary William Andrews arrived in the Mohawk Village bearing the Queen Anne silver. As a missionary he proved a bad choice, showing scant understanding or sympathy for the people to whom he was sent. Three years later he had 20 children in school but acknowledged that he had to bribe them with food to keep them there.

It would seem that the Mohawks decided to have fun with Andrews, for some of them told him that they would come to his services if he would give them a draft of rum. Others expressed the opinion that baptism was all that was required to make anyone a good Christian, and thus they did not need to come to his services. One man, whom Andrews had excommunicated for "drunkenness, sabbath-breaking, cruelty in biting off a prisoner's ears and other offenses," threatened to shoot the missionary. Andrews' departure was prompt, and it was some time before the Indians had another missionary.

About this time a rush of German immigrants invaded the Hudson and Mohawk River valleys. While the Mohawks bitterly complained about the European encroachment, the British provided scant relief.

Few Mohawk Remained Unbaptized

A real turning point came in 1735 when Henry Barclay was sent to Fort Hunter. He dove fervidly into evangelizing, promptly learning their language and beginning a lasting translation of the Book of Common Prayer. Unlike his predecessors who lingered long in the growing Albany community Barclay gave his all upriver to the salvation of the Mohawks.

Within six years he reported that only a few of the Mohawk remained unbaptized! Small Anglican chapels appeared all along the banks of the Mohawk River which meanders eastward through the slopes of central New York to the Hudson. Barclay journeyed further westward and made a beginning in the conversion of the Oneidas. However, Barclay departed for a far more prestigious appointment. He became rector of Trinity Church in New York City and SPG reports over the next decade are filled with complaints about the "dissolute lives" of the Indians.

It was in this period that the French and Indian War of 1755-1762 was fought to determine control of what is now the eastern United States. Though the Mohawks fought as a loyal ally of Great Britain, they did not receive the rewards of victory. Instead, settlers arrived in ever-increasing numbers and occupied Mohawk territory.

It was also in this period that Sir William Johnson, first as a trader and later as the Crown's Indian Commissioner, with the powerful leader of the Mohawk Nation, Captain Joseph Brant or Thayendanegea, cemented a solid bond between the Mohawk and the British Crown and Church of England which would survive the American Revolution.

Sir William wrote the Archbishop of Canterbury, Thomas Secker, urging that the church establish a school for Indians similar to that which Eleazar Wheelock was building at Hanover, New Hampshire (now Dartmouth College). The archbishop, who had corresponded with a number of colonials on schemes for the evangelization of Indians, had at first been in favor of sending Indian youths to Wheelock's school (which had received numerous contributions from English churchmen), with a view of their being episcopally ordained after completing the courses. But the missionary at Cambridge strongly discouraged the proposal with the suggestion that all the Indians would turn out to be Presbyterian. Secker was much alarmed at such a prospect. He advised SPG to set up a rival school but nothing came of the notion.

Myles Cooper, president of King's College (later Columbia), and Charles Inglis, then an assistant at Trinity, traveled up to visit to Sir William in early 1770, and while enjoying the commissioner's famed hospitality at palatial Johnson Hall, they were called upon by a deputation of Mohawks from both principal Mohawk villages, Fort Hunter and Canajoharie. The Mohawks crossly complained that the Roman Catholic Indians of Canada, who had formerly been enemies of the English, had been allowed to have their own Anglican minister, but they, the Mohawks who had always been friendly, had none. Fort Hunter still had its little, old chapel, built in Queen Anne's time. The Canajoharies, upriver, had set about raising one hundred dollars toward building a chapel for themselves. Sir William contributed the rest. Just up the hill from Joseph Brant's house, it was a handsome little chapel in which the Mohawks took pride.

Joseph Brant: Loyalist

Likely the best known American Indian of the 18th century, Joseph Brant lived and died loyal to the Crown and the Church of England. He was a younger brother of the bright and lively Molly Brant, loyal consort of Sir William Johnson who served as the Crown's Indian Commissioner from 1746 until his death in 1774. Molly (baptized Mary) was born around 1736 and at age 23 came into the household of Johnson where she eventually was recognized as the lady of the manor, running a huge household of slaves and servants. While it was reported that Molly and Sir William were eventually legally wed, first in Mohawk ceremony and later in the Anglican chapel at Fort Hunter, no record of the marriage has ever surfaced. The couple had at least nine children and Molly was described as an able hostess who helped Sir William entertain a steady stream of distinguished white and Indian guests at Johnson Hall, the stately white manor house built in

1763 and which yet stands at the end of a graceful tree-lined avenue.

Joseph, who was several years younger than the high spirited Molly, was baptized at the Mohawk town of Canajoharie, a settlement of some 300 Mohawk about 50 miles upriver from Schnectady. He was further educated by the English at the Connecticut school of Eleazar Wheelock. While at the Wheelock school, young Joseph instructed a young minister who was having difficulty in mastering the Mohawk language. The young Puritan minister was Samuel Kirkland, who is best remembered as the Oneida's missionary and fervent supporter of the American Revolution.

The Mohawk's long hoped-for resident missionary arrived just before Christmas of 1770. He was John Stuart. The earnest young man had just returned from the long hard voyage to England for his ordination. He preached his first sermon on Christmas Day at the new church at Canajoharie and in the afternoon visited the home of Joseph Brant, who became Stuart's translator and instructor in the Mohawk language. Soon the two would begin work on translation of some portions of scripture and Anglican liturgy. The two became close friends. Stuart would within a year console the young Brant in his grief at the death of his first wife, Peggie. Again, years later, he would console Brant, the renowned tribal leader and British warrior, in his bitterness following the Revolutionary War.

Sir William, who influenced the nations of the confederacy to fight with the British in the protracted French and English clashes along their colonial borders, died on the eve of the American Revolution. When the war came, the British again sought the assistance of the Iroquois; the Continental Congress sought their neutrality. When the question came to the Council of the League, a decision was ultimately left to each nation. In the course of the war, Kirkland, Brant's old classmate from Wheelock's school, delivered the Oneida and Tuscaroras to the side of the colonists; the Mohawk, Onondaga, Cayuga and Seneca all eventually took up the king's cause. Kirkland was cited by George Washington for his efforts on behalf of the colonists; Brant lived out his life in exile from the ancestral homeland of the Mohawk as a result of his allegiance to the crown.

July 29, 1776, found Captain Brant returning from England, where he had been sent to resolve land disputes between the Mohawks and encroaching white settlements along the Mohawk River. His London negotiations had been successful; he had been quite the sensation and was presented to King George III (though he eluded kissing the king's hand). Soon the settlement question would be moot; the Mohawks would be chased from the Mohawk valley by the Colonial army and the Oneidas.

Joseph Brant (Mohawk) [1743-1807].
1797 painting by Charles Wilson Peele.
Courtesy of the Independence National
Historical Park Collection, Philadelphia.

Upon docking at British-held Staten Island, the young Mohawk must have gazed across the bay at New York City, then held by the rebels. Within the past three weeks the 13 colonies had formally declared their independence and his Anglican clergy friends were at peril. In fact, the rebels would burn Trinity Church, now served by Charles Inglis, who had aided the Mohawks in acquiring Stuart as the Mohawks' missionary.

Captain Brant, who had served the British well in the French and Indian War, offered his services to the British command under General Howe and the loyalists. In the late summer of 1776, Brant distinguished himself in the Battle of Long Island as both a soldier and a strategist. Subsequently, the British command granted his request to slip through the American lines in disguise to return to the Iroquois where he was given a hero's welcome. Captain Brant rallied warriors of the Iroquois to take up the cause of the king and in doing so he split the confederacy and uprooted the Great Tree of Peace.

Iroquois bloodshed followed. The colonists confiscated Johnson Hall at the beginning of the war, dispossessing Molly and her children, who fled to her old home at Canajoharie where she continued to encourage the Mohawk to support the crown. Rebel colonists, escorted by a band of Oneida, swept down the Mohawk valley in the autumn of 1777 and raided Molly's Canajoharie home. She escaped with her children to the Onondagas, but the inventory of items "liberated" by the colonial army included the fancy ball gowns of Molly Brant, the powerful Mohawk matron.

John Stuart, the missionary, continued his efforts along the Mohawk River, reading prayers for the king until patriots placed him under house arrest in Schenectady for three years, fined him and confiscated the church property. The beautiful little Canajoharie chapel was turned into a bar. Stuart, denied permission to teach school to support himself, experienced great hardship. Like many other Anglican clergy, Stuart eventually emigrated to Canada in a prisoner exchange, and with him to Quebec went many of his Mohawk parishioners. He reported baptizing 104 Mohawks in 1784 alone.

Before the American Revolution the six nations of the Iroquois lived in some 30 thriving villages scattered from the Mohawk River to Lake Erie and into the Ohio country. In the unusually bitter cold winter of 1779-80, hundreds of displaced Indian families huddled around Niagara, begging rations from the British garrison. Only two towns stood by the spring of 1780; the others were in ashes or empty, moldering in rain and wind. When the war ended, the Iroquois were the major losers—the Treaty of Paris in 1783 was mute on Indian interests. The United States negotiated at gunpoint with the Iroquois, Delaware, Shawnee and other nations and tribes of the east in the Treaty of Fort Stanwix in 1784. The United States demanded cession of the land—all of the land except for pitiful fragments called reservations, which shrank steadily for the next century.

Two hundred years would pass before the Mohawks again gained a toehold on their ancestral land. It was in the summer of 1993 that the community of Kanatsiohareke, which means "the place of the clean pot," purchased 322 acres of land on the Mohawk River in Montgomery County. By regaining a land base in the heart of the home of their ancestors, late 20th century Mohawks aspire to again fulfill the role of "Keeper of the Eastern Door." Mohawk traditional people dream of restoring peace in the conflict between the nation's scattered fragments—at Akwesasne, Kahnawake, Kanestake, Six Nations and Tyendinega in Canada and the United States.

Joseph Brant, recognizing conclusive defeat during the negotiations in 1784 at Fort Stanwix, left in disgust before the treaty was signed. The Canadians granted their ally a tract of land on the Grand River in Ontario, 60 miles west of Niagara Falls, on which Brant settled pro-British Mohawk and other Iroquois followers. After all the years of toil of the Anglican Church among the "Keepers of the Eastern Door," all that remains of the first major Anglican-Episcopal mission in the United States is an abandoned cemetery on the St. Regis-Akwesasne Reservation at the northern tip of the State of New York.

The Queen Anne Chapel on the Mohawk River was destroyed by American Army Engineers during the 1812-1814 war with England. The stone blocks from the chapel were used to build a lock in the Erie Canal, remnants of which may still be seen.

From 1971 until 1994, the Rev. S.G. Horne served Christ Church (the Royal Chapel) and Queen Anne Parish on the Canadian Mohawk reserve at Tyendinaga (Bay of Quinte) in the Diocese of Ontario. The retired priest generously filled in the history of the Anglican Mohawks and the Queen Anne communion silver:

> In 1783, the Mohawk tribe left the Mohawk Valley in Upper New York State after the War of Independence. The Mohawks had fought with the British Forces and were no longer welcome. They travelled to what is now Lachine, Quebec, under the leadership of Captain John Deyserontou and Captain Joseph Brant, two natives who were commissioned in the British Army. After a stay of about one year a large group under these two leaders travelled west along the St. Lawrence River and the Bay of Quinte. The group under John Deyserontou stopped at the Bay of Quinte about mid-way between what is now Kingston and Belleville in Ontario. The other group under Brant travelled along the north shore of Lake Ontario until they finally settled on the Grand River near present-day Brantford, named after Joseph Brant.
>
> The Mohawks of the Bay of Quinte landed at their present site on May 22, 1784. The first Church to be built at the reserve on the Bay of Quinte, was a log building erected in 1784. The Parish was officially established in 1792. Ministrations were under the leadership of a native catechist. In 1798 King George III of England gave the Parish a Triptych, a Bell, and a Royal Coat of Arms, officially declaring said church a Royal Chapel, and it remains so to this very day . . .

The Mohawk who found refuge in Canada had no sooner established a site for their church than they sent back two men and a woman to the Mohawk River valley to recover six pieces of the Queen Anne communion silver which they had buried before fleeing with the loyalists a year earlier. Three pieces went to Joseph Brant's band at the Six Nations Reserve near Brantford. The other three pieces, consisting of a flagon, a chalice, and a paten, stayed with the Mohawks of the Bay of Quinte for the use of Christ Church. A beautiful stone building, erected in 1843, it suffered from a fire in 1909 which destroyed the tower. Among the losses was the Royal Coat of Arms. The tower was restored in 1919 and King George V of England replaced the Coat of Arms. Mohawks of the Bay of Quinte still receive communion on occasion from the gift of Queen Anne.

Molly Brant remained as loyal as her brother to the English cause and was forced to flee her Mohawk homeland before the war's end. In recognition for her services to the king, British officials built Molly a home near present-day Kingston, Ontario, and provided her with a yearly pension of £100. As an older woman, Molly was glimpsed sitting in the pew of the Anglican church in Kingston "appearing very devout and attentive to the sermon." She died at age 61 on April 16, 1796. The Canadian government issued a commemorative postage stamp honoring Molly Brant 190 years later.

Described by his old teacher, Eleazar Wheelock, as a man of "sprightly genius," Joseph Brant was a forerunner of generations of native peoples who would be caught inextricably in the clash between white and Indian cultures. He had been born and educated in traditional Mohawk ways, but he had also received an education from the English missionaries. While he was equipped to "walk in both worlds," he was never really accepted—except as a curiosity—in the white world nor was he any longer, in an unqualified sense, a Mohawk.

During the last 25 years of his life, Captain Brant resided in baronial graciousness on the Grand River (or Six Nations) Reserve in Canada. Here he translated the Anglican Book of Common Prayer and the Gospel of St. Mark. A chapel was built on the Reserve—identified today as the "First Protestant Chapel in the Province of Ontario"—and on its grounds Joseph Brant was buried. The Queen Anne communion silver is yet used at special services at the Mohawk chapel on the Grand River.

Williams: the Lost Dauphin of France or St. Regis Mohawk?

The War for Independence devastated American Indian missions of the Church of England. Anglican activity ceased; financial support to mission programs—the SPG—disappeared. Almost half a century would pass before any work among Indians was begun under the banner of the new Protestant Episcopal Church in the United States.

The Reverend Eleazar Williams [1788-1858], likely a
Mohawk but claimed to be lost dauphin of France.
Portrait by George Catlin.
Courtesy, State Historical Society of Wisconsin.

The work began among the Oneida, who the English Church left to the Congregationalists and Samuel Kirkland.

Grandfather to American Indian Episcopal mission was John Henry Hobart, Bishop of New York. His grandson, William Hobart Hare, a half century later would become shepherd to the Great Sioux Nation of the Northern Plains as Bishop of Niobrara. The elder established the first Episcopal Indian mission; the grandson established more than 90 new Sioux missions.

Bishop Hobart, consecrated in 1811, was conscious of Anglican heritage among the Iroquois Nations through the work in generations past by the British. He looked at the Oneida, residing to the east of the Finger Lakes region, to initiate his Indian mission, and within four years from his consecration, he had begun the first Indian mission of the Protestant Episcopal Church. Bishop Hobart's work would be the only Episcopal Indian mission for the next 37 years.

A key figure in developing the Oneida mission was a man of much mystery, Eleazar Williams, whose origins have been argued interminably. Some believed—and he himself apparently believed—that he was the son of Louis XVI and Marie Antoinette, the Lost Dauphin of France, and brought to America as a child to escape death in the French Revolution.

Old Episcopal publications, including early editions of *The Spirit of Missions,* identify him less romantically:

> Born at St. Regis, New York . . . May 1788. Son of Thomas and Mary Ann Williams, and a descendant of Eunice Williams, a survivor of the historic Deerfield [Massachusetts] Raid in 1704, who had been carried into captivity and became the wife of an Indian chief. Early in life Eleazer was interested in evangelizing the Indians of New York, and in 1815 went from Oneida, Central New York to take counsel of Bishop Hobart, who received him with great cordiality. In 1822, Williams led his people from New York to Wisconsin. He was made a lay reader, catechist and school master by Bishop Hobart. On July 18, 1826, he was ordained a deacon in Vernon, Oneida County, NY, and advanced to the priesthood on August 28, 1828.

It is now generally believed that Williams was indeed a descendent of Eunice Williams, a member of a distinguished Massachusetts family—Williams College bears their name—who with her family was stolen in the Deerfield Raid by French soldiers and their Indian allies in 1704. Several family members, including her Puritan father, the Rev. John Williams, were later ransomed, but Eunice was adopted into a Roman Catholic Iroquois family, married a Kahnawake (Canadian Mohawk) Indian named Arosen, and declined repeated entreaties to return to her own people. Several of Eunice's descendants were glimpsed with avid fascination in journals of the 18th century; some became traders and one probably became an Episcopal priest.

Indians are left with an unsolved riddle. If, in fact, Williams was a Mohawk, then he was the first Indian priest of the Episcopal Church rather than the venerated Enmegahbowh, the Ottawa of Minnesota. As the question was discussed some years ago, an Indian elder proclaimed, "If he [Williams] didn't want to claim us, we don't want to claim him as one of us."

A few irrefutable facts are: It was from the St. Regis Reservation that Eleazar Williams first surfaced. He had attended school in New England and returned to St. Regis to teach Mohawks for the Roman Catholics. He appears to have been a spy for the Americans in the War of 1812, gathering information from Canadian Indians on movement of British troops. He was wounded at the Battle of Plattsburg in New York. Next he appeared on the Oneida Reservation, sought an interview with Bishop Hobart and laid out a plan to bring the tribe into the Episcopal Church. The Bishop was impressed, and commissioned him as catechist and lay reader. Williams rearranged Joseph Brant's Mohawk prayer book and had it published. He was a man of exceptional gifts. He wrote music and poetry and preached "excellent sermons of great length and earnestness."

Within the short span of three years the Oneida Nation moved toward broad acceptance of the Protestant Episcopal Church, and Williams became a postulant for the diaconate. A little church, built by the Oneida themselves, was consecrated in 1819 under the name of St. Peter's. On this occasion, Bishop Hobart confirmed 56 persons and baptized two adults and 46 infants.

The Oneidas were not long to enjoy their little church building. The early 1800s brought the forced migration of eastern Indians. While many of the Oneida were totally opposed to removal, Williams encouraged it, extolling prospects of new hope in the West. In 1822 the Oneida acquired from the Menominee Tribe a 100-square-mile reservation located at Duck Creek, 10 miles west of Green Bay, Wisconsin. A small stream ran through the valley which the Oneida named "the place of many ducks," and their reservation was long called the Duck Creek Reservation.

In 1823 Williams accompanied Chief Skenandoah and the Oneidas to their new home. At first, each Sunday the Oneida gathered to worship beneath the trees on Duck Creek. Then, in 1825, the first church building in all Wisconsin was erected. By special permission, the Oneida named their church for their "father" back in New York, Bishop Hobart. In 1828 Bishop Hobart made the long journey from New York to visit the Oneidas at Green Bay and consecrate the small hand-hewn log Hobart church. He confirmed 97.

Soon after the Oneidas were moved to the dense forests of Wisconsin they gave the young Episcopal Church 70 acres of land on which to build a mission. For reasons not clearly detailed, Williams departed the Oneida mission in 1830 and was succeeded by Richard F. Cadle. One of the old church publications suggests: "Mr. Williams went west with the Indians to Wisconsin and continued to work among them until someone persuaded him that it would be more profitable to capitalize on his striking facial resemblance to the Bourbons by posing as the Lost Dauphin. Thereafter the work had to be carried on by less romantic characters." Harper's Magazine published a story, "Lost Prince," which became the foundation for much speculation on whether the clergyman in Wisconsin was in fact the dauphin. But minute inquiries failed to substantiate Williams' claims, and the excitement gradually subsided.

Eleazer Williams died in obscurity at St. Regis, New York, August 28, 1858. Originally buried at the Akwesasne Reservation, a cryptic reburial at Holy Apostles took place in 1947, leaving Indians with yet another unsolved riddle about the man who was likely the first ordained Indian.

Jackson Kemper, Missionary Bishop

For a full generation after the Revolutionary War focus of the fledgling Episcopal Church was on its own formation. When a steady onslaught of settlers crashed westward, the Episcopal Church stood aside, weighing options as whether to define itself as a small, self-satisfied denomination clinging to the eastern seaboard or to emerge as an active player in this spectacular national expansion. In the first quarter of the 19th century it left the task of evangelizing the frontier to fervent, more fundamentalist preachers whose emotional style proved well adapted to the religious needs of a rough and adventurous society. However, after major debate the 1835 General Convention of the Episcopal Church entered into a evangelization mode and chose its first missionary bishop, Jackson Kemper. The cleric was handed the awesome challenge to plant and organize the Church from Indiana westward. The choice was wise; Kemper was known for his deep spirituality, gentle character and affectionate interest in his family, parishioners and friends. Moreover, from his first visit to the Oneida, he harbored a lifelong love and concern for Native people.

Bishop Kemper made that first visit to the Oneida in 1838 traveling by horseback across the forests of Wisconsin to lay the cornerstone for a new frame church which would replace the original old log structure on Duck Creek. The visit aroused great excitement among the Oneida, and the bishop, who kept fascinating journals, wrote of having been met "about five miles from the mission by a large number of chiefs and warriors on horseback" who welcomed the bishop with zest and enthusiasm. The service began by chanting the Te Deum in the Oneida language. At the close of the service the congregation formed in procession, and with the bishop and clergy went to the site of the new church, which was on an elevation overlooking the settlement:

> The services at this place were solemn and impressive. The deposits were placed in a tin box under the stone by the chief orator of the tribe. A memorandum was placed with other documents as follows: "This corner stone was laid on the 7th day of August, A.D. 1838, by the Rt. Rev. Father in God, Jackson Kemper, Bishop of Missouri and

Indiana, the first Missionary Bishop of the Protestant Episcopal Church in the United States." Four of the chiefs then
took hold of the stone at each corner, and placed it in its
proper place. The Gloria in Excelsis was then sung . . . the
service closed with the Bishop's benediction.

The following year Bishop Kemper again visited Oneidas to consecrate the new Hobart church, "the first Episcopal Church in the
Territory of Wisconsin." At the close of the service the chiefs and head
men of the nation came in front of the chancel, each placing his hand,
as he came up, on the shoulder of the other, and in this way forming a
half circle in the presence of the bishop, who stood within the railing.
The missionary, Solomon Davis, read on behalf of the Oneidas:

> The Chiefs of the Oneidas cannot suffer you to depart from
> their nation without expressing their sincere thanks for your
> kindness in visiting them . . . His presence has made our hearts
> glad . . . Our house is now "Holy Place." It is our choice that as
> God's chief minister, you should preside over us . . . We now
> extend to you the hand of the nation . . . and will hereafter
> hold on to you as our lawful Bishop.

Bishop Kemper, who eventually made his home at Nashotah,
visited the Oneida nearly every year until 1870.

One of Kemper's visits to the Oneida was to ordain two young
deacons to the priesthood. They were James Lloyd Breck and William
Adams, the founders of Nashotah House Seminary. On a visit to General Seminary in New York, Bishop Kemper awakened Breck and
Adams along with John Henry Hobart, son of the bishop of New York,
to a broader vision of the role for Anglicanism in evangelizing the
American West. These three young men, in a spirit of adventure and
challenge, set off in 1841 for the newly opened Territory of Wisconsin
intent upon organizing a religious house in the tradition of high
churchmanship and later markedly affected by influences of the Oxford
Movement.

When time came for their ordination, the Nashotah House
founders were resolute in their wishes to be ordained in a consecrated
church building. At that time there were only two such buildings in
the whole Territory of Wisconsin—the Oneida's little frame church
and another in Green Bay. So Breck and Adams set off on foot for
Oneida. With an occasional lift in a lumber wagon, the journey required
four days each way. As a memorial of the event the Indians gave them
the old bell "Michael" which for many years was hung in an oak tree
at Nashotah.

Throughout the long ministry of Bishop Kemper—he lived productively until age 81—he kept in close touch with the Oneida mission. The venerable figure who organized six dioceses, consecrated a hundred churches, ordained 200 men to the ministry and confirmed upwards of 10,000 people, cast a long shadow on the character of Minnesota Territory, which would prove to be the next site of Episcopal mission among Native peoples.

At the thriving Duck Creek mission, the Rev. Solomon Davis, or "Priest Davis," followed Cadle. Davis also kept journals, painstakingly written in the old-fashioned character and condescending mien of the times. But his reports do give a first-hand glimpse of 1843 life at the Duck Creek mission. The following was dated April 22, 1843:

> The Oneidas, at the present time, occupy a tract of land containing 64,500 acres. Duck Creek, on which they are settled, is a stream of considerable importance, passing through the centre of this Territory . . . On it are errected [sic] two sawmills belonging to the tribe. The land, for fertility of soil, is not surpassed by any in the northern part of the Territory of Wisconsin . . .
>
> When your Missionary came to them, in 1836, he found them struggling under much embarrassment . . . the Nation was deeply enveloped in debt; the title to their land had not been secured . . . They were restless and uneasy . . . An appeal was made by a delegation of their chiefs to the Domestic Committee of the Board of Missions, who authorized the missionary and one of their own members, T.A. Cushman, Esq., to proceed to Washington and urge their claims upon the government . . . The effort was successful.
>
> . . . From that time their improvement, in both a spiritual and a temporal point of view, has been greater than could have been anticipated. Their settlement now wears the appearance of a thriving agricultural community . . . Strange as it may seem, here are Indians inhabiting neat frame houses, with good barns and out buildings, enjoying most of the comforts of civilized life. The heavy forest is being cleared and the quantity of land cultivated, yearly extended, the fruit of their own toil and industry.
>
> . . . It should be mentioned, that on their first settlement at Duck Creek, their attachment to the Church and veneration for her service was manifested by erecting a house for the worship of God. This building was of hewn

logs . . . the fact more interesting is that it was the first Protestant house of worship erected in the Northwestern Territory . . . The log building has been replaced . . . the church bell which cost a little less than $300 was a donation from one of their chiefs.

. . . The number of the tribe is now 650 souls, one hundred and twelve of whom, including a majority of the chiefs, are in communion with the church. During my ministry here, one hundred and fifty three adults and infants have been baptized, and ninety one have ratified their baptismal vows in the Apostolic rite of confirmation.

"Priest Davis" would "settle over" the Oneidas for 11 years, until 1847. Apparently a learned scholar, he experienced personal anguish when a fire at the mission rectory destroyed his 500-volume library.

Cornelius Hill: First Oneida Priest

The Nashotah founders, Breck and Adams, after journeying to the Oneida mission for ordination, took back with them three Oneida lads. One of the young Oneidas, Cornelius Hill, would in future years play a major role in the life of the Oneida mission. The promising 12-year-old would become the youngest chief and first Oneida priest. While at Nashotah he was made a chief of the Bear Clan at age 13. When he returned to the Oneida a national feast was given in his honor at which all the clans were present. The new chief took on the name and place of one of their oldest chiefs, *Onau-gwat-go* (Great Medicine).

A staunch supporter of the missionaries throughout his life, Chief Hill also led his people in a successful opposition to a further move west. When much pressure was put on all the chiefs to sell their lands and relocate, Chief Hill made a strong reply: "We will not sign your treaty; no amount of money can tempt us to sell our people. You say our answer must be given today. You shall have your wish—and it is one that you will hear every time you seek to drive us from our lands—NO!"

He served as interpreter and organist in the Oneida church through many years and on June 27, 1885, he was ordained a deacon. For reasons unexplained, it was not until 1903 that the Indian was ordained to the priesthood. Two hundred guests and the Oneida brass band appeared for ordination day, which was both a happy and sad day for Chief Hill. His son, who died of whooping cough, was buried on the same day. Father Hill died in 1907, only four years after his priesting. The life and work of this unusual man may best be summed up in his obituary, which was published in *The Spirit of Missions* in 1907:

> The Rev. Cornelius Hill, a chief of the tribe, who through many years, as interpreter, deacon and finally priest, was a spiritual leader among his people. He died on January 25 at age of 75 years, and was buried on the 30th in the Indian cemetery [on the Oneida Reservation].

> Sixty years ago, when a boy of fifteen, Cornelius Hill became a hereditary chief of the Oneida tribe; at nineteen he took his place as a member of the tribal council, which was the supreme authority in managing the affairs of the nation, and during all the latter years of his life he was its sachem, or president. Through a long and faithful life, he served and guided his people well. With changing conditions the authority of the chieftainship was greatly circumscribed and its influence diminished; indeed, with his death it passes finally and completely away. The tribal relations are broken up, and the old romantic chapter is closed. The last of the sachems—those picturesque and striking figures of history and story—has gone the way of all flesh. For years the office had been a shadowy one; now it ceases altogether.

> Sachem he was—but something more and better. Educated at Nashotah in the early days of Breck and Adams, he finally in later years was ordained deacon and priest, and in the spiritual leadership of his people found a sphere of influence in which he wrought patiently and well; for in the Church he believe he saw the one power which could help his people in the critical days of transition from the life of the old days to that of the new. Cornelius Hill: the last of Oneida sachems, the first of Oneida priests.

Beneath a large Celtic cross, Cornelius Hill is buried in the churchyard at Holy Apostles. (For reasons unknown the mission changed its name from Hobart Church to Holy Apostles in 1897.) His wife, Cecelia Skenadore Hill, was buried beside him in 1940.

The Visit of Bishop William Hobart Hare

Within weeks after his consecration as Bishop of Niobrara with jurisdiction over the Great Sioux Nation, William Hobart Hare visited the Oneida on his way to Dakota Territory and conducted his first confirmation service on Easter Sunday, 1873. He was obviously moved by the historic significance; his grandfather had begun the Episcopal work with the Oneida. Hare wrote, "Many whom Bishop Hobart confirmed in New York state fifty years before brought their grandchildren to be confirmed by his grandson."

Hare's reminiscences of his first Oneida visit provide a glimpse of the character of the mission:

> My first impressions of the condition of the Indians here were not gained under very favorable circumstances. The day was one of the dreariest of cloudy, chilly spring days. I had been on the railroad most of the night, and when I arrived at the Reservation at ten o'clock, was still breakfastless.
>
> . . . They have been on their present Reservation, none more than fifty and many less than twenty five years. When they came to it it was a dense forest. They have cleared nearly 20,000 acres of it with their own hands, and now thousands of acres of it are the very best farming land. They have put up hundreds upon hundreds of miles of rail fence. They have cast aside their wigwams, and have erected houses of logs and often of sawn boards, which are quite equal to those of the white settlers upon the frontiers.
>
> . . . Opposite the church is the school-house, where the Missionary and his excellent wife hold a day-school (number of children on the yearly roll, 125; number attending, on the average, 49) . . . Passing along the road beyond the church and school-house, we soon come to the cemetery, where there are many <u>marble</u> headstones. Beyond this we come to what was, a few years ago, the scene of an execution. The Indians have a keen sense of law, and have their own tribunals. In this case they arrested the man on whom suspicion fell, appointed two of their number attorneys, one for the people and the other for the defendant, the native interpreter was chosen as judge, and the chiefs served as a jury. They patiently heard the evidence, and, though the defendant belonged to an influential family, and every effort was made to shield him from condemnation, they adjudged him guilty, sentenced him to be hanged, and with solemn propriety carried the sentence into execution.
>
> . . . I beheld the ONEIDA BRASS BAND of eight pieces, the musicians and their leader all full-blooded Indians. I heard them play by note quick-step after quick-step, with

Oneida brass band, 1923
Courtesy, Archives of the Episcopal Church.

an accuracy of time and a harmony of sound quite equal to that of country bands in the East.

. . . on our right, is the church. It is a frame building, painted white, and will hold, say two hundred and fifty people. It was preceded by a log church, erected by the Indians themselves. The present church cost $7,500, and was paid for by the Indians out of money received from the sale of some of their land . . . There is a project on foot to build a larger and more substantial edifice. The Indians have already prepared some of the requisite timber, and have quarried and hauled large quantities of stone. Labor as they may, however, this new church must require a large outlay of what is with them very scarce, money. Probably not less than $5,000. They spoke of their need in this line in the Council held to-day, and I told them that I was quite sure their Christian friends in the East would help them, provided I could tell them that the Indians were trying to help themselves.

Bishop Hare's appeal for funds for the new church building netted certain help but it was primarily the Oneidas themselves who were responsible for the handsome stone church building which was begun in 1870. Stone for the building was quarried from the reservation and Oneida men each week gave one day's wages toward its building fund. Women and children picked berries to be sold in the neighboring towns, and women made and sold handicrafts to contribute to the building fund. Eventually, after 14 years, $6,000 had been raised, but the Green Bay bank, where the building fund was deposited, failed and all was lost. An appeal throughout the diocese netted $5,000 and work was continued. Finally, in 1886, the cornerstone of the new church was laid by John Henry Hobart Brown, the first Bishop of Fond du Lac, and a member of the family of Bishop Hobart of New York.

The Last 100 Years

The 1890s brought new vitality to the Oneida congregation. A hospital was built after Solomon S. Burleson arrived as the new missionary. This learned man had studied medicine, dentistry and the law before ordination. His little daughter, with 36-cents, started a fund to build the hospital. The hospital was completed in 1893 and its physician was Dr. Josiah A. Powless, an Oneida, who had studied at Milwaukee Medical College. After Powless departed, the hospital became a dispensary. Burleson, whose son later became Bishop of South Dakota, also established a boarding school and was instrumental in at last getting a bridge built across Duck Creek.

In 1898 the Sisters of Holy Nativity, Fond du Lac, sent two of the vocation to work among the Oneida. The sisters built their own home and a tiny little chapel for their own devotions and a room where Indians came for spiritual instruction. Deaconess Sybil Carter, who organized a lace-making industry among Indian women around the country, sent a representative to the reservation and by September, 1899, over 75 Oneida women had made more than 500 pieces of lace.

In 1920 the beautiful church was struck by lightning and all but its stone walls was destroyed. Restoration began in less than a year and on Trinity Sunday, 1922, the restored church was consecrated by Reginald H. Weller, Bishop of Fond du Lac.

In the first hundred years of Episcopal mission among the Oneida in Wisconsin—1823 to 1923—only 10 served as vicars for the congregation, indicating an unusual lengthy time average for the era. Cornelius Hill, with the questionable exception of Eleazar Williams, appears to have been the only Indian priest to minister among the Oneida. In 1950 Edmond R. Webster was ordained but did not elect to work among Oneidas. In 1990 two Oneidas were ordained to the permanent diaconate—Russell Johns and Edmund Powless. The latter, like the esteemed Cornelius Hill, assists with the work at Holy Apostles.

For more than a decade beginning in 1980, the Rev. James H. Dolan served as assistant, then vicar, for Holy Apostles. A native of Wisconsin, he was quite visible in support of the Chippewa position on fishing rights issues which surfaced in the late 1980s. He was active in the ecumenical advocacy organization, HONOR, based in Milwaukee. He retired in 1993 and was replaced by the Rev. John T. Splinter, also a native of Wisconsin.

In the high church matrix cast by Bishop Kemper and assiduously nurtured in the Diocese of Fond du Lac, the Church of the Holy Apostles is an Anglo-Catholic stronghold. Gone are the hospital, the school, the Oneida brass band, and the convent of the Sisters of the Holy Nativity. In fact, in 1994 the church returned an historic building, formerly used as a school, with a parcel of two acres, to the tribe. In 1975 a 10-acre tract was restored to the tribe to be used as a ballpark. Under guidance of a new diocesan bishop, Russell E. Jacobus, the largest and oldest congregation of Indian Christians—the Church of the Holy Apostles on the Oneida Reservation—survives in near unbroken continuity since the reign of Queen Anne of England.

In early spring of 1996, the great-great-grandmother of all Episcopal Indian missions, Holy Apostles, hosted the eighth annual Paths Crossing, a gathering of Episcopal Indian and non-Indian partner congregations. Holy Apostles welcomed representation from 15 tribes and 25 dioceses, Alabama to Wyoming, California to Connecticut. At first view of the great grey gothic tower of Holy Apostles, an awestruck Oklahoma-born Potawatomi priest exclaimed, "This must surely be the cathedral for all Episcopal Indians!"

Present Mission among Iroquois in New York State

Though the Episcopal Church went west with the Oneida in the early 19th century, mission began and has survived in New York State among two of the nations of the old Iroquois Confederacy—the Onondaga and Seneca.

While the Onondaga congregation can trace its Anglican heritage back to Queen Anne, it was not until 1868 that the Episcopal Church opened mission among them. The white frame Church of the

Good Shepherd on the Onondaga Reservation was consecrated in 1870 by Frederic Dan Huntington, the first Bishop of Central New York. Across the state near the shores of Lake Erie is another Good Shepherd, on the Seneca Cattaraugus Reservation, established in 1900.

In colonial days, when Queen Anne was dispatching SPG missionaries out among the Iroquois, she sent communion silver to the Mohawks and the Onondaga. To the Onondaga she sent a chalice, two flagons and three patens with the following inscription:

THE GIFT OF HER MAJESTY
ANNE
BY GRACE OF GOD,
QUEEN
OF GREAT BRITAIN, FRANCE AND IRELAND, AND
ALL HER PLANTATIONS IN NORTH AMERICA
TO HER INDIAN CHAPPELL OF THE ONONDAWGUS.

The gift of the gracious queen was untimely; the chapel on the Onondaga, though commissioned, was never built. The queen's silver reposes, yet, to the considerable dismay of many Onondaga, at St. Peter's Episcopal Church in Albany. The Church of the Good Shepherd on the Onondaga Reservation has sought unsuccessfully to reclaim the gift of Queen Anne; the Albany church has continued to claim ownership.

Episcopal Onondagas were in 1990 for the first time ever communicated from the silver at a festive service at St. Paul's Cathedral in Syracuse. Onondagas were joined by American Indians traveling from as far away as Alaska for the service and to pay honor to David Pendleton Oakerhater, the Cheyenne warrior who became the first Indian listed on the Episcopal calendar of saints. Oakerhater had been baptized, confirmed and ordained in the Diocese of Central New York.

The Church of the Good Shepherd on the Onondaga Reservation had been established for over a decade when Oakerhater came to Syracuse and nearby Paris Hill for study. There is, however, no record of his having visited the reservation congregation.

Scant records were found which informed of work of the Onondaga mission during its early years. Old newspaper clippings indicate good relationships between the people of the Christian community and people who practiced the Longhouse religion, a faith which combined certain Quaker religious tenets and traditional Iroquois ways.

A 1925 edition of *The Spirit of Missions* said that Good Shepherd then had 80 communicants, a church school of 40 and a font role of 33. The article further said that the first Indian troops of Boy Scouts and Girl Scouts were formed at Good Shepherd on the Onondaga. A social worker, funded by the United Thank Offering (UTO), secured the first tuberculosis clinic on the reservation.

Widows of former priests were vital to continuity of the mission and lived on the reservation to serve the congregation on a day-in, day-out basis. The widow of the Rev. W. D. Manross, a resident of the mission from 1919 until 1937, started the first health clinic for children; Mrs. Charles Harris Jr., resident from 1941-1952, raised funds to build a mission hall, still used for reservation community services. Work of these two women was highly respected among the matrilineal Onondaga.

The Episcopal community at Onondaga nurtured a little girl born in the 1950s who grew up to be the first American Indian missionary of the Episcopal Church as well as the first Indian woman elected to the church's Executive Council. Virginia (Ginny) Doctor, whose mother is Mohawk from the Six Nations Reserve of Canada and whose late father was Onondaga, spent her childhood on the Onondaga Reservation. She was baptized and confirmed at Good Shepherd, where all her family was active. Her Onondaga grandmother, in fact, was the mission's matriarch. In matrilineal societies, descent is reckoned through the female line; all children are counted as members of the tribe or clan of the mother. Shortly after the death of her father, friction surfaced on the Onondaga Reservation and all persons who were not Onondaga were evicted from the reservation. The Mohawk mother with her family of seven moved to nearby Syracuse.

However, as a young woman, Ginny Doctor continued activity with the Good Shepherd and eventually served on its vestry. Her vision broadened in a few years and she accepted appointment of the Presiding Bishop to serve on the National Committee on Indian Work. Soon she was called on to carve time from her busy professional responsibilities as director of Syracuse's Indian Center to serve on other national Episcopal commissions, including the committees dealing with Indian and women's ministries. She was appointed to the Episcopal Council of Indian Ministry (ECIM) in 1990 and elected its chairperson in 1992.

As a member of the Oakerhater Evangelism Team in 1991, she traveled hundreds of miles on the Yukon River as part of the "floating revival" sponsored by ECIM. Touched by the spiritual needs of Native Alaskans and enchanted with the pristine land, the merry-eyed Mohawk woman spent the summer of 1992 as a mission volunteer on the Yukon. The following year she resigned her job in Syracuse and signed on for three years as a lay teacher and counselor—in the role of full-fledged missionary—at the village of Tanana on the Yukon River.

Her commitment and multiple skills offer a bright ray of hope for native peoples all across the Anglican Communion.

Good Shepherd on the Seneca Cattaraugus

The Seneca, "Keepers of the Western Door," had largely resisted the considerable early missionizing efforts of both the French Jesuits and Anglicans. Even Samuel Kirkland, the Puritan and patriot who exercised great influence with the Oneida, made little headway in either evangelizing the Seneca or convincing them to fight the British.

Traditional lands of the Seneca encompassed much of western New York and from the 1600s through the Revolution they were victims of the power struggle between nations of Europe. During the Revolution, the Seneca to a certain extent joined the Mohawks in loyalty to Britain, and as a result the Seneca sustained awful devastation at the hands of the colonial army which marched out with orders not only to over-run but destroy. General John Sullivan razed 40 villages and burned 160,000 bushels of corn, leveled orchard after orchard and field upon field.

Iroquois power never recovered. But out of the demoralization came a hope for the future advanced by the Seneca prophet, Handsome Lake, who brought vision of a new religion which combined certain tenets of Christianity with traditional Iroquois ethos. The Code of Handsome Lake—often called the Longhouse religion—was quickly accepted, not only by the Senecas, but by others of the old Iroquois League.

Some Senecas chose the Christian religion and in May, 1900, under direction of an archdeacon in the Diocese of Western New York, the first service of the Episcopal Church was held in a little schoolhouse on the Mile Strip Road, near Irving, on the western edge of the Cattaraugus Reservation. Records say that the first baptism was that of Lillian Warren Pierce, daughter of Bemus and Annie Pierce, and the first confirmation was that of Glennis M. Jimeson. (Jimeson, with its several variations of spelling, is a well-known name among the Seneca, extending back to a kidnapped child of the Colonial era).

Weekly services for the Seneca for the next three years were maintained by the Laymen's Missionary League. Church people in Buffalo and Rochester contributed to erect a frame building at the outskirts of the hamlet of Irving on the western edge of the Cattaraugus Reservation. Consecrated in December, 1903, the Church of the Good Shepherd stands in several wooded acres surrounded by a large cemetery.

One of the best known deaconesses of the Episcopal Church, Harriet M. Bedell, began her lifelong commitment to serving Indian people among the Senecas. A public school teacher in Buffalo, New York, she journeyed from time to time to the Cattaraugus Reservation and taught Sunday school at the Seneca Indian Mission at Lawtons, assisting a missionary named T.H. Clough. At age 30, she heard a missionary to China speak at her home parish during the winter of 1904 and decided she, too, would become a missionary in Hankow, China.

Miss Bedell never got to China but she worked the rest of her long life with Indians, first with the Cheyenne in western Oklahoma from 1907 to 1916, next with Alaska Natives on the Yukon River— stationed, in fact, for a time at Tanana, the village Ginny Doctor would serve generations later. Lastly, Harriet Bedell worked among the Seminole of Florida from 1933 onward, long after official retirement, until her death in 1969 at age 94.

A landmark event occurred in the winter of 1992 when Good Shepherd on the Cattaraugus saw one of its own ordained to the transitional diaconate. The congregation of approximately 100 baptized communicants went through a discernment process in 1991 to identify Roland Cooper, a 34-year-old blue-collar worker, to train for ordination under special canons that allow members of small communities of common ethnic, language or cultural ties to "hold up" one of their own for ordination. A layreader at Good Shepherd for 12 years, Cooper studied several years under senior priests of the diocese and at a special study program at St. George's College, an Anglican institution in Jerusalem. Cooper's family was long active with the congregation. His grandmother, Virginia Snow, served for many years as senior warden. Cooper's ordination service, held at St. Paul's Cathedral in Buffalo, included a Native American dance, hymns sung in the Seneca language and the passing of a peace pipe. In 1995 Cooper became the first Seneca priest of the Episcopal Church.

Two Missions after Seven Generations

The Church of England made its first feeble move to evangelize the world at the Virginia colony. Intent became reality, however, in the New York colony where within a generation prior to the American Revolution almost all of the Mohawks, the eastern-most of the six nations of the Iroquois Confederacy, were baptized as Anglicans.

The Anglican Church's missionaries did their most persistent and effective work among the Indians in New York. But the Episcopal

Church helped to dispatch the first fruit of its evangelizing effort—
the Oneida—westward to Wisconsin. After seven generations, from
the time gospel was "preached and planted" among the Iroquois, the
Episcopal Church's six dioceses within the State of New York have
established and maintained mission among the 62,651 New York Indians only in two small missions—the Good Shepherd churches on
the Cattaruagus and Onondaga reservations.

3

MINNESOTA: WELL-SPRING
OF WORK IN THE WEST

Jackson Kemper, the Episcopal Church's first missionary bishop, un-
capped the well-spring which would surge up in Minnesota and flow
out into the northern plains of the Dakotas to nurture Episcopal Indian mission for the next century.

Kemper, whose cure initially included virtually everything west
of Ohio, was sorely aware of the consequences ahead for the Native
peoples as a result of the national frenzy of western expansion and
the human deluge pouring into Minnesota Territory. A full generation
had passed since the Episcopal Church founded mission among the
Oneida; but scant thought seems to have been given to initiating mission elsewhere. In 1835, shortly after his consecration, Kemper wrote
that the "needs of the red men are a weight upon my soul."

To look after those needs Kemper first sent his devoted disciple
James Lloyd Breck to Minnesota, then occupied primarily by two Indian nations which were historic enemies and spoke entirely different
languages. Frequent skirmishes occurred between the Lakota/Dakota
(Sioux) plains people and the Ojibwa (Chippewa) of the north woods.

A lilliputian lake in the northeast corner of South Dakota bears
the lyrical name of Enemy-Swim-Lake, said to be site of a serious
skirmish between the old foes in which one or the other, depending on
who tells the story, escaped certain slaughter by plunging into the
lake and swiftly fleeing.

Though the territorial contest had persisted far back beyond
memory, the rivalry was intensified immeasurably when in the 1700s
the Ojibwa acquired guns and the Sioux acquired horses. The Ojibwa

swapped thousands of rich beaver pelts to French traders for fire-arms, and the Sioux upon obtaining the horse (left behind by the Spanish conquistadors of the 16th century) became immediately trans-formed from hungry foot-slogging wanderers into the proud knights of the plains and, for a brief moment in time, the greatest buffalo hunters the world would ever see.

Among the several legends on derivation of the word "Sioux" is a story that early French explorers asked their Ojibwa guides about the people who wore great feathered headdress and rode fast ponies. The Ojibwa described the Dakotas as "Na-do-wed-sue," a word which translates as enemy or snake in the Ojibwa language. "Ah," concluded the Frenchmen, "these people are Sioux," adopting the French spell-ing. The United States government, in its tangled and often embittered relations with the many Lakota/Dakota bands—who spoke different but related languages—identified them as Sioux. So did the Church.

There is also a story on how the Ojibwa came to be called Chippewa. The word is a misbegotten pronunciation of a denigrating Dakota word translating as "people of the puckered moccasins." Many Ojibwa people today prefer to be called Anishinaabe, meaning in their own language, simply, "the people."

Ojibwa Mission: 1852-1862

After launching the original monastic community in Wisconsin which evolved into a training center for teachers and preachers preparing for the sacred ministry, Breck grew restless and with the cordial ap-proval of Bishop Kemper and financial aid from the East, he laid plans to establish new work further westward. With two clerical associates and a seminarian Breck set out on a 500-mile trip westward, eventu-ally crossing the Mississippi by canoe and touching Minnesota ground on June 24, 1850.

Breck first set about establishing an Episcopal mission in St. Paul, a crude settlement of 1,600, mostly rough lumbermen and sleazy rum-sellers. The missioners lived two months in a tent until they could build themselves a log cabin. Soon a small church was erected and a school opened.

Through Breck's school in St. Paul two churchmen met and their meeting would change forever the course of Episcopal ministry among American Indians. This historic meeting occurred when an Ottawa Indian named Enmegahbowh brought his son in 1851 to St. Paul to be educated at Breck's mission.

It was Enmegahbowh, in fact, who first invited Episcopal mission among the Indians of Minnesota. Born of Ottawa parents who lived with the Rice Lake band of Ojibwas located north of Lake Ontario, Enmegahbowh—his name means One-who-stands-before-his-people—was living near the village of Peterborough when he first came to the notice of an Anglican clergyman. The minister, identified only as Mr. Armour, persuaded Enmegahbowh's reluctant parents to allow the young boy to live in his home to be educated with his sons. Within three months Enmegahbowh had learned to read and to speak English, but homesickness drove him to return to his own people. He ran away in the night and traveled on foot for two days.

He later attended a Methodist mission school and worked as an interpreter for the Methodist mission at Sault Ste. Marie. With his cousin, George Copway, and another convert, Peter Marksman, Enmegahbowh established a Methodist mission at Lac Courte Oreilles, near present-day Hayward, Wisconsin. In the fall of 1837 the trio entered Ebenezer Manual Labor School in Illinois. Following his graduation, Enmegahbowh met and married Charlotte, an Ojibwa woman whose parents exacted a promise that the couple would not leave Ojibwa territory. Charlotte belonged to the family of Hole-in-the-Day, a wily head chieftain of the Ojibwa. Though her family's religion was the *Midewiwin* (Grand Medicine), Charlotte was baptized prior to their marriage.

Sketchy accounts next provide a glimpse of Enmegahbowh in northern Minnesota where the Methodists ordained him deacon under the name of John Johnson. They expelled him from their ranks following an incident in 1849. It is said that a white man insulted Charlotte, and that "Enmegahbowh knocked the scoundrel down and held him while his wife gave the worthless scoundrel a sound thrashing."

Following the incident, Enmegahbowh came into contact with an Episcopal chaplain serving with the U.S. Army at Fort Snelling, the then-last outpost in the "northern wilderness," standing on a commanding bluff above the Mississippi River at its confluence with the Minnesota River. Through the chaplain Enmegahbowh learned of Breck's mission and school at St. Paul. Within a short time, Enmegahbowh with his young son appeared on Breck's doorstep.

After the Methodists banished him, Enmegahbowh joined Hole-in-the Day's band of Ojibwa on Gull Lake—located near today's Brainerd, some 150 miles to the north of St. Paul. When he returned to Gull Lake he sent the well-known appeal to the Episcopal church:

Come you. Come and teach. Everybody say, Come you,
Come and teach . . . There might be some little translation

of the Liturgy, and some of the forms of Prayers, etc. It would do a great deal of good at present . . .

Bishop Kemper instructed Breck to join Enmegahbowh at Gull Lake, named in *Ojibwa Ka-ge-ash-koon-si-kag*, (the place of the little gulls). Together, in 1852, they established St. John's-in-the-Wilderness which would later become St. Columba's, the mother mission of Episcopal Indian work west of the Mississippi River and the oldest surviving Indian Christian congregation of Minnesota.

Breck looked at St. Columba's mission as the grand entrance into the "Indian field" and envisioned a vast jurisdiction which possibly could become an Indian diocese with its own bishop. This was not to happen in northern Minnesota but the vision would be adapted 20 years hence in the jurisdiction of Niobrara serving the Sioux.

In August of 1853 the untiring Kemper trotted his grey horse across the great distances to Gull Lake to dedicate the little log church to St. Columba, the Scottish abbot dating from the sixth century, and to confirm the first class of Ojibwa Indians. Undaunted by the awesome responsibilities of covering his enormous jurisdiction, Kemper traveled constantly, usually on horseback—"his saddle-bags contained his worldly goods, his robes, his communion service, his Bible and his Prayer Book." His dairy records the events of the day:

> We had the whole consecration service, parts of which were translated by Johnson, with whom I had gone over the whole in the morning. There was then the confession in Ojibwa; I pronounced the absolution. Breck read two lessons from the N.T., which were interpreted. The Creed in Ojibwa, One chant & one hymn in Ojibwa. I read, Johnson interpreting. There was talking at times, & some boys outside made a noise, drumming on the sides of the church . . .

In a 1911 biography of Kemper, Grenough White wrote:

> He [Breck] had a class to present for confirmation, and in a neat log chapel at *Kaygeeashkoonsikag*, the site of the Chippewa mission, Kemper confirmed Mary Medemoyan Statelar, Rebecca Odohbenanequa Manitowab, Charlotte Pewahbekokethegoqua Johnson, David Kahsequa, and John Annegahbowk Johnson . . .

The biographer neglected to note that "Annegahbowk" was also known as Enmegahbowh, who would 15 years thence become the first American Indian priest of the Episcopal Church.

The mission at Gull Lake flourished. By the end of the first three years nearly 100 men, women and children had been baptized, an

Enmegahbowh (Ojibwa-Ottawa) [1810-1902]
recognized as the Episcopal Church's first Indian priest.
Courtesy, Smithsonian Institution.

average of 50 were attending daily morning and evening prayer, and the school had 35 students. Breck, eagerly assisted by Enmegahbowh, rapidly transformed the Ojibwa Christian community. Disarranged wigwams were assiduously replaced by tidy log cabins bordered with neat vegetable gardens. Men, "including chiefs and braves," were toiling with ax and hoe; women were sewing and scrubbing. Children were engrossed in book learning.

Other Ojibwa bands invited Episcopal mission but initial work among the "wild" Pillager at Leech Lake failed and Breck was driven out. In fact, Breck on a visit to the Pillagers was roused in the middle of the night and ordered to abandon the mission. Reasoning that he could serve neither the church nor God by "remaining to be murdered by drunken savages," Breck speedily departed.

Breck's tendency to alter career courses saw him shortly withdraw from Indian work and set off in 1858 to found Seabury Divinity School in Faribault, leaving Enmegahbowh to run the fledgling mission at Gull Lake. Enmegahbowh was substantially assisted by missionaries of the Church of England working in Canada, who shared an Ojibwa translation of the prayer book, the four gospels and later the complete New Testament.

The following year Enmegahbowh was ordained to the diaconate. He had formally applied to Bishop Kemper to be admitted as candidate for Holy Orders on May 5, 1854. During the next five years Kemper included Gull Lake in his annual visitation of Minnesota and when the convention was called in 1856 to organize a diocese, Enmegahbowh was a deputy. Kemper, at the age of 70, then resigned his missionary responsibilities to devote himself wholly to work in Wisconsin. On July 3, 1859, as one of his last acts as the provisional bishop of the Minnesota diocese, Kemper ordained Enmegahbowh to the diaconate.

First Bishop of Minnesota

Continuity of the mission among the Ojibwa, now entirely under Enmegahbowh, was ensured in 1859 when there burst onto the Episcopal scene one of the most dynamic and picturesque men ever to sit in the House of Bishops, Henry Benjamin Whipple, first Bishop of Minnesota. Only 37 when he became bishop, the native New Yorker would head the Minnesota diocese for 42 years and almost single-handedly awakened the Episcopal Church to a social consciousness about Indian affairs.

An Oberlin College dropout, Whipple had worked in the family business in upstate New York and dabbled in Democratic politics before setting himself a three-year course of home study for the ministry. He was ordained priest in 1849. After serving the Rome, New York, church for six years he was called to set up a "free church" parish in the working-class southside of Chicago, then a robust frontier settlement and railroad center.

He had visited Minnesota Territory at least once prior to being elected bishop and had observed the disappearing domain of the Indian. Also, for health reasons, he wintered in Florida where he was stirred by first-hand stories of the U.S. government's despicable treatment of the Seminole chieftain Osceola, captured under a flag of truce and imprisoned.

At Whipple's consecration services, a missionary to Africa who was home on leave handed the young bishop $70 saying, "Before I left Africa, our Christian black men gave me money to carry the gospel to the heathen in America. I give it to you for Indian missions." His course was thereby set, and during the lights and shadows of his long episcopate he became known far and wide as the champion of Indians in their dealings with the government of the United States, as well as their chief pastor and friend.

Traveling to his new post by riverboat, Whipple stopped off at Red Wing on the Mississippi to baptize a baby of Wabasha, hereditary chief of the Lower Sioux. Within a year, the chief himself would be confirmed and would remain Whipple's lifelong friend and ally.

Whipple arrived to assume oversight of his jurisdictions at a crucial hour in Indian-white relations. The federal government's Office of Indian Affairs was abysmally corrupt; the doctrine of manifest destiny was poised for its last and final thrust; the lakes and woodlands tribes were barely subsisting in unbelievably destitute conditions, while the plains peoples were engaged in a last desperate resistance to the white conquerors.

A scant month following his consecration, Whipple set out with Breck to visit Enmegahbowh at the Gull Lake Mission. The bishop wrote of his first visit:

> No words can describe the pitiable condition of these Indians. A few miles from St. Columba we came to a wigwam where the half naked children were crying from cold and hunger, and the mother was scraping the inner bark of the pine tree for pitch to give to her starving children . . .
>
> Our Indian affairs are at their worst; without government, without protection, without personal rights of property, subject to every evil influence, and the prey of covetous, dishonest white men, while the fire-water flowed in rivers of death . . .

During the visit to Gull Lake Whipple confirmed eight Indians—including an aged couple bearing single names of Abraham and Sarah—and wrote of the joy he experienced at the first Indian communion. His spontaneous joy turned quickly to sober resolve. In his autobiography he wrote:

> I was saddened upon my return when good men advised me to have nothing to do with Indian Missions, on the ground that the red men were a degraded, perishing race. Our late presiding bishop, the Rt. Rev. John Williams, said at my first missionary address in his diocese, "They are a heathen people and the picture is very dark . . . they are a perishing people, but the Son of God came to save a perishing world; and if the red race is perishing, the more reason to make haste and carry to them the gospel." I resolved that, with God being my helper, it should never be said

that the first Bishop of Minnesota turned his back upon the heathen at his door.

Whipple was so angered by conditions that he wrote President Buchanan the next spring citing specific recommendations for a policy change in Indian affairs. In the autumn of 1860, the bishop journeyed to Washington to follow up on his letter in person, urging, among other things, that "different bands of an Indian tribe be concentrated in one reservation."

Dakota Mission: 1861-1863

When the first white men came to present-day Minnesota, the Dakota were still living in large numbers in the lake country, using wild rice as a staple in their diet. These eastern-most Dakota people were the Santee and by 1700 had divided themselves into four well-defined bands—the Mdewakanton, Wahpekute, Wahpeton and Sisseton. The far-ranging Teton ("dwellers on the plains") had gradually drifted westward and divided themselves into the seven Lakota bands—the Brulé, Oglala, Hunkpapa, Minneconjou, Blackfeet, Two Kettle and Sans Arc. The Nakota, or middle group, included the Yankton and Yanktonais. Dialects of the Dakota, Lakota and Nakota differ.

By 1850 white encroachment and depletion of game caused the Dakota to agree to relinquish their homelands and settle on reservations which lay along the Minnesota River in the south central part of the state. The reservation was originally 20 miles wide and 140 miles long. But by 1858 the surviving 6,000 Dakotas were coerced into relinquishing their ten-mile strip of fertile land north of the Minnesota River. The Redwood or Lower Sioux Agency was established to serve the Mdewakanton and Wahpekute bands and further up the river Yellow Medicine or Upper Sioux Agency served the Sisseton and Wahpeton bands. A fortified army post, Fort Ridgely, was strategically positioned across the Minnesota River some 15 miles below the Lower Agency.

Adjustment to the role of farmers and wards of the government had been difficult for the Dakota. Grievances mounted against frontier encroachment, rigged treaties and traders' practices which included inflated debts and an ever-present threat to cut off credit. The trader at the Lower Sioux agency, Andrew Myrick, refused hungry Indians credit with the statement: "Go eat grass." Myrick was among the first casualties of the Dakota Uprising; grass was found stuffed in the mouth of his dead body.

As resentment grew toward practices of greedy shopkeepers, a social order internally was maintained only through the old Dakota "head-man" or chieftain organization. There were nine Mdewakanton bands including those headed by Little Crow, Shakopee, and Wabasha.

In June, 1860, Whipple visited the Lower Sioux Agency. The head-chief, Wabasha, along with *Wa-kin-yan-waste* (Good Thunder) and Taopi, invited him to establish a mission among them. These three men figured strongly in both the establishment of the Episcopal mission and in the tragic events to befall the ill-fated Santee. Whipple wrote that the Presbyterians had a mission at the Upper Agency but that he "planted a mission among the Lower Sioux where there had been no mission of any kind."

At the time of the Whipple visit, the agency had several stone buildings, a boarding school, sawmill and stables, and gave the appearance of a well-ordered little village. The government had built houses for the agent, interpreter, physician, carpenter and blacksmith. Among the people of the village were both Anglo-Dakotas and Franco-Dakotas, the latter being offspring of French traders. Whipple, in *Lights and Shadows of a Long Episcopate*, wrote:

> I visited [the Lower Agency] in June, 1860. This visit was at the time of the annual payment and 2,500 Sioux had gathered at the Agency. The head-chief, Wabasha, Good Thunder and Taopi came to see me with a sad story of their wrongs.
>
> They had sold the Government 800,000 acres of their reservation—a country 30 miles long and 10 miles wide—and had been promised $8,000 a year for schools, but the government had not paid them for their land nor had they any schools. They asked for a school and a missionary, which I promised if I could find the man and obtain the means.
>
> When I returned to Faribault, Samuel D. Hinman, one of my divinity students from the diocese of Connecticut, came to me and said: "Bishop, you know I have been holding services for the Sioux near Faribault. I want to be a missionary to them." I had found my man . . . I ordained Mr. Hinman deacon, September 20, 1860, and he began services at the Mission of St. John at the Lower Agency.

The Rev. Samuel Dutton Hinman, along with his young bride, Mary, knowing little of the language or customs of the Dakota, set out undaunted to pursue what would prove to be their life-long work. Accompanying the Hinmans was another missionary, Emily West, a native of Minnesota, who would also dedicate the rest of her life to work among the Santee. Susan Salisbury, the bishop's niece, went as a teacher.

During their first year at Redwood, the missionaries established a school and by the next spring had 50 students enrolled and seven persons prepared for confirmation, including Taopi, Wabasha, Good Thunder and his wife Snana. Good Thunder was, in fact, the first adult Sioux that Whipple baptized and Good Thunder's life was ever after entwined with the Episcopal Lower Sioux mission. Snana (also called Tinkling and Maggie Brass) was educated in a Congregational mission school and, at age 15, she married Good Thunder. Her account of her marriage is recorded:

> An Indian man whose name was Good Thunder offered some special things to my mother for me to be his wife . . . But I insisted that I would marry legally in church; so we did, and were married in the Protestant Episcopal Church. Some years after we got married, we were the first ones to enter the Christian life, which was in 1861. We were confirmed in the same church. On account of our becoming Christians we were ridiculed by the Indians who were not yet taught the gospel of Jesus and who could not yet understand what Christianity meant.

Episcopal mission was not unanimously welcomed at Lower Sioux. Bitterly opposed to Christianity was another of the Mdewakanton chiefs, Little Crow, leader of the so-called "hostiles." Taopi, Wabasha and Good Thunder were identified with the "farmers" or Christian peace party. Though Whipple's sympathy and support toward the Dakotas was unfailing, he wanted, without doubt, to see them abandon their religion and culture and become farmers. When Whipple visited the agency in July, 1862, to lay the cornerstone for the Church of St. John, he was appalled to find a scalp dance in progress near the mission house. It was during the Civil War, shortly after the Battle of Gettysburg. He immediately confronted Wabasha, who agreed it to be inappropriate for the Dakota to celebrate the taking of a scalp of a Winnebago horse thief caught in the act. The bishop then described what followed:

> . . . the chief was smoking, but took his pipe from his mouth, and slowly blowing a cloud of smoke into the air said, "White man go to war with his own brother; kills more men than Wabasha can count all his life".

The work at the Lower Sioux Agency was disrupted in tragedy on August 18, 1862, in the early hours of the Dakota Conflict. The annuity payment was delayed, and delayed again. July passed—the time for their annual buffalo hunt—and still they huddled around the agency awaiting the treaty-obligated annuity. Wise men knew confrontation was inevitable, yet the white man still reneged. The land was gone, the buffalo was going and the treaty-guaranteed food supply failed to arrive. Whipple wrote:

> Four years ago the Sioux sold the Government part of their reservation, the plea for the sale being the need of funds to aid them in civilization . . . Of ninety-six thousand dollars due to the Lower Sioux not one cent has ever been received . . . In June, at the time fixed by custom, they came together for the payment. The agent could give no satisfactory reason for the delay . . . The Indians waited at the Agencies for two months, dissatisfied, turbulent, hungry, and then came the outbreak . . . The money reached Fort Ripley the day after the outbreak. Who is guilty of the causes which desolated our border? At whose door is the blood of these innocent victims? I believe that God will hold the nation guilty.

The bitter outbreak was triggered by a trivial incident which involved a nest of eggs on a white man's farm. Four young Indian hunters of Shakopee's band returning from an unsuccessful hunt passed near a white settlement and found the hen's nest. What began as a dare among angry young men on a Sunday afternoon to steal eggs ended with a challenge to test manhood. Before sundown five white settlers were dead. The young hunters rode rapidly to the Agency and told their story to a group of Mdewakantons whose resentment over broken promises was already at the boiling point. Through the night the Santee chiefs argued. Wabasha argued for peace. He lost.

A band of warriors, crazed with excitement and long-harbored resentment against the whites, galloped through the night to Little Crow's home, awakened him, and urged him to put on his war paint and lead them into a conclusive showdown against the hated whites with a direct assault against Redwood Agency. Though staunchly anti-Christian, Little Crow had tried to live like a white man—even adapting the white man's way of dress: trousers and a brass-buttoned jacket. Though resentful of the government's theft and fraud against his people, Little Crow at first urged that the reckless young men who had killed the settlers be turned over to the military at Fort Ridgely. Someone during the long night called him a coward, an affront no Dakota warrior could tolerate. Before daybreak, he agreed reluctantly to lead his people against the white settlers and soldiers.

The attack on Redwood Agency began at 7 o'clock on the morning of August 18. Hinman, the priest, was sitting on the steps of the mission house at the Lower Agency talking with a man who was working on the new Episcopal church building, when he heard rapid firing at the trading post a quarter of a mile away. Within minutes, Little Crow appeared, running at full speed toward the government barn where he and his party shot the blacksmith and took government horses and fled.

Hinman hastened to the interpreter, who lived nearby, to notify him of the outbreak. Mrs. Hinman was absent from the mission, but Miss West, the missionary, was advised to rush down the bluff to the ferry to cross the Minnesota River. Near the ferry she was joined by a white woman and child. Right after crossing the river, they met a party of Indians in war-paint and feathers, who greeted them pleasantly with "Ho! Ho! Ho! You belong to the mission. *Washte!* (Good). Where are you going?" Miss West pointed to a house in the distance and they said, "No, we are going to kill them," and motioned her to take the road leading to Fort Ridgley. They threatened to kill the other woman, but after Miss West explained that she had promised to take care of her and the child the warriors answered, " Ho! Ho!" and departed.

Taopi's account of the early morning events is found in Whipple's autobiography:

> On the morning of the 18th of August, 1862, I was preparing to go down to the [Episcopal] Mission House, the residence of our minister, the Rev. Mr. Hinman. He had promised to go with me to assist in laying out our burial lot near the new church. My child had been buried but a few days before. As I was starting, an old man came to my house and said, "All the upper bands are armed and coming down the road." I asked, "For what purpose?" He said, "I don't know . . . They are killing the traders . . . The Rice Creek Indians [Shakopee's band] have murdered the whites on the other side of the Minnesota River, and now they are killing the traders."

> As soon as he was gone I heard the report of guns. I went up to the top of my house and from there I could hear the shouts of the Indians and see them plundering the stores. The men of my band now began to assemble at my house. We counselled, but we could do nothing to resist the hostile Indians because we were so few and they were between us and the settlements . . .

> I sent Good Thunder with a message to Wabasha, but he could not reach his house on account of the hostile

Indians . . . Good Thunder came back and brought news that nearly a whole company of soldiers from the fort had been killed at the ferry . . .

Then, on foot and on horseback, the warriors led by Little Crow, continued down to the traders' stores. Some explained to bystanders that they were looking for Chippewas, the traditional enemy of the Dakotas. Soon after daybreak the warriors began entering the stores. A Winnebago chief Little Priest, who had been visiting among the Dakotas for several weeks, and his men killed the much hated trader, Andrew Myrick. Twenty-three white men were killed and 10 women were taken captive. Hinman, along with a majority of the surviving white people of the agency, managed to reach the ferry and cross the river and hurry toward Fort Ridgely.

Little Crow dispatched a message to the Upper Agency, summoning the Sisseton and Wahpeton bands to join in driving the whites from the Minnesota River valley. Only the young hotheads responded; the Christian Indians voted neutrality and herded 62 white people into a warehouse for protection and then escorted them to safety. Within the next few weeks raids took place over the whole surrounding area, fanning out 20 to 30 miles from the reservation, surprising people in their houses and fields. Hundreds were slaughtered. Little Crow led large numbers of warriors against Fort Ridgely and New Ulm, a town settled primarily by Germans. Here the fiercest battle of the war occurred on August 23. The townspeople withstood a powerful Dakota assault and though Fort Ridgley at one point had a troop strength of only 40 men, reinforcements arrived in time to deter the Dakotas from overrunning the outpost.

A violent battle occurred across the Minnesota River from the Redwood Agency, at Birch Coulee, which had been selected as a campsite by a burial detail. The Dakotas surprised and nearly annihilated the 80-odd men in a vicious two-day fight. Under the command of Colonel Henry Sibley, former governor of Minnesota, an army of more than a thousand men then set out to relieve the burial detail and moved on to crush the Indians. On September 23, Sibley's army defeated a contingent at the battle of Wood Lake. This defeat ended the dream of expelling the settlers from the Minnesota River valley. Little Crow and some 200-300 of his followers hurriedly folded their tents and stole quietly away into the Dakota prairies, leaving behind 269 white captives.

Sibley moved with a vengeance, scouting the country to collect every Indian in sight—peace party members as well as hostiles. Sibley's forces paid scant attention to the fact that many whites were saved by Christian Dakotas. Taopi alone is said to have saved 255 captives. Other Episcopal converts who acted to save lives of white captives included Wabasha, Good Thunder, Iron Shield, Simon A-Nag-mani, Lorenzo Lawrence, Other Day, Thomas Robertson, Wakin-yo-ta-wa and Paul Mazakute, who would become, in 1868, the first Sioux ordained to the diaconate in the Episcopal Church and in 1871 ordained priest.

Sibley ordered a military tribunal of five officers of volunteer regiments to examine evidence regarding Indian participation in the war. By November 5 the tribunal had tried 392 men, handling as many as 40 cases in one day, and sentenced 307 to be hanged. Trials of some lasted no more than five minutes. Defendants in the trials had no lawyers to represent them and were not allowed to bring in witnesses in their own defense. Despite the fact that few of the men on trial knew the English language and interpreters had to be used, the interpreters were not sworn in. At no point in the trials did anyone intervene on behalf of the defendants.

Then the prisoners, numbering about 1,600 people, were moved, chained together, down river. The miserable train of humanity measuring some four miles in length, passed through towns and hamlets crowded with angry, cursing, shouting and crying white men, women and children armed with guns, knives, clubs and stones. On occasions before the soldiers could interfere, the crowd rushed upon the Indians as the train passed by and succeeded in pulling many of the old men and women and several children from the wagons by the hair of the head, and beating them, and otherwise inflicting injury upon the helpless creatures. Samuel J. Brown, a mixed-blood Sisseton, testified that he saw an enraged white woman rush up to one of the wagons and snatch a nursing baby from its mother's breast and dash it violently upon the ground. He informed:

> The soldiers instantly seized her and led or rather dragged the woman away, and restored the papoose to its mother—limp and almost dead. Although the child was not killed outright, it died a few hours after. The body was quietly laid away in the crotch of a tree a few miles beyond Henderson . . . I witnessed the ceremony, which was, perhaps, the last of the kind within the limits of Minnesota; that is, the last Sioux Indian "buried" according to one of the oldest and most cherished customs of the tribe.

The condemned were imprisoned at Mankato to await hanging. The others continued the woeful journey to Fort Snelling where they would spend a miserable winter in the flats below the old military post. Even the most embittered white visitors were appalled by the terrible conditions at the Dakota camp. A high fence was put up around their camp. Measles broke out. Sometimes as many as 50 died in a day and were buried in a trench. Among those prisoners were Good Thunder and his wife, the lovely Snana. Two of their children died at the winter camp.

Hinman, the newly ordained Episcopal clergyman, accompanied the Santee to Fort Snelling, and enduring malevolent vengeance of the inflamed white population, moved into the compound with the Indians, placing himself in serious jeopardy. On one occasion a band of vengeful thugs broke into the stockade and beat him unconscious. Hinman and Congregational missionaries Stephen Return Riggs and John P. Williamson, were denounced in the press as mawkish sentimentalists or "contemptible fools."

Whipple was the solitary bulwark between desperate Indians and white hostility that prevailed all across Minnesota. Whipple never wavered in his support, even when anti-Indian sentiment became so intense that a frontiersman was overheard saying, "We must go down to Faribault and clean out that bishop." In his autobiography Whipple reports that after he confirmed Santee prisoners at Fort Snelling, a newspaper account shrieked:

> God was mocked and his religion burlesqued by the sol
> emn farce of Bishop Whipple administering the sacred rites
> of baptism and confirmation on a horde of treacherous fiends
> at Fort Snelling . . .

After the unduly speedy trials had convicted 307, Whipple intervened directly with President Lincoln, showing that the Indians had ample cause for hostility. The President then ruled that those condemned to die merely for fighting in a battle should be treated as prisoners of war. This left 38 to be hanged.

On the morning of December 26 the condemned painted their faces and broke into their death songs as their arms were pinioned with cords and their wrists were tied. At ten o'clock they were marched from the prison to a huge scaffold upon which they were all to stand together in one group to be hanged. Nooses were placed around their necks and white hoods were placed upon their heads. Three slow measured beats were sounded on a drum. A rope was struck. The 38 Dakotas fell to their deaths. It was the largest mass hanging ever in the United States.

As the condemned 38 walked to their execution, it is said they sang the Dakota chant memorialized in Hymn 385 in the present-day Episcopal Hymnal. All but two had accepted Christian baptism. The

*Henry Benjamin Whipple [1822-1901],
first bishop of Minnesota.*

bodies were buried in shallow graves nearby, from which they were shortly exhumed for use as cadavers by local physicians.

Two or three of the executed turned out to be fatal mistakes in identity. Bishop Whipple recounted the sad incident of a man who had been executed and later turned out to be a 16-year-old white youth who had been raised by Indians.

Robert M. Anderson, Minnesota's bishop 1978-1993, recently wrote:

> There have been times in Minnesota history when racism, broken treaties, and repression reached such a climax that Indian people were subjected to starvation, death and imprisonment. The ultimate humiliation came on December 26, 1862.

Even after the mass execution at Mankato, the groundswell of public opinion shrieked for expulsion of all Indians from Minnesota. Bishop Whipple, while acknowledged as the most respected churchman in the state, was publicly censured. He and his missionary weathered public outcry for their ministry to the miserable Santee at the Fort Snelling compound and found themselves caring for as many as 300 Indians. Hinman opened a school within the compound and baptized 149. Whipple visited the prison almost weekly and during the melancholy winter months he confirmed 100 Santee.

The old people would tell stories for many years of the hardships experienced by the Santee Sioux following the Minnesota Conflict. Amos Ross, who became an Episcopal priest, was a youngster of 10 living with his family in far northern Minnesota, near the Canadian border, when the Sioux uprising took place. His family was wholly unaware of the fighting going on in the southern part of the state; their band had had nothing to do with it. Yet, one morning the soldiers came and ordered them to march, leaving behind everything, even their tepees and horses. For two weeks they marched. At the end of the journey moccasins had worn out and people were walking on bloody feet. They were locked up in a military prison at Fort Snelling. Missionaries came and baptized; Hinman kept an Old Testament in his hand to supply himself with names.

The Upper Sioux—the Sisseton and Wahpeton bands—largely innocent of any role in the massacres, fled their roughly hewn log cabins and newly created small farms along the Minnesota River before the advancing army of General Sibley and scattered into South Dakota Territory in the eastern region around Lake Traverse and Big Stone Lake.

In the months following the Uprising, a host of warriors who had fled with Little Crow were ranging in the northern plains, primarily around Devils Lake, and into Canada. Throughout the winter Little Crow sought to mold the western Sioux bands into an alliance that would resist the whites, but the plan came to naught.

As for Little Crow, his end was inglorious. He died not on the battlefield but in a blackberry patch. With his followers, diminished to a mere 16, the hapless warrior who had been coerced simply to save face into the futile fight set out from Canada on a marauding expedition to the settlements in Minnesota and was killed on July 3, 1863, while picking berries near Hutchinson.

The white settlers of Minnesota savored their hour of vengeance when Congress passed legislation which abrogated all treaties entered into by the four bands of Sioux Indians, stripped them of any lands within the State of Minnesota, and expelled them to a then-undesignated location. The legislation, approved February 21, 1863, also called for the removal of the uninvolved Winnebago tribe which had not taken part in the Uprising.

An earlier proposal called for removal of all Minnesota Indians, who numbered some 47,000—Sioux, Winnebago and Chippewa (Ojibwa) tribes—to Isle Royale in Lake Superior, to survive or starve as best they could. Ultimately only the Sioux and Winnebago were deported.

Ojibwa Mission: 1862-1870

The Ojibwa escaped banishment from Minnesota partly because of Bishop Whipple's passionate intercession with powers in Washington and partly because of white gratitude to Enmegahbowh who walked through the night down the Gull River to warn the settlement and garrison at Fort Ripley of an impending Ojibwa attack. When Enmegahbowh learned that the Ojibwa chieftain, Hole-in-the-Day, was joining his old Sioux enemy, Little Crow, to drive out the hated white settlers, he first sent messages to warn the garrison at Fort Ripley, located 40 miles south of Gull Lake, then he sent a messenger to the Mille Lacs Ojibwa band, imploring them to send warriors to protect the fort. More than 100 Mille Lacs warriors sped to the fort.

Lastly, Enmegahbowh hastily collected his family and set out afoot to give warning. Whipple in *Lights and Shadows of a Long Episcopate,* wrote of the consequences of Enmegahbowh's costly alliance:

> He walked all night down the Gull River, dragging a canoe containing his wife and children, that he might give warning to the fort. Two of his children died from exposure . . .

Enmegahbowh paid dearly for his role in warning the whites. Not only did two of his children die as a result of the night of the long canoe trip, but St. Columba's mission was destroyed in the aftermath, leaving the deacon without a church for the next five years. To escape the wrath of Hole-in-the-Wall and his followers, all Christian Ojibwas were obliged to depart Gull Lake. St. Columba's was wrecked and ransacked and the little gardens of the converts were destroyed.

Enmegahbowh brought his Christian group to the white settlement of Crow Wing some days' journey distant. Under the trees of the forest, he conducted Ojibwa language services every Sunday. Eventually, Enmegahbowh was engaged to accompany a treaty delegation to Washington to act as interpreter but for the most part, he and his large family were virtually destitute as he was without employment.

In 1867 Whipple took a step not heretofore taken. Seventy-three years after the consecration of Samuel Seabury as the first bishop of the American Church, the first American Indian was ordained to the

Chippewa Chief Hole-in-the-Day.
Courtesy, Smithsonian Institution.

priesthood. Enmegahbowh's ordination took place in the Church of the Good Shepherd at Faribault, where Kemper had made him a deacon eight years before. Whipple wrote:

> It was one hundred miles to the nearest priest, and the Holy Communion could be administered only at my visits. Enmegahbowh had a good English education, was devout, and well-read in the scriptures and in Church history.
>
> With consent of the Standing Committee, I gave him a dispensation for the Greek and Hebrew . . . My Indian did not miss an answer in his examinations by three of the ablest men in my diocese. I ordained Enmegahbowh to the priesthood in the Cathedral at Faribault, and I knew my red children could henceforth receive the Christian bread.

Enmegahbowh was then placed in charge of the mission at Crow Wing. He reported that in the next few months ". . . to the great comfort and joy to our heart, I have baptized one adult white man and one white child, and on the death of two whites, I have performed the burial services."

His work at Crow Wing concluded before the end of the year, 1867. Though the Ojibwa did not suffer the fate of banishment accorded the Santee, they were made to leave their ancestral Gull Lake home for a newly established reservation at White Earth, some 60 miles to the northwest, deep in the north woods of Minnesota. Enmegahbowh with about 40 of his parishioners set out brokenhearted on the journey. He wrote an account thirty years later of the sorrow of removal:

> Another trouble came on. It was the Removal . . . the most terrible trouble that could come . . . To describe the feelings and sayings of my people would fill many sheets of paper. I will pass them over . . . My people have gone away broken hearted . . . To leave the little graves of our dear children . . . It was a long time before I could get my wife away from the little graves.

Enmegahbowh was warmly welcomed by several of the chiefs and head men who had already settled at the new reservation, including his old nemesis, Hole-in-the-Day. Though the aging chieftain's anger over Enmegahbowh's "betrayal" in warning the white military had cooled, Enmegahbowh always had to be wary until, about 1868, Hole-in-the-Day was assassinated by some of his own men.

Enmegahbowh found several factors at White Earth which hindered immediate acceptance of the Episcopal tenets. There had been a Roman Catholic presence among Ojibwa bands since the 1600s and those who had been born into Roman Catholicism saw no reason to change. They were, in fact, puzzled that the white men "with one Bible had so many religions." The principle factor that inhibited conversion was that the majority Ojibwa practiced the traditional highly ritualistic native religion, *Midewiwin,* called the Grand Medicine Lodge. Centered on health and healing and a staunch moral code of conduct, *Midewiwin* was said to be a sacred gift to the Ojibwa from *Gitche Manitou* (Creator).

Though he was not immediately swamped by converts, Enmegahbowh soon began efforts at St. Columba's to build a handsome stone building and to train several young Ojibwas for ordination, including Fred W. Smith, who succeeded him when he retired after serving for 20 years at the White Earth site.

Whipple Awakens the Church to Indian Advocacy

Unconscionable practices were rampant across Indian Country when Whipple came to Minnesota. In a letter to the bishop who would become known as "Apostle to the Indians," Enmegahbowh provides one example of dishonest dealings and deliberate deception heaped upon Ojibwas on the brink of starvation. Indians from all the Mississippi lands—Mille Lacs, Gull Lake, Leech Lake and Pokeguma—assembled for government rations and Enmegahbowh wrote his bishop:

> The old Sandy Point was covered with wigwams. The first day they received their well-colored flour hard with lumps, the pork heavily perfumed. The old chief brought me some of both and said, "Is this fit to eat?" I said, "No, it is not fit to eat."
>
> But the Indians were hungry and they ate it. About ten o'clock, the first gun was fired. You well know, Bishop, that Indians fire a gun when a death occurs. An hour after another gun was fired, then another and another, until it seemed death was at every wigwam. That night, twenty children died, and the next day as many more, and so for five days and five nights, the deaths went on.
>
> Bishop, when these dear victims strewed along the pathless wilderness shall hear the great trumpet sound and shall point to those who caused their death, it will be dreadful!
>
> My friend, Chief Pakanuhwaush, has just come in. I asked him how many died at the payment at Sandy Lake. He said, "Over three hundred."

A tall ruddy-faced man with a determined chin and generous mouth took on the challenge of reform of the U.S. government's Indian policy, carrying the cause of Indians far beyond all tribal agents and commissioners to the desk of the President of the United States, the halls of Congress and into the deliberations of General Conventions of the Episcopal Church. Whipple pressed the buttons that energized the Episcopal Church to a highly visible advocacy role which by the late 1800s was unmatched across the Christian Church.

When the war to abolish slavery ended, the nation launched into a fit of westward expansion. At the very same time that the huddled masses of the poor and oppressed of Europe were welcomed to the American shores, the American Indians were systematically and ruthlessly robbed of their land and lifestyle. Land-hungry farmers, exploiters and speculators demanded further Indian removal or outright extermination. The-only-good-Indian-is-a-dead-Indian mindset prevailed and the Indian Service, housed until 1849 under the Department of War, was inconceivably corrupt.

Such was the national climate when Whipple strode into an Episcopal Board of Missions meeting in 1866 in New York City. He wrote:

> The Board had made no appropriations for Indian missions. A friend offered a resolution to express cordial sympathy with the Bishop of Minnesota, in his efforts to carry the Gospel to the Indian race. I had just come from Indian Country, where I had witnessed its sorrows and degradation, and was ill from exposure . . . I arose in response to this resolution and said, "If the object of this resolution is to help Indians, it's not worth the paper on which it's written. If it is to praise the Bishop of Minnesota, he does not want it. It is an honest fight, and if any one wants to enlist, there is room . . ."

A resolution was then passed initiating action and setting the stage for an astonishing acceleration of the Episcopal Church's Indian work. The next decades saw both clergy and laity organized more effectively than in any other denomination to work for reform in Indian affairs across the entire federal system.

The year 1871 stands out in the annals of Indian affairs. It was the year that the government of the United States, after negotiating some 650 treaties with the various tribes, decreed an end to treaty-making. An ineffectual man, Ulysses S. Grant, was President of the United States. General George Armstrong Custer, driven by presidential ambitions, was on a rampage in the West.

However, the year 1871 saw the Episcopal Church take forward actions in Indian advocacy. The House of Bishops established the missionary jurisdiction of Niobrara for Indian work, an act accepted by General Convention the following year. This non-geographic jurisdiction was assigned oversight for most of the northern plains Indians.

A second turning point was marked when General Convention created a Standing Committee on Indian Affairs, and elevated the unit to the same level as all other domestic missions. Named to the committee were six prominent laymen. Its chairman was William Welsh, who was from an eminent Philadelphia family. The family would further distinguish itself through Herbert Welsh, a young humanitarian instrumental in founding in his father's parlor the Indian Rights Association, a leading Indian advocacy organization from 1882 until the mid-1980s.

Whipple and other leaders of the Episcopal Church were proponents of President Grant's controversial peace plan. Initiated by the

Quakers, the peace plan included a church-related Board of Indian Commissioners. William Welsh was named the board's chairman. The plan placed churches in control of Indian affairs. A goal was to reform the corrupt Indian Bureau by placing committed Christians in direct contact with the tribes. Motive, however, stemmed more from hope of avoiding further Indian wars than from benevolent altruism or care and concern for the indigenous peoples.

The second tier of Grant's program was the outright apportionment of Indian Tribes to various Christian denominations. Indians were provided no choices. Denominations were allotted various tribes to "Christianize and Civilize." The 1872 apportionment assigned the Episcopal Church primary responsibility for the Dakota or Sioux, with lesser work among the Shoshone-Bannock in Wyoming territory and the Ponca in Nebraska.

Churches were to appoint Indian agents and receive federal funding for operation of mission schools. There would be no separation of church and state in the realm of Indian affairs. The idea was not radically new; as far back as 1819 Congress had voted a permanent "civilization fund" with a $10,000 appropriation which would increase annually. The "civilization fund" was administered by the American Board of Commissioners for Foreign Missions (ABCFM) for its mission purposes.

William Welsh in 1870 had visited the various reservations and made a detailed report of his travels and his talks with the chiefs. Welsh made recommendations to the Secretary of the Interior and he also reported to the Episcopal Church, where he made pleas for missionaries and money. The church responded to his eloquence and three missionary organizations, the Domestic Committee, the American Church Missionary Society and the Indian Hope Association of Philadelphia, all turned over monies from their treasuries to Welsh's Indian Commission.

In an incredibly brief time period—1871 until 1882—the Episcopal Church sent out 80 new missionaries to Indian country and ordained 20 Indians to the diaconate and two to the priesthood.

The government looked to the churches to transform its Indian agencies into missionary outposts, to send strong honest men as agents, and committed men and women as teachers. Corruption would cease, the political sinecures would disappear, and furthermore, the Indian would be "civilized." That was the dream. Utopia proved illusive; political pressures did not dissolve and the various missionary societies were not prepared to handle the tremendous responsibilities suddenly thrust upon them. Though funding flowed from the government, it was insufficient and many of the church denominations had to compete with "foreign infidels" for missionary funds. By 1882 all the churches had withdrawn from responsibility of agency operation. However, the apportionment system was well established and it has cast a long shadow.

Though the bishop of Minnesota was a strong advocate for the Indians, he too presupposed that for an Indian to be a Christian he must cut his hair, wear shoes, get behind a plow and wholly subscribe to the white man's firmly held tenets regarding private property. Most of all, he thought that the "little red brother" must firmly renounce all trappings of "pagan" spirituality. It is ironic that Whipple also stated in his autobiography:

> I have never known an atheist among North American Indians . . . They believe unquestioningly in a future life. They believe that every thing in nature—the laughing waterfall, the rock, the sky, the forest—contains a divinity.

As an Indian advocate in the whirlpool of public policy, Whipple was unsurpassed, but the bishop was a product of his time. His writings are rife with paternalism and enshrouded in ethnocentrism. Whipple shared a conviction held by "reformers" and cultural imperialists of the era that acculturation was in the Indians' best interest. That Whipple advocated the reservation system is known; the extent to which he influenced the congressional action in 1877 that illegally took the Black Hills from the Sioux Nations of South Dakota is not known. Before the aspirations of human relations of the late 20th century censures Bishop Whipple, it must be remembered that for a decade or more following the Sioux Uprising he stood firmly as the single bulwark between white malevolence and Indian desperation.

"Straight-tongue" was a name given him by the Ojibwa because, as one said, "he has never spoken to us falsely." He crashed through the forests and backwoods on foot and by canoe; he sped across the prairies in wintry weather—with temperature as low as 30 degrees below zero—in a sleigh pulled by his coal black horse, Bashaw. When possible, he wintered in Florida where he interacted with local Seminoles in the Everglades and the miserable Plains Indian prisoners at St. Augustine. There is a persisting but undocumented story that Whipple influenced the Christian conversion of several of the Plains prisoners including David Pendleton Oakerhater, the Cheyenne saint.

Ojibwa Mission: 1872-1902

Bishop Whipple in 1872 sent Joseph Alexander Gilfillan to supervise the work at St. Columba's and open new ministry among the Ojibwa.

Gilfillan would remain with the Ojibwa for 25 years, and eventually be named the first Archdeacon for the Indians. Born in Ireland, he came to speak the Ojibwa language better than any other white man. He traveled up and down the country on foot, on pony-back and by canoe, and made a regular 300-mile circuit of his missions in all seasons and weathers. He designed and built little churches, won woodsmen to temperance, started children's boarding schools, and safeguarded Minnesota forests from destruction. One of his notable works was translation of the Episcopal prayer book into the Ojibwa language. His language teacher had been Enmegahbowh.

Envisioning St. Columba's as the centerpiece of missions among the Ojibwa, Whipple looked first at Red Lake Reservation, some 80 miles into the backwoods, for expansion. On the bishop's first visit, the Red Lake headman, *Madwaganonint* (One-Who-Has-Spoken), asked the bishop to send a teacher and build a school, but made no promises that he would convert to Christianity. In 1876 Bishop Whipple dispatched two recently ordained Ojibwa deacons, *Nabicu* (Samuel Madison) and *Kadawabide* (Frederick Smith) to begin the new mission, St. Antipas.

In a scant two years, new work had opened at nearby Redby and shortly the old headman, *Madwaganonint,* received baptism, instruction and confirmation. He stood by the chancel rail to make sure that others of his band kept their promise to be confirmed and by the 1880s his village consisted entirely of Christians.

Episcopal missions opened at Leech Lake in 1880 and at Cass Lake in 1881. A second lasting mission was opened on White Earth Reservation in 1893 when Samuel Memorial Episcopal Church was established at the hamlet of Nay-tah-waush. It was named for Samuel Madison, the deacon, who was given by his father, a Grand Medicine Lodge man, to Dr. James Lloyd Breck "to raise in the white man's way." Provided with a good education, Samuel showed much promise before his life was cut short by consumption; he died in 1877, a mere decade after his ordination. The Samuel Memorial congregation, which celebrated its centennial in 1993 by hosting the convocation of the Minnesota Committee on Indian Work, has had a long history of Indian ministers, often of different denominations—Louis Many Penny, Edward Kah-O-Sed, William Rice, George Smith, Floyd Keahna (a member of the Sac and Fox tribe), Alan Kitto (a Sioux), and a well-loved native son, Doyle Turner.

Deaconess Sybil Carter was invited by Whipple in 1890 to visit Minnesota with a view to bettering the condition of the Indian women. Remembering what had been done among the Irish peasantry and the poorer women of Northern Italy, she introduced the lace industry among them. The deaconess spent 30 years in Minnesota and the lace work of the Indian women became world renowned. Whipple presented a piece of their lace to Queen Victoria at Windsor Castle and later lace work from the Episcopal Mission on the Lower Sioux Reservation near Redwood was presented to Queen Alexandra of England.

In 1897 the Missionary District of Duluth was set off from the Diocese of Minnesota (to be reattached in 1942) and all the Ojibwa mission stations fell within limits of the Duluth jurisdiction. James Dow Morrison was named bishop, a position he held until 1922. He appears to have honored the wise choices of Whipple in founding the work among the Ojibwa. By the time of Morrison's consecration the work was soundly established at four of the Ojibwa reservations— Cass Lake, Leech Lake and Red Lake, as well as White Earth. In the early 20th century the Ojibwas were victims of lamentable timber frauds and land losses resulting in factionalism persisting into the present day.

Old records hint of a larger degree of charitable leniency in Minnesota toward traditional Indian religious beliefs than was evidenced in other sections of the American Church in the early part of the 20th century. The Ojibwa traditional religion, *Midewiwin,* or Grand Medicine, was referenced in old Episcopal publication as "an ancient Indian faith proclaiming sound ethics and definitely making for a fairly high type of citizen when this code is adhered to."

At the end of the last century, it was surmised that one-third of the Ojibwa held to the Grand Medicine belief, one-third were Christians and one-third had no religious standards or beliefs.

Enmegahbowh lived to bury not only his "dear companion" Charlotte, with whom he had lived for more than 50 years, but also all 12 of his children, one of whom, George Johnson, he had seen ordained to the diaconate. Most of the family had been victims of consumption, a much-feared form of tuberculosis which ravaged many Indian communities all across America. After Charlotte's death Enmegahbowh's affection centered on a small grandson, but the child died within a year or so and the old man was left alone. Finally he married a second wife who tended him faithfully and with affection until his own time came.

Enmegahbowh died at age 92, on June 11, 1902, after serving his church for 44 years, and surviving his beloved bishop by only nine months. He is buried on White Earth Reservation at St. Columba's, the mother mission of the Episcopal Church's Indian work west of the Mississippi River. His grave is marked by a grey granite stone for which Congress appropriated funds in acknowledgement of his role as conciliator in the 1862 conflict. The present-day Minnesota Council of Indian Work added his name to their calendar of saints, recognizing him as the first American Indian priest in the Episcopal Church. The diocese was poised to present his name for the Episcopal Church's calendar of saints at the 1997 General Convention.

Rekindling Sioux Mission: 1862-1909

The Lower Sioux suffered diaspora after the treaties were abrogated; the Upper Sioux fled in fear and eventually settled in the northeast corner of South Dakota near their traditional homeland around Lake Traverse. A few of the Upper Sioux drifted on further north and west to Devils Lake, North Dakota.

In the aftermath of the Uprising, Whipple did what he could to relieve the anguish of the Episcopal converts, especially those who, at personal peril, had aided white captives during the conflict. He was able to rescue a handful, including Taopi, from banishment to Dakota Territory, and quartered them for several months at the farm of Alexander Faribault, himself a mixed-blood. Sibley, the U.S. Army's commanding officer, issued a writ on behalf of Taopi:

> The bearer, Taopi (Wounded Man), is entitled to the lasting gratitude of the American people for having, with other Christian Indians, during the outbreak, saved the lives of nearly two hundred white women and children.

By 1866, however, anti-Dakota sentiment still raged to such an extent that Faribault asked the bishop to remove the Santee from his land, and most of them were dispatched to the new Santee Reserve in Nebraska. Whipple held a farewell service for them and the Indians said their last goodbyes. He was able to get Taopi dispensation to stay in Minnesota. In 1869 Taopi received an offer from the government to live on an 80-acre tract of land on the old reservation. However, by that time, Taopi was on his deathbed.

Wabasha, the second of the Santee chieftains who stepped forward to become an early Episcopal convert and who stoutly sought to avoid the conflict, was, nonetheless, sent west with the Mdewakanton band. A hereditary chief of the Mdewakanton for a quarter of a century when the uprising occurred, and a rival of Little Crow, Wabasha had been at the wrong place at the wrong time; he was on the scene at the battles at Fort Ridgely, New Ulm, Birch Coulee and Wood Lake.

Good Thunder, the youngest of the early converts, joined the Sibley expedition as scout in the spring of 1863, and his wife, Snana, was among those who were given refuge at the Faribault property.

There has long been a touching story that Mrs. Good Thunder, at the time of the 1862 outbreak, seized the Bible from the church, buried it, and sent word to the bishop that she had saved "the Great Spirit's book" (she thought it to be the only one existing). Eventually Snana separated from Good Thunder and within a few years she joined the Santee in Nebraska where she married Charles Brass, a Dakota man, with whom she had two sons and an adopted daughter. She died in 1908 in Nebraska.

Though Episcopal mission at the Lower Agency on the Minnesota River closed with the ill-fated 1862 Uprising, eventually efforts were rekindled among the eastern Dakotas in Minnesota after scattered remnants quietly drifted back to their ancestral homes. The old Chief Good Thunder, the first Sioux warrior whom Whipple baptized, eventually reappeared at his old home where the missionary, Hinman, had established the first Episcopal mission among the Sioux. When Good Thunder was able to buy 80 acres of land, he promptly went to see the bishop and gave 20 acres for the Birch Coulee mission, located across the Minnesota River from the Birch Coulee battle site, near Morton. The mission continues to serve the Lower Sioux community.

The first priest-in-charge at Birch Coulee was Henry Whipple St. Clair, the son of George Whipple St. Clair, who was the first Sioux that Bishop Whipple ordained to the priesthood. At the laying of the cornerstone, Good Thunder presented a request from the Indians that the new church be named St. Cornelia's, to honor the wife of their beloved bishop. Though not on the exact site of the original, the new church building used much of the stone from St. John's which was near completion at the time of the uprising.

At the dedication of St. Cornelia's, July 15, 1891, Bishop Whipple told about Wabasha, Good Thunder and Taopi asking him 33 years earlier to send them a minister, and that he had sent them Samuel Hinman who valiantly went west with the expelled Santee. Hinman's troubled life found him often in conflict with fellow clergy and his dispute with William Hobart Hare, bishop for the great Sioux Nation, resulted in banishment. In 1886 Hinman sadly returned from Dakota Territory to the vicinity of the Lower Agency to resume work at the mission he had begun almost a quarter of a century earlier. After his wife, Mary, died in 1876 in South Dakota, Hinman married his second wife, Mary Myrick, the mixed-blood daughter of Andrew Myrick, the despised trader from Lower Agency.

Hinman was not present for the dedication of St. Cornelia's; he died on March 24, 1890, and was buried near the grave of Wabasha in the churchyard. Hinman's son, Robert, was placed in charge of the government school at Birch Coulee in 1891 and remained in the post for 30 years.

Though all Sioux were banished from Minnesota in 1863, census a decade later counted 237 Sioux scattered across southern Minnesota. Some were hapless souls who had not participated in the 1862 conflict but were doomed to wander homeless. Others were exiles who had drifted back from South Dakota to their ancestral home areas. In 1886 Congress authorized the purchase of land for these people, establishing the Lower Sioux and Shakopee-Mdewakanton Sioux Prairie Island Indian communities. It was to the Shakopee Prairie Island community that Episcopal ministry next moved.

Approximately 125 miles east of the Birch Coulee mission, the white Episcopal communicants at Red Wing for several years had observed Indians from Prairie Island appearing at church. *The Spirit of Missions* in the early 1900s condescendingly reported:

> It had not been an uncommon sight, at the celebration of the Holy Communion, to see five, ten, fifteen, or even twenty Indians, waiting until their white brothers had received, and then coming forward reverently to take their places at the Lord's table.

Prairie Island, one of the largest islands in the Mississippi and comprising some 25 square miles, is located 12 miles above Red Wing. As the Sioux wandered back to their ancestral homes in the late 1800s the government finally provided small allotments of land, consisting of from seven to 15 acres apiece. Some 60 Sioux were living in shacks on Prairie Island at the turn of the century. For the most part they are wretchedly poor; however, when Bishop Rowe of Alaska visited Red Wing in the winter of 1905, Sioux women from Prairie Island walked 12 miles to the city to bring him a gift of two dollars for his work in Alaska. In 1906 *The Spirit of Missions* related:

> Within the last five years, it has been evident that more direct spiritual oversight must be given to these neglected red brethren, and arrangements were made by which Henry Whipple St. Clair, then a student at Seabury, was able to hold service among them twice a month. A little over a year ago the Diocese of Minnesota assumed the responsibility for this work, but it still remained under supervision of the rector of Christ Church, Red Wing.
>
> . . . they but rarely come into contact with others of their race. The nearest school is 200 miles away. These people— the remnant of a great race—have been left amidst poverty,

ignorance and disease. They have houses that are utterly inadequate for shutting out the winter's cold, and so many of them have put up their old style tipi and are living a life half native, half civilized.

And yet these people have vision, out of their penury, they brought to the rector of Christ Church about a year ago, the sum of $50, requesting him to hold it for them until they had enough to build a chapel of their own. There was a little unused church at Point Douglas, not far above the settlement, which the bishop presented to the Indians. The funds for taking this down, purchasing necessary new materials, and erecting the new building on Prairie Island were provided by the American Church Building Fund Commission, Bishop Edsall and other interested friends in the diocese.

So last spring as soon as the river was open, the little church with its windows and furnishings was brought down the [Mississippi] river. The building is very simple, the interior being finished in natural pine. The chapel has been beautified by a rood-screen, the gift of Mrs. Whipple, in memory of our great-hearted bishop, who lived and cared so tenderly for his red children.

The Chapel of the Messiah was built on an acre of ground deeded by one of the Indians, Thomas Williams. At the service of consecration, October 10, 1906, the bishop was assisted by Henry Whipple St. Clair, who was assigned to come from Birch Coulee monthly to hold services. At the services, the bishop confirmed seven and set apart two lay readers, Thomas Whipple and Thomas Roulliard. The missions publication said:

The entire service (except the prayer of consecration) was in the Sioux language. St. Clair read the epistle. Thomas Roulliard, a young Indian from Carlisle School, who is to enter Seabury next fall, played the organ. [Roulliard would not be ordained until 1925 at age 60.]

Ojibwa Mission: 1925-1994

Whipple had chosen a capable enabler when he named Gilfillan the first Archdeacon for the Indians. He not only established missions but he gathered around him young Indian men and trained them for the work of ministry among their fellows. He clearly set the stage for

Prairie Island Chapel of the Messiah, 1906.
Bishop Edsell and congregation at consecration.
Courtesy, Archives of the Episcopal Church.

the next generation, and by 1925 the Diocese of Duluth had the second largest Indian work in the American church, second only to South Dakota. It counted 2,000 baptized Indian members, 17 mission stations and 11 Indian clergymen and catechists.

In 1924 the old government school on Cass Lake was purchased for a church school for Indian boys but the building burned before the purpose could be realized.

Five hundred came to Convocation in 1924 at Cass Lake. The Rev. W.B. Heagerty, M.D., Superintendent of Indian Missions for the Diocese of Duluth, wrote in *The Spirit of Missions:*

On a Friday in the middle of June Indians began to arrive at the Convocation grounds on the shore of Cass Lake. All Saturday they came, in the early part of the day by team, towards night by auto, until on Sunday, the opening day of the Convocation there were more than 500 present. This included men, women and children—the whole family came. All the time tents of all sorts and conditions were going up on the camping ground. It had become a place teeming with Indian life and custom; here a group of the older men, sitting on the grassy ground smoking and evidently discussing something of interest in the native tongues; here a group of younger men or boys laughing and talking in English as they renewed acquaintance; here a grandmother rocking the baby in her arms as she hums an Ojibwa melody, while the young mother is cooking over the fire outside the tent. Children run around and play, shouting sometimes in English, sometimes in Ojibwa. A native clergyman is lining up his people to have them sign the register.

An immense kettle is boiling and emitting savory odors over the trench of wood coals. It contains a stew of many ingredients; the Indian women in charge stir it occasionally with the large wooden paddle and perhaps add more ingredients. Some men are tending the fire. The bell rings and the "crier" calls in Ojibwa "dinner is served."

. . . altar built of peeled pine logs varnished to a silvery white; the cross and candlesticks of peeled cypress and the bishop's rustic chair. But listen—the tune is familiar but the words are Ojibwa. We recognize "The Church's One Foundation" in the distance. The procession has started: a catechist with the beautiful brass cross from St. Columba Mission leads . . . Part of the service is in Ojibwa, part in English; the sermon in English, translated by an interpreter . . .

Edward C. Kah-O-Sed, a Canadian-born Ojibwa, was ordained in 1926. Kah-O-Sed made a new translation of the prayer book and Hymnal into the Ojibwa language and was an inveterate traveler on behalf of the Church across all northern Minnesota. Other Indian clergy names in the mid-1920s included Charles Wright, Frank Waukazo, Louis Manypenny, Fred Smith, Mark Hart, William Losh and James Rice. William Boyle, a graduate of Seabury Divinity School, became the second Archdeacon of the Indians and the first Ojibwa named to the post. By the mid-1930s there were 1,800 baptized Ojibwas on the northern Minnesota reservations.

It was about this time that George Alvin Smith was seriously considering vocation. A grandson of Enmegahbowh—Father Smith's grandmother, *Ne-gon-e-shig-o-quay* (First Day Woman), was Enmegahbowh's second wife—really did not have to ponder vocation seriously. His mother told Kah-O-Sed when George was about 10, "My son will be a priest someday." "Thus," he commented in 1992 at the fiftieth anniversary of his ordination, "I was promised to the ministry." The eminent senior Indian priest of the diocese was born on the White Earth Reservation in 1915, and baptized by Kah-O-Sed. He served reservation congregations across northern Minnesota—White Earth, Leech Lake, Cass Lake, Onigum, Squaw Lake, Redby, Red Lake and Bemidji.

In the late 1960s Smith was chosen as first chairman of the National Committee on Indian Work, formed in response to a group of articulate young Indian men who challenged the Episcopal Church to become more involved in the lives of American Indian people. At the time, Smith was serving a congregation in Bemidji. The vestry asked for assurance that he could be in the pulpit three Sundays a month. "That fourth week will allow you the time to be away to head NCIW, and your absence will be St. Bartholomew's missionary outreach," said the senior warden.

In October, 1991, the amiable elder became the first recipient of a new diocesan award for service and ministry, the Bishop Whipple Cross. In 1968 Seabury-Western Theological Seminary awarded him the doctor of divinity degree. Though long retired, the tall and stately senior priest sometimes attends NCIW convocations. He came in 1993 to Nay-tah-waush on the White Earth Reservation to dedicate a revised edition of the Ojibwa Hymnal.

In the north woods of Minnesota the spring of 1994 saw an extension of an Ojibwa Lenten practice which had its origins so distant in the past that no one knows when it began. It is the "Ojibwa Song Service." Bishop Whipple a century ago had commented that he had "never heard a sweeter service than that sung in the Chippewas' musical tongue." By custom, each Sunday night during Lent people from the three northern Minnesota reservations—Leech Lake, Red Lake and White Earth—meet at the home of a host family and sing in the Ojibwa language, often until well past midnight. The services proved so popular that it was agreed in 1994 to do them on other holy days.

The Torch Passes

When Whipple died in 1901, Enmegahbowh wrote:

> Our bishop was all love. He preached always, from the beginning: Love, love, love. Love the Great Spirit, love one another, love all other tribes. His one great aim has been to unite us by close connection, Indians and whites, in Christian fellowship.

Henry Benjamin Whipple, remembered as one of the most striking figures of the Episcopal Church, is buried on the grounds of the
Cathedral of our Merciful Savior in Faribault, the first church building erected in the Episcopal Church as a cathedral.

Whipple, the man, was not without characteristics of cultural
imperialism. He saw "detribalization" as a necessary part of the Chris-
tianizing process. He favored the reservation system, an isolation
strategy with Indians concentrated in one spot. His 562-page autobiography is not without ethnocentrism. His references to "our little
red brother" do not endear him to the 20th century Native American.
Yet, the book, intentionally or otherwise, provides cherished glimpses
of character, humor and wisdom of Indian people of that era.

In 1993, nearly 90 years after Mrs. Whipple gave the Chapel of
the Messiah a rood-screen, the Presiding Bishop of the Episcopal
Church, the Most Rev. Edmond L. Browning, visited Prairie Island
and participated in the dedication of a new parish center. In fact, the
Executive Council of Episcopal Church, which met in Minneapolis,
drove some 30 miles to Prairie Island where they viewed the casino of
the Shakopee-Mdewakanton Sioux tribe, a revenue-producing enterprise of incredible proportions. The Church leaders were briefed on
concern about the nearby nuclear storage facility, built in the late
1960s by Northern State Power Company. Indian people of Prairie
Island were never partners in the decision to place the facility in their
community and have no say in how the radioactive nuclear waste material is disposed of.

The legacy of Robert M. Anderson's episcopacy (1978-1993) was
that of enabling Indians to design and devise ministry to respond, to
their needs. Coming as bishop in 1978, Anderson consistently brokered
views of the Native constituency across the diocese and beyond. He
championed a progressive strategy in Indian ministry, moving from
the old "missionary model" which was blind to Indian beliefs toward a
new examination of old values and concepts of the Native heritage.
The 14 predominantly Indian congregations of the diocese were dis-
mayed when Anderson announced plans to retire in 1993.

Bishop Anderson's tenure brought a new generation of Indian
clergy to the diocese. He ordained three Ojibwa during his episcopacy: Doyle Turner (1986) and George Ross (1989), who are vicars for
White Earth Reservation congregations, and Johnson Loud Jr. (1988)
of the Red Lake Reservation. In the early 1990s two other clergy were
called to serve Ojibwa congregations. Mark MacDonald came as vicar
of the Red Lake congregations and Indian theological trainer for the
diocese. Michael Smith, an Oklahoma Potawatomi, came as vicar for

Samuel Memorial on the White Earth.

Sioux clergy ordained by Anderson include Virgil Foote (1982), Gary Cavender (1983), Melanie Spears (1993, the first Dakota woman ordained to the priesthood) and John Robertson (1993). Another Sioux clergyman, Lyle Noisy Hawk, served the historic Lower Sioux mission for six years beginning in 1990.

A highly visible Sioux priest, Philip Allen, was the third Archdeacon for Indian Work in Minnesota, from 1990 until his retirement in 1995. Also serving as vicar for All Saints' in metropolitan Minneapolis, Allen three times headed Minnesota's deputation to General Convention—1988, 1991 and 1994. He served on Executive Council 1988-1994. Allen's record in national Indian work dates from 1974 when he served as chairperson of the National Committee on Indian Work, a responsibility again assumed in 1987. Subsequently he chaired the Episcopal Council of Indian Ministry (ECIM), successor to the NCIW.

Another Anderson—Howard—dedicated a decade to bridge-building between Indian and non-Indian constituencies in Minnesota and neighboring North Dakota. He encouraged passing the torch when Indians were primed to take responsibility. The Minnesota Committee on Indian Work (MCIW) became the vehicle to take responsibility. MCIW underscores compatibilities of native spirituality and the Christian faith. Many of its leaders participate in traditional Dakota vision quests, sweat lodge and healing ceremonies. Additionally, MCIW has achieved a harmonious working relationship between reservation and urban Indian communities as well as between historic rivals, the Dakota and the Ojibwa.

Of all the dioceses with major Indian ministry, only Minnesota has consistently funded its Indian work from diocesan budget and endowments rather than through funding from the national church. In fact, almost one out of every four dollars of the diocesan budget goes to support the work of a vital and strong MCIW.

The present Minnesota bishop, James L. Jelinek, consecrated in 1993, named three canons for Indian ministry: Doyle Turner, John Robertson and Mark MacDonald. Keyed on moving from "maintenance to mission," MCIW in early 1994 began a new program for leadership training, inaugurating a two-year Indian Ministries Diploma Program through United Theological Seminary (UTS), New Brighton. Headed by MacDonald, the innovative program graduated its first student, Robert Roy (Ojibwa), in 1996.

The Minnesota model for alternative training attracted the attention of national Episcopal Church leaders seeking to discover why persons of color were not putting themselves forward for ordination. By mid-summer of 1996, a five-year covenant had been reached among Jelinek and ECIM, other Indian leaders, and the Congregational Ministry Cluster of the Episcopal Church Center, aimed at establishing a training institute for the next millennium.

An imprint of countless committed Christian men and women—both Indian and white—is stamped on the history of the Episcopal Church in mission among the Ojibwa and Dakota people in Minnesota. The legacy lives, left by Enmegahbowh and Whipple; Good Thunder and Gilfillan; Kemper and Kah-O-Sed; James Lloyd Breck and George Smith; and continued by Anderson, Anderson, Allen, Jelinek, MacDonald, Robertson and Turner.

4

NIOBRARA: THE GREAT SIOUX NATION

Springtime finally came to Minnesota in 1863 after the horrendous winter for some 1,600 Santees who had been confined in deplorable conditions in a stockade in the flats below Fort Snelling. The vast majority had not been involved in the massacres in the Minnesota River valley; they were judged guilty simply of being Santee. One hundred and thirty had died that winter in the stockade while federal officials deliberated future disposition of all Indians—some 47,000 Sioux, Ojibwa and Winnebago—in Minnesota.

On May 4 federal troops marched 771 Santees, mostly women and children, to the Mississippi River landing and put them aboard the Davenport. Accompanying the miserable throng was a military escort of 40 men and Samuel Hinman, the Episcopal missionary. The Northerner, pulling three barges of Santees, departed the following day. Wretched and homeless, all their treaties abrogated by the U.S. government, classified as prisoners of war, their destination was Crow Creek on the Missouri River in Dakota Territory.

After considering the Dry Tortugas off the Florida Coast, desolate Devils Lake in present day North Dakota, and an island in the middle of Lake Superior, officials in Washington eventually settled on Dakota Territory. Actually, the Indians were already on their way while Indian Agent Clark W. Thompson was threshing about in the dry and barren terrain seeking the precise site to dump the unfortunate lot. He chose an uninhabitable spot 80 miles upriver from the formidable old Fort Randall and eight miles above the mouth of Crow Creek. His hastily made choice proved a disastrous mistake.

The Indians' journey was harrowing and many more died. Overcrowded conditions, unfit even for livestock, required sleeping in shifts. Near St. Louis they were transferred to railroad box cars—as many as 60 to a car—and transported overland to the Missouri River where they were loaded onto one steamboat. John P. Williamson, a Congregational minister, accompanying the refugees along with Hinman, wrote that congested conditions were "nearly as bad as the Middle Passage for slaves . . . fed on musty hardtack and briny pork, which they had not half a chance to cook."

Upon at last reaching Crow Creek at the end of May, 1863, the Santee met unspeakable hardship, to be endured for three long years. Virginia Driving Hawk Sneve, in her history of the Diocese of South Dakota, describes the westward exodus and arrival at their bleak and barren reservation:

> They reached Crow Creek on May 30th [1863], and in a matter of days, the hills around the agency were covered with the graves of women and children who had died as the result of the over-crowding on the small boat, and who had no medical attention on their arrival at Crow Creek. The situation at Crow Creek was one of the worst ever inflicted on prisoners in the United States.
>
> It was a horrible region, filled with the petrified remains of the huge lizards and creeping things of the first days of time. The soil is miserable: rain rarely ever visits it. The game is scarce, and the alkaline waters of the streams and springs are almost certain death.
>
> The Indians arrived too late to plant crops, which would not have produced enough harvest in that arid land to support them. The government had to feed them and this was difficult because of the distance from the source of supply.

Prospects of mass starvation loomed; government agents hastily contracted with Mankato suppliers 300 miles away for beef cattle, pork and flour to save the Santee from extinction. When the supplies finally arrived the cattle were emaciated. The pork and flour, though condemned as unfit for consumption, was nonetheless ladled out to hungry humanity. Bishop Whipple's autobiography tells that the women the first bitter winter picked up half-digested kernels of grain in horse manure and boiled the kernels for soup. Other women turned to prostitution as the final measure of keeping themselves and their children from starvation.

The Indians were not allowed to leave the stockade to hunt. Not only were they restricted by the federal troops, they were, in fact, fearful of venturing from their confines into the vast prairie where hostile Sioux kept vigil. Their cavalier cousins, the Tetons, looked with contempt on the Santee, who had surrendered.

It was a time of astounding transition for the once-nomadic, numerous and proud Lakota people of the plains, where the diverse bands of Lakota/Dakota were in the last throes of resistance to the American republic's doctrine of manifest destiny.

At the time of early European contact the various bands of the Sioux were ranging from the Great Lakes area westward—the Santee (Dakota) to the east, the various bands of the Tetons (Lakota) to the west, and the Yankton and Yanktonai (Nakota) in the middle, mostly along the Missouri River.

A treaty in 1825 affirmed the Dakota domain over the vast northern plains extending from the Mississippi River to the Rocky Mountains. Each successive treaty reduced that domain. When Episcopal mission arrived in South Dakota the Sioux still held vast territory spilling into Montana, Nebraska, Wyoming and the Dakotas.

The Fort Laramie Treaty, signed in 1868, five years after the Episcopal arrival, reduced the Sioux lands but stipulated a reservation which included nearly all of the Dakota Territory west of the Missouri River, and in addition, the lands east of the Bighorn Mountains, which were designated as unceded Indian territory where the Sioux could hunt and roam. The treaty's major concession to the Sioux was the stipulation that whites were explicitly excluded from this territory and all military forts closed. Agencies, to issue rations and other annuity goods, were established within the reservation: three on the Missouri on its eastern edge, Standing Rock on the north, Cheyenne River and Crow Creek further down, and the Spotted Tail (Rosebud) and Red Cloud (Oglala or Pine Ridge) agencies in the southwest corner.

With western expansion of white settlers, railroads, and wanton slaughter of the buffalo—primary source of food, clothing and shelter for the Sioux—the bands by 1863 were clustered around the agencies, except for certain unreconcilables under Sitting Bull and Chief Gall who never deigned to approach them.

A peace commission inspected conditions at Crow Creek in the autumn of 1865, reported on the drought conditions, grasshopper plague, and "semi-starvation" the surviving Santee had withstood for two years, and recommended they be again moved. The site eventually selected was in northeast Nebraska Territory at the confluence of the Niobrara with the Missouri rivers. In the spring of 1866 the missionary Hinman accompanied the surviving Santee, as they slowly trudged 100 miles southward in decrepit wagons, on horseback and by foot, to their new reservation. Around 1,000 made the journey.

Arriving on June 11, they received a hostile reception from white settlers whose lands had been appropriated by the government for the new Santee reservation. Except for minor moves of a few miles along the Missouri River, there the Santee would remain until the present day.

The small Santee Reservation proved to be the springboard for Episcopal mission in the high plains, and out of it would come 45 clergymen and the first Indian bishop of the Episcopal Church.

Since a near mass conversion to Christianity in their traumatic period in stockades and prisons back in Minnesota, the Santee had undergone a radical transformation. In effect, they abandoned their own cultural identity, societal order and process for leadership selection. The chieftain traditionally chosen by heredity, was now chosen by popular election. When a chief of the Brulé visited the Santee he scornfully reported that the Santees had "placed themselves absolutely under the control of their missionaries, and they had little thought for anything in the world beyond piety."

Hinman's work at Fort Snelling and subsequent work at Crow Creek laid the foundation for the later strength of the Episcopal Church among the Santee and subsequently among other Sioux bands of the plains. Hinman and Whipple had ardently ministered to the Santee in Minnesota, baptizing all the chiefs of the Lower Sioux and caring for 300 at Fort Snelling. Bishop Whipple on a single occasion had confirmed 100.

With the help of his wife, Mary, and the Minnesota-born missionary, Emily West, Hinman continued fervently with his mission among the Santee in their new home. He lived among them without any financial aid from the Church Mission Board, relying solely on voluntary gifts from white persons in the east who felt kindly towards the Indians.

As part of President Grant's new Indian policy, which assigned tribes and bands to the overview of Christian denominations, the Santee Sioux in 1869 were assigned to the Society of Friends (Quakers). However, Hinman continued his work untroubled by decisions in distant Washington.

Under his direction, the Santees built the first chapel for Episcopal services among the Sioux of the future Diocese of South Dakota. The worshipers in this little log chapel on Bazille Creek became the first in what would eventually grow by the year 1935 to be 97 Indian congregations in the diocese. It was here on Bazille Creek that many Santee learned to read from Hinman's new translation of the Book of Common Prayer.

Wabasha, hereditary chief and loyal friend of Bishop Whipple, gave land for a second Santee mission six miles away, and soon a school was opened with Miss West and Mrs. Hinman as teachers.

In Minnesota Whipple had been the Santee's bishop and patron. In their new home their bishop was Robert H. Clarkson, who had been rector of a prestigious parish in Chicago when Whipple was founding a new "southside" free church. The scholarly Clarkson was appointed Bishop of the Missionary District of Nebraska and Dakota in 1865, giving some relief to the aging Joseph Cruikshank Talbot, who called himself the "bishop of the all outdoors." Whipple, who managed to escape the overarching high church-low church row of the era, characterized Clarkson as a "high churchman."

With a bishop who had little experience in Indian affairs and lived in far-away Lincoln, Hinman appears to have gone about his labors in a detached and autonomous manner, a factor which likely figured when he later came into immediate conflict with his next bishop.

Always able to interact comfortably with Indians, though his relations with whites would prove more and more strained, Hinman moved rapidly to train helpers immediately upon arrival at the Nebraska reservation. By the time the new log chapel was built at Bazille Creek, no less than five Santee were preparing for holy orders—Paul Mazakute, Daniel C. Hemans, Luke C. Walker, Christian Taopi, and Philip Johnson Wahpehan. Clarkson sent Walker, the most promising of the quintet, to study at Philadelphia Divinity School. The team of postulants assisted Hinman in a further translation of a large part of the Book of Common Prayer into the Santee dialect.

Times were hard, but the Santees settled in on the sandy hills of their new reservation and started farming the poor soil—somewhat to the disgust of their proud relatives of the buffalo range, the Tetons— and began sawing timber to build houses, schools and churches.

They prevailed after a series of set-backs relating to their chapel. The first chapel was flooded and all records destroyed; the second, described as the most beautiful small chapel in the west, was blown away by a tornado. The third, known as the Chapel of Our Most Merciful Savior, would survive.

Mazakute Ordained: Yankton Mission Opened

Though his ministry would last only briefly, Paul Mazakute (Iron Shooter) will be long remembered as the first Sioux to be ordained in the Episcopal Church. Mazakute, who Whipple cited for risking his life to "save helpless women and children," came west with the expelled Santee but did not tarry long at Crow Creek, moving on to the Yankton agency to work at a sawmill. As a catechist he soon began holding services and instruction classes for the large Yankton band, and is recorded as having held services for the ill-fated Ponca Indians in Nebraska.

When Clarkson ordained Mazakute to the diaconate in 1868 he assigned the Santee to the Yankton Reservation where his early efforts laid the foundations for the work of the Episcopal Church on that reservation, out of which would come some of the Church's strongest leaders.

This ordination in the remote sandhills of Nebraska broke ground for a transformation into what was recently described as the "the genuinely Dakota Church." The Rev. George Preble Pierce, who served 16 years in South Dakota missions and headed the Church Army until his 1994 retirement, contends that the Christian movement started among the Sioux by the evangelistic efforts of the missionaries in a time of great turmoil was "a people's movement." In his doctoral dissertation, "Leadership in Crisis: The Lakota Religious Response to Wounded Knee, 1973," Pierce writes:

> The Dakotas who were converted became leaders among their people. They initiated a new way of life by which one could survive in the new circumstances in which they found themselves . . . As Christ became the new center of Dakota culture, Dakotas were strengthened to reshape attitudes and habits. The transfer of core Dakota values into the institutions of the Christian faith effected a deep level of contextualization of theological truth . . .

Mazakute's ordination, in retrospect, signaled a milepost. Soon the Episcopal Church, with small presence in the vast prairies and plains, would be reaching out beyond its work with the Santee exiles. Its first outreach was to the nearest neighbor, the Yanktons, whose 400,000-acre reservation was a dozen or so miles upriver from the Santees, on the opposite side of the river between Choteau Creek and the Missouri River.

The Yanktons and Santees had had some dealings with each other when Santees were still in Minnesota and there had been some contact when the Santee were at Crow Creek. Yanktons had roamed over a vast territory of Dakota, western Iowa and Nebraska and being centered along the Missouri River they had long had a relatively cordial relationship with white traders, primarily French. In fact, it was French traders who sought out Jesuits to journey from time to time up the Missouri to baptize their half-Indian children. In the 1840s Father Pierre Jean DeSmet made his first visit to the Yanktons and he returned in 1849 for extensive visits with the Ponca, the Arikara and various Sioux bands.

The Yanktons had observed the Episcopal mission and school at Santee and one of its headmen, Francis Deloria, reported to Hinman, "I am sent by four chiefs, four head soldiers, and eight sons of chiefs, to pray you and the brethren of your holy fellowship to build up a mission among our people."

Hinman was aware of internal friction between parties at Yankton. Some wanted a Roman Catholic mission, another large group wanted no mission at all, and a third segment was attracted to the Episcopal Church for the "simple beauty of her services, the singing, the instruction of the children, and the use of vestments by the minister when celebrating divine services." Hinman wisely replied that it was essential that the Yanktons were united in their desire for Episcopal mission. Time passed. Deloria reported back that there was accord.

Hinman received a formal request for a mission on April 30, 1868. At that time the Episcopal Church was unable to respond to the Yanktons' request because "the men and means" were not available. The Congregationalists sent the Rev. John P. Williamson.

Meanwhile, events in Washington would change forever the Episcopal Church's involvement in Indian ministry. Primarily it was the Peace Policy legislation pressed through by President Ulysses S. Grant and enacted in 1869 which sought to curb profiteers on Indian supplies. The plan gave church groups responsibility for recommending Indian agents and it apportioned tribes to specific denominations. Yankton Reservation, as well as six other Sioux nations, were assigned to the Episcopal Church.

The new law, in addition to stipulating that Indians would be placed on reservations and taught agriculture, established a Board of Indian Commissioners. Appointed as head of the Commission was William Welsh, a Philadelphia philanthropist and prominent Episcopal layman. The next year, Welsh made an extensive trip to visit reservations and make recommendations to the Secretary of Interior. He visited Santee and Yankton and when he heard the Yankton's request for Episcopal mission, he offered sufficient encouragement that the Indians began hewing logs for a church and mission house at the Yankton Agency. Bishop Clarkson assigned his new Santee deacon, Mazakute, to the Yankton site and sought a second trained white clergyman to assist Hinman.

In 1870 the Rev. Joseph W. Cook became the first—after Hinman—to answer the call for a white missionary to work among the Sioux of Dakota Territory. Scores would follow. Cook had been a missionary in Wyoming and had an extensive knowledge of medicine and thus quickly gained a reputation among the Yanktons. His work continued among the Sioux for 30 years.

A group of Santees, with skills in building, came over from across the river to prepare the timbers for the Yankton Church, and under Mazakute's supervision the Indians had a building by the time the new white missionary arrived. The *eyapaha* (crier) was sent out several miles to cry aloud to the people that the church was ready and to come to services. It was this structure in the hamlet of Greenwood—Church of the Holy Fellowship—that Bishop William Hobart Hare chose for his cathedral church when he arrived in 1873.

Meanwhile, back at Santee in the autumn of 1870, the first convocation of the Dakota missions was held. The event took place at the house of Wabasha, the crafty old survivor. The handful summoned by the missionary Hinman could little guess that this gathering would become for the next century and a quarter the most distinctive institution of American Indian Episcopalians—the Niobrara Convocation. Resolutions passed at the first convocation spoke to social structures in family life, superimposing patriarchal practices over traditional Sioux social standards. For instance, one resolution read, ". . . Indian custom of regarding the daughter as belonging to the mother, even after marriage, is destructive of the authority of the husband . . ." Another stated, ". . . that the husband is the head of the wife should be enforced . . ." Polygamy was forbidden; divorce was unrecognized except on grounds of adultery; betrothal without consent of both parties was nixed.

In 1871 Clarkson made his last visit to the Sioux and ordained Mazakute to the priesthood and Daniel Hemans and Luke C. Walker to the diaconate. The bishop confirmed 24 in what would be the first confirmation in Dakota Territory. The bishop sent Hemans to Yankton as interpreter and assistant to the new white missionary, J. W. Cook.

Work at the Yankton Reservation moved briskly. The white priest with Mazakute and Hemans conducted the first service of baptism for a Yankton Indian. Soon there was the first Christian marriage, first service of Holy Communion and the first Christian burial. In addition to the Chapel of the Holy Fellowship at the Agency, Church of the Holy Name was opened in 1870 on Choteau Creek with Mazakute originally in charge. St. Matthew's, near *Magaska* (White Swan) opened in 1871 with Philip Johnson Wahpehan in charge.

Cook moved rapidly to open schools on the Yankton Reservation. Sisters from Memorial House of Philadelphia—Lizzie Stiteler and Anna Prichard—arrived and were joined by Sophie Eymer. Miss Stiteler married William Joshua Cleveland, one of the original "back east" clergy recruits of William Welsh, and the two were sent to found

The "Bough Church" and rectory in 1872
of Paul Mazakute [?-1873], first Sioux ordained
in Episcopal Church.

the work at Lower Brulé. Miss Eymer also married a clergyman, the Dakota deacon Walker in Greenwood in 1872. The Walkers served the Episcopal Church long and well, in later years on the Crow Creek Reservation. His special contribution was that of revising translations of the Book of Common Prayer.

However, the first ordained Sioux would not serve the church long. Paul Mazakute, shortly after ordination, contracted tuberculosis and had to resign work on the Yankton and return to the Santee Reservation. During his years at the Yankton mission Mazakute likely influenced the life of the Deloria family, who became leaders for generations in the life and body of the Episcopal Church. Francis Deloria, half Yankton and half French, the first of the Yanktons to request Episcopal mission, enrolled his son, Philip, in the mission school. The lad grew up to leave a yet unparalleled mark on the Episcopal Church in South Dakota.

Mazakute, after returning to Santee, continued with his ministry, building a "bough house" for his church, and using a tepee as his rectory. The Iron Shooter left his own account of his work:

In 1862 I made my Christian vows. For seven years I was a Catechist, and for five years I have been a Minister. One year I was a Deacon, and for four years I have been a Priest. I went to the Yankton people [1869]. Though I never been far away, yet among Dakotas—at Yankton Agency, and White Swan, and Choteau Creek, at Ponca, at Santee, and on the Bazille—six villages I have proclaimed the glad tidings of the Gospel.

A women's organization in New York heard of Mazakute's work and raised money to build him the Chapel of the Blessed Redeemer and a log cabin for a home on Bazille Creek (later known as Howe Creek), a still active mission on the Santee Reservation. After only a few months in the new mission and just four years after ordination, Mazakute succumbed to his illness on May 12, 1873. Today in Minnesota one of the two Indian congregations within the Twin Cities worships at Mazakute Memorial Mission, a remembrance befitting this first among many notable Dakota priests.

Bishop Clarkson, responsive to the pastoral needs of the growing throngs of white settlers, resigned his authority over the Indian field in 1872 to devote full energy and time to the white field. General Convention had just established a single missionary jurisdiction among Indian tribes and named the jurisdiction Niobrara.

The Bishop of Niobrara

In the 1860s, when few spoke out on behalf of Indians, one who did was a young eastern Episcopal clergyman. The rector of a Philadelphia parish was visiting on the shores of Lake Superior during the summer of 1863 when he saw a crudely-lettered sign:

$250 REWARD
FOR THE HEAD OF A DEAD SIOUX INDIAN.

He immediately wrote to the Sunday school pupils of his parish back home informing them of conditions of Indians:

I saw numbers of them every day. Sometimes they were picking berries in the woods, sometimes lounging about the streets, and at other times paddling their canoes along the shore of the lake. But no one seemed to take any interest in them. They wandered about like sheep without a shepherd.

The young man did not realize it then, but he was entering his first plea for what would be his own future flock. The signature to that letter was William Hobart Hare. His flock, beginning a decade thence, would be the Great Sioux Nation, and his episcopacy would be the non-geographic jurisdiction called Niobrara, named for a river flowing out of northeast Nebraska into the Missouri.

Though the first hand view of the displaced Indians in the lake resort community may have awakened Hare to the cause to which his life would be directed, he likely already possessed a broader understanding of Indians than much of the American Church. Certainly the subject of the Indian was discussed in family gatherings. His mother was the daughter of John Henry Hobart (1775-1830), Bishop of New York, who in 1814 had founded Indian mission in the young Episcopal Church, re-establishing among the Oneida the Anglican Christianity which had come and gone with British rule.

Born in Princeton, New Jersey, May 17, 1838, Hare, on each side of his parentage, was a son of the Protestant Episcopal Church, but he also sprang, two generations back, from New England Puritans and Pennsylvania Friends. A maternal ancestor had come from England with William Penn. His father was rector of Trinity Church and an eminent biblical scholar. His mother was the daughter of the 11th in succession of American bishops. Her lineage also included a New Jersey cleric highly vocal in support of a colonial episcopate and, opposed to the American Revolution.

By 1843 the family had established itself in Philadelphia where William was afforded the best of education. From boyhood he had been prepared to be "a clean and perfect Christian gentleman," and his progression into the ministry was more or less a foregone conclusion. In 1862 he was ordained to the priesthood by Alonzo Potter and became rector of St. Paul's in the Philadelphia suburb of Chestnut Hill. He married a clergyman's daughter who died four years later leaving one son, Hobart Amory. Following his wife's death, Hare became secretary for the Foreign Committee of the Board of Missions of the Episcopal Church and "deeply immersed, body, mind and heart, in the work of making known the Gospel among the heathen in distant lands . . ." He would later despair that the church was derelict in "making known the Gospel to heathens not far off but lying cold on the church's bosom."

No sooner had the House of Bishops' vote been tallied on All Saints' Day in 1872 creating the new missionary district in the west than Bishop Henry Whipple rose to nominate William Hobart Hare as Bishop of Niobrara. Hare was consecrated the 100th bishop in the

American episcopate. His friends felt his place to be in "centers of learning, not in the destitute and dangerous west among hostile Indians."

By saddle and buckboard, Hare came to his new assignment in April, 1873; his jurisdiction was not over a territory or a region but over a people—the Sioux Nation. En route to his new post Hare visited the Oneidas in Wisconsin and made a wide detour in his journey to visit the "semi-civilized Indians before going to the wilder tribes of the Northwest, and therefore first made a visit to the Indian Territory of the Southwest." Unfortunately, his journals provide no further information on his journey into Indian Territory. He reached Yankton City on April 29, 1873:

> My arrival in Yankton occurred just after one of the most memorable storms that Dakota has ever known, and the effects of it were plainly to be seen in the carcasses of cattle which had perished in it, and in huge banks of snow which lay still unmelted. The storm had overtaken Custer's celebrated cavalry, while they were encamped about a mile or so outside of Yankton.
>
> From Yankton I passed up the Missouri River along which the main body of the missionary enterprise of our Church among the Indians was then located. I found that missionary work had been established on the Santee, Yankton and Ponca Reserves, and three brave young deacons, fresh from the Berkeley Divinity School, had, the previous fall, pressed up the river and begun the task of opening the way for missionary effort among the Indians of the Lower Brulé, the Crow Creek and Cheyenne River Reserves. Altogether, there were, besides three natives, five white clergymen and five ministering women.

The three Native clergy on hand to greet their new bishop were Mazakute and deacons Daniel C. Hemans and Luke C. Walker. Though the Dakota clergy would become the cornerstone to Hare's work in the Niobrara, only one of the three would be alive within six months of his arrival; Mazakute would die within a month and Hemans was victim of a smallpox epidemic which swept across the Santee Reservation in 1873 and took the lives of 105.

Within months prior to the bishop's arrival two other Santee deacons had died. One was Philip Johnson Wahpehan, called Philip the Deacon, at the Yankton mission; the chapel at White Swan was renamed the Church of Philip the Deacon after his death in a terrible blizzard. The other deacon was Christian Taopi, once a fierce warrior, whose name—Wounded One—was earned when as a youth he had been injured in a Santee-Ojibwa battle back in Minnesota. He, too, succumbed to tuberculosis in 1872.

Also on hand to greet the new bishop, in addition to Hinman, were five white clergy who had responded to an earlier appeal for young missionaries to come west to work among "hostile" Indians. Welsh, the Philadelphia philanthropist, had created interest and generated eastern funding to enlist help from seminary-trained clergy. His eloquence at the Episcopal Church headquarters established an Indian Commission which delivered both missionaries and money.

Joining Joseph W. Cook, who was first to arrive, were Henry Swift, William Joshua Cleveland and Heckaliah Burt, all recruited from Berkeley Divinity School, and the deacon and linguistics scholar, J. Owen Dorsey, working among the Ponca, whose reservation was beside the Santees'.

Hare's immediate attention was to the challenge presented in the federal government's plan for Episcopal oversight of seven more reservations. While on the surface there was humanitarian and evangelistic motivation in the new policy, the grand scheme was to lead the Indians along the path to "civilization."

Agencies assigned to the Episcopal Indian Commission were:

Agency	Tribe/Band	Estimated Number	Language
Yankton	Yankton	2,500	Dakota
Crow Creek	Yanktonais	1,200	Dakota
Crow Creek	Lower Brulés	2,200	Lakota
Cheyenne River	Two Kettles, Sans Arcs, Minneconjous	2,000	Lakota
Red Cloud's (Pine Ridge)	Oglala	2,500	Lakota
Spotted Tail's (Rosebud)	Upper Brulés	2,500	Lakota
Ponca (Nebraska)	Ponca Tribe	750	Ponca
Shoshone and Bannock	Shoshone/Bannock Tribes (Wyoming)	1,500	Shoshone Bannock

SIOUX LAND CESSIONS

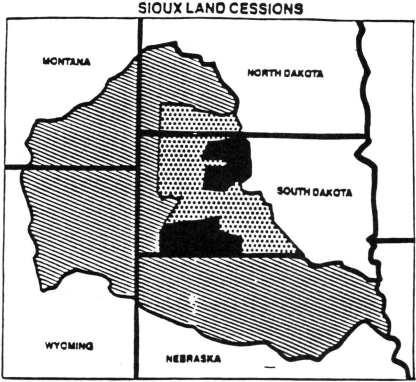

⬚	1868	The Fort Laramie Treaty outlined the Great Sioux Reservation and the unceded Sioux territory.
⬚	1876	The Great Sioux Nation after the United States illegally took the Black Hills and the unceded Sioux territory.
⬛	1889	The Great Sioux Nation after the United States government broke the Nation up into smaller reservations for the various Sioux bands.

Two bands on the east side of South Dakota—the Traverse Band of Minnesota exiles which were settled at the Sisseton-Wahpeton Reservation and the small Flandreau Colony—were assigned to the Presbyterians. The Roman Catholics assumed mission at the Standing Rock agency (which included the Hunkpapa, Sitting Bull's people) on the far north as well as virtually all of the Montana tribes.

The Expulsion of the Ponca

Hare, within a year of assuming spiritual authority over the peaceful Ponca tribe, wrote them off. Related linguistically to the Omaha whose homeland was further down the Missouri River, the Poncas were a sedentary farming people forced to move twice in a decade. By 1865 they were about 20 miles from the Santee where they were subjected to constant Sioux harassment. Even before the Ponca tribe was assigned to the Episcopal Church, Hinman was sending Mazakute to minister to them, and when Welsh visited the Ponca in 1870 he returned to New York with a strong plea for a missionary for them.

Dorsey, the brilliant young deacon from Maryland, responded to the call and went to the reservation in the spring of 1871. Dorsey quickly acquired their language, similar to the Omahas, translated the Lord's Prayer and the Apostles' Creed and taught many to read the McGuffey reader. By 1872 a mission house and chapel had been built and on July 19 Dorsey baptized 29 persons including 17 adults. The next year Dorsey contracted malaria and had to return east to recuperate. Later, working for the Smithsonian Institution, he did major linguistic studies on the Omaha and Osage.

Hare chose to abandon the Poncas, writing, "It has seemed advisable to suspend our work among the Poncas, pending their proposed removal . . . It is probable that the Poncas will be removed to a Reservation not under control of the Church." Due to pressure, likely from Welsh, Hare permitted Dr. Richard Gray, candidate for ministry and a practicing physician, to take charge of the Ponca mission in 1874.

Within three years of Hare's arrival, Congress authorized the Interior Department to remove the Poncas to Indian Territory to make way for the Brulé Sioux, who declined ever occupying it. The Poncas were not consulted; they first learned of the plan when they went to church one Sunday morning and Gray informed them that he had heard that they were to be driven from their homes and sent far to the south, never to come back. He said he was exceedingly sorry for them as they had been honest, industrious, frugal, hard working, and had just gotten themselves nice houses and farms.

The Ponca said they would rather die than leave their homes and frantically pled for support. The government, on advice of Hare, went forward with removal, sending a detachment of 25 soldiers to force their expulsion to the Quapaw River of Indian Territory. Six hundred and eighty-one persons, led by their chief, Standing Bear, started their long walk in the heat of summer during which the forlorn little band experienced torrential rains, swollen rivers, and even a tornado. No preparation had been made to receive them and some did not survive. They constantly begged for permission to return home.

Hare's advice for the Ponca removal was apparently based on his assumption that he knew what was best for them—a long and sad assumption of western European mindset in Indian relations. No Episcopal mission accompanied the Ponca to what would become Oklahoma, nor are there records of Episcopal ministry among the 170 Ponca who returned to Nebraska after a landmark decision in Indian law several years later. It is noted, however, that Nebraska's bishop, Clarkson, was active with the Ponca Relief Fund.

Expulsion of Samuel Hinman

While Samuel Hinman had the respect of the Indian clergy, he did not get along with the white missionaries. Almost immediately, conflict, which would last for nine years, arose between Hinman and Hare. The missionary was accused of "gross immorality, misconduct and the dishonest and unfaithful use of money entrusted to him for the work of the mission." The conflict brought charges and counter charges and included a $10,000 libel judgment rendered against Hare in a New York court. An appeal reversed the lower court and ordered the case to be arbitrated by "wise and judicious mutual friends." Thus, the case came in 1887 to the offices of the Presiding Bishop. Eventually, the conflict resulted in Hinman's expulsion from the diocese. The man who went into the wilderness with the Santee was, thus, himself expelled.

Whipple welcomed him back to Minnesota, but further difficulty followed when the luckless missionary was later accused of improper conduct in a position as interpreter with the U.S. Census Bureau. He died a broken man in 1890 in Minnesota and was buried at Birch Coulee not far from the spot where his missionary work among the Dakota had begun 31 years before. Years later Edward Ashley wrote of the Hare-Hinman episode, "It is not for me to say anything in regard to the merits of the case, except this: Bishop Whipple of Minnesota stood by Mr. Hinman."

The conflict created a split in the Santee mission Indians. A certain capricious bent of Bishop Hare surfaced when he expelled from the church Indians who supported Hinman, the man who had initially brought Christ to the Dakota and who had stood by them in their most desolate hours during the expulsion from Minnesota.

Other Niobrara Work Founded

With the Ponca sent south, the Santee and Yankton work well launched, the new Bishop of Niobrara set about nurturing the work begun before his arrival among the Yankton. A fourth chapel was opened, Holy Comforter, in 1873 at Point of Timber, six miles below the Agency, with the Rev. George Young (whose full name appears to have been H. St. George Young) recruited by William Welsh to direct St. Paul's School.

St. Paul's School at Yankton Agency, the first of the esteemed old Episcopal boarding schools, opened in 1873 with an initial class of six Dakota youth which included four future leaders of the church and the Yankton Nation. The Rev. Joseph Cook hand-picked the six lads. The number was limited at first because of a shortage of bedding and clothing; later the school would serve 124-140 boys. The six included Charles S. Cook, the half-Indian son of a Virginia army officer, who chose to be called by the priest's name; Felix T. Brunot, a young chief who later exercised major influence on his people; Alfred C. Smith, who became a respected government day school teacher at Yankton and other reservations; William T. Selwyn, the single disappointment to Cook, and Philip J. Deloria, chieftain, priest, legend.

Brunot, 20; David Tatiyopa, 21, and Deloria, 19, in the summer of 1873 organized *Wojo Okolakiciye* (The Planting Society), which initially focused on reconciliation between Indians adopting the new agricultural life and those who sought to continue the nomadic life of their ancestors. The young men, all Christian converts, began farming and building log houses to replace the traditional tepees. The "hostiles" mocked their efforts and raced their horses across the gardens of the brotherhood to trample their corn and potatoes. Later known as the Brotherhood of Christian Unity (BCU), the Planting Society prevailed and eventually spread to every reservation in South Dakota. It once had a membership of 1,000.

Bishop Hare next concentrated on initiating new work among the Yanktonais and Lower Brulés at Crow Creek Agency, the several bands at the Cheyenne River Agency, the Oglalas at Pine Ridge and the Upper Brulés which eventually became the Rosebud Sioux.

Additionally, Episcopal work would spread to Flandreau and Sisseton-Wahpeton, initially assigned to the Presbyterians.

Crow Creek

Crow Creek Episcopal work first came and went with the saddened Santee exiles who disembarked from an overcrowded boat from Minnesota in 1863 to "this horrible region, filled with petrified remains of huge lizards and creeping things." When Welsh visited in 1870, he reported that the buildings at Fort Thompson had been taken over by the bands of Two Kettles and the Lower Yanktonais who were then "living peaceably and trying to farm." Hinman accompanied a delegation from the National Council of the Church in 1872 to the site and held in the Dakota language the first service many of the Indians had ever heard.

Heckaliah Burt, one of the three Berkeley Divinity School recruits Welsh had persuaded to serve among the Sioux, was sent to Crow Creek in late 1872 and held services near White Ghost's camp. In May, 1873, Christ Church and a new school were built.

Hare visited in 1875 and a few years later an account was written which epitomizes cultural destruction sought by church leaders of the era. A convert named *Iewicaka* (Truth Teller), age 35, had been designated as keeper of the drum of the Order of the Grass Dance. The bishop extolled Truth Teller's act when the convert declared "his purpose to abandon all Indian ways and adopt those of the white man, to give up all heathen rites and ceremonies and worship only the God of civilization." Whereupon Truth Teller, to attest his sincerity, presented the drum of the Order of the Grass Dance saying, "I part with the feather and the drum and all Indian ways forever."

Off and on Heckaliah Burt served the Crow Creek Mission for 45 years. In 1881 when settlers and Dakota newspapers demanded that the reservation be abolished and the land be opened for settlement, it was said: "The only friend the frightened Crow Creek Indians seemed to have left was their Episcopal missionary, the Reverend Heckaliah Burt."

Lower Brulé

Just across the Missouri River from the Crow Creek Reservation was the agency for the Lower Brulés, who were described as "perfect Ishmaelites, wandering in small bands, thousands of miles over the prairies; treacherous beyond all other Sioux and most apt to commit most of the rascalities which occur in this district." To them in 1872 was sent another of the Berkeley Divinity School recruits, William Joshua Cleveland. Soon after his arrival he wrote:

> We found an utterly raw and wild field in which neither the government nor any religious body had yet undertaken aught in the way of civilizing or Christianizing enterprises. No farming or stock raising . . . no schools . . . they were camped together in the brush, spending their time wholly in dancing, the hunt of the buffalo, and the war path.

Cleveland expressed optimism but later had to admit that the prospects were not encouraging. Teachers arrived to open a school and, while the effort was not successful, Cleveland married one of the teachers, Miss Lizzie Stiteler. The work was temporarily abandoned to be reopened in January, 1875. Later Heckaliah Burt came from Crow Creek and the Church of the Savior was built. In 1878 the Santee priest Luke C. Walker arrived to remain until 1921. A large portrait of Walker hangs on the wall of the white frame building housing the Church of the Holy Comforter.

Cheyenne River

The agent for the Cheyenne Agency described his charges (Minneconjou, Sans Arc, Two Kettles, and Black Feet Bands of the Teton Lakota) as "wild and roving, with real hatred for the white race." In fact this hostility manifested itself in 1876 when an Episcopal priest, R.A.B. Ffennel, was murdered by an Indian who had vowed to take the life of the first white man he saw in revenge for injury he had suffered from the military.

Ffennel's predecessor, Henry Swift, the third of the original Berkeley Divinity School recruits, opened the Cheyenne River work in 1872 using post quarters at Fort Sully until a mission building could be built. After three years Swift saw considerable progress. One of the leaders, Charger (who would later at baptism take the name of Martin), and his band settled at the Little Bend across from Fort Bennett. The Indians soon helped build a boarding school. Eventually Edward Ashley was sent to Cheyenne River and remained in charge of seven mission stations until 1924. One of the priests serving under him was Good Teacher, a Santee, who had been ordained in 1898.

Rosebud, Spotted Tail's Brulé

After *Sinte Gleska* (Spotted Tail) visited Chief Wabasha on the Santee Reservation and saw their schools, chapels and hospital, he wrote William Welsh on November 15, 1870:

MY FRIEND:

> I wish you to send us a missionary, as I find out it will be for the good of my people, and my white relations have recommended it. I have three villages—one of Ogalalla, say 200 lodges, Black Bear is their chief; the *Brulé Wanagi* (Ghost), 150 lodges, Red Leaf is their chief; the Upper Brule, 225 lodges, Spotted Tail is their chief. We wish to have some of our own people to instruct each band, and also an interpreter for each.

He expressed a need, as well, for a garrison of soldiers to keep away bad whites and whiskey peddlers. "To us, whiskey is death," he wrote. Welsh, acting on his own, purchased the holdings of the trader-bootlegger and promised Spotted Tail a missionary "as soon as the Upper Brulés were assigned a permanent home." Soon a school was opened for 150 children of Spotted Tail's tribe, run by the wife of the agent, and sponsored by the Church.

Spotted Tail, reconciled to the overpowering strength of the white man, exerted his influence as a peace chief. As a young man he was a warrior of note but after being held captive by General William S. Harney following a series of skirmishes, he recognized that resistance to the white onslaught was futile and signed the Fort Laramie Treaty along with Kicking Bird of the Kiowa and Black Kettle of the Cheyenne.

Bishop Whipple described Spotted Tail as "a picture of manly beauty, self-possessed, with piercing eyes." Bishop Hare, while serving on a government commission, experienced his moment of greatest fear:

> The commissioners met with several thousand of the disaffected Sioux in counsel. The commissioners sat in chairs with the cavalry mounted behind. The chiefs and leaders sat in a great semi-circle in front. Back of them were hundreds of young bucks galloping madly hither and thither. Spotted Tail finished a spirited speech in which he virtually told the commissioners to go back East and mind their own business. He suddenly gave a signal and every unmounted Indian ran to his horse and flung himself in the saddle, grasping his gun.

Hare in 1875 sent the Clevelands and two other teachers to the Spotted Tail Agency, then located five days from the nearest railroad. The work progressed rapidly and within two years, "a school house built to hold 75 was bursting at the seams with 150 students on the roll." Within a decade St. Mary's school, likely the best known of all the Episcopal boarding schools, was located on the Rosebud Reservation.

The government moved Spotted Tail's Agency several times. Finally the chief said: "We have been moved five times. I think you had better put the Indians on wheels, and then you can run them about whenever you wish."

There came in 1889 as priest-in-charge at Rosebud Mission Aaron Baker Clark with his wife, Sarah; they founded a dynasty of clergy and dedicated laity, generations of whom would work among Sioux and, subsequently, Navajo Indians in Episcopal mission. The eldest Clark son, the Rev. John Clark, succeeded his father at Rosebud Mission. A second son, the Rev. David W. Clark, was Superintending Presbyter at Crow Creek and Lower Brulé mission from 1919 until 1942 when he transferred to Navajoland. Clergymen named Clark served more than 60 years in South Dakota; they, indeed, "came to stay."

Flandreau

A solid example of Indian initiative emerged to establish Episcopal ministry at Flandreau in 1869. Chief David Weston, an Episcopal catechist, led 25 families away from the Santee reservation eastward 140 miles to the fertile Big Bend valley of the Big Sioux River, an unoccupied area more similar to their Minnesota ancestral home. Their journey was arduous, but upon arrival the Episcopal converts built a log cabin as their chapel and held regular worship services led by Weston.

Within the next year, 40 other Santee families, apprehensive about the permanency of the Nebraska site, had joined the Weston colony. A primary motivation for the bold and independent step was the group's aspiration to "live like white people," breaking away from tribalism and Indian agents. Among these emancipated Santee were men who had served three years in the Iowa prison, experienced religious conversion and psychological transformation. The latter included a craving for individual ownership of farms, and so the Flandreau filed land claims under the Homestead Act. By 1872 there were 257 people living in 51 log cabins; their living conditions were scarcely different from their Norwegian neighbors.

Shortly after Hare arrived in his jurisdiction the Weston band sent a delegation to invite the bishop to visit. Hare was reluctant to infringe on Presbyterian-assigned territory, but eventually, after the Indians demonstrated their own commitment to a mission by acquiring eight acres of land, the bishop elicited funding from St. Thomas Church, New York City. The money was used to build St. Mary's Chapel, named to honor Mary (Mrs. Samuel) Hinman, who died in 1876. The church was consecrated on April 20, 1879, during a roaring gale which fanned a prairie fire. The bishop stopped in the middle of his sermon, shed his robes and joined the firefighters. He later wrote, ". . . the flames came within fifteen feet of our holy and beautiful house." Services resumed in the evening and eight were confirmed.

Eventually an agency was established for the Flandreau colony, referred to as "Sioux of different tribes," and a boarding school was opened. In 1894 the white members separated and built a separate chapel. St. Mary's served the Flandreau Indian School until 1972.

Sisseton

Bishop Henry Whipple visited the Sisseton Wahpeton people here in the fall of 1868 and was so shocked at the conditions of hunger among the people that he personally issued food and clothing to our people and did not require them to work for this food as so many were too weak from hunger to work.

These were the words of a young tribal officer, Michael I. Selvage, as he welcomed visitors to the 120th Niobrara Convocation at St. Mary's Episcopal Church, Old Agency, on the Sisseton-Wahpeton Lake Traverse Reservation in June of 1992. As he recounted the suffering of his people in the aftermath of the Minnesota Conflict, he stressed the role of the Bishop of Minnesota in advocacy for the Lake Traverse Sioux. The young tribal officer, who is not an Episcopalian, continued:

In the 1876 a group of Sisseton and Wahpeton men walked all the way to the Yankton Reservation, asking the Episcopal Church to come to Sisseton; yet at that time, President Grant's Peace Policy would not allow the Episcopal Church on the Lake Traverse Reservation.

In February 1881 the reservations were opened to other denomination[s] and Bishop Hare came to Sisseton and authorized establishment of St. Mary's Church at this

Agency. This occurred on Easter of 1882. From this Church many leaders of our people went, and from this Church leaders continue to come. An example was set forth over a hundred years ago, and we now need to recall that example of faith, hope and charity.

The Sisseton delegation did, indeed, come to the sixth annual Niobrara Convocation, walking over 300 miles and taking 10 days to do it. Hare, reluctant to trespass onto a Presbyterian-controlled reservation, did not act. Four years later, however, Hare visited the Sisseton and sought permission from both the agent and the Presbyterians to establish a church. Women from the east sent building money to erect St. Mary's first small frame chapel, which still stands. The bishop sent Edward Ashley, who arrived on June 1, 1881, to begin work with a membership of 13. Within four years three other chapels were opened—St. James' at Enemy-Swim-Lake, St. John the Baptist at Brown's Valley and St. Luke's at Veblen. Within a couple of decades communicant strength grew to 287. A 1905 *The Spirit of Missions* article tenderly tells of the faith of Sisseton people:

> One Sunday, when a blizzard came up on Thursday evening and kept up in all its fury until Saturday at midnight, there were immense snowdrifts, some of them 10 feet high, about the mission buildings, but Mrs. Red Earth trudged alone over the two miles through the deep snow, breaking the path as she came, her Prayer Book and Hymnal wrapped up in a handkerchief.

Victor Renville, who was the first Sisseton to be ordained priest in the Episcopal Church, was a 13-year-old student at the Congregationalist mission when the Dakota conflict broke out. His mixed-blood family, living at the Upper or Yellow Medicine Agency, was taken captive but released without harm. After serving as a scout for several years, Renville relocated on the Sisseton-Wahpeton reservation.

Standing Rock

Though the huge Standing Rock Reservation, spilling over into North Dakota, was initially missionized by the Roman Catholic Church, Episcopal mission began there in 1883 following an investigation by Swift who reported to Hare:

> The sentiments of Sitting Bull's people are strong and set for *our church* to build on the Grand River.

In 1890 Mrs. John Jacob Astor provided funds to build St. Elizabeth's Church, to which Philip J. Deloria, then a deacon, was sent. The St. Elizabeth's boarding school opened soon afterward, located near Wakpala on a high bluff overlooking the valleys of the Missouri and Grand Rivers.

The work at St. Elizabeth's is closely associated with the name Deloria. The best-known of all the Indian priests of his era, Deloria was in charge of the Standing Rock mission until his retirement in 1925. It was here that he raised his family of high achievers—one daughter, Suzzane, became a well-known artist; another daughter, Ella, a noted scholar and writer; a son, Vine, esteemed priest of the church and Archdeacon of Niobrara.

Chief Gall, who fought beside Crazy Horse and Sitting Bull at Little Bighorn, lived as an old man near St. Elizabeth's. Deloria in 1918 related a story about the old warrior:

> My people are essentially religious people. When once they understand the Christian teaching, they prove to be devoted and faithful followers. As an example, I cite the conversion of Chief Gall. This man was a prominent chief. Because he fought on the Indian side, the soldiers were after him. One day the soldiers surrounded his camp and caught Gall. They ran their bayonets into his body, one into his head and one into his back. Because he fell in deep snow, they left him, thinking he was dead. Afterwards he regained consciousness and recovered.
>
> Later in his life he came to live a half mile away from my chapel. He used to come to the services, sit in a chair in the rear of the chapel, and simply listen. One day he invited me to come and see him. He said, "Many years back soldiers thought they had killed me. But God gave me power to recover. He sent me to live near this church. All I hear have combined to make my poor heart see a Man in these services. He is called the Son of God. This Man lived rightly towards this earth. His words are truth. His deeds are kind, loving and merciful. I have made up my mind to spend the rest of my life following him. I believe that at an appointed time He will take away my spirit and then I want my poor body returned to dust with Christian burial.
>
> According to his wish, Chief Gall was baptized and confirmed at the next visit of Hare, and upon his death given Christian burial. He sleeps in St. Elizabeth's Cemetery, a third of a mile away from the chapel.

Red Cloud's Oglalas of Pine Ridge

Bishop Whipple of Minnesota once said, "There are many men of mark among the Sioux; Red Cloud was a born leader of men, one who had the faculty of clothing truth with a terseness which stamped it upon the memory of the listeners." Having been asked for a farewell toast at a public dinner, Red Cloud arose and said:

> When men part they look forward to meeting again. I hope that one day we may meet in a land where white men are not liars.

Red Cloud, the great war leader of the Oglala, thoroughly distrusted the white man. When the Fort Laramie Treaty, which stipulated that federal military posts would close, was presented, Red Cloud withheld his signature until he saw the posts actually evacuated and burned by the rejoicing warriors.

The Episcopal Church was "invited" to begin mission in nearly all of the South Dakota reservations. Records show that Yankton people, through Frank Deloria, requested a mission: ". . . pray you and the brethren of your holy fellowship to build up mission among our people." Flandreau petitioned for mission; a woman even gave a horse to help fund the work. Sisseton sent a delegation 300 miles to plea to "have the Protestant Episcopal Church here in this place to teach us and our children that great law . . ." One finds no records, however, of an invitation coming from the fiercely independent Oglala people of Pine Ridge. The Rev. Nevill Joyner, superintending presbyter on the Pine Ridge from 1908 until 1940, wrote in a 1924 edition of *The Spirit of Missions* in fusty but nonetheless revealing language:

> What people inhabit the Pine Ridge Reservation? The Oglala band of the Great Sioux Nation, the most war-like of all American Indians and the last to submit to the dominion of the white man.

For several years, William Joshua Cleveland had traveled monthly 40 miles from his Rosebud station to hold services on the Pine Ridge Reservation. In 1874 Hare, at the government's request, visited the Oglalas as head of a commission to determine the cause of the Indians' unrest, but it was not until 1887 that the bishop actually established a mission among the Oglalas. He then sent Luke C. Walker with an eastern educated deacon, John Robinson, to begin a school and establish a mission. They arrived six days after Crazy Horse had been killed and found the Oglalas in a furor over the young chief's death. The mood of people did not daunt them; they immediately began the work which Robinson would carry on for 12 years at Pine Ridge.

By 1880 the Church of the Holy Cross at Pine Ridge village had been completed, again a gift of Mrs. John Jacob Astor. The bishop visited the next year to confirm seven.

The Pine Ridge mission, which by 1910 had grown to 26 chapels and stations, saw more and more Indians in clergy roles. First there was Joseph Marshall, a mixed-blood deacon who opened a school in a tepee at the Wounded Knee settlement in 1879, married one of the first Pine Ridge confirmands, and served Pine Ridge 38 years. Then came William T. Selwyn, Yankton Indian, as a teacher.

Another noble name in the Indian clergy roster was that of Amos Ross who shortly joined the Pine Ridge mission staff. He was born in 1852 at a Santee winter camp near St. Paul and came with his family to Crow Creek and thence to the Santee's Nebraska reservation. He became a catechist after four months' study in 1872 in Davenport, Iowa. After long study, he was ordained to the diaconate. He married Lucy Gayton, mixed blood Ponca in 1877; she came with him to Pine Ridge, where he first served at Orphan's Camp, which he renamed St. Andrew's, at Wounded Knee. At the 1892 Niobrara Convocation Ross, along with Philip Deloria, was ordained to the priesthood and put in charge of the growing Corn Creek District of the Pine Ridge Mission.

In 1885 the first eastern-educated and seminary-trained Sioux, Charles Smith Cook, arrived on Pine Ridge. A mixed blood Yankton, Cook graduated from Trinity College, Hartford, Connecticut, in 1881 and received a master's degree from Trinity in 1887. He then earned a theology degree from Seabury Divinity School, Faribault, Minnesota. The son of a Virginia military officer and a Yankton woman, his foster father was the Rev. Joseph Cook of the Yankton Mission. Charles Cook became superintending presbyter of the Pine Ridge Mission.

It would be Charles Cook's sad duty to bury victims of the Wounded Knee massacre—30 soldiers and 20 Indians who died in his guild hall, hastily converted into an infirmary. He contracted tuberculosis and died on Good Friday, 1892.

Theft of the Black Hills

Though English-born Edward Ashley is credited in the old *The Spirit of Missions* publication with "understanding the Indians far better than any white man," he counted the Lakotas' archenemy, George Armstrong Custer, as his friend. A story in *The Church at Work,* October, 1923, tells of the celebration on the occasion of the archdeacon's having completed 50 years of ministry among the Sioux:

He is the sole white survivor of that group which opened the Black Hills to white settlers, stripped the Indians of their hunting grounds and led to the Custer massacre of the Little Big Horn.

Hare, however, is on record in a letter to President Grant opposing the 1874 expedition led by General Custer to explore the Black Hills to ascertain whether rumors were true that there was "gold at the roots of the grass." Custer led 1,200 troops into the Black Hills in direct violation of terms of the 1868 Fort Laramie Treaty, which guaranteed to the Sioux the land from the Missouri River west to the Wyoming-South Dakota border, with an even larger western area to remain "unceded Indian territory" upon which the Indians could hunt and from which whites were excluded. Hare informed the President of the United States that he feared the Custer expedition into the Black Hills would:

> . . . provoke an Indian War and would seriously imperil the existence of the struggling but numerous missions, which encouraged by your policy, that the Episcopal Church is nourishing among the Sioux, and endanger the lives of her missionaries.

Gold, of course, was discovered in the Black Hills, whereupon no power on earth could stop the onslaught of greedy white prospectors or the last desperate assault of the Plains Indians on a Montana creek called Little Bighorn. As miners poured into the Black Hills, skirmishes broke out and the Sioux were ordered onto reservations. Sitting Bull and Crazy Horse refused to bring in their people. Outraged by unjust attacks and invasion, Sitting Bull said:

> We are an island of Indians in a lake of whites . . . these soldiers want war. All right, we'll give it to them.

The fatuously ambitious General Custer led a 7th Cavalry unit into Montana intent upon irrevocably subduing the "hostiles." On June 25, 1876, referred to in certain Indian circles as Sioux Victory Day, Sioux and Cheyenne warriors, led by the Oglala Crazy Horse, along with Sitting Bull and Gall from Standing Rock, annihilated the Custer column. Not a single soldier in Custer's immediate command of 250 men survived. The Indians then split into bands to escape more easily. Some, including Sitting Bull's band, fled to Canada. Before the end of the century Crazy Horse and Sitting Bull were both betrayed and slaughtered. Chief Gall, however, lived to be an old man on the Standing Rock Reservation as a confirmed Episcopalian.

Retribution for the Little Bighorn victory came swiftly. Within two months commissioners came riding up with the demand that the Sioux surrender the Black Hills, the "unceded" Powder River country, and remove to Indian Territory. Spotted Tail actually went with a delegation to inspect the country of Indian Territory and found the Creeks courteous and hospitable. The removal proposal was dropped after fervent outcry from Texans and Kansans who were likely looking at grabbing chunks of Indian Territory for themselves—which, of course, they did. So, the Sioux were spared a Trail of Tears to the Territory, but the land cessions were forced upon them.

The Fort Laramie Treaty had provided that any ceding of lands would require approval of 75 percent of the adult male Indians. By mid-August Congress voted to cease subsistence until they relinquished all claims to the Black Hills. By 1877 the "sign or starve" tactics brought certain Sioux leaders to their knees and an agreement was signed. However, only ten percent—not 75 percent—of male Sioux adults ever signed the agreement. Within six months Congress passed an act confiscating the Black Hills region and the unceded territory.

In 1980, 103 years after the Sioux lands were unlawfully taken, the Supreme Court ruled the seizure to be illegal and the Court, in uncommonly terse language, stressed:

> . . . a more ripe and rank case of dishonorable dealing will never, in all probability, be found in our history.

The Supreme Court recommended compensation for the land plus interest. Congress appropriated $17 million which included interest since 1877. The tribes of the Great Sioux Nation said, "No! We do not want the money; we want the Black Hills." The issue is yet unresolved and over $350-million, including accrued interest, sits in the U.S. Treasury awaiting resolution.

In the early years, the Episcopal Church's role in the Black Hills theft was not without taint. However in recent decades, atonement has been evident. Niobrara Convocation in 1987 voted in support of the Sioux Nation Black Hills Act, known as the Bradley Bill. The Detroit General Convention of 1988 and the Phoenix General Convention of 1991 called for fair and just settlements of Indian claims. In 1989 Presiding Bishop Edmond L. Browning led an alliance of church groups in calling upon congressional leaders to form a high-level national commission to recommend resolution of the Black Hills issue. Such legislation was considered by Sen. Daniel Inouye, chair of the Senate Select Committee on Indian Affairs, but was stoutly opposed by the South Dakota congressional delegation. At even the suggestion of

studying the Black Hills issue, a torrent of calumny rose from the
state's non-Indian populace, including ire within segments of the Episcopal Church. The South Dakota bishop's house in Sioux Falls was
fire-bombed on the night of May 14, 1991. Fortuitously, there were no
physical injuries and but scant structural damage.

Had the Episcopal Church raised up a hue and cry in the last
century before the Black Hills were illegally confiscated, the outcome
might have been different. Records indicate that Hare refrained from
direct participation in the Government's maneuvers, but he assigned
clergy, including Hinman broadly trusted by the Sioux to serve on a
commission "to negotiate for purchase of the Hills." In recent times
the august Whipple of Minnesota has been accused of "engineering
the government's theft of the Black Hills, finally breaking the back of
Sioux resistance." Whipple's protracted autobiography does, indeed,
reveal that in the aftermath of the Sioux victory at the Battle of the
Little Bighorn, he traveled 200 miles in a jolting wagon with a treaty
commission which met with the Sioux Chief Spotted Tail. Perhaps
Whipple, with his past record for friendship with Indians, was the
persuasive pivot as the commission moved about to the various agencies apprising the chiefs of the government's terms and extracting
their signatures.

Slaughter at Wounded Knee Creek

A pitiful postscript to Sioux Victory Day was written in 1890, at
Wounded Knee Creek on the Pine Ridge Reservation when the 7th
Cavalry slaughtered scores of half-starved Minneconjou, struggling
through a bitter December morning to reach Pine Ridge Agency for
rations. Nearby, Christmas greens were still hanging at the Episcopal Church of the Holy Cross. The Episcopal ministers and
congregation cared for the wounded and buried some of the dead—30
soldiers and 20 Indians. The 376 other dead Indians, of whom 207
were women and children, were buried on a hilltop in a mass grave.

Trigger-happy 7th Cavalry troopers acted both to avenge the
death of Custer and to stop further spread of the Ghost Dance religion, a messianic movement which swept across western Indian
country promising the return of the buffalo and departure of the whites
from the land of the Lakota.

An unconscionable undercount of Wounded Knee casualties—
149—was given in history books for a full century. Descendants of
survivors and victims, in cooperation with the Nebraska Historical
Association, have identified 376 victims. These included 106 children,

Gathering the dead at Wounded Knee Battlefield, 1890.
Courtesy, Smithsonian Institution.

age 16 and under; 101 women and 169 men. There were 14 unidentified children, 13 unidentified women and three unidentified men. Names of the victims were read December 29, 1990, to memorialize the centennial of the tragedy in a pre-dawn service at Calvary Cathedral in Sioux Falls. To the muffled cadence of a Sioux drum the Rev. Martin Brokenleg and other participants lit a votive candle as they read the name of each victim.

Bishop Hare's Chapels, Churches, Clergy and Schools

By 1885 Episcopal chapels, churches and schools were sprinkled across the nine Sioux Reservations. Many of these chapels yet stand—in virtual isolation from a settlement, a village, a stream or a tree—and on Sunday mornings their bells still peal out across the vast prairies summoning to worship fourth, fifth and sixth generation Sioux Episcopalians. Mainstay at today's chapels are commissioned licensed lay readers because Lakota/Dakota clergy often serve as many as six or seven congregations and, thus, appear only once or twice monthly to hold the service of Holy Eucharist.

From the beginning of work among the Lakota/Dakota people, the Episcopal missionaries founded schools. Hinman immediately started a school at Santee and Joseph Cook opened a school at Yankton Reservation for 125-140 Indians up to age 40.

No sooner had Hare unpacked than he, too, inaugurated boarding schools, believing value would be gained in "isolating the children from heathen influences." He also justified the boarding school system with a conviction that the Church had responsibility not only to convert the Indians but to train them in practical ways to prepare for their future, whatever that would be. The government cooperated—its agenda was complete acculturation—and stipulated that rations would be issued only to those children who regularly attended school. Before his first anniversary as diocesan, Hare had founded St. Paul's for boys and St. Mary's for girls. St. Mary's, though it would experience several moves, lasted while others came and went. It was not until September, 1986, that St. Mary's, the last of many Episcopal Indian boarding schools, ceased operation. For generations many mannerly Sioux matrons referred to themselves as "St. Mary's girls," and many married Sioux clergymen. Hare looked to the boys' boarding schools as a supply source for Episcopal Church Lakota/Dakota leadership and he chose men who first became helpers, then catechists, and after training, deacons and priests. Hare felt that only by the aid of its own people could the Indians be effectively evangelized.

Retired Suffragan Bishop Harold S. Jones, the church's first American Indian bishop, was the grandson of an early native priest trained by Hare. Bishop Jones, a Santee, said several years ago that 45 native priests came out of his small reservation, "the place where the Episcopal Church was first planted among the Sioux."

The Venerable Vine Deloria (1901-1990), one of the great story tellers of his time, had much praise for Hare's way of training the Sioux clergy. "Hare taught them the Bible and the Prayer Book and gave them a little booklet on how to run a parish. That's all! But the teachings of these early Indian ministers were simple, sound, sincere, solid, stimulating and stabilizing! The teachings were effective; Hare had 10,000 souls settled in 100 chapels on the ten Sioux reservations ministered to by the Indian clergy and catechists, with only half dozen well-chosen white clergy. Some of the Indians were sent away to study; others were trained at home."

Amos Ross, whom Deloria described as his uncle, was an excellent example of the home-trained, faithful old Sioux clergy. A youngster at the time of the Sioux uprising, he was force-marched with his northern Minnesota band to Fort Snelling and while interned he was baptized by an Episcopal missionary. Young Amos survived the perilous journey west with the Santee exiles and became a skilled carpenter and worked at the agency at the new Santee settlement. Bishop Clarkson became interested in the young man and sent him and another Indian, John Rouillard, to study for four months in Davenport, Iowa, and then the bishop designated him as a catechist. After long study he was ordained to the diaconate and finally—in 1892—he was ordained to priesthood and put in charge of the growing Corn Creek District of Pine Ridge Mission. At the time he retired he had nearly 1,800 members in 11 churches in the sparsely populated eastern end of Pine Ridge Reservation.

For decade after decade, the brightest young men on the Sioux Reservations, men who in an earlier time would have been hunters and warriors, had but three career choices: teach, preach or work for the Bureau of Indian Affairs (BIA). Many became Episcopal priests, some of whom served their people for more than 50 years, including Luke C. Walker, Amos Ross and Philip J. Deloria.

By 1925 Lakota/Dakota communicant strength grew to 5,183 in 97 congregations. While community strength lessened, the number of congregations held steady for the next decade. On the Pine Ridge reservation the high point in communicant strength was reached with 2,090 in 1945.

Magnificent Lakota/Dakota names appeared on clergy rosters of the Diocese of South Dakota. Clergy and catechists listed in a 1937 roster included the names of Brings the Pipe, Charging Cloud, Winter Chaser, White Plume, Standing Elk, Driving Hawk, and many others including a priest whose name was Christian B. Whipple, named to honor the first Bishop of Minnesota. The 1992 roster of active deacons and priests included American Horse, Bear's Heart, Blue Coat, Brokenleg (father and son), Makes Good, Moose, Two Bulls, Two Hawk, Turgeon and Tyon, along with less lyrical names such as Brown, Campbell, Mesteth, Potter and Robertson.

The Legendary Delorias

The Deloria name appeared on the clergy rolls of South Dakota for 98 years. Philip J. Deloria, whose Dakota name was *Tipi Sapa* (Black Lodge), was ordained to the priesthood in 1892. His son, Vine V. Deloria, was ordained in 1913 and died in 1990. He had retired as archdeacon of Niobrara Deanery in 1968.

The story of the conversion of Philip Deloria been printed and re-printed in old church publications across the years. Though it is a bit simplistic and quite likely not totally true, it is a charming story. Hugh L. Burleson, South Dakota's fourth bishop, relates the story in a 1920 issue of *The Spirit of Missions:*

> Tipi Sapa was riding by a chapel (at Greenwood) in full war regalia when he heard the congregation singing, "Guide Me, O Thou Great Jehovah," and he stopped to listen to the words. He did not enter the chapel but rode back later another day to hear the same hymn being sung. Apparently a great impression was made on the young chief. He had understood the words as the hymn was being sung in Dakota. Finally he went to Bishop Hare and stated he wanted to become a Christian. The Bishop told him he must give up his chief's position and cut his hair and become a simple man. Tipi Sapa refused to do this, stating he was a powerful chief. He returned later, however, and was baptized.

Young Philip may have been a bit more acquainted with the Episcopal Church than the story indicates. Records show that Philip was baptized at age 16 in 1874, the same year the Episcopal missionary came to Yankton Reservation. Paul Mazakute, for the previous seven years, had been on the Yankton Reservation holding services, first as a layperson and then as a catechist and deacon.

Vine recounted his family's history. Vine's grandfather, Francis, was the son of a Yankton Sioux woman and a French father whose name was Philippe des Lauriers. Francis possessed strong spiritual powers and became, among other things, a medicine man, after a vision quest in which a black lodge appeared. This name, *Tipi Sapa* (Black Lodge), he gave his son, born of his Standing Rock wife. Francis had three wives. "I had three grandmothers," said the aged Deloria, "a Standing Rock grandmother and a Rosebud and Crow Creek grandmother, and between them there were 23 children." Francis, according to Vine, "had all his children and grandchildren baptized." But because he had more than one wife, Francis postponed presenting himself for baptism until he was quite old.

Francis sent some of his children to the new mission school. The missionaries saw that young Philip showed much promise and he was sent away to Shattuck Military School at Faribault, Minnesota. At Shattuck, Philip was a special student who concentrated on learning English and mathematics. After his graduation, he returned to Dakota, became a catechist, and then was ordained deacon at St. Stephen's chapel on the Cheyenne River reservation. He was then sent to establish St. Elizabeth's School, and after his ordination to the priesthood, became superintending presbyter of the Standing Rock Reservation.

After 40 years on the Standing Rock, Philip returned to the Yankton reservation in 1925, and the Church built a home for him at White Swan. In recognition of his devotion, his figure was included among the 98 "Saints of the Ages" in the reredos of the high altar of the National Cathedral in Washington, D.C. He was one of three Americans so honored.

Besides his son, the archdeacon, Philip Deloria left other descendants of distinction. They have included a daughter, Dr. Ella Deloria, who became a noted scholar, and a grandson, Vine Jr., who is recognized as one of the foremost American Indian authors of the 20th century.

Hare's Successors

For 36 years Hare worked among the people of South Dakota. When he died in 1909, there were 100 congregations where there had been nine, 26 Indian clergy where there had been three. In 1883 the House of Bishops discarded the "Niobrara" name and established boundaries of his jurisdiction to coincide with the present-day state. *Zitkana Duzahan* (Swift Bird), as Hare was sometimes called, then became bishop of the missionary district of South Dakota with white settlers as well as the Sioux under his jurisdiction. It was not until 1971 that South Dakota was classified as a diocese. Hare, a widower for 43 years, was buried in Sioux Falls.

His immediate successor was his assisting bishop, Frederick Foote Johnson, who served two years as diocesan and then was translated to the Diocese of Missouri. The House of Bishops elected Rowe of Alaska as the South Dakota diocesan. Rowe declined. In the spring of 1912, George Biller Jr., dean of Calvary Cathedral in Sioux Falls, was named South Dakota's third bishop. He had been born in London and began his missionary work in the United States in the Choctaw Nation, Indian Territory (present-day Oklahoma), where his mission was mainly among white settlers or "sooners" who had moved into Choctaw Nation prior to statehood. He served as South Dakota bishop only three years before his untimely death at age 41.

The fourth missionary Bishop of South Dakota, Hugh Latimer Burleson, had been ordained at the Hobart Church on the Oneida Reservation in Wisconsin where his father was a missionary. A seasoned priest prior to becoming bishop, Burleson had worked in New

*The Reverend Philip Deloria [1854-1931] (seated) with the
Venerable Edward Ashley, Archdeacon of Niobrara.*
Courtesy Vine Deloria, Jr.

York on the staff of the Presiding Bishop and served as editor of *The
Spirit of Missions*. Burleson's lasting imprint on Indian ministry included creation of the office of Archdeacon of Niobrara to which he
appointed the Rev. Edward Ashley. In 1930 Burleson created Niobrara
Council to handle issues in the Indian field. Heading the South Dakota church from 1917 until 1931, Burleson was aided by two
successive suffragans, one of whom, W. Blair Roberts, would succeed
him.

The depression years were hard for South Dakota; fund short-
ages forced the national church to reduce its subsidy by 10 per cent.
In 1943 the Indian work of North and South Dakota was consolidated
and placed under the Rev. John B. Clark, who worked out of Mobridge.
The work remained combined until 1951.

In the early aftermath of World War II, Bishop Roberts spoke to
a new unmet need in the Indian world, the emerging urban Indian
population. "In Rapid City," he said, "the problem is great . . . over
3,000 Indians moved here . . . comparatively few of these people attend

Emmanuel Church." He appointed the Rev. Levi M. Roulliard to work among Indians not only in Rapid City but in Huron, Sioux Falls, and other cities and towns.

The House of Bishops in 1945 elected Conrad H. Gesner, a godson of Bishop Burleson, as coadjutor, a position he would hold for nine years before being installed as diocesan. He served until 1970. During Gesner's episcopacy, three Presiding Bishops came to Niobrara Convocations, Church Army personnel appeared and the number of native clergy increased. Lyman C. Ogilby served as coadjutor from 1964 to 1970, and stepped aside to allow South Dakota Episcopalians to choose Gesner's successor.

Canadian-born Walter H. Jones served for 13 tumultuous years, years which saw the 71-day occupation of Wounded Knee by the American Indian Movement (AIM) in 1973. In the May issue of *The Episcopalian,* Jones wrote:

> Let us share with everyone the fact that Christians and Episcopalians have taken a stand. It is not for one day for the TV cameras . . . it is not a stand for rhetoric or impossible resolutions. It is not a stand for or against any individual.
>
> It is a stand beside the person who, in fear, left his home and had need of food, clothing, and a place to stay. It is a stand beside the people who, regardless of their political views, need insulin, or medication or wounds bandaged—yes, and even Pampers.
>
> Nearly 100 years ago the Episcopal Church of the Holy Cross was used to house the victims of Wounded Knee. Today it is again being used to house the homeless and the stranger who heard something was going on in Wounded Knee and drifted in.
>
> We share with you the resolutions drawn up by the Niobrara Deanery: there must be a careful and thorough study of the treaties and their guarantees; there must be open and fair hearings of injustices, problems and particularly what are the needs of the Indian people; and finally, there must be an educational program which clearly sets before all people the tremendous cultural values and contributions that the Native American has made to this nation.
>
> The Episcopal Church, because it is at Wounded Knee, . . . has in its membership persons who are on every side. Members who are tribal chairmen, employees of the BIA, members of Public Health, and yes, even Russell

Means who on March 31, 1940, was baptized at Holy Cross
Church . . .

In a journey to the village of Wounded Knee, a hamlet of bitter
memories, two decades after the occupation, it was hard to envision
the armored personnel carriers that rumbled across the terrain. Looking across the wind-swept hillocks of the lonely countryside, it was
hard to picture some 300 Indians barricaded in the now demolished
Roman Catholic church, surrounded by 300 federal agents. It was difficult to internalize that major strategy sessions took place in the
modest and small Church of the Holy Cross in the village of Pine Ridge.

To this edifice built a century ago with money from Mrs. John
Jacob Astor, came the National Council of Churches' chief trouble-
shooter, John Adams, who asked for and received the support of the
Rev. George P. Pierce, superintending Presbyter for the Pine Ridge
Reservation. Pierce, an Episcopal priest who eventually headed the
Church Army, had served in South Dakota Indian ministry for more
than a decade and was known and trusted by traditional Lakota
Church people.

In his doctoral dissertation, "Leadership in Crisis: the Lakota
Religious Response to Wounded Knee, 1973," Pierce wrote:

> Our home and Holy Cross Church became center for NCC
> activities for the next three weeks. Adam's main objective
> was to establish negotiation between the government and
> AIM. For this purpose he traveled back and forth between
> the federal command post in Pine Ridge and the AIM head-
> quarters in Wounded Knee . . . In order to establish trust,
> Adams used his vast network of contacts through the
> churches . . . Basic sanitation, blankets, and food were pro-
> vided for the demonstrators . . . Margaret Hawk, a Lakota
> Church Army sister, and myself, in particular concern for
> the residents of Wounded Knee, carried food into the
> perimeter . . . This latter action had been approved by a
> group of local clergy who met the first week of the occupa-
> tion.

> It was important that the church maintain neutrality in
> this conflict. From the standpoint of the reservation com-
> munity, this was, in part, a fight between Russell Means,
> the leader of the AIM occupation, and Dick Wilson, the
> Tribal Chairman, both of whom had been baptized at Holy
> Cross.

First American Indian Bishop

A high point in the tenure of Walter Jones was election of the first American Indian bishop, Harold S. Jones. The April 1972 edition of *The Episcopalian* described the January 11 event:

> In a ceremony in which two cultures blended . . . priests wore white albs with scarlet stoles, designed and worked in Indian motif especially for this services. The new bishop's vestments were rich with symbolic Indian designs . . . Much of the service was bilingual. Hymns and prayers burst forth in both English and Dakota, sung simultaneously. St. Joseph's Roman Catholic Cathedral, a massive church, was filled with a strangely beautiful interplay of sound . . .
>
> Numbers of Indians took part. The master of ceremonies was the Rev. Martin Brokenleg, a young priest from Sioux Falls. His father, the Rev. Noah Brokenleg of [the town of] Mission, was attending presbyter. The Rev. Wilbur Bear's Heart, associate director of the Dakota Leadership Training Program, read the Litany . . . An Indian layman, Kent Fitzgerald, executive director of the National Committee on Indian Work, preached the sermon . . .

This first American Indian bishop, Harold Stephen Jones, was born at Mitchell, South Dakota, December 24, 1909, educated at Seabury-Western Theological Seminary, ordained to the diaconate in 1938 and to the priesthood in 1941, and consecrated bishop on January 9, 1972. Upon returning to South Dakota after seminary, the young priest served stations, chapels and churches on the Pine Ridge and Cheyenne River reservations. Later he served at Wahpeton in North Dakota, and three years among the Navajo at Good Shepherd Mission in Fort Defiance, Arizona.

Bishop Jones, who had been reared at Santee, tells of his early assignments after graduation from Seabury at age 29. The superintending presbyter, Nevill Joyner, said that pay would be $40 a month and that the young clergyman would serve three chapels which were located 23 miles apart. Jones asked how he was to travel between mission stations. "Walk," pronounced the Rev. Mr. Joyner.

The tall and distinguished bishop tells a story about how he arrived at his first clergy assignment, Christ Church, Red Shirt Table, on the Pine Ridge Reservation. "I caught a ride on a watermelon truck," he said. "I sat in back among the watermelons in the rain."

The rectory at Red Shirt Table, which yet stands, was a tiny one-room cottage to which Harold Jones brought his bride, the late beautiful and gracious Blossom. "Our first home was furnished with 21 apple crates," said Mrs. Jones. "We had no electricity or water for the first eight years after Harold was ordained."

At the mid-point of the tenures of the two bishops named Jones, it was reported that 15,000 to 20,000 Sioux of South Dakota were Episcopalians in 80 congregations of the Niobrara deanery. "Bishop Harold" had to resign in 1976 because of a stroke. He would, however, continue occasional visitations for many more years. "Bishop Walter" resigned in 1983 to return to his native Canada where he became the archbishop and metropolitan of the Province of Rupert's Land.

The Niobrara Cross

Two monumental symbols and events in the Lakota/Dakota Episcopal community descended from the earliest mission among the Sioux—the Niobrara Cross and the annual Niobrara Convocation.

Early in his tenure, Hare designed a symbol for his charges as a token of their obligation to Christianity. The symbol of confirmation among Dakota people is the Niobrara Cross. In the early days few of the converts could read, so certificates of baptism and confirmation meant little. The bishop recognized the Indian cultural use of symbols and designed the Niobrara Cross with four tepees, symbolizing the four winds. On top of each tepee is a cross. In the very center of the cross are Christ's words: "I am come that ye may have life." Since 1873 every Indian has received the Niobrara Cross at confirmation as a symbol of the truth found in Christianity. In 1975 the Niobrara Convocation voted to share the Niobrara Cross with non-Indian confirmands of the diocese.

Niobrara Convocation: A Distinct Institution

Begun prior to Hare's arrival was the Niobrara Convocation, the single most distinctive institution of American Indian Episcopalians. The first Niobrara Convocation was held in October, 1870, at the Church of Our Most Merciful Savior on the Santee Reservation. Attending were two white and three Indian clergy, four lay delegates, four catechists, representatives of Santee bands, one Ponca, and five head men of the Yanktons. And, since 1870, with but rare interruptions, this summer gathering has been held annually.

President and Mrs. Calvin Coolidge attended the 1927 Niobrara Convocation at Pine Ridge. He appears to have been routinely silent; he is not quoted.

The character of Niobrara Convocation is described by Virginia Driving Hawk Sneve:

> The Niobrara Convocation, although it has no Indian ceremonials with it, has served the same social function as the old Sun Dance, when friends and relatives came together in the summer from all directions. The convocation custom of the Indians from the different reservations camping together was not unlike the traditional affairs held in the camp circle each summer by the various tribes.

The 1923 Niobrara Convocation was described in fusty but nonetheless revealing language in *The Spirit of Missions* in an article written by Roger Daniels, thought to have been a staff person of the national church headquarters. He told of the his arrival to the site on the banks of the Moreau River near White Horse on the Cheyenne River Reservation. He wrote:

> Fully two thousand Indians were encamped there for three days. They came by prairie schooners, in spring wagons, in buggies, in autos, on horseback. As fast as new arrivals came, tents sprang up mushroom-like, and campfires crackled and pots began to boil . . .
>
> Then would sound the call of the camp herald announcing in the Dakota tongue that time had come for prayer. The chief of these heralds is Spotted Rabbit, who as a young man of nineteen joined himself with that nomad group of Sioux who were attacked by Custer and later turned to annihilate his body of troops to the man. Spotted Rabbit took part in the battle of the Little Big Horn, being given the honor of riding onto the battlefield unarmed in an attempt to take Custer alive. His mission failed when his horse was shot from under him. Custer died a moment later. Now Spotted Rabbit calls his brothers to prayer . . .
>
> The program of the Convocation is in the hands of a special committee which holds its final meeting the night before the meeting opens. All regulations are made by this committee. Much has been said about Sioux dances. It seems worthy of note that a contribution toward the Convocation expenses which had been raised at an Indian dance was turned down by this committee.
>
> A large class was confirmed by Bishop Burleson and several catechists were licensed. But the special interest of this Convocation centered round the fact that it marked

*Niobrara Convocation, ca. / 1920, camp due east of Episcopal
Church on southern border of Pine Ridge village.*
Courtesy Vine Deloria, Jr.

the completion of Archdeacon Ashley's fifty years of service
among the Indians. The Ven. Edward Ashley, LL.D., is the
sole remaining white man who witnessed the signing of
the Black Hills treaty . . .

In the summer of 1986, The Church of Our Most Merciful Savior
hosted the convocation, attended by 500, and two elder clergymen
captivated a crowd of visitors as they reminisced about the 50th
Niobrara Convocation in 1920 when 4,000 Sioux assembled at the
Santee site. The old priests told of a thousand tents dotting the hillside, sloping north to the Missouri River. The two elders laughed, and
joked, and told stories about the convocation herald or crier (*eyapaha*)
in 1920 who rode horseback around the encampment and with his
long wooden lance nudged stragglers into meeting sessions.

These two aging clergymen, who sat straight on the backless
wooden benches under a vast arbor—an open-sided pavilion roofed
with boughs—were among the most revered Indian clergy of the Episcopal Church. The awe-inspiring pair were Vine Deloria Sr. the retired

archdeacon of Niobrara, (1901-1990), and Harold Jones, the first American Indian bishop of the Episcopal Church, born in 1909.

At the 50th Niobrara Convocation, five Sioux men were ordained deacons; at the 114th, the first Native American couple was ordained. Charles and Cheryl Montileaux of Pine Ridge were made deacons by Bishop Craig Anderson, and at the ordination, Naomi, their five-year-old daughter, carried a thurible filled with sweet grass, whose burning is part of a Plains Indian tradition. The young clergy couple offered much promise but, tragically, a scant two years after her ordination Cheryl Montileaux died of cancer at age 31. Her grief-stricken husband would soon stop functioning as a clergyman.

The Presiding Bishop Attends
the 1987 Niobrara Convocation

Presiding Bishop Edmond L. Browning came to the 1987 convocation, the 115th, as did 2,100 others. The convocation was held deep within the Rosebud Reservation at Mission, a village of 900 with but two small motels.

Throughout an afternoon the Presiding Bishop sat quietly, unattended, on a wooden plank propped by concrete blocks, beneath a vast brush arbor, and listened to concerns of the people of the grass-roots. He personally carried communion wafers and wine to the ill and hospitalized; he visited the domestic violence shelter operated by White Buffalo Calf Women's Society in one of the buildings of the Bishop Hare School; he observed a cross-section of Reservation life dispirited by neglect.

The Primate's observances were perhaps key to transition and unprecedented reorganization in the national Church's structures relating to Indian ministry. Within ten months, during a meeting of Executive Council in South Dakota, Bishop Browning would charge his Blue Ribbon Task Force on Indian Affairs to bring forth recommendations on "what we ought to be doing [in Indian ministry] and how to do it."

During the 1987 three-day Convocation, 85 persons were confirmed, two received, three baptized, 77 commissioned as lay ministers, one couple married, and 119 clergy "laid hands" at the priesting of Charles Montileaux. Business meetings produced resolutions supporting return of Black Hills land to the Sioux Nation.

In the great Sunday morning procession, hundreds walked down the hill from the beautiful old St. James' Chapel behind colorful banners of many of the 86 reservation chapels as well as the banners of Indian congregations from neighboring dioceses. Three bishops walked in the procession. Leading them was the retired Santee suffragan, Bishop Jones. Walking together, in full Sioux head-dresses, were the tall and fair diocesan bishop and the sensitive and caring Primate, who within the first 18 months of his tenure had participated in Native American gatherings in Navajoland, Oklahoma, Niobrara and Minnesota, had met with National Committee on Indian Work at Church Center in New York, and had broken all records in the number of American Indians appointed to national Church committees and commissions.

Services were held in the open air, beneath an enormous brush arbor. Hymns were sung in Lakota and English. Splendid star quilts, hung behind the altar, served as the dossal. The Primate of the Episcopal Church sat in the rugged hand-made tall chair that had been the chair of Bishop Hare. In his sermon Browning gently called for reconciliation and harmony; he spoke of his own ministry as one of servanthood as he seeks to understand the concerns and special visions of all the people of God and his whole creation.

The convocation was not without its lighter moments. Browning stood in the center of a great circle of American Indians in the twilight of the longest day of the year on the grounds which had been the Bishop Hare School for Indian Boys, and in solemn ritual—as old as time among the peoples of the plains—he was honored in a name-giving ceremony. The Very Rev. Clyde Estes, Lower Brulé Sioux, with drum, dignity, and scriptural reference, proclaimed the name of the Presiding Bishop to be *Inyan Wichasa* (Man of Rock). The traditional Lakota/Dakota giveaway followed. Browning linked arms with Marie Rogers and Christine Prairie Chicken to dance the honoring dance at the end of the ceremony. Browning was visibly moved as he accepted the many magnificent hand-crafted gifts which included eight star-quilts, a beautiful beaded stole, and a splendid chief's head-dress with full-length trail. The latter, in resplendent scarlet, perfectly matched the beaded moccasins which had been presented to the Presiding Bishop at his 1986 installation by the Ven. Noah Brokenleg, senior priest of the Rosebud Mission.

Respected figures of the Indian world and visitors from the Fiji Islands, Germany, South America, Puerto Rico and 18 states of the union participated in sunset prayers, healing services, and hymn singing in both Lakota and English languages. Dr. Ben Reifel, former Congressman and the only Sioux ever to serve in the U.S. House of Representatives, traveled from Florida to visit with old friends and former constituents. Dr. Helen Peterson of Portland, Oregon, former executive director for the National Congress of American Indians, also returned to her origins as chair of the National Committee on Indian Work.

The Ven. Vine Deloria Sr. journeyed from his retirement home in Tucson for the 1987 Niobrara Convocation and immediately was the center of a circle of listeners for his lively and enchanting stories. It would be his last convocation.

Subsequent Niobrara Convocations

The following year blistering heat confronted some 450 participants at the 1988 convocation hosted by Gethsemane Chapel at Wanblee on the Pine Ridge Reservation. Two Indian clergymen were honored in recognition for their 25th anniversary of ordination, and for the first time a lay woman—the author—was preacher. The following summer the Seminole bishop, William C. Wantland, was preacher for the 117th convocation held on the Cheyenne River Reservation. Senior Catechist Norman Blue Coat was ordained to the diaconate and a lay man from the Sisseton Reservation, Vernon Cloud, was elected *Itancan* (chairperson).

At the century-old rural church of St. John the Baptist, located on the high prairies and lake country of the northeast corner of South Dakota, the 118th convocation paid tribute to the life and ministry of Vine Deloria Sr., who died the previous winter. Forty years previously the Lakota leader had served as vicar at St. John's and four other congregations of the Sisseton Mission before moving on to other congregations, thence to the national church New York headquarters in 1954-1958, and concluding his distinguished vocation in 1968 as archdeacon of Niobrara.

Returning from distant places to host the memorial dinner and traditional give-away were several members of the Deloria family. Vine Deloria Jr., Sioux author, academician and attorney, was guest preacher at Sunday morning Holy Eucharist. Sometimes described as an iconoclast regarding western European Christianity, the author of *God is Red* (1973) warned the several hundred assembled that the Supreme Court decision which held against religious practices of the Native American Church threatens all people of religious convictions.

A call for a suffragan bishop of Indian descent for the Diocese of South Dakota was issued at the 1990 convocation. There was also affirmation of a proposal for positions of archdeacon of Indian work and youth coordinator of Niobrara. Special recognition was accorded two Sioux priests who were celebrating their 28th anniversary of ordination, the Rev. Wilbur Bear's Heart and the Rev. Noah Brokenleg.

Holy Spirit Church near remote Fire Steel, South Dakota, on the Standing Rock Reservation, was the site for the 1991 convocation. Guests included a delegation of New Zealand Maori, headed by the Rt. Rev. Whakahuihui Vercoe. One of the Maori visitors, the Ven. Ben Te Haara, who in 1992 was consecrated as one of the three new Maori assisting bishops, described the convocation:

> The setting in the wilderness, the climatic changes of hot and cold wind, the make-shift shelter, the lonely solitary stone building of Holy Spirit, a historic church, and its task of feeding 300 people . . . An aged grandmother's dream to gather her family together to host the convocation . . . reminded me of the struggle we have . . . So much to be discovered, so much spirituality which has yet to be authenticated by the Christian Church.

Steven Charleston (Choctaw), new Bishop of Alaska, was guest preacher and a Standing Rock Sioux, Leland Brown, a recent graduate of Seabury-Western Theological Seminary, was ordained to the diaconate. The Brokenleg family hosted a feast in thanksgiving for the return to the Episcopal Church of their son, the Rev. Martin Brokenleg, reinstated to the priesthood on Maundy Thursday.

Some 739 were welcomed to the 120th Niobrara Convocation in 1992 at St. Mary's on the Sisseton Reservation by a young tribal officer, Michael Selvedge, who paid homage to the early Episcopal missionaries who aided the Traverse Lake band when they most desperately needed help. The subject of the selection of a suffragan bishop dominated discussion. After the 1990 convocation calling for election of a suffragan, diocesan convention and General Convention had approved and the search process had been well launched. Within weeks following Niobrara Convocation the diocesan bishop had been named to head General Theological Seminary in New York. The suffragan search became moot.

The 121st Niobrara Convocation in 1993 was at Mission on the Rosebud Reservation and its guest preacher was Diane Porter, senior executive for program at the Episcopal Church Center in New York. She preached a message of hope for the Niobrara deanery and the diocese as they launched the search for their new chief pastor.

Anderson, a highly energized California-born theology professor, was elected at age 42 as the diocese's eighth bishop. Shortly after his consecration in the 1984, he decreed a change in differential in the salary of Indian and non-Indian clergy in the diocese. Indian clergy had been paid significantly less than non-Indians. He launched a major fund-raising campaign which netted in excess of $1 million as an endowment for clergy support. He served on several national church commissions and committees and chaired the Presiding Bishop's Task Force on Indian Affairs which after a year's study recommended creation of the Episcopal Council of Indian Ministry, a predominantly Indian umbrella organization responsible for apportionment of national church funds to dioceses for Indian work, replacing a predominantly non-Indian coalition as agent for apportioning funds. He served on the South Dakota Governor's Commission on Reconciliation and was highly visible in seeking resolution of the Black Hills ownership question. It was shortly after he had made an appeal for the Senate Select Committee on Indian Affairs to call for a presidential commission to recommend redress, that his home in Sioux Falls was fire bombed. His tenure, however, saw notable decreases in the numbers of active Indian clergy and of Indian congregations across the diocese.

The New Sioux Bishop

A Sioux Indian was elected to succeed Anderson. Creighton Leland Robertson, 50, a member of the Sisseton-Wahpeton band, became the first Indian diocesan bishop of South Dakota, which ever since Hinman brought the Episcopal Church west with the exiled Santee 131 years previously, has had a majority of Indian communicants.

The sun was merciless on that June day in 1994 when Robertson was consecrated in an open air service a dozen miles distant from the site of the Church of the Holy Name on Choteau Creek, which was founded in 1870 by Paul Mazakute, the first ordained Sioux. Cicadas sounded in tall, old-growth trees nearby, shading dozens of campers and vans. Outside the arena were seven white tepees, raised primarily for ceremonial purposes. In the procession many Indians walked behind bright banners of distant congregations in Minnesota, Montana, Idaho, Nevada, Colorado, North Dakota, Utah, Oklahoma, and elsewhere. Four hymns and the Sanctus were sung in the Dakota language; an unscheduled honor song with Sioux drum was offered.

Beside Robertson as he knelt before the Presiding Bishop was an 85-year-old elder, standing tall and straight with the aid of a cane. He was Harold Stephen Jones, the retired suffragan of South Dakota and the first Indian bishop.

The new bishop has stressed the need for more Indian clergy, recognizing that there were 10 to 15 more Indian priests in the diocese a decade ago. The large soft-spoken man looks to alternative approaches to clergy training such as the extension program of Vancouver School of Theology, in which several Indians of his diocese have begun study. He has said, "We are technically still a mission district; in terms of funds, we depend on the national church." Annually the national Church allocates more than a half-million dollars to the diocese which has a communicant strength of slightly over 50 per cent Indian.

Robertson springs from a family with Episcopal roots extending back to the Sioux Uprising in Minnesota. A mixed-blood Scottish and Dakota ancestor was a student at Seabury Seminary, Faribault, Minnesota, when the Dakota war broke out. Another ancestor, Thomas A. Robertson, left a vivid account of his experiences as a courier between Little Crow and Colonel Sibley. After the conflict, Robertson's ancestors were among the Sisseton and Wahpeton Indians moved to the reservation near Lake Traverse in Dakota Territory, settling near Veblen. St. Luke's was founded in 1886 around the Robertson family. Most of the gravestones in the old cemetery bear the Robertson name. Sadly, one of the new bishop's first tasks was officiating at the closure of St. Luke's, his ancestral home parish where a grandfather, Sam Robertson, long served as catechist.

Robertson spent his early years near Veblen and other hamlets on the Sisseton Reservation. He served as an acolyte at Trinity Church in Wahpeton under Harold Jones. Though sensing a call to ordination, Robertson studied law and later practiced in Webster, South Dakota, acting as legal counsel to the Sisseton-Wahpeton tribe. After working for the State Department of Labor in Pierre for six years, he responded to the call to the ordained ministry and entered Sewanee. Ordained priest in 1990, he was assigned to be priest-in-charge of the Santee Mission, serving Blessed Redeemer and Our Most Merciful Savior, churches established by Hinman, the first Episcopal missionary to the Sioux, the cornerstones of continuity of the Episcopal Church in South Dakota.

God is 'Wakantanka'

Driving Hawk Sneve, in her history of the Diocese of South Dakota, succinctly characterized the appeal of the Episcopal Church to the Sioux. In her chapter entitled "God is 'Wakantanka'" she says:

Religion permeated every aspect of the Dakotas' life. It was impossible to differentiate between the social, economic, and religious phases of the Dakota culture. Religion was inextricably interwoven with every pattern of individual behavior.

The early missionaries insisted that their converts repudiate the most basic elements of their culture. To the Dakota, a man was destined to be a warrior and hunter. To refuse to fight or hunt and agree to plow the land was a sign of weakness. The male who voluntarily submitted to these shameful things—which he must do to become a Christian—made great personal sacrifices in the face of degrading ridicule from his people. Women became the first converts, for their acceptance of Christianity did not mean an abandonment of their former role as wife and mother.

The Dakotas acceptance of Christianity was at first an acceptance of the God of their conquerors and a search for the white man's power, without completely abandoning the old beliefs. The missionaries attempted to make it easier to reconcile the different beliefs by calling the Christian God 'Wakantanka', the Dakota name for the Great Spirit.

The color and richness of the Episcopal ritual appealed to the Dakotas because they could associate such with their native ceremonies. Feast Days and holidays were important in the Church, and provided festivities to a people who needed diversion to relieve the drab drudgery of their days.

In addition, the Church had ceremonies for the transition from one stage of life to another, which the Dakota could relate to their native ceremonies. Baptism for the babies and confirmation for those who were passing into adulthood were acceptable substitutes for the Hunka and Puberty rites. The service of the Burial of the Dead had within it the proper honor and mystery which the Dakota gave in their old funeral ceremonies. The Church also permitted the giveaway and final feast given by relatives of the deceased to be held in church guild halls.

It was unfortunate that the early missionaries believed that the Dakota had to change his entire way of life to become a Christian [rather than] using the native religion as a frame of reference. Instead, the missionaries were determined to eradicate the traditional religion of the Sioux.

5

THE NORTH DAKOTA MISSION

When Little Crow fled the Minnesota River valley to Dakota Territory, he took with him some 200-250 Mdewakanton Santees and their families. "There," he said, "my people will scatter over the plains like buffalo and wolves." Little Crow's fugitives were joined by a sizable number of Sisseton and Wahepeton refugees who had dodged the fighting but feared retribution. Several groups pushed on to Canada but a number spent the winter of 1862 at Devils Lake, an oasis of sorts in the middle of the vast northern plains, and frequented by the Yanktons, Yanktonais and Tetons.

Colonel Henry H. Sibley, fearing an alliance of the western Sioux, made plans to invade the Devils Lake stronghold. Several skirmishes occurred on the North Dakota plains in the summer of 1863 with more than 100 Indians killed. By fall, following the death of Little Crow and reluctance of Sissetons and others to join in further warfare, the Dakota Conflict came to a close.

In 1867 a treaty was signed which provided a reservation between Devils Lake and the Sheyenne River (the lack of an apostrophe for the lake's name and the spelling of the river with an "s" instead of a "c" are holdovers from early map-makers). The Devils Lake Reservation was to be home for the fugitive Santees and the Cuthead band of the Yanktonais who already claimed the area as home. By winter of 1867 some 250 Sioux on the south shore of the lake were living in great destitution, "having eaten their horses and those of the mail carriers." Relief efforts were carried out by the agent at Sisseton but as the game completely disappeared during the next two years, more and more half-starved homeless Indians wandered in.

Once more, it was Bishop Whipple of Minnesota who came to the rescue. Upon his urging, Congress appropriated $15,000 for the Devils

Lake group in 1869 and placed the bishop in sole charge of the expenditure. An inspection found a population of over 400, but only 90 were men. The next spring the Fort Totten commandant provided seed corn but no tools. The dauntless women planted the corn with elk and deer horns and pointed sticks. But frost came early and no harvest was had. Starvation at Devils Lake was not uncommon.

When a newly appointed agent appeared, he was baffled by the cultural diversity of the dwellers of Devils Lake Reservation. Homeless wanderers drifted in from as far away as Montana. The Cutheads had scant exposure to agents or missionaries and cared little for either. Groups of Santee, drifting back from Canada, appeared to make their living in summertime by robbing supply trains, then coming in to winter at Devils Lake. Having retained a bit of religious training from missionaries in Minnesota, the Santee reportedly chanted psalms around their campfires and on occasion substituted some of Isaac Watts' hymns for their own songs at scalp dances.

Early Day Overview

The Anglican prayer book was first read in the present-day Diocese of North Dakota at stations of the powerful Hudson's Bay Company and later at U.S. Army posts scattered across the northern plains for the purpose of subduing the Indians. There is a brief reference to Indian evangelizing efforts of the Hudson's Bay Company which for a century and a half ruled a vast empire from Hudson Bay to the Rocky Mountains. In 1820 the company dispatched a chaplain to a Red River settlement of Scots in the northern-most reaches of today's diocese. The Rev. John West, former curate of White Roding, Essex, was allotted an extra £50 annually for work among the Indians, but there is no record of how well he earned his extra stipend. However, there is a record that West, after a brief two-year stay among the Scots, moved to Winnipeg where he started St. John's College, and this institution for generations supplied clergy for North Dakota missions and parishes.

Indians first evangelized Indians in North Dakota. On three out of the four big reservations of the diocese it was Indians who first brought the gospel to their tribes. Though old church chronicles, by and large, give this fact scant attention, it was the young students coming home to Standing Rock Reservation from distant places such as Hampton Institute in Virginia who brought the Episcopal prayer book and set about sharing it. Later, Standing Rock Episcopalians went up the Missouri River to bring the gospel to the Arikara at Fort

Berthold, and an Episcopal missionary finally came to Turtle Mountain because of the persistence of a determined old Chippewa named Rising Sun.

It was for the purpose of Indian work that the banner of the Episcopal Church was raised in South Dakota. Two decades later the Episcopal Church came into North Dakota with the singular intention of ministering to the white settlers swarming onto the windswept prairies.

From the outset, Indians were largely ignored in North Dakota. In the financial crunch of the 20th century's depression years the diocese abandoned its Indian work on the big Standing Rock Reservation and turned responsibility over to South Dakota. For 20 years, 1931-1951, the Rev. John B. Clark administered mission work from Mobridge, South Dakota. From 1943 until 1951 mission on the three other North Dakota reservations was turned over to Clark, a second generation member of the steadfast and stalwart missionary family which came from New England to South Dakota in 1889 to work among Indians.

North Dakota's First Bishop

The buffalo was slaughtered, the west was "won" and railroads were built. The General Convention of 1883 voted an ecclesiastical division of the Dakotas and William D. Walker of New York City was chosen the first bishop of North Dakota. He arrived in 1884 in the Territory of North Dakota—statehood came in 1889—to be confronted by the dual difficulties of meager national church funding and formidable local prejudice against Indians.

By the time the bishop arrived, the native peoples of the northern plains were living in abject poverty in small pockets of reservations. The Chippewas were virtually isolated at Turtle Mountain Reservation near the Canadian border. Remnants of three tribes, the sparse survivors of smallpox and other European-inducted epidemics, were squeezed onto Fort Berthold Reservation along the upper Missouri River. These tribes were the Arikara, Hidatsa and Mandan who in the early part of the century had hosted the Lewis and Clark explorers. Several Sioux bands were squatting on crumbling fragments of their former holdings. At Fort Totten were the Devils Lake Sioux (named for the deep and spirit-filled lake on whose shores they resided). Included in their numbers were Sisseton and Wahpeton refugees from Minnesota. Other Sissetons lived in the far southeast corner of Walker's jurisdiction; a sliver of the Sisseton Reservation wedged up into North Dakota and it was here that the government would build a major boarding school. The largest North Dakota reserve was west of the Missouri River, the Standing Rock Reservation, home of the Hunkpapa, Sitting Bull's people, straddling the North and South Dakota border.

Prejudice toward the territory's 8,000 Indians was rampant among land-hungry white settlers; a climate of latent hostility prevailed across the plains and was especially keen in the communities bordering the five reservations. The Episcopal Church never "caught on" among the North Dakota tribes as it did on the South Dakota reservations. For instance, in 1918 half of South Dakota's 20,000 Indians were baptized Episcopalians. In the same year in North Dakota there were 7,000 Indians on four reservations. The Episcopal Church was represented on all of them but could claim only 312 baptized persons and 187 communicants.

Lack of funding was a factor. During the crucial transition era, major opportunity for evangelization among the Natives of the Northern Plains was lost. During the years 1886-1893 the Episcopal Church allocated, over the entire country, a total of $107,146 for Indian education. The Roman Catholic Church expended $1.5 million, and the Presbyterians allocated $150,000 for a single year. The bishop's work in the Turtle Mountains, for instance, had to be funded entirely by money that the bishop garnered in bits and pieces from wealthy eastern parishes.

The eastern parishes in 1889 subscribed to a custom-built 60-foot railway chapel for the North Dakota bishop at a cost of $3,000. Cornelius Vanderbilt made the first contribution. Eighty persons could be seated on portable chairs in the "Cathedral Car of North Dakota," which not only had a "transept" but also an organ which the bishop played at services on sidings across the state.

Rising Sun: the Persistent Chippewa of Turtle Mountain

Sometime in the 1860s, long before the church sent the New York-born bishop to the territory, Rising Sun, a staunch old Chippewa, took upon himself a near life-time quest to bring the gospel and lasting Episcopal mission to his people, a band of Ojibwa which had moved west from Minnesota into the Turtle Mountains of north central North Dakota. Rising Sun's group is still known as the Turtle Mountain Chippewas.

New information uncovered suggests that Rising Sun, whose

name memorialized the fact that he had first seen the light of day just as the sun rose in the east, had drifted north into Canada and worked for the Hudson's Bay Company. He came into contact with the Anglican Church and was baptized. When he returned home to Turtle Mountain, he wanted to bring his whole tribe into the church.

Rising Sun is first glimpsed in 1869 when he set out in the company of several other chiefs for the White Earth Reservation, located 175 miles away in Minnesota. The party was seeking to recruit an Episcopal missionary. They had heard of the work in Minnesota of the indefatigable Enmegahbowh, who two years earlier had been ordained as the first Native American Episcopal priest. When Enmegahbowh was unable to produce a missionary for the Turtle Mountain band, Rising Sun is next seen trudging on to distant Faribault, nearly 300 miles south of White Earth. There is a story that Bishop Whipple awoke one morning to find Rising Sun curled up on his threshold, nearly buried in snow. He told the bishop how he and his wife had set out in a cart but the horse had died on the way, and that they had pulled the cart by turns. When his wife's strength gave out he had left her by the roadside with the cart and had walked on alone.

Sorrowfully the bishop explained that he had no one to send but urged Rising Star to stop at White Earth and prevail upon Enmegahbowh to teach him the Creed, the Ten Commandments and the Lord's Prayer. By 1873 the Turtle Mountain people had made three more fruitless pleas for an Episcopal missionary. The dauntless Rising Sun, despite disappointments, continued his lonely efforts to bring the gospel to his people, and historians provide a vignette of Rising Sun counting the days, and each seventh day, teaching his people all he had learned from Enmegahbowh.

In 1875 Dr. David Buel Knickerbacker, later bishop of Indiana, appeared in the Turtle Mountains with a treaty commission. The Turtle Mountain chiefs gathered and there were council fires, peace-pipes and all the time-honored ritual that extended for the better part of a week. Sunday arrived. Knickerbacker walked around the camp and saw a group of Indians listening to one who was addressing them in the Chippewa language with which he was somewhat familiar. Now and then from the people around the speaker there burst forth a chorus of response. He listened. The words appeared familiar, and all at once he realized that he was hearing a Christian service. It was Rising Sun teaching as best he could the truths of the Christian faith as taught him by Enmegahbowh.

He reported to Whipple that he had discovered "Forty seven Chippewas trying to be 'good Indians' . . . keeping up prayer and singing . . . but feeling the need for someone to be with them to lead and teach them." The Minnesota bishop was still unable to send a missionary to the Turtle Mountain Chippewas.

Nine years after the Knickerbacker report, Bishop Walker arrived in North Dakota territory. Once again Rising Sun, then about 60, tramped across great distances in pursuit of a missionary. This time he had carefully laid his strategy to succeed in his 15-year quest. As companions to call upon the North Dakota bishop, he chose his seven-year-old grandson, a young chief named Little Elk, and one of the tribal elders who spoke a little English. More importantly, Rising Sun decided to prevail upon Enmegahbowh to accompany the Turtle Mountain emissaries, so first the little party made a very long detour to the White Earth Reservation. Enmegahbowh did agree to go with them, and the group set out on an 11-day walk from White Earth to the see city of Fargo. Old documents provide a fleeting glimpse of the stalwarts along with description of the eclectic clothing they had acquired to impress the new bishop:

> They had traded beadwork for "civilized" clothing, and one of the group wore checkered trousers, another wore a vest, and the lad wore a long linen duster which trailed the ground. The old chief, Rising Sun, donned a battered white top hat . . . Bishop Walker warmly received the emissaries; they are recorded as having enjoyed his cakes and candies.

The initial meeting lasted through the night to early morning, and the Chippewas at last wrung from the Episcopal Church a commitment for mission. True to his word, during the ensuing year the bishop from his meager funding erected the Church of the Resurrection at Belcourt. In the following year he sent to the Turtle Mountain Chippewas a teacher, Wellington Jefferson Salt, a Canadian of mixed Indian and white ancestry. Son of a Methodist minister, Salt had been working in Minnesota lumber camps when he made his decision to offer his services to Walker. Salt arrived at Turtle Mountain Reservation on May 2, 1888. During his first year he enrolled 20 pupils at the school which he established at the Belcourt church building. Though he later was engaged to teach at the government school, Salt continued to conduct weekly lay services and at intervals Enmegahbowh traveled the 175 miles from White Earth to administer Holy Communion. Bishop Walker's diary recorded:

> In my mail today there was a very touching gift of four dollars for North Dakota missions. It came from old Rising Sun, a Chippewa Indian who lives in the Turtle

Rising Sun with his wife in front of their home.
Courtesy Smithsonian Institution.

Mountains . . . Nobody who has not seen—as I have—this old man, roughly dressed, sitting in a log hut bare of furniture, can estimate the magnitude of his gift. Nobody can estimate the generosity of this gift.

In 1901 an outbreak of smallpox closed the Turtle Mountain government school and Salt was transferred to a South Dakota government school. His departure spelled doom for the Indian community at the Church of the Resurrection and the little building was soon hauled 12 miles away to Rolla, a white community.

Rising Sun, who lived to reach the approximate age of 110, did not even then lose hope for lasting Episcopal mission among his people. From his first government annuity check, he and his wife purchased $30 worth of lumber for a future Episcopal chapel and kept the lumber stored in their tiny home for six years. He then gave land from his allotment, near Dunseith, for an Episcopal mission. A full decade would pass before his gifts would be accepted, but in 1911, reckoned to be Rising Sun's 99th year, the faithful old Chippewa saw his dream

become reality. Salt was ordained to the permanent diaconate, returned to Turtle Mountain, and on October 15 the little chapel was
named and dedicated to St. Sylvan's (or as it is in old French patois,
St. Sylvane, from the Latin, Sylvanus) after a mission which Rising
Sun had seen in Canada. St. Sylvan's was ably served by Salt until
his death in 1920.

There briefly appeared in the Turtle Mountain mission one of
the most colorful characters of North Dakota's clergy roster—Aaron
McGaffey Beede. A man of many skills, by his own labor, he built the
chapel on Rising Sun's land. The chapel was "built of logs set upright
on the foundation." Beede, at the time serving white congregations at
Rolla, began conducting regular services for the Chippewa and wrote
of his outrage at finding the "40-odd members in a deplorable
plight . . . crowded into smaller and smaller areas of the impoverished
reserve by land-and-cattle-hungry white settlers." In 1903, Rising Sun,
then 90, was robbed of his tribe's last calf and its only pony. The federal government, which would not take measures to protect the
Indians, distributed among them every two weeks a dole of 10 pounds
of flour and 10 pounds of pork per person. On his monthly visits, Beede
often brought some of his own food and clothing for them and was
able to have nine of their children placed in the Fort Totten school.

Through the years, St. Sylvan's has held out unfulfilled promise
for growth. But the diocese has rarely been able to fund resident clergy
for the Turtle Mountain Chippewa. After Sioux Church Army Captain
Robert Dudley and his Navajo wife, Linda, transferred in 1994 after
serving two years, St. Sylvan's was without trained leaders. The faithful are served on occasion by the Arikara priest, Duane Fox, who resides
half-way across the state at the Fort Berthold Reservation.

St. Sylvan's stands forlorn and lonely on a high elevation of land
as a monument to the faith, perseverance and devotion of Rising Sun,
who for nearly half a century knocked on Episcopal doors seeking
help to bring the gospel to his people and, who in his quest, once donned
a battered white top hat in an effort to impress a young bishop from
New York.

Fort Totten Mission at Devils Lake

By 1872 the ofttimes transient Devils Lake population had soared to
1,000. In the same year the Northern Pacific Railroad inched westward
from Fargo to within 82 miles of the agency. Up until then, no serious
Christian missionizing efforts had been made, but when the Grant Peace
Policy was set in motion, Devils Lake Reservation was assigned to the

Roman Catholic Church which in 1874 opened a school under auspices of the Sisters of Charity, known as the Grey Nuns of Montreal.

By 1890 the U.S. government decided the Indian threat was forever behind and abandoned the Fort Totten military post, turning over to the Indian Bureau some 39 buildings, which were pressed into service as an Indian residential or boarding school. From all across the northern plains, lonely young students were gathered up for industrial training. The bureau retained the strict Grey Nuns to teach at the huge government-run school.

It was to Fort Totten that the first bishop of North Dakota next turned after launching his initial Indian mission at Turtle Mountain. He purchased the deserted old trading post and sent William D. Rees to minister to Indian students. Soon, Rees, who readily learned the Dakota languages, had as many as 100 students regularly attending his Sunday school. By the end of the century he had baptized 305 Indians and presented 276 for confirmation. He was assisted by a mixed-blood Sioux catechist and postulant for Holy Orders, John S. Brown.

The mission at Fort Totten, St. Thomas', dates back to 1898 when *Iyayukamani* (He-Follows-Walking) loaned his home for services in the Dakota language. Years later, a woman in Rochester, Minnesota, donated $1,000 to build the Margaret Breckenridge Memorial Chapel on land acquired from *Iyayukamani*. The chapel, completed in 1923, was initially located atop Raven Hill, but subsequently moved to the town of Fort Totten.

The first North Dakota Indian to be ordained to the priesthood, William Skala Cross, worked at St. Thomas in the 1930s. Born on the Standing Rock Reservation, Cross became a lay reader in 1908, was ordained deacon in 1925, and priest in 1928. Another esteemed Sioux priest, Moses Mountain, came from South Dakota as catechist, and following his ordination in 1954, he was priest-in-charge at Fort Totten until 1957. Then he was transferred to the Fort Berthold congregation of St. Paul's, where he served with distinction until his death in 1984.

Though Devils Lake Reservation knew famine and crop failure in the transition years when the government pressured warriors to become farmers, present day economy is somewhat better than that of many reservation communities. Two tribally owned plants provide jobs and one tribal industry in 1990 was declared Minority Business of the Year. The big Catholic church appears dominant but St. Thomas' Church still stands. Although it has not had resident clergy for many years, an English-born priest and physician drives 90 miles from Jamestown to celebrate Holy Eucharist at St. Thomas' once or twice a month.

The Episcopal Start at Standing Rock

Indians had a major role in generating Episcopal mission at the huge Standing Rock Reservation. Two young Dakota students—Azuyetawa and Young Eagle—led the way to launching Episcopal mission on the North Dakota side of Standing Rock. These students along with many other plains Indians were sent to Hampton Institute in distant Virginia for education. While in the east the two students had become acquainted with Episcopal services and the prayer book. Both of today's North Dakota Standing Rock congregations—St. James' at Cannon Ball and St. Luke's at Fort Yates—can trace their beginning back across a full century to the return of these young men in 1887 to Standing Rock Reservation, home of Sitting Bull's people, the Hunkpapas.

The students had come into possession of a Dakota translation of the prayer book. Likely the translation came from Bishop Hare's mission at St. Elizabeth's on the South Dakota side of the Standing Rock. The students called upon the Episcopal chaplain at the military post at Fort Yates, and with his assistance regular services were begun for 50 or more persons. A brief reference to the Standing Rock mission in the history of North Dakota diocese says:

> Their chapel was a rude log hut built by one of their group. These native lay readers, after instructing some Indians for baptism, sent a letter to Bishop Walker asking him to visit Standing Rock. In the summer of 1891, the bishop went to the reservation and at Cannon Ball baptized 13 persons—three infants, six boys and girls and four adults.

By the summer of 1892, with Chaplain G.W. Simpson of Fort Yates working with them, between 125 and 150 identified with the Episcopal Church. Nearby, the Sioux built a long guild house with clay roof and earthen floor. Services, held on Friday and Sunday, were attended by 100 men and a like number of women.

While there is no recorded evidence of Bishop Walker's further support to the fledgling mission at Standing Rock, note is made of the fact that at Cannon Ball—so named because of unique rock formations found in the vicinity—a small frame chapel was erected, partly funded by donations from Trinity Church, Newark, New Jersey. Subsequently, mention is made of the 30 families at Cannon Ball aspiring to build a stone chapel, "but by 1904 their building fund had reached only $6.50."

Then, in 1908 Beede came to the Standing Rock Reservation and built with his own hands a church building which "will withstand anything but a number one cyclone." This brilliant and colorful Episcopal clergyman had been in turn a New England Congregationalist minister, professor of Greek, and college president. He was first assigned to white missions but quickly became absorbed with Indians, working first with the Turtle Mountain Chippewas. Bishop Cameron Mann, recognizing Beede's extraordinary capabilities, appointed him General Missionary in charge of Indian work. Soon, wearing moccasins with his clerical garb, "the Venerable Beede" was full of Indian history and folklore and after seven weeks of intensive study was able to read the Dakota prayer book.

Beede built still another chapel. Wasulatusa (Red Hail), who had been present at the Custer battle, returned to Cannon Ball and converted to Christianity through influence of Charles Prettyflute, a native layreader. Red Hail (said to have been born during a great meteoric shower), for whom the Sioux camp was named, aspired to build a chapel on the lower Cannon Ball River. The Indians entrusted their entire building fund of five dollars to Bishop Mann with the request that he give them a church. Under supervision of Thomas P. Ashley and the camp's layreader, Martin Prettyfeather, they cut cottonwood logs along the river and put up a chapel in which 75 worshipers could stand. The log building, whitewashed inside, had neither seats nor other furnishings, not even a stove for heating. After June of 1903, John Brown and Prettyfeather conducted the Episcopal services in the Dakota language.

Red Hail sensed need for a frame building and in 1905 launched a building fund with forty-five cents and a two-cent postage stamp. Again, it was Beede who did the actual construction of St. Gabriel's. Forty years later it was reported that the little frame building had withstood a major flood. St. Gabriel's mission, however, was eventually abandoned. Through the years, the diocese retained title to the property and in 1996 a church camp, called St. Gabriel's, was being established with financial assistance from the Church Center in New York, ensuring perpetuity of the generosity of the faithful Red Hail.

A footnote on Beede discloses that after long playing the advocate's role in Indian affairs, generally through self-denial and personal sacrifice, he was incensed over an incident involving eastern criticism of the manner in which he distributed shipments of old clothing and goods. It seems that touring Episcopalians in 1916 questioned his distribution of their largess and protested to New York Church authorities. The fiery Beede held strong opinions about churchmen who could afford transcontinental vacations yet questioned disposition of cast-off clothing. He resigned in a monumental huff.

However, Beede remained on the Standing Rock Reservation—he was at the time vicar at St. James, Cannon Ball—and began the study of law. Soon he was elected county judge and performed civil marriages from the Episcopal prayer book.

Beyond the laity, Azuyetawa and Young Eagle, an impressive roster of Indian successors can be sketched. First on the list is Thomas P. Ashley who came from South Dakota as catechist and was placed in charge of the Cannon Ball chapel. Later ordained to the permanent diaconate, his career is recorded as having been cut short following divorce in 1907. John S. Brown is listed as a mixed-blood candidate for Holy Orders. Among others associated with the Standing Rock mission were Charles Prettyflute, Alexander His-War, Martin Prettyfeather (who changed his name to Martin See-Walker, memorializing a visit with the bishop), Paul Bear Paw, Julia Bear Paw, Lucy Shoot-the-Buffalo and William White Feather. Others would be Red Hail, whose grandson was the Rev. William Skala (White) Cross, the first North Dakota native priest.

A Sioux priest who took the name of Herbert H. Welsh to honor the philanthropist and Indian advocate, was long associated with both St. James' and St. Luke's. During the period that Indian work of North and South Dakota was consolidated, Sidney Bear's Heart was sent from Santee to serve Cannon Ball. Sidney U. Martin, a Standing Rock native, served from 1949-1956. In more recent years an Oglala from Pine Ridge Reservation, Harold Eagle Bull, served the St. James' mission.

In 1969 the Rev. Innocent Goodhouse, born on the Standing Rock Reservation, became vicar of St. Luke's and continued his ministry 22 years until his 1990 retirement. He died of cancer July 5, 1991. One of the first graduates of Dakota Leadership Program, Goodhouse, along with Moses Mountain, was among the distinguished Indian leaders of the diocese in contemporary times. John F. Floberg, a young non-Indian priest, replaced Father Goodhouse on the Standing Rock Reservation in the summer of 1991, soon after his graduation from Bexley Hall.

Fort Berthold: Indians Evangelize Indians

What is perhaps the most striking example of Indians evangelizing Indians occurred at Fort Berthold. St. Paul's Mission traces its beginnings back to the last year of the last century when a group of 20 Standing Rock Sioux Episcopalians set out far up the Missouri River on a preaching mission to the Arikara people at Fort Berthold

Reservation. Leaders of the Indian missionaries were the native deacon, Thomas P. Ashley, and a layreader, William White Eagle. Likelihood of success could scarcely have been anticipated because Yellow Bear, principle Arikara leader, vehemently opposed all aspects of white civilization, and especially Christianity.

Records fail to provide details, but the Standing Rock missionaries reached the defiant Arikara chieftain and to the amazement of both the Episcopal Sioux and his fellow tribesmen, Yellow Bear was converted. At his baptism he added Paul to his name in honor of the early Christian saint. When a chapel was erected it, too, honored St. Paul. Paul Yellow Bear, throughout the remainder of his life as a layreader, reinforced Episcopal presence at Fort Berthold.

While Paul Yellow Bear and Annie Dawson Wilde led the Fort Berthold Episcopalians living on the east bank, John Brown, the native layreader, with Henry Red Dog as helper, was working on the opposite side of the Missouri River. Since there was no chapel, Red Dog held services for St. John's Mission in his home.

The mission at Fort Berthold was unique in that it was a spontaneous growth and entirely the work of Episcopal Indians. There was a series of visits back and forth between the faithful of Cannon Ball and Fort Berthold. A group of Arikara appeared at Standing Rock in 1903 seeking a layreader's license for Red Dog. Cannon Ball people raised $19.75 to assist the Fort Berthold build a chapel. By 1906 the mission consisted of 19 adults and a large number of children of the Sioux, Mandan, Gros Ventre and Arikara tribes.

However, the work at this mission to the Indians from the Indians soon suffered a reversal as a result of the activities of a native prophetess known as "Winnie," who claimed she had been ordained to overthrow the white man's religion. With the help of her uncle, Enemy Heart, the prophetess compelled Roman Catholic and Congregationalist converts to renounce Christianity. Of the smaller group of Episcopalians, only Yellow Bear and his family and Red Dog remained with the church. Once when the bishop visited, he found the 15 former communicants cold to his advances and only Red Dog attended his service. Yellow Bear, fearful for the safety of his family, moved to the other side of the Missouri River. Even after the prophetess threatened Yellow Bear with death by lightning, he continued conducting services from the Dakota prayer book, though his language and that of his people was Arikara. There had by 1913 been no Arikara translation. Eventually the influence of the prophetess waned and Red Dog by 1912 was ministering to seven communicants on the Fort Berthold Reservation. His stipend of $30 was contributed by the Dakota Indians of Standing Rock.

Moses Mountain arrived at St. Paul's in the aftermath of a sweeping upheaval which victimized and displaced the Fort Berthold people. In the 1950s a decision was made in Washington to build Garrison Dam across the Missouri River. The gigantic dam was to provide flood protection to down-river white interests. The Indians had no say in the decision. The reservoir eventually inundated the fertile bottom lands of the reservation. Many of the Fort Berthold people slid down the economic scale from stability as small farmers and ranchers to welfare recipients. The communicants of St. Paul's experienced a special wrench; their chapel and cemetery had to be moved from the wooded lowlands to a barren windswept plain overlooking the huge artificial body of water stretching over 100 miles upriver.

With the death of Mountain, St. Paul's at White Shield was served by a part-time non-Indian priest. In 1988 the first Arikara, Duane Fox, was ordained. For the first few years of his priestly ministry he was assigned to Turtle Mountain, but in 1991 he was sent back to his own people.

Indian "Field" Overview

The Episcopal vicar at the town of Wahpeton did outreach work with students at the big Indian school located there. Old periodicals tell of two descendants of Sacajawea, the heroine of the Lewis and Clark expedition, being among the 44 persons confirmed in 1932. For 12 years—1956 to 1968—a very distinguished Santee Sioux was vicar of Trinity Church in Wahpeton. He was Harold S. Jones who would become the first American Indian bishop with his election as suffragan of South Dakota in 1972.

The diocese's first archdeacon for Indian work was appointed in 1922. He was Homer R. Harrington, who trained Herbert H. Welsh (Hawk Shield) for ordination and several lay readers, including Paul Bear Paws, George American Horse, Martin See Walker and George Two Bears. Harrington continued in the position until 1930. Jeremiah Johnson, listed as either Cree or Chippewa, born on a Canadian reserve, served non-Indian North Dakota congregations for five years in the 1920s.

North Dakota suffered severe hardships as a result of the depression of the 1930s; drought, dust storms, grasshoppers, crop failures and bank failures brought about a major exodus of population. A 32 percent cut in appropriations from the national Executive Council in 1932 seriously impacted the Indian field in the diocese. In fact, portions of the Indian field of North Dakota was for a period of

20 years given over to South Dakota.

Thus it remained until the election in 1951 of Richard R. Emery, 41, of Minneapolis, as seventh North Dakota bishop. Clark was finding that distances from the other three North Dakota reservations—Fort Totten was 250 miles away—made his work extremely difficult. The new young and energetic North Dakota bishop shortly assumed responsibility for the Indian communicants of his diocese. Potential was envisioned for a spirited new commitment to the Indian field in Emery's tenure, but he met a tragic death in a train crash in 1964.

Old literature of the North Dakota Episcopal Church is rife with references to its displeasure with traditional Indian ceremonies. One convocation voted to cut off free food (during the depression years) to Indians who participated in traditional dances. There was a reversal of such policies when the ninth diocesan bishop was elected. Harold A. Hopkins Jr. brought a thoughtful and sensitive respect for Native American spirituality and in 1985 became the first Episcopal bishop to "go up the hill" on traditional Dakota vision quest. Throughout his tenure (1980-1988) he honored his covenant to empower Indians to take programmatic ownership at the diocese and national church levels.

Hopkins raised the North Dakota Committee on Indian Work to a vital decision-making role in coordinating all Native American mission and ministry in his diocese. On the national level, Hopkins advocated changes in structures which would serve the interests of Indians, and out of a series of consultations in which Hopkins provided leadership came in 1989 the new umbrella organization for Indian work of the church, the Episcopal Council of Indian Ministry (ECIM).

A further contribution to native ministry evolved when Hopkins named Howard Anderson as coordinator for Indian Work, a joint appointment with Minnesota. During the years of the Hopkins-Anderson team North Dakota Indian work saw a vigorous resurgence.

Vision of Future North Dakota Mission

A man with years of experience among Alaska natives, whose perspectives are vastly different from native peoples of the plains, was elected in 1989 as North Dakota's tenth bishop. Andrew H. Fairfield had been among the adventurous young men recruited in the late 1960s by Bishop William Gordon to serve in rural Alaska. Immediately upon completion of studies at Church Divinity School of the Pacific, Fairfield began nine years' work in native villages along the Yukon River. Then he worked twelve years out of the diocesan office. Taking a cue from the flying Alaskan bishop, Gordon, Fairfield became a pilot, a skill which served him well when he came to his large new diocese.

Since Fairfield's arrival new urban Indian outreach has emerged in Bismarck, initially sponsored by St. George's parish and administered by a Sioux lay woman, Carol DeWall. A joint diocesan urban ecumenical project in the border cities of Fargo, North Dakota, and Moorhead, Minnesota, has continued. As Indians have moved away from reservations into urban areas, primarily for employment, more Indians are appearing for services in congregations of Fargo, Grand Forks, Minot and Williston as well as Bismarck.

The five predominantly Indian congregations of the diocese—at Dunseith, Fort Totten on Devils Lake, Fort Yates, Cannon Ball and Fort Berthold—in 1969 were served by two resident Church Army professionals, two Indian priests and one trained Indian layreader. A third Indian priest, Harold Jones, served a mixed congregation at Wahpeton. Twenty-five years later the Indian field had but one Indian priest, the Arikara Duane Fox, serving two widely separated congregations, and a non-native, full-time priest at Standing Rock.

Though no Indian postulants had surfaced by the mid-1990s, several Indian aspirants had been identified. Under tutelage of seminary-trained Father Floberg, diocesan-based theological training programs had been activated with expectations for future involvement with the Vancouver School of Theology Native Ministry Degree Program, the Trinity TEEM 100 program, and other courses.

The North Dakota Council of Indian Ministry had renewed zest by the mid-90s, and elected an energetic lay woman, Ardis Shaw from Fort Totten, as its chairperson. While within the diocese tension between native and non-native communicants still exists, lay leadership growth surged in the last decade, moving such individuals as Carmine Goodhouse of Standing Rock into national Church decision-making roles. For the first time ever, NDCIW was to host the diocesan convention in the autumn of 1996.

6

OKLAHOMA: TOO LATE WITH TOO LITTLE!

The Episcopal Church first appeared in Indian Territory (Oklahoma) seven years after passage of Andrew Jackson's loathsome Removal Act of 1830, which forcibly uprooted from their ancestral domain the five great tribes indigenous to the southeast United States—the Choctaw, Chickasaw, Cherokee, Creek and Seminole—and ruthlessly expelled them to a wilderness region west of the Mississippi River.

Between 1837 and 1846 four Episcopal bishops who came riding into Indian Territory intent on bringing Episcopal mission went away baffled, and wrote reports saying that the Presbyterians or Methodists or Baptists had already settled in and were solidly missionizing the tribes who had traversed the Trail of Tears.

The Episcopalians had come too late with too little!

First of the bishops to make the arduous journey to Indian Territory was the heroic Jackson Kemper, who came twice on horseback across the plains from Wisconsin and Minnesota. The Episcopal Church's first missionary bishop, whose jurisdiction was literally everything west of Ohio, is seen in 1837 shivering in a violent summer hailstorm in the prairies of Kansas. The following year a lonely forlorn figure rode his tired grey horse 20 miles in an early November snowstorm.

Kemper was in pursuit of the Anglican Iroquois, missionized three generations previously by the British back east. He had heard that a band of Mohawks had wound up in Indian Territory and were reportedly "reading services from the Anglican prayer book, given their ancestors back in New York by the Society for the Propagation of the Gospel."

A small band of Mohawks was indeed among the 67 tribes uprooted and swept into Indian Territory. By 1837, when Kemper came into Indian Territory, Choctaws had already walked the Trail of Tears. Chickasaws had followed. Contentious Creeks were making new homes west of the Arkansas River. To the east of the Arkansas River large contingents of the Cherokee had already arrived and were by then building plantations, mission schools and printing presses. The remainder of the Cherokee would struggle westward under military escort within the year. Only the Seminoles had not yet capitulated to the inevitable and were continuing a struggle of resistance in Florida swamps.

The quiescent Choctaws were the first to walk the Trail of Tears, from the deltas of Mississippi to the distant Indian Territory; 18,000 were force marched and 6,000 perished on the way. Alexis de Tocqueville, the French literary genius, in *Democracy in America,* provides a haunting image of the Choctaw removal:

> . . . I was on at a place named by the Europeans Memphis . . . there arrived a numerous band of Choctaws . . . endeavoring to gain the right bank of the Mississippi, where they hoped to find an asylum which had been promised them by the American Government. It was then in the middle of winter, and the cold was unusually severe; the snow had frozen hard upon the ground, and the river was drifting huge masses of ice. The Indians had their families with them; and they brought in their train the wounded and the sick, with children newly born, and old men upon the verge of death. They possessed neither tents nor wagons [sic], but only their arms and some provisions. I saw them embark to pass the mighty river, and never will that solemn spectacle fade from my remembrance. No cry, no sob was heard amongst the assembled crowd: all were silent. Their calamities were of ancient date, and they knew them to be irremediable . . . One could not watch without feeling one's heart wrung . . .

With the Choctaws had walked Presbyterian and other missionaries sent out by the American Board of Commissioners for Foreign Missions (ABCFM). Other Christian denominations and mission boards had championed the Five Tribes' legal battles. A Congregationalist missionary named Samuel Worcester sweated three years in a dank Georgia prison for his honorable principles and became the principal in the 1832 decision, *Worcester v. Georgia,* the landmark case of all Indian law.

In a stance uncharacteristic of the Episcopal Church of the era, the stalwart Kemper wrote, ". . . needs of the Red Men are a weight upon my soul." Time and again he would demonstrate his conviction. He vowed to "do everything in my power" to establish missionary posts as he set out in search of the Mohawks in Indian Territory.

His first stop in the territory was Fort Gibson, a mean little frontier outpost known as the "Hell Hole of the Southwest." In the 1830s the fort was little more than a collection of crude log buildings and noted for nightly poker games and drunken celebrations. A nearby boarding house provided cramped quarters for an ever increasing number of travelers such as George Catlin, Washington Irving, and Sam Houston, former governor of Tennessee and future president of the Republic of Texas. One assumes that Episcopal bishops lodged at the boarding house as well.

Accompanied by the Rev. Henry Gregory who had been engaged by the Board of Missions of New York for the impossible task of missionary for all Indian Territory, Bishop Kemper found the Mohawks living with a small band of Seneca Indians on Cowskin Creek in the northeast corner of present-day Oklahoma. The Cowskin Creek site was inundated when the Grand Lake of the Cherokees was built. The churchmen learned that some 50 Mohawks until recent years had been reading the gospels in Mohawk and using the Book of Common Prayer and singing Anglican hymns. But the Mohawks, perhaps disillusioned, had now defected from the Anglican beliefs. The churchmen had arrived too late.

Kemper and Gregory then sought out the neighboring Senecas with whom the Mohawks had settled around Sandusky, Ohio, after being driven from their ancestral home following the American Revolution. The Seneca with the little band of Mohawks had made an eight-month journey westward, arriving in the summer of 1832 at their new reserve on the Cowskin Creek.

The churchmen got audience before a council of Senecas, making a somewhat dramatic appeal for renewal of Episcopal activity. Reminding the Indians that the Church of England had brought the gospel to their forefathers and that the Episcopal Church had descended directly from the Church of England, they asked that an Episcopal missionary be permitted to work among the members of the tribe. The Seneca, who had been the least accepting of Anglicanism of all the Iroquois, showed little enthusiasm for the proposal. In 1840 they gave a firmly negative answer. The Episcopal Church had arrived too late!

Gregory's final report—he departed his post at Fort Gibson in 1839—expressed doubt as to whether much headway could be made among the Senecas. He did believe, however, that good missionary work might be done among the Shawnees and Quapaws who lived in the same area. He added, "Among the Osages I cannot say that I see a favorable opening at present." Gregory's final gesture toward the Indian missionizing effort was to send back to Indian Territory six Mohawk prayer books which he obtained in New York.

Gregory's replacement was the Rev. William Scull, an army chaplain stationed at Fort Gibson. In 1840 he affirmed that conditions were "not favorable for mission among the Seneca" but offered a hope for establishment of an "extensive literary institution" among the Cherokees as many "sects," including the Moravians, were at work among the Cherokees.

The procession of Episcopal bishops who journeyed out into Indian Territory conducted, in today's language, a "feasibility study." Some were accompanied by church headquarters personnel who wrote detailed and sometimes overly optimistic reports. Their laudable endeavor to establish mission among the Five Tribes was unsuccessful.

After Kemper's visit, came Leonidas Polk, Bishop of Arkansas and the second missionary bishop. Polk, better recalled as a general who was killed leading forces of the Confederate army, made several trips into Indian Territory, traveling extensively in the Cherokee Nation where he visited Chief John Ross at Park Hill.

Ministry Sought with the Choctaw

Bishop Polk also ventured into the large Choctaw Nation, which covered the southeast quarter of present-day Oklahoma, and with whom there had been a Christian mission since 1818. Polk is reported to have conducted services at Doaksville, a major settlement in the Choctaw Nation. By the time of his 1840 visit the Choctaws had recovered from their arduous removal journey, and had written and adopted the first constitution within the limits of Oklahoma, and had established an educational system that would produce within a few years the highest English language literacy rate of the western world. The Episcopal bishop was shown courtesy but got no converts. He had arrived too late.

The "civilized" Choctaws, who had welcomed the missionaries not so much for the salvation of their souls as for a serious quest for language literacy, apparently held out a certain appeal to the Episcopal leaders. Bishop James H. Otey twice journeyed into the Choctaw Nation. In 1844 he made an exploratory trek by way of the military trail to Fort Towson, a crossroad outpost near a Red River ferry and riverboat landing.

Successor to Polk and specifically assigned to southern Indian

Territory, Otey was accompanied on his second journey among the Choctaws by N. Sayre Harris, secretary and general agent of the Board of Missions. At the old Presbyterian mission, Wheelock Academy, they were met by the Rev. Alfred Wright, Presbyterian missionary whose church had 116 members and three candidates for the ministry among the Indians. The Episcopalians were assured by Peter Pitchlynn, a Choctaw leader and future tribal chief, that they would find friends in the area and that they would have been able to establish missions had they come two years earlier.

Otey and Harris then made their way north to Fort Smith, Arkansas, and parted. Harris went on alone, traveling by steamer to Fort Gibson where on Easter Day of 1845 he conducted services for military personnel. He then proceeded over into the Creek Nation. He probably traveled by boat to the vicinity of present-day Tulsa. He is next found calling upon Roley McIntosh, chief of the Creek Nation. Though the Creeks had once severely punished native converts for taking up the Christian religion, the Creek Council had allowed the Baptists to begin missionary efforts in 1829.

Harris proceeded with an extraordinary proposition, holding out the potential of a separate Indian bishopric! Catching a whiff of certain discontent among Indians because of the existing missions' exclusive use of white preachers and religious leaders, Harris opened debate with flattery, commending McIntosh for his reputation for having great interest in the progress of his people. Harris then pointed out to the chief that an all-Indian Church had never been tried. Devoid of canonical authority to do so, Harris painted a picture of an experiment which would rely solely on Indians for its ministry, its catechists, and all its local officers. He rested his case with the proposal of the possibility of an Indian bishop.

At the time of Harris' conversation with the Creek chief, the Episcopal church had not yet ordained a single Indian and it would be another 14 years before Enmegahbowh would be a deacon.

The wily and wise McIntosh, who sprang from a family of Creeks who against formidable odds had survived and emerged as leaders, heard the proposition. He indicated some interest. He did nothing. Harris left the territory discouraged.

First Cherokee Confirmations

George W. Freeman was elected Bishop of Arkansas and Indian Territory in 1844 and served for 14 years. Freeman's first planned trip into the territory was thwarted in 1844 due to disturbances in the Cherokee Nation. It was, in fact, a reign of terror with rising factionalism, assassinations and murder because of a political feud between the Ross and Ridge families.

By 1846 the Cherokee civil strife had abated and Freeman set forth for Fort Gibson with the Rev. Mr. Townsend as his companion. Townsend reported that they had found "a convenient and comfortable post chapel at Ft. Gibson. Sunday crowd had filled to overflowing, much interest in Episcopal service." He wrote:

> Half a dozen were baptized and eleven confirmed: a colonel, an officer's wife, several soldiers and two Cherokee females, one of them a lady of great respectability and refinement. The other, a young girl, was confirmed in a separate service because she had been too shy to step forward at the time of confirmation of the group. Finding the girl sobbing bitterly following services, the bishop made haste to arrange for her early confirmation.

Heartened by reaping "first fruits" with the Cherokee confirmations, Freeman and Townsend set out in February of the following year intent upon visiting Fort Wayne in the Cherokee Nation and Forts Washita and Towson in the Chickasaw and Choctaw Nations. February weather brought impossible roads and they had to limit their visits to Fort Gibson, where they spent four days "conducting five worship services, three of them including sermons by the bishop . . . five children were baptized; four more persons confirmed." Townsend further wrote:

> With a commission for sending the teachings of the gospel to every creature in the world, the church has three ministers among the wide-spread multitudes of these western frontiers, two chaplains at military posts, whose line of duty *excludes* Indians; and one solitary missionary . . . whose health is insecure, means exceedingly limited and whose anxieties are about equally divided between those around him who pleaded for the privileges of the gospel with their expiring breath and the church whose slumbering ears seem to be sealed against such appeals.

Townsend, the solitary missionary, is heard of no more; concluding, apparently, that other denominations had preempted the obvious missionary opportunities with the Five Tribes and that the Episcopal Church had arrived too late with too little.

Lost Opportunity with Chickasaws

It was in 1848 that the Chickasaws contacted the Episcopal Church's New York headquarters through the Commissioner of Indian Affairs, asking assistance with founding a school. The Chickasaws, whose new home was located to the west of their "cousins," the Choctaws, had applied for a manual labor training school and the commissioner had quoted federal regulations which would, under specific guidelines, fund the school. The government would advance $6,000 to erect buildings for the project and an equal amount would be forthcoming annually.

However, there was a stipulation; the annual payment would be granted in the form of fifty dollars for each Indian child. It was further stipulated that the money would be paid only after the reception of pupils at the school.

Both Bishops Otey and Freeman, who had so long sought a toehold among the Five Tribes, were willing to take a chance even though this meant that the Church would be required to raise sufficient funds and locate personnel for the project. From Tennessee Otey gave his full support to the project, offering to surrender the services of a prospective deacon whom he described as one who would "sit admirably for such an enterprise as the one contemplated among the Chickasaws." An appeal was made universally to church members calling for contributions toward "availing ourselves of the most important and favorable opportunity which has ever been presented for establishing missions among the aborigines west of the Mississippi River . . ."

The appeal fell on deaf ears. Henry Whipple had not yet brought the Indians' message and awakened the consciousness of the Episcopal Church. Bishop Freeman, therefore, had to report that the appeal had not been met with adequate support or encouragement. The Chickasaw Council then looked to the Methodist Church and the Chickasaw Manual Labor School for Boys opened near the Chickasaw capital at Tishomingo in 1851.

Thus ended all attempts of Bishop Freeman to establish missions in Indian Territory. Then came the Civil War which abysmally divided the Five Tribes internally. The Cherokee especially suffered. While the war did not break down the organization of the Episcopal Church or divide it, north versus south, the war put a halt to missionary activity for a dozen or more years.

In 1870 Henry Niles Pierce became Bishop of Arkansas and Indian Territory, holding the position for almost 20 years. Pierce made only an occasional trip into the territory to visit army posts. He played no part in the establishment of the first and most significant work among Oklahoma Indians, sponsored by a parish in the distant Diocese of Central New York.

The Sainted Oakerhater

In 1881, the first time in more than 30 years, an Episcopal missionary arrived in Indian Territory. In fact, three missionaries arrived—a white priest from Paris Hill, New York, named John Barrett Wicks, accompanied by David Pendleton Oakerhater, a Cheyenne deacon, and Paul Zotom, a Kiowa deacon. The latter two, newly ordained, were returning home after spending three years in a Florida prison and three years studying under the white priest in New York. Wicks' health failed within three years and he returned to New York. Zotom more or less dropped out of sight. But Oakerhater would serve his God, the Cheyenne people and his church for yet a half century, until his death in 1931. For almost a decade, his was the only ordained Episcopal presence in all Indian Territory. A century after the deacon's return to the Cheyenne, he would become the first American Indian listed on the calendar of saints in the Episcopal Church.

Born in the mid-1840s, Oakerhater was reared on the high plains in a non-white, non-European culture. His people, once proud and free, were gradually crushed by the pressure of an alien government which desired the land and even the life of Indian America. The peace loving Cheyenne, led by Black Kettle, were attacked under a flag of truce in 1864 by John Chivington, colonel of the Colorado volunteers and an ordained Methodist minister, at Sand Creek in southeast Colorado. This unprovoked attack slaughtered 140 Cheyenne women and children in the camp, together with some 60 men. Black Kettle escaped.

Four years later, on a cold Thanksgiving morning of 1868, Black Kettle's band was murderously annihilated in a pre-dawn raid by Colonel George Armstrong Custer and the Seventh Cavalry at Washita Village in Oklahoma. Black Kettle, the Cheyenne peace chief, was killed. Men, women and children were mercilessly killed, the village destroyed, and 600 Indian ponies shot on the spot by order of Colonel Custer. Some Cheyenne warrior survivors went north to relish victory eight years later at Little Bighorn.

As Oakerhater was a member of Black Kettle's band, it is likely he was present at either or both Sand Creek and Wichita Village. The full-blooded Cheyenne—whose name roughly translates as "Making Medicine"—had, as a young man, distinguished himself for bravery as a member of an elite Cheyenne warrior society. His final moments

Ordination picture on June 7, 1881,
of David Pendleton Oakerhater (Cheyenne) [1884-1931].
Courtesy Episcopal Archives, Diocese of Oklahoma.

in the role of warrior were played out on June 24, 1874, in the barren
red cedar breaks of the Texas Panhandle at the Battle of Adobe Walls,
among the last of the Texas skirmishes in the long series of Indian-
white confrontations.

Adobe Walls was a camp of buffalo hunters. The Plains Indians
had watched as the once-endless herds of buffalo had been wantonly
destroyed. One June sunrise in 1874, 700 warriors of five tribes—
Kiowa, Comanche, Wichita, Cheyenne and Arapaho—futilely attacked
the camp. With long-range buffalo guns, the hunters methodically
picked off the circling warriors. The attack failed. Warrior leaders,
including the 30-year-old Oakerhater, were later arrested by the U.S.
Army. Nine Comanches, 26 Kiowas, two Arapahos and 33 Cheyennes,
including Oakerhater, were hauled away, without trial, from Fort Sill,
Oklahoma, restrained by heavy leg chains in a creaking army wagon
en route to military prison at Fort Marion at St. Augustine, Florida.
They were in the custody of Lieutenant Richard H. Pratt, who would
later influence Oakerhater's life.

Early in Oakerhater's prison years, Bishop Henry Whipple of

Minnesota is said to have conducted a week-long preaching series for the imprisoned Indians while on one of his several Florida journeys. Researchers have futilely sought details on the bishop's interaction with the Indian prisoners. Though some researchers suggest that the dynamic Whipple may have led Oakerhater to convert to Christianity, Whipple's autobiography makes no mention of any encounter with the prisoners and the extent to which Oakerhater's life was influenced by the bishop is unknown.

Lieutenant Pratt, however, is known to have shaped Oakerhater's Christian development. Connection with Senator George and Mrs. Pendleton of Cincinnati was doubtless made during the prison years. Likely the link was through archery instruction for the Pendleton daughter and through art. Oakerhater, along with other non-English speaking prisoners, began drawing on ledger paper supplied by Pratt. Their art work "talked" not only to whites, but served as communication with people back home. The ledger drawings, an outgrowth of traditional symbol or pictographic art, were to become national treasures and are found today in private collections and several museums, including the Smithsonian. The drawings of Oakerhater bear a glyph meaning "Sun Dancer."

Mrs. Pendleton, a daughter of Francis Scott Key, was attracted to Oakerhater's drawings. She arranged for Oakerhater to receive a Christian education in upstate New York, "taking up expense of tuition for three years at $115 per year." With Pratt's assistance, four former prisoners departed Florida to began studies under the auspices of Mary D. Burnham, a deaconess in charge of the House of the Good Shepherd in Syracuse, New York. The deaconess planned a three-year course of study for Oakerhater and placed him under the charge of Wicks.

Oakerhater was baptized on October 6, 1878, in "an impressive service" at Grace Episcopal Church in Syracuse by Bishop Frederic D. Huntington. Confirmation followed on October 20. At the time of confirmation, the Cheyenne chose the name of David Pendleton Oakerhater, a gesture honoring the family of his benefactor.

In 1879 Pratt was named superintendent for a new educational institution in Pennsylvania which would come to be known as Carlisle Indian School. At Pratt's request, Oakerhater returned to Indian Territory to recruit for Carlisle, and while in the west, he reunited with his wife and small son whom he had not seen since his imprisonment. Oakerhater's little family returned to Syracuse with him. Tragically, his wife and son did not survive the cold upstate New York winter of 1880. They were buried in the cemetery of St. Paul's at Paris Hill.

Four Indians went to New York for study. In addition to

Oakerhater and Zotom, there were two others: John Wicks Oksteher (sometimes referred to as Ostei), a Cheyenne who died in New York in 1880, and Henry Taywayite, whose tribe is unknown. The latter failed to enter missionary work and returned to the territory as a layman.

Bishop Huntington ordained the two Indians to the diaconate at Grace Church, Syracuse, on June 7, 1881. On that same day they joyfully undertook the long train ride to Indian Territory. The missionary priest accompanying them, John Barret Wicks, recorded that "the boys were going home and were merry hearted."

The missionaries arrived in Indian Territory at the beginning of the demise of tribal life. Only a quarter-million had survived the 400 years of European invasion and "manifest destiny." More than half of the surviving Indians were residing in Indian Territory. White agitation to break up Indian reservation life came to fruition before the end of the century with the Dawes Severalty Act, commonly called the Allotment Act. The year 1889 would see the Oklahoma Land Run. By 1907 Oklahoma would be a state, the Indian nations dismantled.

Wicks' correspondence described the Cheyenne Nation as "a land of prairie wolves in nightly concert and curious antelope." The missionary trio arrived in time for a great gathering of the Cheyenne for a Sun Dance. (Within a decade the government banned the sun dance along with all tribal religious practices.)

Wicks described Oakerhater as about 30 and "tall and straight as an arrow with a fine open countenance that would attract attention in any company." He was as gentle, said his teacher, as he was faithful; his faithfulness had made him a legendary figure in the Florida camp. Wicks was to discover, upon their arrival in Oklahoma, that Oakerhater was also a legendary figure among his own people, holding a prominent place in his tribe. Wicks listened with both the pride of a mentor and awe as an observer when the deacon made his first address before his Cheyenne kin:

> Men, you all know me. You remember when I led you out to war I went first and what I told you was true. Now, I have been away to the East, and I have learned about another Captain, the Lord Jesus Christ, and He is my leader. He goes first, and all He tells me is true. I come back to my people to tell you to go with me now on this new road, a war that makes all for peace. and where we [ever] have only victory.

The record book for the Episcopal mission established at the Indian agency at Darlington shows a beginning date of June 16, 1881. Oakerhater sponsored and witnessed the baptism of Mary Star, age 11. A few days later, on June 25, Oakerhater conducted the first Christian burial service ever known among the Cheyenne, a child of Big Horse, a Cheyenne chief. Later on that summer Cheyenne agent John Miles, writing to the Commissioner of Indian Affairs in Washington about the returned Fort Marion prisoners, said that David P. Oakerhater was preaching in his native tongue and no better example of Christian manhood was to be found. Early converts included *Wah-Nach,* mother of Oakerhater, and Whirlwind, the chief of the Cheyenne and son of the Cheyenne peace chief Black Kettle.

Independent of the Board of Missions in New York, and supported wholly through funding generated by Deaconess Burnham, the mission venture grew. Oakerhater lived and worked in the vicinity of the Darlington agency and Zotom moved on to a site near Anadarko. Wicks worked at both places, erecting a chapel at the Kiowa Agency and a home and mission facilities at Fay, near Darlington. Wicks' reports told of conducting services regularly at Indian camps and of building a mission house in Anadarko into which he proposed to move his wife and family. By the following year the missionary team had initiated regular services in two school houses. A report from P.B. Hunt, an Episcopalian who was in charge of the Kiowa, Comanche and Wichita agency, alluded to an expressed interest in the work by the bishop of Arkansas and Indian Territory, who suggested "if possible, adding to the work force."

First Cheyenne Confirmations

Bishop Pierce made a visit in 1882 and for the first time in 36 years an Indian was confirmed in Indian Territory. The last Indian confirmation of record had been in 1846 when Bishop Freeman visited Fort Gibson and confirmed a Cherokee "woman of refinement." At the Cheyenne and Kiowa missions, the bishop reported having confirmed 25 persons—15 at Darlington, nine at Anadarko and one at Fort Sill. His report fails to say how many of the confirmands were Indian, but certainly some were. The following year, Wicks reported that construction was underway in Anadarko on a new church building which would seat 200! Twelve confirmations as well as baptisms were recorded.

Oakerhater in 1884 would find himself alone in the western Oklahoma work. Wicks' health failed and he returned east. The work founded by Zotom soon failed and the Kiowa was eventually deposed from the ministry. Bishop Pierce sent no help. Oakerhater continued alone and for nine years was the only active ordained representative of the Episcopal Church in Indian Territory.

These were years of major transition for the Cheyenne. The buffalo was gone. Game was scarce on their big reservation, which stretched along the two Canadian rivers and upper reaches of the Washita. Sometimes the rations were low-grade or spoiled; sometimes the rations did not arrive on time. They camped near the Agency at Darlington where their children were in day school and where rations of food and clothing were issued. But the social exchange was good, with visiting back and forth. It was almost like the old days at the great summer encampments. Then the government began pressing them to plow and plant and grow livestock. The disturbing orders came in 1886. The Cheyenne would move to farms in the far reaches of the dry reservation. In the next year came notice that under the Dawes Act the Cheyenne would have to accept allotments of 160 acres per individual and that the remaining land would be opened to white settlement. Not only were the Cheyenne forced into farming, but worse still, their children would go to government boarding schools, often many miles away. These were problems of daily life that the Cheyenne Episcopal deacon dealt with in ministering among his people.

Missionary District of Oklahoma and Indian Territory

General Convention created the Missionary District of Oklahoma and Indian Territory and Francis Key Brooke was sent in 1893 as its first bishop. Prior to his arrival only three other missionary efforts, besides the Cheyenne and Kiowa work, are on record.

One finds no reference to a Caddo mission in Episcopal records, but Muriel H. Wright claims such occurred. Long considered by many a major authority on Indians of Oklahoma, she was the granddaughter of Allen Wright, principal chief of the Choctaws (1866-1870). Miss Wright in the 1951 edition of *A Guide to the Indian Tribes of Oklahoma* sketched the abominable treatment to which the peaceful Caddo were subjected when pushed from their ancestral home in Louisiana and northeastern Texas. Eventually located in 1854 on a small reservation along the Brazos River in Young County, Texas, the Caddo became prey for land-greedy Texans. In 1859 all surviving Caddos, 1,430 of them, were force-marched in severe August heat to Indian Territory and placed on the Washita River, without military protection "against attacks of hostile Comanche and Kiowa." Miss Wright wrote:

> The Episcopal church placed a mission on the [Caddo] reservation in 1891, and another was established by the Roman Catholic Church in near present Anadarko.

The Roman Catholic mission survives in Anadarko.

In the research of the Rev. Sam L. Botkin, published in a 1958 edition of *The Chronicles of Oklahoma,* is mention of an unnamed Arkansas priest having started Oak Lodge Episcopal Mission among the Choctaws in 1891. Site of the mission was Skullyville, destined to become a ghost town, but once the bustling northern district headquarters of the Choctaw Nation, founded in 1832 near the Swallow Rock boat landing on the Arkansas River. Annuities due the Choctaws were paid at Skullyville; the name is derived from the Choctaw word *iskuli,* meaning money.

Another Episcopal ingress was made into the Choctaw Nation in the McAlester area, site of rich and extensive coal fields which were leased to white operators and worked by imported miners, primarily from Italy. The Episcopal Church opened All Saints' Hospital in South McAlester in 1895. Land was provided by a "citizen of the Choctaw nation" and building funds were raised through donations from easterners for the first hospital in Indian Territory.

An English-born clergyman was the hospital's superintendent, chaplain and missionary. The Rev. George Biller Jr. resigned that post in 1903 and 10 years later was consecrated as South Dakota's third missionary bishop.

The third bishop of Oklahoma, Thomas Casady, writing in 1930 to Miss Helen M. Brickman of New York City, responding to her inquiry, tells of other Indian mission in the state:

> We now have definite work among Indians at Eufaula and are just beginning work at Pawnee. The prospect in the latter place is uncertain, owing to the long continued opposition of white people to joint services with the Indians. On the other hand the Indians rather resent segregation, but we are making the experiment. At Pawnee we have several Indian communicants who come to church occasionally but the white people will not tolerate Indians at any church social function. In October I am opening exclusively Indian work at Watonga under an efficient and experienced deaconess. This looks hopeful.
>
> In Pawhuska a fine Indian man is treasurer and a member of the choir. In Eufaula and McAlester the President of the Bishop's committee is a half breed Indian. Both men are of fine standing in the community. In the Western Archdeaconry we have an Indian lay reader but as yet he has not been overly successful. The whole problem is very difficult in Oklahoma because of prejudice and because of

past experiences. I am having to start from the bottom and on entirely new lines.

In probably one-third of our parishes and missions we have people of part Indian blood who are regular attendants and communicants. We have no full blood Indians in such relations with the Church except at Pawhuska, El Reno and Sapulpa so far as I can remember. My own feeling is that the separate Indian work is wrong in principle although it is the only method available to us in some places.

One notes the scant reference to the Indian mission of half a century among the Cheyenne. However, Casady's predecessor had admirably demonstrated his support to the Cheyenne work. He solicited funds in the east and brought on board the Rev. David Sanford, who knew the Cheyenne language, to assist with work at Darlington and Bridgeport. Later, a chapel was erected at Bridgeport where Sanford made his home. This was likely an especially happy period in Oakerhater's life. He married Minnie about 1898 and their home was the church facility.

Cheyenne School

The government had established the first school for the Cheyenne in 1872 near the Darlington Agency. Later, in 1897, it was moved to Fay on Chief Whirlwind's allotment. The Whirlwind school was named for the famous old peace chief, one of the Cheyenne spokesmen at the Treaty of Medicine Lodge. Oakerhater carried the Episcopal mission to these children and their families camped nearby. The government closed the school in 1901 and the children were dispatched away to government boarding schools. The widow of Chief Whirlwind, an Episcopal communicant, gave the old government school building to the Episcopal Church for a mission day school which the agency allowed to be established "for the care of those unhealthy children who are debarred from the government school." Sanford was placed in charge. Cheyenne parents resisted sending their children away to boarding school and complications with the government officials developed when healthy students appeared to attend the Whirlwind school. The white missionary was targeted for strong criticism by government officials and after several delaying actions the bishop eventually had to let Sanford go.

The Rev. James J.W. Reedy succeeded Sanford. As non-resident priest-in-charge, Reedy visited the mission once a month to hold communion services, but the general religious work was ably handled by the deacon, Oakerhater. Bishop Brooke recognized help was necessary with the school and sought a teacher through the National Council.

Harriet Bedell and the Cheyenne

Harriet M. Bedell, who aspired to serve as a missionary to China, was recruited to teach at Whirlwind Mission where she would be the only white woman for miles in every direction. In late December of 1907, Miss Bedell—within a few years she would be "set apart" as a deaconess—departed from her native New York by train for Watonga, Oklahoma. The rest of the journey she would make by wagon to the hamlet of Fay, and thence to Whirlwind where she remained for a full decade and earned a Cheyenne name of *Vicsehia* (Bird Woman). Her salary was $400 a year.

Miss Bedell, who was filled with zeal for the Indians, soon became one of the most prominent writers for the national Episcopal periodical *The Spirit of Missions,* providing frequent sidelights of work among the Cheyenne. In 1910 she wrote:

> We live in an Indian camp, and come in very close contact with the people. There is a church day school of thirty-nine pupils, ranging in age from five to seventeen years, and all our work goes hand in hand with work in the homes. The Indians live in tepees, in a most primitive way. Beds are of covered dry grass, and the cooking is done on a fire made in a hole in the ground . . . Among the older people many of the old-time customs still prevail, such as wailing at funerals, burying all belongings with the dead, the cries of the medicine man, calls for feasts from the hills, and the old kettle-drum ceremony, lasting all night.
>
> . . . Both men and women wear their hair long, in two braids over the shoulders, the men's only differing in having a third very small braid from the middle of the back of the head in memory of the old "scalp lock." The women wear short, loose gown with flowing sleeves, belted in at the waist, with fancy metal belts or twisted colored scarves. The men wear white man's dress, except for the moccasins, heavily beaded in beautiful Indian designs. Many still paint their faces, and during their festive times still like to wear feathers.

Whirlwind Mission Chapel with tents in the background.
Courtesy, Episcopal Diocese of Oklahoma.

Miss Bedell wrote of her visits with Bishop Brooke to Chilocco, an Indian boarding school run by the government near the Kansas border in north central Oklahoma. She wrote in 1913 that a priest was in charge of the Chilocco work which had "about 100 members." In another 1913 article she wrote:

> Several visits have been made to Deer Creek to care for sick Indians. Visits to Big Horse, Little Elk and White Buffalo were such interesting ones and as a result Pipe Woman and Sun Maker are candidates for baptism. It was hard for Sun Maker to give up the old ways, but he finally did and was ready for anything. The change was complete. He asked if he must cut off his braids. I said, "No, you can be just as good a Christian with long hair." This pleased him, as the Indian takes great pride in his hair.

Miss Bedell's many stories published in *The Spirit of Missions* provided glimpses of the Cheyenne in daily life. She wrote sensitively of the changes occurring in the lives of the people, but one observes that at least on one occasion the good lady was duped! She wrote in 1913 of the "Willow Dance." What she described was the Sun Dance, which the federal government in its firm resolve to make the Indian "give up the old ways" had outlawed in 1883. The Cheyenne and other western Oklahoma tribes simply changed the name and continued the tradition. Thus, she was invited to witness the Sun Dance from the periphery, but not the ceremony itself:

> I have just returned from the Washita River, where about 3,000 Indians were assembled—Cheyennes, Arapahos, Comanches, Kiowas and Pawnees. They camped around a fifty or sixty acre space. The scene was very picturesque— the white tepees with men and women in gay attire going in and out . . . They gathered for the Willow Dance, which was held in a tent erected with much ceremony in the center. The purpose was to invoke the Great Spirit's blessing on the medicine men, and their medicine, which they made in a large tepee . . . After a parade the dance began. It consists of just the bending of the knees. They danced for nearly two days
>
> *I did not witness the dance itself* [but] the Indians made me very welcome, and several have promised to send their children to our school . . . School opens the first week of September . . . Mr. Sherman Coolidge, a full-blooded Indian priest, with his wife, are to be with us.

Coolidge was a Northern Arapaho priest who had already served on the Wind River Reservation in Wyoming for 25 years. Since the Oklahoma mission was on the Cheyenne-Arapaho Reservation, one wonders if Coolidge had been brought in to do specific work among the Southern Arapaho; if so, it never materialized. Little can be found about Coolidge's ministry in Oklahoma except for his signature on baptismal, marriage and attendance records over a two-year period.

Minuscule traces of the faithful Oakerhater are occasionally uncovered. There is a shameful little reference to the 1914 diocesan convention in Oklahoma City during which the Indian delegation, including Oakerhater, was housed not at a hotel but with a family "where, it was felt, they would be more comfortable."

In 1916, after serving 36 years a deacon, Oakerhater retired on a small pension. Within a year the Whirlwind school closed and Miss Bedell was transferred to Alaska. Later, after very devoted work along the Yukon, she tried to develop work among the Seminoles in Florida. The following year a new bishop came to Oklahoma who would give no specific attention to Indian ministry, stating in *The Spirit of Missions:*

> There are many Colored folk, and also a lot of Indians. But you would not know many of them as Indians . . . they do not wear feathers . . . The Indians are not, except in a very few cases, the wards of the Government. There is very little distinctive Church work being done among them. This is because that have so intermarried with white people that, except for a few isolated instances, they can take their places in church work along with the white people.

Oakerhater in "Retirement"

Though officially retired, Deacon Oakerhater continued to work alone, functioning as a Cheyenne peace chief and "holy man," marrying and burying the faithful, baptizing and preaching among the population, and training layreaders to carry on the work of Christianity. He trained Stacey Riggs and his own son, Frank, as well as Archie Walker. Brief glimpses of the aging deacon and the Cheyenne mission are provided in *The Spirit of Missions* and Oklahoma diocesan papers. For instance, at a convocation attended by "at least 80" in 1927, the Rt. Rev. E. Cecil Seaman, acting bishop of Oklahoma, wrote:

> . . . the four-room house of the Rev. David Oakerhater and his good wife was the center of much activity. In the afternoon I baptized two children, granddaughters of Chief Turkey Legs. Our Indians had come from all directions, in wagons and cars. Some had brought their tepees, and set them up in the yard . . . Holy Communion was administered from a portable folding altar . . . the sermon was interpreted by Howard Bird, who was trained by the Church in South Dakota, where he was baptized and confirmed. Later he was a Carlisle student and football player. A man and three children were baptized.
>
> Before we left Chief Turkey Legs presented to the Church, subject to approval of the Indian agent at Concho, two additional acres of land for a cemetery.

Chief Turkey Legs of the Cheyenne.
Courtesy, Archives of the Diocese of Oklahoma.

Oklahoma Committee on Indian Work

Fifty years after Chief Turkey Legs' gift, the land would be returned to the Cheyenne Nation. On recommendation of the Oklahoma Committee on Indian Work (OCIW) Bishop Gerald McAllister in 1983 deeded back the land which was no longer needed for cemetery use. This gesture pre-dated a national movement by a full decade. In 1992 churches were called on to return tribal homeland to tribal ownership and control as a measure of appropriate observance in 1992 of the 500th anniversary of the voyage of Christopher Columbus.

In 1977 a handful of Oklahoma Episcopal Indians organized the Oklahoma Committee on Indian Work, and it has become the longest sustained diocesan Indian advocacy program of the Church, with the exception of Niobrara Council of South Dakota. In the early years the outward and visible purpose of OCIW was to gain feast day recognition of David Oakerhater. The core purpose of OCIW, however, was to gain the attention of non-Indian pew mates for Indian issues—treaty rights, sovereignty, culture and history—and to garner non-Indian support in advocacy.

The Episcopal Church of Oklahoma, without asking Indians, had for generations magnanimously preached "acculturation" of Indians. The Oklahoma Church had embraced an elaborate rationale based on the "superiority" of white economy, culture and religion. Consequently, destruction and exploitation of Indians emerged out of what was intended to be philanthropy and assistance. For instance, a 1925 Church publication noted that there were 120,000 people of Indian blood in Oklahoma, that they were still a "peculiar" people, but that they were rapidly being absorbed in the nation.

Some 3,400 of these "peculiar" people are baptized Episcopalians and represent approximately 15 per cent of the baptized members of today's Diocese of Oklahoma. They have been sent forth as leaders to the broader church; two of the four American Indian bishops were Oklahoma-born, as were four out of seven national staff officers for Indian ministry. Additionally, at the invitation of Bishop McAllister, Oklahoma diocesan 1977 to 1989, the national church's field office was housed in the splendid new Oklahoma diocese center. From 1986 until 1994 a Caddo woman served as the national church's Indian ministries field officer; during a portion of her tenure, a Pawnee served as support staff.

The OCIW's major contribution to both Indians and non-Indian Episcopalians has been the efforts—primarily by one small frail-looking indomitable Creek woman—to gain official recognition for David Pendleton Oakerhater. Lois Clark, a retired public school teacher, began the effort by detailed research and writing a booklet entitled *God's Warrior* in which she said:

> He was never raised to the rank of priest and therefore never had the privilege of celebrating Holy Communion among his flock; yet, when he died on August 31, 1931, he had served the Episcopal Church in Oklahoma longer than any of its clergy.

She wrote of Bishop Brooke's comment that the Cheyenne deacon was the "remnant of the first attempt of our Church to do work among the [Oklahoma] Indians." Mrs. Clark further expounded, "What the Bishop left unsaid was that the Church hierarchy had abandoned its work among [Oklahoma] Indians, but Oakerhater had not."

In the closing hour of the 68th General Convention in Anaheim in 1985, both houses voted to include the name of the Cheyenne among the notables of the Episcopal Church. Mrs. Clark stood proudly before the convention to express the gratitude of Indians across the nation. In an air of gracious authority, she presented an icon of Oakerhater to the National Cathedral and blankets to the incoming and outgoing

Lois Clark [1910-1985], (Creek).

Primates of the Episcopal Church. This was to be the last public appearance of Lois Clark, a woman who gave distinguished service to the Episcopal Church at parish, diocesan and national levels. Two months later she died at home on November 19 at age 75.

First Oakerhater Feast Day

Oakerhater was honored in the noblest way Episcopalians know: his first feast day, September 1, 1986, was celebrated at the National Cathedral in Washington, D.C. The Bishop of Washington, John Thomas Walker, was celebrant. The preacher was William C. Wantland, a member of the Seminole Nation of Oklahoma and Bishop of Eau Claire. Lawrence Hart, a traditional peace chief of the Cheyenne Nation, as well as a relative of the deacon and a Mennonite minister, stood in the great cathedral attired in traditional Cheyenne clothing and read the Gospel in the Cheyenne language. The Rev. George Smith (Ojibwa) of Minnesota, first chairperson of the National Committee on Indian

Work, was a participant in the liturgy, as were three native-born Oklahomans: the Rev. Barnett Jackson (Cherokee), Owanah Anderson (Choctaw), and Tim Tall Chief (Osage).

Members of the Oakerhater family were present for the celebration as were delegations of American Indians from Oklahoma and elsewhere. They walked proudly in procession. They heard the collect:

> O God of unsearchable wisdom and infinite mercy, you chose a captive warrior, David Oakerhater, to be your servant, and sent him to be a missionary to his own people, and to exercise the office of a deacon among them: Liberate us, who commemorate him today, from bondage to self, and empower us for service to you and to the neighbors you have given us; through Jesus Christ, the captain of our salvation, who lives and reigns with you and the Holy Spirit, one God, for ever and ever. *Amen.*

Wantland, the second American Indian bishop of the Episcopal Church, concluded his powerful sermon on the occasion:

> On August 31, 1931, Oakerhater died as he had lived, with full faith and trust in his captain, the Lord Jesus Christ. A busy non-Indian Church soon forgot the work of this saintly man. More than 30 years passed. But in the early 1960s, a family of Episcopalians moved to Watonga, Oklahoma, and finding no Episcopal community there, with cooperation of a nearby priest placed a newspaper advertisement inviting all persons interested in the Episcopal Church to attend a meeting on a Sunday afternoon at the home of the new family.
>
> At the appointed date and time, over 30 loyal Cheyenne Indians appeared. These Churchmen had been nurtured in the Episcopal Church by David Oakerhater, and after his death by the Lay Readers that he had trained. After half a century, the Whirlwind Mission of the Holy Family emerged from the underground, and is again a mission of the Diocese of Oklahoma, and a living memorial to David Pendleton Oakerhater.

In late August for the next several years at Roman Nose State Park, in the red and craggy hills of the old Southern Cheyenne Reservation near where Oakerhater ministered, the Oklahoma Committee on Indian Work sponsored the Oakerhater honor dance.

The 1992 Oakerhater event was marked with new activity in

the old Cheyenne Nation. Only a week before, the Rev. Jim Knowles, the new Indian missionary for the diocese, had opened the doors of Oakerhater Episcopal Indian Ministries Center located 10 miles from the pow-wow grounds on the outskirts of Watonga, Oklahoma. Knowles, a Cherokee deacon, serves as director for a social ministries and referral service program as well as for the Whirlwind Mission worshiping community. Fifty-four Indians appeared for the first event of the new center, which was the 50th birthday party for a member of the Oakerhater family.

Knowles trained and presented the first class for confirmation in a generation in 1993. Among the confirmands were direct descendants of the deacon.

Potawatomi's Cedar Lodge Jubilee Center

A picturesque white frame Quaker mission house has stood for more than a century on a gentle sloping hillside in the present-day Citizen Band Potawatomi tribal headquarters in central Oklahoma near Shawnee. Of Algonquin stock, the Potawatomi were pressed ever westward from their traditional homelands on the upper shores of Lake Huron, eventually locating in Kansas. Subjected to grossly unfair treatment in Kansas, a segment of the surviving Potawatomi opted to relocate in Indian Territory in 1867 on lands between the North and South Canadian Rivers. The Potawatomis eventually became neighbors to the Kickapoo and Absentee Shawnee, with whom the Society of Friends (Quakers) had mission since 1875. In fact, the Friends had been interested in the Shawnee since the time of William Penn in Pennsylvania.

The old Quaker mission house became a focal point of the Episcopal Church's first and only mission outreach to Central Oklahoma tribes. The initial mission began to unfold in 1990. Catalyst was a young Potawatomi deacon, Norman Kiker, who was chosen as the tribe's chaplain and spiritual adviser. He had been ordained the previous year through the diocesan perpetual deacon training program. With the blessing of both Emmanuel Episcopal Church of Shawnee, his home parish, and his diocesan bishop, Kiker cast about for a more definitive involvement of his church in tribal life.

First, Kiker began weekly worship services, billed as non-denominational. Within a few months the old Quaker mission was renovated and renamed Mission Hill Indian Church. In the summer of 1992, over 100 came to a special service in which another Potawatomi clergyman participated. He was the Rev. Michael Smith, a graduate of

Seabury-Western Seminary, who was ordained to the priesthood in January 1992.

Secondly, Cedar Lodge Center evolved to serve Indian people of all tribal and spiritual traditions. Kiker applied for Jubilee Center designation of the Cedar Lodge program which offered family counseling, life-skills development and chemical-free vision. Out of Cedar Lodge came a special Court Appointed Special Advocate (CASA) volunteer project. Cedar Lodge Center received Jubilee designation and thus became the first Jubilee Center in the Diocese of Oklahoma.

7

THE EPISCOPAL CHURCH IN
NAVAJOLAND

Introduction: The Culture

The Navajo call themselves *Diné* [Den-AY]—The People. Their creation story maintains that The People emerged from an underground
world north of the Gobernador Canyon in northern New Mexico. Anthropologists hold that the Navajo descended from the Athabascan
peoples of the Yukon basin of Alaska and Canada. Their highly difficult languages are similar and, in fact, to an extent interchangeable.

While the Athabascan remained in the Yukon regions, the Navajo drifted southward, and by the time Columbus set sail westward,
the Navajo were firmly lodged on the wind-swept deserts of Arizona,
New Mexico and Utah. The People express an interminable affinity
for the harshly beautiful environment that is their homeland, a 25,000-
square-mile area bordered by their four sacred mountains and
approximately the size of West Virginia.

The relationship between land and mystery, nature and God,
constitutes the character of Navajo tradition. The extended family, or
clan, is the bulwark of Navajo life, and each of the more than 75 clans
is traced through the female line. Marriage within a clan is forbidden.

The philosophy on which the *Diné* founded their culture is based
on a poetic metaphor which projects a dichotomy between good and
evil—good, harmony and beauty on the one side of reality, and evil,
chaos and ugliness on the other. Thus, while aspiring to attain balance and harmony, the Navajo must deal also with a world inhabited
by evil, personified by witches and skin-walkers, damned humans who

are seen on the roadside at nightfall draped with deerskin and antlers. Navajo believe that evil happens when people are out of harmony with nature; the remedy for getting back in balance with oneself and one's surroundings is to see a medicine man for appropriate healing ceremonies. The term "medicine man" is a *biligaana,* a non-Navajo term; the Navajo word for the traditional religious leader, *Hataathlii,* is more appropriately translated as "chanter, singer or healer." Incidentally, there are also women who are *hataathlii.* Traditional Navajo religion, with its 35 different rituals, including sandpainting, demands the chanter to study many years to memorize the ceremonies.

The role of beauty is reflected in their creative ceremonies and in their art. Dancing and singing have always brought families and clans closer together. The *Kinaaldá* is the puberty ceremony for girls; the *Yeibichai* takes place in the winter and lasts nine days; the Squaw Dance or Enemy Way brings young men and women together for several special days of summer. Along with its social aspects, the Squaw Dance is a profoundly serious healing ceremony for one who has been away from the confines of the four sacred mountains living among whites or fighting in a war. In the summer of 1991, women for the first time were participants in the purification ceremonials of the Enemy Way; a significant number of Navajo women had served in the Gulf War.

THE BEAUTY WAY

In Beauty, may I walk. All day long, may I walk.
Through the returning seasons, may I walk.
On the trail marked with pollen, may I walk.
With grasshoppers about my feet, may I walk.
With dew about my feet, may I walk.
With Beauty, may I walk.
With Beauty before me, may I walk.
With Beauty behind me, may I walk.
With Beauty above me, may I walk.
With Beauty below me, may I walk.
With Beauty all around me, may I walk.
In old age wandering on a trail of beauty, lively, may I
*   walk.*
In old age wandering on a trail of beauty, living again,
*   may I walk.*
It is finished in beauty.
It is finished in beauty.

—Navajo Beauty Way Prayer

NAVAJOLAND AREA MISSION

Episcopal mission among the Navajo had an inauspicious beginning. There were, in fact, three beginnings in widely separated regions of the vast and rugged Navajo Reservation which spreads across state boundaries of Arizona, New Mexico and Utah. The beginnings were in quarter-century increments. First, to Fort Defiance, Arizona, in 1892 came an Episcopal lay teacher soon followed by a woman who built a hospital; 25 years later a medical mission was opened in the New Mexico region, and in another 25 years to the remote Utah region in 1942 came a Connecticut Anglo-Catholic priest who is said to have baptized 10,000 Navajos.

By the middle of the 20th century the three missions were sharing the gospel with the Navajos—Good Shepherd at Fort Defiance, San Juan near Farmington, New Mexico, and St. Christopher's near Bluff, Utah. Each had its own outstations and each had determined its own character.

Until 1977 Episcopal mission among the largest Indian tribe was under jurisdiction of three Episcopal dioceses—Arizona, Utah and New Mexico. Thoughtful Church leaders agreed that the separation of the Church's missions into three dioceses was not in harmony with other Navajo tribal activities, and that the unique language and culture of the Navajo people required a unified plan for mission. A plan, however, was slow to evolve.

General Convention of 1976 voted to unify Navajo work into a single jurisdiction as an area mission, a structure requiring appointment—not election—of its bishop. Navajoland's deputies to General Convention had voice but no vote until the 1997 General Convention.

The decade—1977 to 1987—was a transitional period in Navajoland. Canonical organization absorbed the early years Otis Charles, then Bishop of Utah, was named the first Bishop-in-Charge. Assets and property titles were transferred to the new entity by the bishops of Arizona, Rio Grande and Utah.

During the years when jurisdiction was being designed a young Navajo was growing up in a tiny community called Coalmine, eight miles from Fort Defiance. He was Steven Tsosie Plummer, born in 1944 in a hogan near St. Mark's mission, a concrete block chapel perched on a barren slope on which herds of goats graze. Plummer came from a non-English speaking home. His father was a miner at the nearby gigantic Peabody open pit coal mine. Steven worked awhile at the mine after dropping out of school as a ninth-grader. After considering whether to study to be a medicine man, like his grandfathers, he decided to prepare for the priesthood of the Episcopal Church, and his decision had high impact on the Episcopal Church in Navajoland. Confirmed at Good Shepherd, Plummer came under the mentorship of a Santee Sioux priest, Harold S. Jones, who was named vicar of Good Shepherd in 1968, serving the mission until he was elected Suffragan Bishop of South Dakota in 1971.

After returning to Albuquerque Indian School, Plummer took courses at Cook Christian Training School, Tempe, Arizona and Phoenix Junior College. In 1975, after two years' study, he was granted a certificate from the Church Divinity School of the Pacific.

Joseph M. Harte, the bishop of Arizona, presided at the most colorful ordination of his long career when Plummer was ordained to the diaconate at the rim of Canyon de Chelly, a site of breath-taking beauty which is revered as a holy place in Navajo tradition.

Frederick W. Putnam, Suffragan Bishop of Oklahoma for 15 years, resigned his post to accept appointment as full-time resident bishop of Navajoland. He was installed in January 1979 at Good Shepherd Mission, Fort Defiance. He moved to Farmington and set up offices at the old San Juan mission compound, initiated several new programs, and played a vital role in launching the new jurisdiction. Upon reaching retirement age, he resigned in 1982.

In the transition years two other Navajos, Eloise Martinez and Yazzie Mason, both from the New Mexico region, were ordained to the diaconate. Yazzie elected to serve in the permanent diaconate; Martinez was ordained to the priesthood in 1979 but subsequently renounced her vows and left the Church.

Presiding Bishop John Allin chose as Putnam's successor the highly energetic bishop of Nevada, Wesley Frensdorff, who would serve from 1983 until his tragic death in 1988 in a plane crash at the rim of the Grand Canyon. Though he was appointed on a quarter-time basis, Frensdorff with his characteristic zest soon had Navajoland moving toward a new vision of "total ministry," which he had effectively initiated in Nevada. He established a structure which provides regional vicars—one in each of the three regions—supplemented by lay pastors for the mission stations. Recognizing indigenous ordained leaders to be essential, Frensdorff introduced the "calling process," in which communities identified individuals for ordained and lay leadership. First fruit of this innovation was harvested with the ordination in 1988 of Buddy Arthur of Farmington.

The Episcopal Church's General Convention in Detroit in 1988 agreed to allow Navajoland Area Mission to select its next bishop, subject to affirmation by the House of Bishops. After receiving recommendations from the Navajoland Council, the Presiding Bishop appointed William Wolfrum, suffragan of Colorado, as part-time

*The ordination of Steven Plummer to the diaconate, 1975,
with Bishop Joseph M. Harte of Arizona.*

Photo by Ed Eckstein.

interim to serve until Navajoland made a choice.

At the June convocation in 1989 Steven Plummer was selected by the Navajos as their next bishop; the House of Bishops in September ratified their choice.

Good Shepherd Mission was the unofficial host for Plummer's consecration in March 1990, an event which joyously blended Anglican liturgy and Navajo ceremony. Fourteen bishops joined in laying hands on the third American Indian bishop of the Church after a Navajo medicine man sang a portion of the "beauty way" chant as he sprinkled corn pollen on the bishop-elect and his family.

Navajoland was joint host with the Diocese of Arizona for the 70th General Convention in Phoenix in July 1991. "Look forward to beauty," chanted Alfred Yazzie, the *Hataathlii* from Fort Defiance, as he gently sprinkled pollen while circling the altar at the opening service. The press acclaimed the American Indian ceremonial worship service, in which some 80 Indians from across America participated, the highlight of an otherwise troubled convention. Among those sharing wisdom of an ancient heritage with an audience of 5,000 were the four Indian bishops of the American Church—retired South Dakota suffragan Harold Jones (Sioux), William Wantland (Seminole) of Eau Claire, Steven Charleston (Choctaw) of Alaska, and Navajoland's Plummer. Highly visible were 40 Navajo and Niobrara (South Dakota Sioux) youth, trainees for 21st century leadership of the Indian Episcopal Church.

Crisis Arises: 1993

An unsettling setback faced Navajoland Area Mission in May 1993 when its bishop was publicly accused of sexual misconduct with a male teenager prior to his consecration. The accusation, which Plummer did not deny, was made by Gary Sosa, a recently ordained deacon in Navajoland, who alleged that Plummer had told him in November, 1990, of the impropriety and that the activity had extended over a two-year period.

The situation was made known to Presiding Bishop Edmond L. Browning by Plummer in 1991, at which time the youth was no longer a minor. Immediately upon learning of the misconduct, Browning, who has jurisdiction over the area mission, sent Plummer for medical and psychological evaluations which indicated he was not "at risk" for repeating the behavior. The youth involved did not come forward and there was no indication that he wished to press a complaint.

Browning in May, 1993, announced that Plummer would take a year's leave of absence and continue a "closely monitored program of therapy" after receiving a resolution from a special meeting of council, standing committee and staff of Navajoland, which expressed desire that Plummer "continue to be our bishop." The resolution, passed unanimously, stated that Plummer had "sought and received help in this matter through Christian prayer, modern psychology and traditional Navajo ways" and that they were convinced that the "past is left behind, and our concern is with the present and the future."

Browning appointed Bishop Wantland of Eau Claire as interim bishop. The Episcopal Council of Indian Ministry in August 1993 asked Plummer to resign, saying "such resignation is, in our opinion, essential for your own healing, for that of your family, and for all our people." While issuing a statement deploring sexual misconduct, ECIM requested that the Primate visit Navajoland to hear directly from communicants before making a decision on Plummer's future.

Browning complied with ECIM's request and following a three-day visit reported that "a large majority of the people favored the return of Bishop Plummer . . . his ministry to the non-English speaking Navajo, his ministry as a bridge between Anglican and Navajo cultures and traditions, and his ministry as a pastor with compassion for his people and a deep spirituality were affirmed at each of the area meetings."

To understand the view of the Navajo, one must ponder the traditional *Diné* ceremonials, including the highly complex curing rites, the aim of which is to restore harmony in the all-inclusive universe. Navajo believe that evil happens when people are out of harmony with nature and that harmony can be restored and balance attained through ceremonials performed by the *hataathlii*, just as Christians believe in confession and forgiveness. Plummer sought out the *hataathlii* and availed himself of healing ceremonials; he availed himself of Christian acts of contrition, and reconciliation with the victim and the accuser. The Christian primate listened intently to the Navajo who live in two worlds—the *Diné* and the *Biligaana*—and made his decision based on evaluation of the needs of Navajoland, the wishes of the people there, and of Plummer's present circumstances and abilities to carry out this ministry.

Browning issued a statement in April, 1994, disclosing that Plummer would return as bishop on June 1 and said that his decision was supported by the House of Bishops, which with the Primate has oversight responsibilities.

Browning, whose 12-year tenure as Presiding Bishop was to conclude at the end of 1997, made a farewell visit to Navajoland at its 1996 summer convocation, extending heartfelt good wishes to the people of the Episcopal Church's uniquely structured jurisdiction. It was during the convocation that announcement was made that four Navajos were new candidates for ordination: Margaret Hardy, Catherine Plummer, Eugene Shirleson and Inez Velarde.

EPISCOPAL MISSION AT FORT DEFIANCE, ARIZONA

Early in the spring of 1892 an Episcopal lay teacher arrived at Fort Defiance, the old military post which had been recast as Indian agency headquarters for the sprawling Navajo Reservation and site of a government school. He was George H. Wadleigh and his was a dual appointment—school teacher and designated presence of the Episcopal Church.

Though Wadleigh was to remain at Fort Defiance for only nine months, his brief stay set the stage for Episcopal work among the Navajo for the next 100 years.

Fort Defiance was one of the many military outposts founded for the sole purpose of subduing the Indian. Established in 1849, in the early aftermath of the Mexican-American War, it was the first fort to be located in the center of Navajo country. Located on the high desert plateau, 6,972 feet above sea level, the original little adobe fort was nestled beside a rare flowing stream surrounded by a grassy green meadow where the Navajo had long grazed sheep.

Fifteen years later, Fort Defiance would become headquarters of Kit Carson who ruthlessly rounded up 7,000 Navajo from the mesas, mountains, and deep red canyons. From Fort Defiance the hapless Navajo men, women and children were herded eastward on the appalling *hwelte*—the Long Walk—of 1864. Across the treeless landscape, the Navajo were marched 300 miles to Fort Sumner, New Mexico, and dumped for four years on a 40-square-mile barren area, known as Bosque Redondo, along the Pecos River.

When the four-year exile ended it was at Fort Defiance that the federal government set up Navajo resettlement headquarters. The old fort then became a center for distribution of food rations, seeds, tools and the sturdy little Spanish "churros" sheep—two animals for every surviving man, woman and child. The government spent $30,000 to replace the sheep that Kit Carson killed in his scorched earth tactics to dislodge the Navajo from their beloved desert domicile. The first desperate decades after resettlement were hard times for the Navajo; starvation was ever threatening. Out of this period grew the famous Navajo weaving and silverwork, both crafted as items for trade.

Under the Grant Peace Policy, within a year after the Navajos were allowed to return home, the Presbyterians sent a young eastern lady, Miss Charity Gaston, to start a school. The government agreed to furnish a schoolhouse and pay the missionary teacher $600 a year. When Miss Gaston arrived in her starched white shirt and long woolen skirt, she found several hundred Navajo families gathered around the old fort, living in dugouts awaiting rations, seeds and tools. Navajos walked as far as 30 miles once a week for rations, each receiving a pound of beef and a pound of wheat or corn for each day of the week. Occasionally a bit of salt and tobacco might be tossed in.

Eventually, a few Navajos sent their children to Miss Gaston's school, but most were wary of exposure to the "white man's magic." At best attendance was irregular; some days three children appeared, other days 33, and often curious adults wandered in, ate the school dinner and departed. Within a year, Miss Gaston also departed. She married a fellow Presbyterian missionary and went to work among the Pueblo people whom she labeled as "more civilized."

Meanwhile, Herbert Welsh, the renowned Philadelphia

philanthropist who had played a major role in Episcopal intercession among the Sioux, rode 300 miles on horseback to visit Fort Defiance in 1890. From a committed Episcopal family whose Indian advocacy in both Church and state spanned generations, Welsh wrote back to his eastern friends, "I am now more than ever impressed with the great needs of these [Navajo] people."

Women of Westchester County

It was through Welsh's connections with New York wealth that women of Westchester County became involved in Episcopal mission among the Navajo. On a memorable day in 1880 a meeting was held at the New York City Park Avenue residence of Mrs. John C. Jay:

> Miss Cornelia Jay presided, assisted by Miss Fanny Schuyler. It was then resolved to inaugurate the work of the "Woman's Auxiliary" in the parishes of Westchester County, the Association to be known as the "Westchester Branch of the Woman's Auxiliary to the Board of Missions." A board of managers was elected, among the members being Miss Schuyler. Miss Jay was continued as president. The first county meeting was held in Rye. Many clergy were present to represent "Home Missions." It was evident from the start that this group was to be especially interested in Indian missions.

In the same year, a report to the Commissioner of Indian Affairs describes Fort Defiance as a collection of old, dilapidated mud pig sties, sheep pens and nothing more. During that year the government built a boarding school for the Presbyterians; the school was described as a dark and dreary musty adobe dungeon, and the expected 60 pupils failed to appear.

In 1887 the federal government declared compulsory education for Indian children. Government agents drove about in their buckboards collecting Navajo children, delivering them to Fort Defiance to attend the government school or, as was often the case, dispatching the terrified children off to schools distant from the purifying sunlight of their desert home.

Five years after the compulsory education act, George Wadleigh and his wife appeared at Fort Defiance. Nearly a century later, a manuscript surfaced which detailed the history of the first 62 years of Episcopal mission among the Navajo. It was laboriously researched and written by the Venerable J. Rockwood Jenkins (1869-1963), who for three decades served as archdeacon of Arizona.

Wadleigh's latchkey to open Episcopal work among the Navajo had been provided by John Mills Kendrick, Bishop of Arizona and New Mexico territories, Herbert Welsh of the Philadelphia-based Indian Rights Association; and the women of the Westchester Branch of the Woman's Auxiliary. The New York women would provide unwavering support to Navajo needs for half a century.

During the hot summer and frosty autumn of 1892, Wadleigh organized a Sunday school, began a boys' choir, and wrote frequent letters to Miss Schuyler. Wadleigh's letters have mercifully been preserved. Some offer a glimpse of daily life around the old fort; others keenly call for cultural extinction of the Navajo.

Shortly after his arrival, he petitioned the Westchester women to fund a disciplinarian, "a male, to control the boys outside the classroom . . . and to send a medical missionary." It would be a few years before the latter saw response, but by year's end the disciplinarian appeared—Jeffrey Goulette, described as "one of Bishop Hare's 'boys,' a Dakota Indian, an Episcopalian, and a graduate of Haskell Institute." His salary was recorded at $50 a month; what eventually happened to Goulette is not recorded.

Bordering on the ludicrous was Wadleigh's plea to Miss Schuyler for a Christmas box which would contain:

> Neckwear . . . something like a Windsor scarf, made of silk or any other neat wash fabric. Like all Indians, bright colors are favorites. Now they have only an occasional red bandanna handkerchief, which they tie around their necks, and the effect is villainous, nor is it good for their health.

Wadleigh later admitted that the Windsor ties were not well received, and that the boys still preferred to wear their "villainous bandannas." In January of 1893, he hinted that he would possibly leave. Posterity records no further word of the man who brought Episcopal mission, albeit briefly, among the Navajo.

Archdeacon Jenkins reports stirring events around the old fort in the autumn of 1892. While the Indian agent, Dana Shipley, was busy trying to enforce the compulsory school act, a brawl ensued with Black Horse, the new headman, in which the agent was seriously injured. This occurred near Round Rock store and involved such well known characters as Chee Dodge, the trader Charley Hubbell and Arthur Hardy. Hubbell's trading post beneath old cottonwood trees today bears a national historical landmark designation and Chee Dodge would figure prominently in reservation politics for the next 50 years.

Agent Shipley was replaced shortly by Lieutenant Edwin H. Plummer of the 10th U.S. Infantry. A devout Episcopalian and a man of fine education and independent means, Plummer's name would be taken by a Navajo family which includes the first Navajo bishop.

In 1894 Bishop Kendrick disclosed in a letter to the Westchester women that the medical service was the greatest need among the Navajo. Expressing his distress at the total lack of medical care afforded the Navajo, the bishop expounded on the fact that the Navajo suffered from epidemics, such as measles, brought by the white man; that there was no treatment for the scourge of tuberculosis nor the dreaded eye disease, trachoma, which caused blindness. He wrote:

> The government will never provide a hospital for these people. The hospital could be made the center of field work over this portion of the Reservation. In time we could connect with this hospital a chapel for religious services. And another reason for locating the work of the ladies here is that it will be but a short distance from a transcontinental railroad line, and it can be visited by some of those who are especially interested in it.

The persuasive bishop had already found the woman to run the hospital the Westchester women would fund. She was Miss Eliza Thackara, daughter of an Episcopal clergyman of the Diocese of Florida. "She has good sense and good health," wrote the bishop:

> She was at one time the matron [of the government school] and is now one of the teachers. I met her here a year ago, and have become more acquainted with her on this visit, and it seems to me that the good opinion expressed of her is well deserved. I think that she will accept the appointment.

Eliza Thackara, Architect for Navajo Mission

Miss Thackara, whom the Navajo would give the name "Woman who laughs," accepted the appointment—she would remain 25 years—and the women of Westchester adopted the Navajo project with munificent generosity and enthusiasm that would span half a century.

Thus it was that the women, carrying dispensary kits and school books, brought lasting Episcopal witness to Navajoland. With Eliza Thackara in the vanguard in the 1890s, a hardy throng of eastern women—medical missionaries and school teachers—left hearth and home in snug New England villages to toil in this distant arid land of high plateaus, deep and abrupt canyons and fierce red rocks. They ministered first to the physical ills of the *Diné*.

When the Episcopal missionaries arrived, the *Diné* yet firmly held on to all the old beliefs centered on sacred mountains and monsters, all-powerful medicine men, myths and mysteries acted out in ceremony, *shin-dees*, skin-walkers and witches. The Westchester women, products of Victorian age finishing schools, had little capacity to fathom the soul of the Navajo. It would be almost a century before the Church would say that a person can be Indian and Christian, too.

When Miss Thackara started building her hospital, the Navajo had been released only a short generation previously from internment, and memories of the travail of the *hwelte* were still fresh. Elders could remember the peach orchards in Canyon de Chelly, destroyed by Kit Carson and his troops as they ruthlessly starved the Navajos toward surrender in a callous scorched earth tactic destroying fields, orchards, sheep, cattle, goats and horses of the *Diné*.

On October 20, 1894, the Indian Council met at the agency to act on the request for land for the proposed hospital. Readily agreeing that it would be "good that the white brothers and sisters were going to build a house for them to go when they were sick," the old chiefs balked on the site proposed by Agent Plummer and Miss Thackara. The Indians exclaimed, *"Shin-dee, shin-dee!"* Some of them walked off as fast as they could go and others drew their blankets over their heads and would not look. *Shin-dee* is one of the beliefs of the Navajo, even today. Miss Thackara recorded her interpretation:

> When a Navajo is about to die, he is carried out of his house, for he must not die in his house. Should any man, woman or child die in a house, it must be immediately destroyed. Should it be left standing, it would be death to anyone who would ever enter it, and so great is the dread of the place where it stood that no Navajo wants to pass near it.

Lieutenant Plummer shrewdly engaged the Navajos in selecting the site for the hospital, and within a couple of hours a sunny slope of the mesa about a mile from the Agency had been decided on as site for the hospital. Soon Miss Thackara would plant rows of cottonwood trees, which yet serenely stand and give off a rustling rhythm to the quiet of the high desert.

Miss Thackara, frequently described in the bishop's correspondence as a "genteel southern lady," supervised every single phase of construction of the hospital. At 7:30 in the morning she was at the stone quarry, overseeing the Navajo workers. The stone was a very white limestone that would eventually turn pinkish as it weathered.

A small and erect woman, Miss Thackara readily earned the confidence and trust of her eastern benefactors, local traders and, more importantly, of the Navajo. She was obviously a determined woman as well. Throughout the time she was overseeing the workmen at the quarry she visited all Indians within walking distance; she had no other way of getting about. However, she soon got a team of horses. An agent was dispatched 150 miles to the San Juan region where the best horses were to be found and at the most reasonable prices. Soon Miss Thackara was traveling in a new farm wagon to visit among the Navajo in their hogans. She must have made an impressive appearance, clad from head to foot in garments suited to the severe winter weather, including long rubber boots to protect her from the deep snow and dampness.

Her first water well proved an abject failure. She paid an expert well-digger $100 to dig 30 feet through the rocky hillside and line the well with stone to protect it from quicksand and cave-ins. The clear cool water, however, proved to be impregnated with alkali. Horses and cattle utterly refused to drink it. "You couldn't even cook beans in it," she wrote Miss Schuyler.

Building material had to be hauled over almost impassable roads. The lumber had to come from the government sawmill 16 miles away and all hardware and other purchased items had to be brought 30 miles from the railroad station at Gallup. In a letter to eastern benefactors in September, 1895, she remarked:

> I am so hopeful that means will come in to finish the buildings, that we may push the work and get in before winter. If the winter sets in early, we may have to suspend work until spring.

Winter did come early. A snowstorm arrived in early November. And work, often accomplished only after bonfires had been lit to keep the mortar from freezing, went on at a tedious slow pace.

1897: Hospital Opens

At last her dreams were fulfilled and her faith rewarded. On March 1, 1897, the doors of the hospital were thrown open. It was considered the finest building on the Navajo Reservation. The stone building shown out as a clear white landmark across the plains. In time the

Navajo would call it *Kin Ligai*—the White House.

The day after its opening the first patient was admitted—a man with a terrible cancer on his arm. It was a critical case, for had he died the superstitious fears of the Navajos would have rendered the hospital a failure. His recovery was rapid and complete, and the success of the hospital was assured. In the early years Miss Thackara, no doubt, found many Navajo unwilling to avail themselves of the facility. Sick Navajos were appalled by the impersonal loneliness of hospital life; they were used to the tender solicitude of a whole family, and by the "sing" which, according to the Navajo beliefs, brought the ill into direct communion with the spirits. Many Navajos yet believe that once a death has occurred in any building, it should at once be burned. Miss Thackara did not burn her new hospital building when a death occurred and certain of the Navajos assumed the building was surely contaminated by evil. In the Navajo ethos, a corpse lost all identity as kin, friend or clan mate, and became, instead, a source of supernatural contagion.

Bishop Kendrick made his first visit to the hospital in August. He held a service in the dining room of the government school; but more significant was a baptism held at the hospital. Two children were baptized—children who had been virtually given to the mission by relatives. One was a small boy named Edward Plummer, in delicate health, who did not live long. The other child was a girl named Glympba, who belonged to the household of One-Eyed Billy, a well-known medicine man. Glympba's mother had recently died and as nobody seemed to want to take care of the child, she was handed over to the mission. Glympba was among the first of many orphaned children who from time to time were brought up at the mission. Some were legally adopted. Miss Thackara was especially attracted to Glympba and it was her hope that she might be educated while keeping in touch with her own people, and thus be of service to them and to the tribe, extending more widely the influence of the mission. Miss Thackara would realize her wish; Glympba went away to Phoenix Indian School and returned to work with her devoted patroness who would later describe Glympba as "very capable and most helpful."

Old baptismal records of the summer of 1902 show that 14 candidates from the mission hospital had been baptized. Among the names were three Gormans, two Gatewoods and Henry Yahkee. One assumes the latter to be the "little" Yah Kee, the Gatewoods to be of the family of the early interpreter, and the Gormans progenitors of the famed Indian artist, R.C. Gorman, whose family came from Fort Defiance. Soon there would be a marriage ceremony at the mission—Nelson Carl Gorman and Alice Peshlaka.

By 1907, which marked a full decade of service, the hospital had gained a true respect from the Navajo. But funding problems continued. In 1907 Miss Thackara wrote a business-like statement of expenses:

> To run the hospital as we have during the past year will cost $5,000 and this does not include any improvements, but covering, I believe, all expenses. It pays the salaries: the doctor, $500; the nurse, $500; interpreter, $300; housekeeper, $420; my own salary, and the Indian assistants we must employ; our drugs, forage, supplies, etc. I would be relieved if I could make my budget at six to eight thousand!

However, after the first decade contributions began coming not only from the Westchester Branch of the Woman's Auxiliary, which from the beginning had consistently and generously sponsored the undertaking, but also from branches in Chicago, Pittsburgh, Detroit, Florida, South Carolina, Eastern Maryland as well as from recently organized branches in Arizona and New Mexico. Sunday school Advent offerings bolstered the cash flow and the old standby, Indian Rights Association, made a special donation.

Constant changes in personnel were a distinct handicap to the work. Bishop Kendrick wrote the Westchester women that some of the helpers had been unsatisfactory and had to be removed. He continued:

> Others have been satisfactory from a professional standpoint, but they were not missionaries . . . the result was that they tired of the work; it was lonesome for them; they were homesick . . . and left as soon as their year was out. They were everything that could be demanded socially, personally and professionally, but the *missionary spirit was not in them.*

Archdeacon Jenkins suggests the mile and a quarter altitude contributed to the constant change in personnel. He wrote:

> With the best intentions in the world on the part of many of the workers when they arrived, adjusting to the climate and high altitude [6,972 feet] was cause for a decided lowering of morale. Added to this was the isolation and extreme remoteness from customary pleasures and social contacts and the amenities of life. All these things together would work on the nerves and produce irritability and even depression.

Ensuing years brought both exhilarating triumphs and dismal disappointments. The bishop records that "powers that be" at Fourth Avenue in New York (Episcopal Church headquarters) were making tedious inquiries. A long sought deaconess proved to be autocratic, "in fact positively cruel." In 1908, 130 patients had been cared for. Many eye cases had been treated because of trachoma, so widely prevalent among the Navajo.

Eventually the federal government erected a well equipped hospital at Fort Defiance and the mission facility was used exclusively for the treatment of eye cases.

Rose Wauneka's Story

Rose Wauneka was among the hundreds of Navajo women who came in the early part of this century to Good Shepherd Mission. Her story was told in "We Walk in Beauty" [*Ho'zho'go Na Shadoo*], a Resource Guide for the 1976-77 Church School Missionary Offering project. Grandmother Wauneka's story likely parallels the experiences of many other Navajo women of her generation:

> I was born at Black Mountain—way up on Black Mountain. I was living with my grandmother since I was small. At Black Mountain we have to go three miles up the mountain to get a jugful of water; and there were so many people at that one small spring that we had to wait 2-3 hours to fill our bucket.
>
> During those years it was hard to get food. The people don't have no flour. They have to grind corn. We had to gather wild tea in the summer. That's all the "coffee" we have, and it wasn't much of anything! We don't know what candy means. But we have plenty of goat's milk to drink with corn bread, made all different ways: blue bread, dumplings and mush.
>
> And we pick all kinds of berries—several kinds you can eat. They grow in certain spots on the mountain and taste salty. There were some fruit trees in Canyon de Chelly. And, of course, pinon: roast, eat raw, and grind.
>
> Later, when I was six or seven, there is a trading post but too darn far and too little money. They just bring home a little from there. Some of the people used to be really wild, so they keep us out of town. Now they know about coffee and sugar and flour. The only trading post was Hubbell's—50-60 miles—all day and overnight trip.

Good Shepherd Mission was a hospital. One of my sisters was there sick. Mother took me to Good Shepherd; and then she said there were some children who were baptized, so she put me in to get baptized in 1908.

They start the school in Chinle in 1911 or 1913. They were hunting for school children around, hogan to hogan. My grandmother had to give me up. I was seven years old. We went to school about five years and they start talking about sending us away to school and ask us where we want to go. I sign up for Sherman Institute. At that time you sign up for three or five years.

We left Chinle in 1920, in May, and of course I went to school three years and my last year I was there I got trachoma—Yuma kids all had it. We caught it. So my time was up and I came back to Fort Defiance, and went straight into the hospital at Good Shepherd and the eye doctor said I had to stay.

There were old sheds for chickens, turkeys and rabbits. We ate that and mutton, mutton, mutton. And I was a patient for three months. Operation on my eyes and I got my sight back better, and then one afternoon the doctor said I was all right and what did I want to do. I thought it over: I thought the Mission had help me in every way through prayer, and I said I would like to come back here and help you with the work because the Mission help me. I took the cook's job for patients about two years. My husband and I, we got married at Good Shepherd Mission, and of course there was no one from his family who knew about coming to church. My husband only went through fourth grade and I used to teach him every night—writing and English.

My husband took sick. And then at the end of his life he told me you should go on with Good Shepherd Mission and don't ever leave your church; he told me, with our little kids standing there. And that made me feel even more that the Mission was important. That was many years ago.

Anne E. Cady.
Courtesy, Archives of the Episcopal Church.

Anne E. Cady—UTO Missionary

Out of Alaska to Fort Defiance in 1915 came a nurse, Anne E. Cady, who had been a United Thank Offering missionary of the Woman's Auxiliary. Due to the severity of the Alaskan climate, Miss Cady's health had broken, but after a few months of rest, she was eager for work again. When invited to go to Fort Defiance, she cheerfully accepted the appointment. She was especially well fitted and qualified for the position because of her former experience in working among Native peoples.

Three years after Miss Cady's arrival, Miss Thackara retired, on October 1, 1919, after 25 years of active service. She could resign with good grace and complete satisfaction, because she could turn over the work to one who was so well fitted to take her place and to carry on with every chance of success. Well might Miss Cady report, "She has left behind her an influence which only the consecrated life of a 'gentlewoman' could leave, and which will be felt for years to come."

Miss Cady propagated growth of the Navajo work until her retirement a quarter of a century later. She initiated a field work program which Good Shepherd has continued. Lively congregations still worship at two outstation chapels which Miss Cady began—St. Anne's at Sawmill, 14 miles north of Fort Defiance, and St. Mark's at Coalmine, eight miles to the east.

In the next decade, little by little new buildings were added and old ones enlarged on the 48-acre plot deeded by the Navajos. Central heating was installed; an electric plant replaced the old hand lamps that had for many years been a menace and nuisance. The Westchester women sent $1,500 to erect a stone entrance to the compound. The entrance, surmounted by a cross, took the place of an iron ranch gate. A legacy from the estate of Joanna Hagan of Philadelphia was used to build, just north of the main building, a stone house containing two bedrooms and a bath which could be used as a guest house for visitors. Many of the old buildings are still in use for the delivery of community social and economic development programs.

The Woman's Auxiliary of West Virginia and Mrs. J. Hull Browning of Newark presented Miss Cady with a new Ford automobile. The many trips to Gallup and across the rough country of the reservation previously had to be made in freight wagons.

Two major events in the life of the mission occurred in the mid-1920s. Miss Thackara came back to Good Shepherd for a wonderful Christmas visit, and remained for several pleasure-filled months.

The second event was far less joyful. A new bishop appeared. Ignoring the fact that women had for three decades founded and funded the Good Shepherd mission, Bishop Walter Mitchell declared that a man must be in charge—"It might be embarrassing for [the chaplain] to serve under a woman!" Miss Cady was obliged to step down from her official position to become assistant superintendent. She accepted the demotion with grace and continued her work. The bishop appointed as superintendent William B. Heagerty, MD, whose medical experience was expected to be an advantage. His stay was brief.

Another transition was quietly occurring. Miss Cady had spoken to the need for a school; a new wing on the main building made room for it. Gradually Good Shepherd became an orphanage. The government assumed more medical responsibilities for trachoma patients, but when the children were discharged many had no home to return to, so they remained at the mission. The reservation superintendent and Chee Dodge, the head man of the whole tribe, heartily approved this new plan and Miss Cady heartily cooperated.

When Dr. Heagerty resigned, the bishop sent Archdeacon Jenkins as temporary superintendent to assume charge of the religious work of the mission with Miss Cady. Rose Crosby (Wauneka), a Navajo, continued as helper. An attractive rectory had been built just across the driveway from the main building. Archdeacon Jenkins and his sister, Miss Lucy H. Jenkins, were the first occupants of the new house, which is yet the home of Good Shepherd's vicars.

In July, 1929, the new superintendent, Walter L. Beckwith, arrived. In connection with the program of the orphanage and school, regular evangelistic visits were made to Indian camps by Beckwith and Miss Cady, assisted by *Tsi-Hi Notah* as interpreter. Though Beckwith soon departed, Miss Cady carried on, setting up clinics and classes at distant trading posts. Archdeacon Jenkins described evangelistic outreach activities:

> One of the most important field stations was at a saw mill, about 15 miles north of Fort Defiance and on very high land, the altitude being nearly 9,000 feet. Here were several good cottages of officials and other employees, and many Indians came from their homes to work at the mill. Miss Cady started visiting this settlement, doing clinical work and holding services in a school house.

In 1932 the bishop sent yet another clergyman, S.W. Creasy, to be superintendent of Good Shepherd Mission. Miss Cady was again demoted to assistant. He stayed scarcely two years.

Miss Janet Waring, vice president for Woman's Auxiliary for the Diocese of New York, wrote an article for *The Spirit of Missions* in which she described a visit to Good Shepherd Mission in 1929.

> The only habitation in which we could take refuge from the sudden and unexpected downpour was the hogan of *Hosteen Nez*, a full-blooded Navajo who in years gone by had worked for the founder of our mission, Miss Thackara. We found the family gathered in the one-room hogan, a low dome-like dwelling built of wattles and clay, with a door and a place for the smoke of fire to escape but no windows and with dirt floor. Furniture there was not, beds there were not, many sheep skins with an occasional Pendleton blanket indicated the sleeping places.
>
> After an hour the rain stopped. Then *Hosteen* harnessed the horses to the big lumber wagon, put boards across for seats. He and his sons waded in deep water above their waists, testing the river bottom, then by forcing the horses through the stream, we made a triumphal passage through the angry waters.

Now we were in sight of the mission and of the belfry tower of the little Chapel of the Good Shepherd. The sun was pushing through heavy clouds and there lay before us a scene as pastoral as any ever seen by the shepherds of Palestine. Before us over a wide stretch of valley were flocks of beautiful white sheep, three to four hundred, enfolded and watched by Navajo women. The Navajo women own and are the custodians of the sheep.

Picturesque are the clothes of the women . . . silver buttons on their tight-fitting waists, and often a silver necklace of remarkable workmanship, as well as bright beads. Their skirts, of which they wear four to eight, are very full and each has a flounce measuring from 12 to 15 yards around. Their long black hair is done in a sort of "bob-knot" at the back of the neck and all wound 'round with a woolen string.

We had arrived at the gateway, surmounted by its stone cross. To the left was the chapel built in memory of Miss Cornelia Jay. Its bell rings out over the silent desert for daily services. The forty acres on which the school stands was deeded to the Church by the Navajos themselves.

It was, I learned, the season for sheep dipping, and Fort Defiance is one of the chief government dips. There are strict regulations obliging the Navajos to bring their flocks here once a year, to be driven through the long deep trough of medicated bath.

Later from my bedroom window in the mission, I looked out on a picturesque encampment spread over the wide country, the Navajo families gathered around their camp fires, sheep skins drying on the sand. A flicker of twenty or more camp fires made an unforgettable picture.

The Mission in the Great Depression

The Great Depression of the 1930s very naturally affected the welfare, not only of the Good Shepherd Mission, but of the Navajo people generally. It was especially felt in 1933 when there was practically no market for blankets or silver jewelry, and no government funds available for providing work for the Navajos. It was a particularly painful time for the Navajo when the federal government launched a controversial stock reduction program, slaughtering the sheep by the thousands "for the good of the economy."

Good Shepherd Mission strained all its resources to provide food in exchange for labor; often Indian men and women would come 100 miles to work for flour, sugar and coffee! Intense grazing had injured pasturage, and there was little vegetation to catch and absorb the scant rains that fell. Erosion rapidly set in and added to the problem. The Government Recovery Program very tardily rectified the erosion to a certain extent; dams were built for flood control, and roads were repaired for travel over the reservation. A new government reorganization plan combined four administrative centers into one, with many sub-agencies, and also the Navajos were given a greater share in administration.

The year 1934 saw yet another clergyman come to take charge. He was Frederick A. McNeil of Phoenix, who would remain two years, to be succeeded by James R. Helms, rector of St. Mark's Church in Mesa, Arizona.

As a result of the depression, cuts had to be made in appropriations from the Board of Missions of the Church, while at the same time living expenses were increased. Yet no children were turned away, and even more were accepted, an act of sublime faith. The government came to the aid of the mission by a special appropriation because the mission was, in fact, caring for so many of the little "wards of the government."

Most encouraging was an unexpected gift from the east. Mrs. Samuel (Ethel Chaney) Thorne of New York had been a great supporter of missionary work in general, and her greatest joy was in the Good Shepherd work among the Navajos. She left in her will the residue of her estate to the Woman's Auxiliary of New York to be used as they saw fit in advancing missionary work. The first and largest appropriation from this fund was made to the Good Shepherd Mission for a Thorne Memorial dining room, kitchen, school, and living quarters building. Construction was initially contracted to a white man who failed to perform. Howard McKinley, known for his foresight and courage, said, "We Navajos can build the building; we don't need a white man." The work began.

Miss Cady retired in 1940 after 25 years of dedicated and devoted service. War came to America the next year and Helms was called to become a chaplain in the Army Air Corps. Then two more clergy came and went—Cecil Harris and Hector Thompson.

The David Clark Decade

In 1943 a clergyman came to stay a full decade. He was David W. Clark, who with his father and brother John had been missionaries among the Sioux Indians in South Dakota. Early in his tenure Good Shepherd entered into yet another phase of service, that of working cooperatively with the newly established Navajo Child Welfare Office which assumed child placement responsibilities. Previously all matters of child case study, admittance and care were investigated, financed and followed through by the mission staff. The new tribal program purchased foster care services from the mission at $40 per month per child for 60 children. Good Shepherd offered children a nurturing and secure atmosphere and supplied their personal needs and clothing during the school year.

Until 1942 the mission had operated a school of eight grades for resident orphan children and a few boarders from a distance. Then the boarding school was closed and the facility functioned as a dormitory for students attending the government school.

With spiritual shepherding by Clark and his helpers, baptisms and confirmations increased. Meanwhile, Bishop Mitchell retired, succeeded by Arthur Barksdale Kinsolving II, a member of a large and influential church family. His father had been Missionary Bishop of Brazil.

In the early post-war years the Division of Town and Country Work of the Executive Council of the Church established an intercultural rural institute for graduate students which operated for 10 weeks each summer. Twelve students worked at Good Shepherd. Additionally, the mission became closely associated with the Committee on Literacy for the Navajos, a project of Home Missions Council of the federal Council of Churches. Under leadership of Howard McKinley, the literacy program headquartered at Good Shepherd worked on translating parts of the prayer book into the Navajo language.

In 1948 the mission launched yet another new program when a school opened for pre-school-age children—a predecessor of Head Start. Twenty children, many non-English speaking, were enrolled. Another innovative approach was pioneered by the mission with a Shepherd's School, an outreach to children who spent their youth in remote areas of the reservation herding the family's sheep. Twenty were brought to Good Shepherd twice annually for instruction and care. Other examples of vitality during the decade in which David Clark served as vicar of Good Shepherd included a scholarship program to assist young Navajos in their studies away from the reservation.

During Clark's tenure, the work at Sawmill and Coalmine experienced significant growth. A community house was built at Sawmill and electricity installed through help of volunteer electricians. The organized work which was so patiently begun and carried on by Miss Cady was appropriately called St. Anne's Mission. Over the New

Mexico state line, at the old coalmine station, where services had been held for 14 years in a tiny house and in an old garage, permission was granted by the Navajo Council to erect a suitable building, and a community house was dedicated on July 10, 1952, as St. Mark's Mission.

From the vicar's progress report, mailed to friends of the Mission:

> In the past 10 years [1942-1952] the church's ministry among the Navajo people has moved forward at Good Shepherd Mission with the cooperation of several thousand people to whom this News Letter is sent. Because of your constant response to the extreme needs of the Navajo People your church has restored the plant of 10 buildings to a useful center for its field program and a mission home for orphans. One hundred thousand dollars have been expended on this restoration, and $33,000 on the Thorne building, which (after many years) is now two-thirds completed and in daily use. At outlying stations, two community houses have been erected. Furnishings for all these buildings have been put in excellent condition.
>
> Five workers now use personal cars, which, with a mission-owned truck and "suburban" (station wagon) have greatly extended the range of our ministry; with these increased facilities for travel, regular work has been established in six outlying areas. The staff of the mission has grown from six in 1942 to 20 in 1952. Our family of orphan children has increased from 25 to 60. The larger parish congregation of Good Shepherd Mission now numbers about a thousand baptized persons, with hundreds more affiliated in one way or another, and seeking to learn more about the kingdom of God among men.
>
> In the past 10 years there have been 819 baptisms and 292 confirmations. The Navajo people are now participating in the organized life of the church. In 1942 there were 10 members in the Woman's Auxiliary; now there are 75 members in four groups. There is a chapter of the Girls' Friendly Society and a junior branch of the Brotherhood of St. Andrew.
>
> In 1942 there were 15 children in Sunday school; now there are 400 enrolled in Christian education classes, with a full-time director of Christian Education on staff. A Bishop's Committee of seven members has been functioning for several years. The annual appropriation by the National Council for work at this mission has been increased

from $3,000 in 1942 to $11,200 in 1952. With a steadily increasing membership, the congregation of Good Shepherd Mission has assumed a greater share in the church's mission to others. In 1944 the combined quota and assessment totaled $63; for 1952 more than $1,000 has been given for the general missionary work of the whole church.

It was also during Clark's tenure that a young New Yorker and Yale graduate came to Good Shepherd as Clark's assistant. Davis Given was a candidate for holy orders and kinsman to the Arthur Vining Davis family. Given eventually became the mission's vicar and superintendent, serving until 1962.

Clark resigned in 1953 and was replaced by Paul L. West, who left after a single year. During that memorable year, however came a gift which would change the landscape of the old mission compound.

Impressive New Chapel

The Arthur Vining Davis Foundation granted $250,000 for construction of a new and larger chapel and clergy residence. The old chapel, built as a loving memorial to Miss Cornelia Jay 44 years previously, had cracking walls and because it had been constructed on partly filled land it was no longer entirely safe. Given in memory of Elisabeth H. Davis by her husband, Arthur Vining Davis, the new chapel had as architect John Gah Meem, whose buildings surround the Santa Fe plaza, and whose father had been a missionary in Brazil, serving under Kinsolving's father, the Bishop of Southern Brazil.

Work was begun in the fall of 1954 and the bishop laid the cornerstone of the partly completed building in January 1955. The chapel was strikingly designed to harmonize with the land and people; Navajo craftsmanship and symbolism are represented in its vessels and furnishings. The first services were held during Holy Week 1955.

On July 10, 1955, the chapel was consecrated by Kinsolving in the presence of the Bishop of Utah and Bishop Coadjutor of the Rio Grande. Among eminent visitors were the donor, the architect, John Gah Meem, the Venerable Vine Deloria Sr. of South Dakota, and superintendents of other Episcopal missions among the Navajo. The three bishops joined in confirming a class of 30 from Good Shepherd and its stations.

The Trail Ahead, published in 1955 by the National Council, describes the consecration of the new chapel:

Four hundred Navajos and two hundred non-Indians

*The 1955 consecration of the new chapel of
the Fort Defiance.*

came together at the Mission of the Good Shepherd, to participate in the dedication of the new chapel. A non-Navajo-speaking Indian clergyman preached; his words were interpreted by a Navajo. After the service there was a procession to the new clergy house which too was dedicated. In the traditional Navajo manner feasting followed, and in the background there was Navajo music by Navajo musicians. The service was one the Navajos themselves had requested as the proper way to launch the use of the new mission buildings.

Unfortunately, the chapel was constructed on shifting soil and two extensive structural repairs have been required, including one as recently as 1990, for which the Arthur Vining Davis Foundation and United Thank Offering provided funding.

20 Priests in 34 Years

Given continued as vicar and superintendent until 1962. Kinsolving also retired in 1962 and was succeeded by Joseph M. Harte, who as a young priest had worked among Osage Indians in Oklahoma. During the next half dozen years the bishop would send a half dozen priests to serve Good Shepherd—E. Jack Fowler, Reginald Rodriguez (the first Indian; he was from nearby Laguna Pueblo), Richard Stinson (who appointed the first Navajo field workers), John R. Davis, DeWitt Smith, and in 1968 a Sioux priest, Harold S. Jones, whose brief tenure is yet reverently remembered. Good Shepherd was served for two years by the new Navajo priest, Steven Plummer, who would later be sent to the Utah region.

Margaret Hardy, an aunt of Plummer, came to Good Shepherd as a baby. Her mother had died when the baby was about 15 months old. Her father felt he could not properly take care of the child, so he took her to the Good Shepherd missionaries. She grew up at the mission and was sent to Phoenix College and returned to work at the mission as a stenographer. Mrs. Hardy, a candidate for ordination to the diaconate after serving many years as a lay pastor, recently spoke of the frequent clergy changes at Good Shepherd:

> Fr. Jones's assistant was Fr. James Thompson. After Fr. Jones left us to be bishop in South Dakota, we had Fr. Edward O. Moore. His brother is Canon Roswell Moore who was Province VIII President. We've seen lots of change!

Philip Allen, an Oglala Sioux, served as Good Shepherd vicar 1979-84. In 1983, Bishop Frensdorff ordained David Jasmer, a scholar and teacher at the tribal high school, as non-stipendiary clergy under special canons. He served for a full decade as assisting vicar for outstations and as supply clergy for Good Shepherd.

Four more interim vicars came and went: John Byron, William Tye, Jack Fowler and David Gipp. In 1986 a young native of Massachusetts who had worked in Tanzania as well as at the Wind River Reservation in Wyoming was called by Good Shepherd. He was George Sumner, who departed after three sound and positive years for doctoral study at Yale.

Sumner was followed by Mark MacDonald, who came as vicar with his young bride in 1989. The couple immediately began study of the difficult Navajo language and within a year MacDonald required less and less services of a translator. The Minnesota native, who has distant Indian forebears, had built a Native American worshiping community at his previous post in Portland, Oregon. During his

Navajoland tenure he rose to national and provincial prominence in cross-cultural liturgical and evangelism initiatives. In his first year as vicar, active communicant strength of the southeast region of Navajoland Area Mission showed a 28 percent growth pattern. However, with the unsettled situation surrounding the bishop's leave of absence and discord in the area mission, MacDonald answered a call in late 1993 to return to his native Minnesota to a joint appointment as Indian theological trainer for the diocese and vicar for churches on the Red Lake Reservation.

Upon MacDonald's departure, William Wantland, the interim bishop, appointed James Speer as vicar. Speer, who grew up in southern California, had attended seminary at Vancouver School of Theology. Following ordination he served 14 years in Canada, working among the Tahltan Indians of North British Columbia and the Cree in Alberta Province. His stay at Good Shepherd was brief and by year's end both Speer and David Jasmer, the non-stipendiary school teacher, had departed. Speer returned to Canada and Jasmer transferred to the Diocese of Rio Grande. Work was carried on primarily by the lay pastors—Margaret Hardy and Pauline Dick—with frequent visits by the Rev. David Bailey of Phoenix, who was appointed by the Presiding Bishop as unofficial assistant or mentor to Plummer in 1995. In early 1996, David Suttcliffe of Milwaukee was called as the 20th vicar in 34 years.

Good Shepherd Mission in 1992 celebrated its centennial and hundreds gathered at Fort Defiance for the celebration at the 17th annual convocation of the Navajoland Area Mission. It was in 1892 that a layman-teacher named George H. Wadleigh came as a forerunner to Fort Defiance. Though his stay was but for a brief nine months, this man, whose subsequent life is wholly lost in history, must have planted seeds that grew in this rugged, obdurate land where the old people at dusk still see skin-walkers moving up mysterious arroyos through pinon and juniper undergrowth.

Leaves of Miss Eliza Thackara's cottonwood trees still rustle in the evening breeze that moves in fits and spurts across the old Good Shepherd compound. Her white limestone hospital building has weathered considerably during its almost 100 harsh winters, but it still serves as the center of a Navajo Episcopal community. Miss Thackara—and the Westchester women—will be glad to know that the ministry she started on this high arid plateau in the southeastern edge of the vast Navajo Nation has withstood adversity and survived. The woman whom the Navajos named "Woman Who Laughs" must surely smile.

NEW MEXICO: SAN JUAN MISSION

On the eve of World War I, a tiny, spunky, Kentucky-born woman found it necessary to flee from her teaching position in Mexico City, barely escaping Pancho Villa's troops, to wait out the political unrest across the border in El Paso, Texas. Mattie C. Peters, barely five feet tall and weighing less than 100 pounds, would never return to her south-of-the-border teaching position. Instead, she would establish a new Episcopal mission among the Navajo called the San Juan Mission, located on the outskirts of Farmington, New Mexico, only a stone's throw from the boundary of the vast reservation.

In 1914 Frederick B. Howden, who served 24 years as Bishop of New Mexico and Southwest Texas (renamed the Diocese of the Rio Grande in 1975), journeyed for three days from Albuquerque to visit St. John's congregation at Farmington, a small trading center of about 1,500. The bishop visited the northeast edges of the enormous Navajo reservation and learned that the government provided no medical services for the nomad Navajos of the region. Approaching native mission from a different perspective than that of his brother bishops of earlier generations, who proposed to superimpose European values on native societies, Howden discerned need for an integrated program of medical, social and religious work among the Navajo which would reflect appreciation for their own religion, culture and customs.

The bishop decided to name the new mission after the mighty San Juan River which rises in the Colorado Rocky Mountains and meanders westward, cutting through high plateaus to join the Colorado River and then charge through the Grand Canyon. In the long dry season the San Juan is a gentle stream; in springtime when snows melt in the mountains, the river is wild and raging.

The bishop told his annual convocation in May, 1916, of his plans for a small hospital in the vicinity of the Navajo reservation. He sought out Miss Peters, who was still biding her time on the border, and offered her the missionary post. This spirited woman rose to the challenge, knowing she would face loneliness, uncertainty and hardships. The bishop then prevailed on the National Mission Board to appoint Miss Peters as the first woman missionary for his missionary district. Her salary was $50 a month.

She arrived in Farmington in bitterly cold December weather in 1916. The bishop had provided a small dilapidated four-room rental house near the San Juan River. With some borrowed furnishings Miss Peters, with a Navajo school girl as her helper and interpreter, by early January, 1917, began the Episcopal work among the Navajos of New Mexico. She acquired a stock of simple medicines and converted one of the rooms of the small house into a combination dispensary and first-aid station where cuts, bruises, minor ailments and a bed patient could be cared for.

The word went out among the Navajo that there was a woman who lived beside the San Juan River who would help Indians, and soon the Navajos, at first hesitant and shy, appeared. Throughout the first year, she worked virtually alone. For critical cases she had the assistance of a skilled local physician and surgeon, Dr. A. M. Smith, who became impressed with Miss Peter's work and volunteered his services without remuneration. It soon became obvious that more facilities were necessary and the bishop sent the priest-in-charge of St. John's Mission to seek funding in the east. Enough money was raised to build two small wards which would accommodate two patients each, a small dispensary, another bedroom for an additional worker, storerooms and a cellar. The bishop found a missionary nurse, Emily Ireland of New York City, and for the first time in 14 months Miss Peters had a professional medical worker.

In 1918 the devastating influenza epidemic reached the Navajo Reservation. The two women were taxed to the utmost to care for the vast number of Navajos who came in from the desert seeking help as the influenza struck more and more families. Blankets were spread on the floors of the mission and soon these valiant women were caring for as many as 30 patients at a time, in addition to dispensing medicine, comforting the bereaved and helping to bury the dead. Dr. Smith helped when he could but the burden was on the two women along with a new volunteer from Virginia.

The San Juan Hospital

No sooner had the little mission survived the influenza epidemic than the San Juan River, swollen by the melting snows and heavy rains in the mountains, went on a rampage and inundated the lowlands. When the water receded it was apparent that the mission buildings had sustained structural damage and were on verge of collapse. A decision was made to move the mission to higher ground and the bishop acquired 78 acres on a mesa up the incline from the original site. Soon money was raised to begin work on a small combined hospital and chapel. Miss Peters went east and raised funds to furnish the new 20-bed hospital through numerous speaking engagements. Meanwhile, Miss Ireland, whose around-the-clock labor did irreparable damage to her own health, departed. The young Virginia volunteer married a desert dweller many years her senior and also departed. Eventually another graduate nurse, Sara McIntyre, joined the staff, and subsequently came Thelma K. Kelm, who had trained at the Good Samaritan Hospital in Los Angeles. In a 1925 issue of *The Spirit of Missions*, Miss Peters wrote:

> It was my privilege to be the first one sent by the Church to this far-away corner of the Navajo country to establish, first of all, a dispensary work and to open a house by the side of the trail, which for seven years was a Mission of hope and help to hundreds of Indians living on the large Reservation . . .

> After six years of hoping and planning, through gifts of United Thank Offering and many friends, the Mary E. Hart Memorial Hospital and Chapel stand today not far from the Reservation line . . . Before we could get the house into any kind of order, we were called upon to open the wards to sick folks.

> An epidemic of measles was raging out on the Reservation and many children, and even men and women, had already died for want of medical help. During the remainder of December we cared for patients in the wards and visited and cared for stricken Indians in nearby camps. Just three days before Christmas, a young girl passed away. She was the fifth child of one family to die within two weeks. Her death cast a shadow over our preparations for Christmas festivities.

> But, by Christmas morning everything was in readiness. We entertained our Indian guests, 150 strong. We did not attempt a full service, but the Christmas story was told through an interpreter. It was a touching sight to see those pagan Indians—as many as could be crowded into the chapel—on their knees while the simple prayers were said.

Because of ill health, Miss Peters had to resign in 1924. During eight years she had brought Navajo mission significantly forward, leaving a well run hospital and two field outstations, at Carson's Trading Post and at Aneth, in Utah. Both were operated by women.

The bishop placed the vicar of the St. John's Mission in charge of the San Juan Navajo facility. Conflict frequently arose between the clergyman and the hospital staff. On one occasion the bishop had to intervene and surprisingly decided against the clergyman. Staff positions and nurses were appointed by the Mission Board in New York and their salaries, pitifully low, were paid by the United Thank Offering of the Women of the Episcopal Church (UTO). Nurses who did volunteer for mission work were far more interested in foreign service than in the isolated loneliness of northern New Mexico. Over several years both clergy and nurses came and went but the little mission managed to survive.

Bishop Howden in 1927 interviewed Robert Yarborough Davis, a native of South Carolina, for a growing parish in New Mexico. After offering him the post in an attractive growing community, the bishop turned the conversation to San Juan Indian Mission, a project which brought the bishop grief, trouble and worry, yet which he loved dearly. Davis, who was looking to work in New Mexico for health reasons, later admitted that he had "only a mild curiosity about Navajo and no intention whatsoever to become a missionary among them." However, by the next day he found himself persuaded to go to San Juan, stay a month, and consider the position. Davis set out from Albuquerque for the two-day journey to Farmington and quickly found himself enchanted with the land which he described as "fantastically beautiful and constantly changing, unearthly heavenly colors." Mile after mile of New Mexico desert was dotted only occasionally by a lonely Navajo hogan, an occasional trading post and strange rock formations. Captivated by the country and the challenge, Davis accepted the position. At a salary of $2,100 a year, he would be chaplain at San Juan Hospital, general missionary to the Navajos, vicar of St. John's in Farmington and have pastoral care of all Episcopalians in San Juan County. He remained in the position for 23 years.

St. Luke's-in-the-Desert

Lena D. Wilcox, who had experience among Indians in both Oklahoma and New Mexico, began work in the mid-1920s at Carson's Trading Post, located 28 miles out in the desert. The usual dispensary, consisting of simple remedies, first-aid equipment and clothes for the needy were provided in this most modest beginning. In writing on selection of the site for the mission station, Miss Wilcox said:

> Since "the people" are nomadic, following their sheep herds, they do not live in villages. The Church, in order to reach them at all, must go to where they do most resort, at a trading post.

The next step was to build a chapel, and the Woman's Auxiliary of the Province of the Southwest raised $1,000 for the project. O. J. Carson, the trader, deeded a 10-acre tract across the Gallegos arroyo from the trading post. It had been decided from the beginning that the house of worship would be in keeping with the stark beauty of the Indian country, with an extremely simple exterior. Small windows would protrude from log beams, a small bell tower would be topped by a cross, and a heavy hand-made door would be painted scarlet. The walls of brown sandstone were quarried from the surrounding country and laid up with adobe mud by the Navajos. The logs were hauled 60 miles over rough desert roads. The cement for the foundations and other materials had to be trucked from Farmington. Even the water for mixing the concrete and adobe had to be carried across the arroyo from the trading post. The chapel had *vigas* (roof-beams) in the old Spanish fashion of the country, and the altar was inlaid with a panel of petrified wood. The candlesticks were handmade from native pine, and the dossal was a Navajo rug.

Howden came in October, 1930, to consecrate the chapel and it was dedicated to St. Luke the Physician, being officially designated as St. Luke's-in-the-Desert. In his book, *The Pilgrimage* (1980), Davis described the dedication:

> Long before the hour of the service, Navajos had gathered from all parts of the desert, coming in rickety wagons, on horseback, on foot and a few in wheezy cars. The headman of the Navajos in that vicinity was present with his family. He had been one of the leaders in donating work and in showing interest in the construction. We paid the men for part of the work . . . When the service began, the little building was packed; the women, girls and children on one side, and the men on the other. Some sat in the Aisle, others stood wherever there was an available inch of space and many were outside, unable to squeeze into the crowded church.
>
> The patrician bishop gave an effective portrayal of the love which Christ has for every race and pointed out that all are one in that brotherhood throughout the world. He emphasized that the chapel, so in keeping with the rich heritage of their own culture and desert country, had been set apart for their own use.

Miss Wilcox described St. Luke's field mission as the only religious, social or medical center in the entire district of about 5,000 square miles. She wrote, "the mission stands in almost the center of this vast tract of sand and sagebrush and there is probably not a Navajo in the entire district who has not at some time, in some way, felt the influence of its ministry."

After Miss Wilcox had lived and worked in the remote outstation for 15 years she wrote a reflective article for *The Spirit of Missions* in a vein exceedingly uncommon to her era. She weighed characteristics of Navajo traditional religion and its quest for harmony, but faulted the "hold" the medicine man had over the people. She gave the opinion that the deplorable disease rate and resulting human suffering justified on-going Episcopal Mission. In 1937, she wrote:

> *Ho, ho, ho, ho.*
> *Ee, hee, hee, hee, yah, hee yah.*
> *Oh ho, ho, ho.*
> *Ee, hee, hee, hee, yah, hee, yah.*
> *Dolah, ah-nee, ee-ee-ee-ee-ee-ee.*
> *Ee, oh, oh, hoh.*
> *Eee yah, hee yah.*
> *Ee, yah, ee, oh.*
> *Oh, ho, hee yah, ee, hee.*

Chanted to the muffled cadence of rattles and the soft thud of moccasined feet, the last song of the Navajo's nine day Night Chant, or *Yabaichai* ceremony, floats in through the desert night, bringing with it the spicy smell of burning sagebrush and the smoke of many fires. For nine nights the Navajos have been holding this great ceremony of healing and supplication to the gods; and now the last of the chants floats in as they conclude the ceremony with the chant to the bluebird, just at sunrise on the last morning.

Across the arroyo in the opposite direction stands the rugged cross of St. Luke's-in-the-Desert, outlined against a sky of turquoise blue. On the one hand, the age-old religion of the Navajos, handed down for generations, their only means of expressing a religious life that is fundamental in the life of all Indians and the Navajos. On the other hand, the new and, to the Navajo Indian, unproven religion of the white man. Just where to draw the line between the two, or how to lead from one to the other, is a question every missionary in the Indian country must face.

Time and again we are asked, and at times I myself have almost wondered as I have watched the intricate making of a sand painting or listened to the reverent and impressive chanting of the medicine man, if it were not better to leave the Navajo to pursue undisturbed his own colorful rites and ceremonies.

The Changing Social Scene

Bishop Howden envisioned an integrated program of medical, social and religious work in the Episcopal mission among the Navajo. Significant progress had been made in the medical and religious aspects of the work but the Navajo was undergoing enormous socio-economic change and the mission staff was present to counsel on coping with the government's new policies and programs. John Collier became Commissioner of Indian Affairs and set out the hated policy of stock reduction as a hedge against over-grazing. The Fruitland Irrigation Project proposed scientific irrigation controls. The new Navajo capital was built at Window Rock. Day schools were opened. Soil conservation projects were put into effect. It was a new day for the Navajo and much was unexplained to the people.

Jane Turnbull, another registered nurse, was recruited as a UTO worker for the San Juan Hospital in 1931. She intended to stay one year but remained among the Navajo until her death in 1984. She had been trained in both surgical and obstetrical work and soon won the confidence of the Navajos with her devotion to duty, deep interest in the Indians and her skill in handling difficult cases. At times she was the only medical help to the Navajos, and she delivered many Navajo babies into the world. An adopted Navajo daughter survived her.

During the period 1930-1932, nearly 500 patients were cared for in the little hospital; hundreds of religious services were held, some in isolated places on the desert; 58 Navajos were baptized; and there were 55 Christian burials. There were several thousand dispensary cases.

In 1932 the hospital had a small two story addition. The upper floor had a three-bed ward for obstetrical cases and a second room set aside for critically ill patients. The two rooms beneath were used for staff workers. Labor and building materials were comparatively low in price and there was an abundant supply of large boulders which were used for the walls. The total cost of the construction and furnishings was slightly over $3,000.

Since the early days Navajo volunteers assisted with the hospital. Katherine Jim was among the first. Her husband, George Jim, was among the last survivors of the crew that laid the stones to build the hospital building. Members of the Jim family have been prominent in the life and body of the San Juan mission and the broader New Mexico region of Navajoland Area Mission.

Davis had many visitors stop by the mission through the years. Among them was a priest from Old Greenwich, Connecticut, who expressed interest in starting a mission somewhere in Navajo country. Davis encouraged the priest to consider the Utah region:

> In 1943, this dream became a reality when Father H. Baxter Liebler resigned his parish, forsook all the comforts of the East and with several volunteer missionaries went to one of the most rugged regions in southeastern Utah and there established a mission. The cornerstone for this mission, St. Christopher's, was laid in June, 1944, by Bishop Moulton.

Davis, who had had to deal with recurring tuberculosis throughout his adult life, by 1950 found his work too difficult. He reluctantly resigned and with his ever supportive wife, Mildred, moved to El Paso.

A Harvard-educated native of Japan, Eugene Botelho, came to work among the Navajos in 1949, first in the Utah region of the reservation at San Juan Bautista, Montezuma Creek. By 1954 he had moved across the reservation to the San Juan Mission in New Mexico. With an unusual gift for language, he was able to preach his first sermon in Navajo 13 months after his arrival. In addition to serving as priest-in-charge, Botelho was administrator for the hospital.

Botelho, who made special efforts to encourage young Navajos who showed unusual potential, became known as "Father B" among the youth of the community. One teen-age boy whom the priest befriended was a basketball player named Benjamin Benally, who lived at the mission and attended Farmington public schools. Benally was starting forward for the Broncos of Central Junior High, and led them to the state championship, whereupon the young Navajo was elected "Basketball King," and was expected to escort the Homecoming Queen, a beautiful *biligaana* (white girl) to the prom. Benally knew only the ceremonial dances and desperately sought help from Father B. The priest had not danced in 20 years, but quickly recruited one of the young mission aides to teach the Navajo teenager to do the twist, the current fad among all youth. The basketball player escorted the blonde beauty to the dance without incident.

The government eventually was forced to take more responsibility for the health of the Navajo and the old San Juan hospital was closed in 1959. By then the compound contained several structures, including a frame rectory and the concrete block All Saints' Chapel. An era of relative quietness settled on the mesa as the church hierarchy continued debate on "what to do about the Navajo."

Botelho made frequent trips east to raise money for the mission, and on at least one occasion Benjamin Benally was among the group of Navajo youth which accompanied the priest. Botelho departed San Juan in the mid-1960s, leaving behind a network of mission stations surrounding San Juan Mission. In addition to St. Luke's-in-the-Desert, there was St. Francis at Crown Point, St. Charles' at Fruitland, St. Mary's in the Hogback area, St. Michael's at Kirtland and St. Augustine's at Shiprock. Bishop Charles James Kinsolving III, a member of a large and influential family of churchmen, retired in 1972 to be followed by Richard M. Trelease Jr., a strong proponent on "Canon Eight" clergy ordination, and soon the new bishop would encourage ordination of indigenous clergy after training in home community.

Trelease appointed Henry L. Bird, a civil rights activist in the 1960s, as vicar of the San Juan Mission with responsibilities to include training Native lay and ordained leadership. Bird's role would take a different turn when the tranquillity of the San Juan mesa was shattered in 1974. Serious racial hostility erupted in Farmington, described by Bird as "an ugly little border-town rife with racism and resentment." The economy of the town was built on Navajo trade but the white political power structure dealt abominably with reservation Navajos.

Chokecherry Canyon Murders

Matters came to a head in the spring of 1974. Three Navajo men were brutally murdered and their bodies cast into Chokecherry Canyon, just outside the city. One of the victims was Benjamin Benally. While Benally had not continued his connection with San Juan after Father B departed, his wife, Rena, was an active member of the San Juan Mission congregation, and it was in the San Juan cemetery that Benally was buried.

The brutal, sadistic, torture murders were committed by three white thrill-seeking Farmington high school students who were later convicted and sentenced to juvenile reform school. The murders and subsequent lenient prison sentences set off a series of clashes between the Navajo people and the city of Farmington.

With experience in non-violent confrontation and with full approval of his bishop, Bird permitted the new advocacy group, Coalition for Navajo Liberation, to hold its strategy meetings in All Saints' basement. Bird, who served San Juan from 1973 until 1979 with the exception of one year, participated along with other community clergy in a series of Coalition for Navajo Liberation marches in Farmington. Eventually, the U.S. Commission on Civil Rights became involved and eventually issued a report stating:

. . . beyond question, Farmington is a racist and sick community which treats its Navajo citizens in many respects like animals . . . Farmington has been shown to be a blight on the state of New Mexico and a parasite on the Navajo Reservations.

It would be a long time before unrest abated in the mean little town. In fact, 20 years later, if one is an Indian, one feels racial enmity as one enters a Farmington restaurant, registers at a motel, or buys gasoline at a service station.

An interesting postscript to the convicted youth: one attempted suicide by drug overdose, one was involved in an inexplicable car accident, and the third was dead as a result of a freak hit-and-run incident in Lubbock, Texas. Some say the three were victims of Navajo witchcraft.

First Indian Woman Priest; First Resident Bishop

Of vital significance to the New Mexico Navajo community in 1977 was the ordination of two San Juan communicants to the diaconate. On Wednesday, December 21, 1977, two bishops—Charles of Nevada and Trelease of Rio Grande—jointly ordained Yazzie Mason and Eloise Martinez. After extensive community-based study, both were ordained under the old Canon Eight. Yazzie, fluent in the Navajo language but limited in English, chose the permanent diaconate and lived in the Fruitland area of New Mexico until his death in 1997.

Martinez, however, became the first Indian woman ordained to the priesthood in the Episcopal Church. Her ordination was held at All Saints' Chapel of the San Juan Mission on November 18, 1979, with Trelease and the new bishop of Navajoland, Frederick W. Putnam Jr., officiating. The preacher was Steven Plummer, who stressed the progress his people have made over the years from "subject people to a place of dignity and responsibility." A social worker for the Navajo tribe, Mother Martinez resided south of Farmington on the mesa. She would experience sorrowful disappointment; her priestly role was not accepted by the constituency and within three years she renounced her vows and departed the Episcopal Church. There would not be another Indian woman priest until 1983 when Anna Frank of Alaska was priested.

On January 27, 1979, the first resident bishop of Navajoland was installed. Putnam chose Farmington as his residence, saying: ". . . because it is a central spot for work in the Navajo reservation."

Episcopal oversight of the Navajoland Area Mission had been initially assigned Otis Charles, Bishop of Utah. Putnam was former Suffragan Bishop of Oklahoma. Appointed by the Presiding Bishop and unanimously approved by Navajo Convocation in the summer of 1978, Putnam's installation was held at Good Shepherd Mission, Fort Defiance, with the Rev. Boone Porter, editor of *The Living Church*, as preacher. A native of Minnesota, Putnam served in several midwest posts prior to his consecration as the Oklahoma suffragan in 1963.

"The Navajoland Area Mission is a new concept in the Episcopal Church," Putnam said. He cited among his goals an enabling "of indigenous ministry and an extensive training program especially suited to training Navajo people for lay ministry. Out of this training we hope will come candidates for the ordained ministry as well."

After Putnam's retirement in 1983, the Presiding Bishop tapped the Bishop of Nevada, Wesley Frensdorff, for episcopal oversight of the Navajos. Frensdorff, early in his tenure as interim bishop, instituted a process whereby communities would identify individuals to study for ordination. After prayer and thoughtful deliberation, the New Mexico region picked Buddy Arthur for ordained leadership. There followed a lengthy theological education by extension and in 1988 Arthur was ordained priest and has since served New Mexico region congregations along with the Rev. Jack Fowler. Fowler refers to himself as a "Navajo in-law" as his wife and children are Navajo. In addition to the All Saints' congregation, today's New Mexico region has St. Michael's congregation at Fruitland and St. Augustine's at Shiprock, as well as St. Luke's-in-the-Desert.

The old stone hospital now houses offices for the Episcopal Church in Navajoland. Lucille Blakesley long served as administrator and a Navajo, Rosella Jim, as secretary. Up a stony pathway from the old hospital is All Saints' Church, fittingly decorated with fine hand-woven Navajo rugs, colorful banners and altar hangings and an arrestingly rustic stylized crucifix, crafted by Victoria John, also a member of the Jim family which helped to build the San Juan Mission.

It was to All Saints' Chapel that the Most Rev. Edmond L. Browning paid his farewell visit to the Navajos at the 1996 summer convocation.

ST. CHRISTOPHER'S MISSION IN THE UTAH STRIP

In the summer of 1942 Harold Baxter Liebler, a middle-aged, black-clad, Anglo-Catholic easterner rode horseback alone across the rugged desert country of that remote part of the Navajo Reservation known as the Utah Strip.

He was looking for a place to establish a mission among the Navajo. He was, in fact, looking for a place and a people who had never come in contact with the Gospel. Liebler deplored the efforts of missionaries who sought to destroy all that remained of the beauty of Indian life and thought instead of sanctifying it and enriching it with the truth and grace of the Gospel.

A half century after his desert quest, a more enlightened and less ethnocentric Episcopal Church has become more and more affirming of Liebler's concepts—viewed at the time, if not heretical, then certainly radical. Liebler proposed a missionary stance which would respect native cultures and advanced a premise that the Gospel could be communicated not as a contradiction but as a fulfillment to Indians' traditional beliefs.

Since his Nashotah House seminary days, Liebler had held an ardent interest in Indian cultures. For years, whenever an extended vacation from his work as rector of St. Savior's Church in Old Greenwich, Connecticut, made it possible, Liebler had gone into the southwest, convinced that somewhere he would find a tribe or group of American Indians to whom he could minister while respecting their own way of life.

In his search he had ridden many days west from Farmington. He had been stranded in the desert when his sorrel horse and pack burro strayed in the night. After a friendly Navajo helped him find the animals, the priest had again been stymied when the stubborn brown burro refused to set foot on the bridge spanning the San Juan River. His ultimate test came when he was stricken with severe abdominal cramps after drinking bad gypsum water. This episode earned him his first Indian name which was Priest-with-Sore-Gut.

Plodding across Monument Valley, he eventually arrived at the ghost town of Bluff, Utah, where he learned that in a 300-square-mile area there was no mission, no school, no medical or hospital facility for the Navajo.

Twelve miles east of Bluff, he located Hyrum's field, a valley nestled between the San Juan River on the south and the cliffs of Cow Canyon to the north. Halfway up the canyon wall fresh water dripped from a slit in the otherwise impregnable and barren sandstone. He

named the valley St. Christopher's. Legend has it that he said his
first Mass at the site on St. Christopher's Day, and here the tall, ur-
bane easterner would live, preach, teach, train, and 40 years later—in
1982—be buried.

Born in Brooklyn into a middle-class family, the St. Christopher's
founder attended select New England summer camps. He was schooled
in New York City and at Columbia University. Upon completing seminary at Nashotah House he was ordained in 1914 and spent the next
three years at St. Matthias in Waukesha, Wisconsin, and a year as
curate at St. Luke's, New York City. Liebler then founded St. Savior's
in Old Greenwich and by the time he resigned to found the Navajo
mission, he had served the Connecticut parish for 25 years.

In preparing to come to Navajoland, Liebler first sought a rudi-
mentary understanding of the difficult Navajo language with its
strange sounds, high and low tones and nasalized vowels, studying at
Barnard College with an anthropology professor who had written a
Navajo grammar. In Liebler's intense but brief study he managed to
perfect his pronunciations and intonations, but his vocabulary was
extremely limited. Later a Navajo would inquire, "Who is this white
man who talks like a Navajo but says only a few words?"

He spent the first half of 1943 setting up machinery for raising
eastern money to support the mission and recruiting volunteers to
run it. It was the Anglican Franciscan friars who became the volunteer mainstay. Liebler shortly recruited Brother Michael and Helen
Sturges, a former social worker and future school teacher, along with
Esther Bacon, a nurse from West Virginia. The devoted Brother Juniper would join the community by autumn and remain with the Navajo
mission for life, as did Sturges.

The missionary party departed New York in the middle of World
War II, which imposed rationed tires and rationed gasoline and a 35-
mile-per-hour speed limit. Sturges drove her heavily laden Plymouth
convertible with Brother Michael beside her, and Liebler drove a sec-
ond-hand Ford pickup. Riding with him were his wife, Frances, and
another volunteer, Catherine Lucas. Nurse Bacon joined the party in
Ohio. They camped and cooked—and frequently repaired retread
tires—halfway across the continent, and nearly two full weeks later
arrived at Hyrum's field where they pitched tents and shortly developed a daily routine which Liebler described:

> Every morning the Angelus aroused us at the first sign
> of daylight. That the bell was a large frying pan struck by
> hammer handle only served to remind us that it was a call

to work and to eat, as well as to pray. Our little portable altar was set up, and Mass began as soon as it was light enough for me to see the pages of the missal.

On the first Sunday two small children astride a small burro sat high on the crest of Cow Canyon and silently watched the party celebrate Mass. The following Sunday a whole family of Navajos, including a baby on a cradleboard, hid in the sagebrush and watched. On the third Sunday several Navajos appeared and there was never again a Sunday Mass without Navajos present. It was in the early days of the mission effort that a Navajo man attached himself and his sizable family to the newcomers. Called Randolph, he served as translator, hired help and friend.

Brother Juniper, the second of the Franciscan friars, arrived in October, 1943. He traveled by train to Grand Junction, Colorado, and by mail truck to Blanding, Utah. There he was picked up by Liebler in the mission truck which was loaded with lumber that stuck up over the cab. The friar wrote his eastern friends:

> We had traveled only two miles before a bumping noise announced a flat tire whereupon we gathered a pile of brush and lit a fire—both for light and for warmth, for it was late October and at an elevation well over six thousand feet. With the tire changed we were off again and about forty-five minutes later we dropped down into a narrow canyon road and turned eastward toward the Mission camp . . . Those at the camp heard us coming, and built up a big camp fire which disclosed an army squad tent, an umbrella tent and a couple of other small tents and an Indian teepee. Far back in the shadows, I could see the outlines of a building without a roof . . . I could hear a roar in the distance which I later learned was the river tossing its gigantic sand-waves into the night.
>
> The next morning I was awakened by a weird sound, and as I sat up, Brother Michael said, "Oh, that's just Randolph, welcoming the dawn. Think nothing of it." Not long after this, the Angelus was rung on what I later learned was an old Pennsylvania Railroad engine bell, now hung on a tripod in the midst of the camp. After Mass and breakfast, I was given my first job: A neighbor had given Father an old outhouse after the CCC [Civilian Conservation Corps] had erected his fancy new privy. I had the job of setting up the thing and putting a door on it . . . this bit of refinement

was a considerable advance over the sage-brush device that had served hitherto.

By spring of 1944 the staff of five—Frances Liebler and Esther Bacon had departed—had built a stone building, improvised a water system, acquired a milk cow and a beautiful black mare, Shioni.

The First Easter

It was with his Good Friday message that Liebler entrenched himself with the Navajo as a man with strong medicine. He had pondered long on how to convey the message of death and resurrection to a people who are loathe even to mention the dead. He later wrote about his first Holy Week among the Navajo:

I needed an idea to put over the crucifixion, and decided to use the sand painting. Few as we were, we carried out the traditional rites with precision and care, and our people attended with obvious reverence. On Good Friday, after the solemn rites were concluded at the altar of the Mission House, Brother Juniper brought in a bucket of light-colored sand and dumped it on the ground in front of the altar; with a bit of board I smoothed it out to cover about a square yard. From the Franciscan Fathers' Catechism, I read short selections of the story of the Crucifixion, and between the readings drew the picture with colored sands, while Brother Michael and Helen sang suitable hymns. First I drew the Cross, in black sand, then the figure of the Crucified in beige-colored sand . . . then, the figures of St. Mary and St. John. The sun was represented by a disk of yellow sand above the cross. When I read of the darkness spreading over the land, I obliterated the sun with black sand.

The grapevine carried the news far and wide—a white man had made a sand painting! All day long groups came in to see it; in modulated tones they discussed it and silently filed out.

The Holy Saturday rites were carried out . . . Towards afternoon clouds appeared in the sky . . . and darkness came on. I was awakened at dawn by the sound of rain beating down on the roof of my tent and leaking through in various places.

We had to stretch a tarpaulin over the altar and then replace the linens before we could start the Easter Mass. The congregation was not large. One young sheepherder brought a day-old lamb with him to church. An occasional bleat—especially while we were singing "Angus Dei"—was not out of place or distracting, but toward the end of the service the lamb broke its tether and made for the sagebrush that adorned the base of the paschal candle. Brother Michael, never at a loss, simply swooped the little beast up with his left forearm, and holding his hymnal in his right hand, continued the stentorian tones through the last Alleluia.

That Easter Day was the occasion of my second sermon in the Navajo language. It might have been a little longer than the one of the previous Christmas. [The vocabulary of the padre had grown!]

Toward noon the rain subsided. The next day Randolph came in while we were still at breakfast. "Faa Leeah, is medicine man living up the river bouth sem mile, he got boy is sick year an a half. He want you go up there and make him well."

"Well, Randolph, I don't know that I can do him any good, but I'll go to see him and do what I can."

"Oh, you can do it all right. All Navajos know now you got strong medicine. They try lawn tine make rain, can't make any. You make big rain . . . rain all roun. You can make at boy well."

By the next Easter, a stone mission house had been completed, and a one-room clinic and a school were operating. The clinic, which eventually grew to eight rooms, primarily served as a baby delivery facility, and for inoculations and diagnostic purposes, with the critically ill dispatched to the Fort Defiance and Cortez, Colorado, hospitals.

The school, housed in a CCC shack dating from the depression days on "permanent loan," was immediately filled to overflowing by young men with jangling spurs, old men wearing their hair in the traditional bun wrapped with yarn, babies in cradleboards, grandmothers and grandfathers, and just about every age in between. Attendance was sporadic but the mission team had come to accept Navajo cultural priorities—sheep had to be herded, and this was generally the task of the children; a healing ceremony for some relative was ample reason to miss school.

Gaining a better command of the Navajo language, Liebler set about translating and teaching catechism, and looked forward to a dozen baptisms on Holy Saturday of 1945. To his astonished disappointment, only two youth—Dan and Pauline—appeared at the

*The Reverend H. Baxter Liebler [1889-1982],
at St. Christopher's original log chapel.*

font and were the first Navajos known to be baptized in the state of
Utah. Late in the afternoon, however, two of the translator Randolph's
children appeared and asked to be baptized. When questioned on why
they had not attended the earlier baptism service, they explained that
they had had to herd sheep. By nightfall, the number of baptized Navajos in Utah was doubled!

However that Easter Eve was to bring other first fruit. An elder,
Hashk'aan, appeared and returned for Mass the next day, and from
that day to his last illness 15 years later he never missed a Sunday
Mass. *Hashk'aan* was one of the first three confirmed when the new
Utah bishop, Stephen C. Clark, visited St. Christopher's in 1945, and
the old man for many years set a splendid example of the Christian
life to the people of the area.

St. Christopher's compound grew. The community of volunteers,
with assistance of two or so Navajo laborers, erected a log church
(which burned in 1964) as centerpiece for a cluster of red native stone
buildings and cloister, surrounded by well-irrigated hayfields,

cornfields and vegetable gardens. Eventually, each of the growing number of volunteers had a sleeping room with a stove, running water in the kitchen and kerosene lamps. Liebler had slept for two years in a plains-type Indian teepee. An army surplus jeep replaced the aged pickup. It was not without considerable effort, but title to the property was eventually obtained through action of the U.S. Congress, and the patent was signed by President Harry Truman. Perhaps most important to the growth of the mission was a steady surge in dedicated volunteers, which would eventually include a priest, identified only as Father Clement, who had been a missionary in the Philippines.

The White Horse Lost Opportunity

In spring of 1946 a patriarch, known as *Tsiithlagai* (White Horse), invited the team to come to his camp on Montezuma Creek to "conduct prayers and give instructions." Knowing only that the patriarch's camp was east of St. Christopher's and located at the mouth of Montezuma Wash—a dry creek except for an occasional flood—and that an abandoned trading post was an unfailing landmark, a trio set out on horseback across trackless rough terrain, keeping an eye to the right for the meandering San Juan River.

It took the trio, Liebler, Helen Sturges and a new volunteer from Chicago, two days to traverse the desert brush and deep gullies; today with a paved road and bridges it is but a 10-mile journey. At last they arrived:

> ... and we saw the ruins of the abandoned trading post, the great peninsula at the confluence covered with a massive stand of cottonwoods, hogans, corrals, pelt racks and other indications of habitation. Our first visit was to two hogans. A vast expanse of sand provided a fine meeting place ... Most of the women brought parasols of vivid hue ... brightly colored shirts of men and boys ... they must have numbered between 60 and 70. The attention span of these people amazed me ... they seemed to grasp the gist of my message and wanted to know when the baptism was to be. I sometimes wonder whether I didn't make a mistake in not taking advantage of the situation.

Liebler, never deviating from Anglo-Catholic regimen, told the assembled that he could baptize only those who sincerely believed and showed promise of perseverance. He did not move on the opportunity to baptize White Horse's entire band. In future writings Liebler appears to question his judgment. A full decade after the White Horse "invitation," a St. Christopher's Christmas Newsletter read:

The great Chief White Horse has gone before us. Readers of our Newsletter back in the mimeograph days may recall how he rode in with twenty or more of his descendants for the marriage of a relative near here. Most of them attended our daily services. White Horse himself came and was deeply impressed. He asked us to come to Montezuma Creek and hold services there. At that time we were just getting started here at Bluff, and it was not easy to get away, but before long three of us went, horseback, carrying all our camp equipment; we took two days finding the place. Had we been willing to let down our standards, we could have baptized fifty or more Navajos at that time—but we had determined to test and try all candidates and see to it that they were adequately instructed . . .

Several of White Horse's great-grandchildren, who later came to our school here at St. Christopher's, were baptized, and only last spring and summer some others of his descendants. In October he announced himself ready, and on the 30th he was solemnly baptized, surrounded by his numerous progeny.

It was his last visit to the church—he was then barely able to mount a burro, let alone walk. A month later, at his home, he received his First Holy Communion; on St. Stephen's Day his Viaticum. His son-in-law brought the news of his imminent death. "White Horse, he call all his relations and he told them 'I'm gonna die' he said, 'and so somebody go and tell Father come here and help me and put me under the ground, God's way,' he said." By sundown all was done as the Chief would have wanted it done . . . After the burial we gathered in the hogan. There was some talk among the unbaptized which implied the existence of a state of *ch'iindi*—the taboo that surrounds everything connected with a Navajo death. The widow spoke up briskly, "Didn't you hear what Father told us? When one is baptized, and the soul is in grace, there is no *ch'iindi*. There is no need to fear, all is peace."

Outstations Organized

Liebler, dubbed the "Desert Priest" by a national publication, eventually expanded work into other regions of the Utah strip. The hamlet of Mexican Hat was regularly visited. A few years later, the team had acquired an Army surplus Dodge weapons carrier and was crashing across the rough country to Navajo Mountain, a rounded, hazy promontory that is a Holy Mountain to the Navajo.

One of Liebler's first outreach stations was in the Monument Valley area in an area of crimson red cliffs known as the Hat Rock area. Services were first held in a deserted road crew shack and it was to this station in its final configuration as St. Mary's-of-the-Moonlight, Oljeto, that Liebler and his faithful followers retreated upon his 1966 retirement. And it was here that Liebler died in 1982.

In the early years roads were non-existent and Liebler and his faithful band demonstrated profound perseverance when again and again they bumped across country to distant outstations. In years to come, Brother Juniper would paint marks on exposed surface rocks to reveal a "road" from Bluff to Montezuma Creek, and it was over this road that Liebler took Bishop Clark by jeep to survey the St. Christopher outstation. The jeep, however, sank up to its headlights in wet sand and the bishop experienced an unplanned overnight campout on the San Juan River and a ride on a borrowed Navajo pony the next morning back to St. Christopher's.

The work at Montezuma Creek flourished. A trader deeded two acres of land for a school, Bishop Clark blessed the site, seminarian summer workers with Navajo helpers put up stone walls, and Father Botelho, with a gift of languages, arrived to run the school. The schoolhouse was smoothly turned into a church for once-a-month Sunday Mass by opening the triptych and revealing the crucifix. Unforeseen was the Navajo need for a boarding school not merely a day school. The children came on the first day bringing their blankets, saying, "It is too far for us to walk to school and back every day. We will stay here until it gets warm again in the spring." Both the Montezuma Creek school and the St. Christopher's school remained operational until the early 1960s.

At the suggestion of Bishop Clark the Montezuma Creek outstation was named San Juan Bautista. Liebler explained:

> Our river, the San Juan, had been named by the Spanish explorers in honor of St. John the Baptist, and as our church and school were within a stone's throw of the river, I thought it well to take on that dedication. But somehow

"St. John the Baptist Church" might create a difficulty in
the minds of any who had heard of a Baptist church.

The Liebler Legacy

Through all his 23 active years at St. Christopher's mission, Liebler
endeavored to generate funds—generally from the east—to support
his work among the Navajo. He gave numerous talks in New York
including one at the Church of St. Mary the Virgin arranged for by
Dr. and Mrs. Bertram Eskell. Mrs. Eskell (Joan), a native of England,
had from time to time been among the mission volunteers. After the
death of her husband and that of Liebler's wife the two were married
in 1979. She survives and drives from Moab, Utah, to attend
Navajoland annual convocations.

In 1966, at age 77, Liebler retreated with three of his flock—
Joan, Helen Sturges and Brother Juniper—to an even more remote
part of the reservation seven miles from a tiny settlement called Oljeto
which means as "moonlight" in the Navajo language. It was here among
the towering monoliths of Monument Valley, approximately 60 miles
southeast of Bluff, that they began to establish Hat Rock Valley Retreat
Center. Within four years the Liebler community of volunteers had
hewn and hauled rocks for a new church building—St. Mary's-of-the-
Moonlight—remotely located in the shadows of fierce red cliffs 12 miles
from a paved road. St. Mary's, styled as a stone hogan and cooled by
wide arched porticos, blends with the rough craggy desert
surroundings.

Liebler died November 21, 1982, at age 93 and was buried on the
grounds of St. Christopher's Mission. His grave, at his request, is near
the high altar of the original log church and watched over by the statue
of the Navajo Madonna and Child which survived the 1964 fire. Helen
Sturges died in 1985 at age 88 and Brother Juniper died in 1990.

San Juan Bautista, eventually known as St. John the Baptizer,
in time would be served by Steven Plummer, who was sent to the
Montezuma Creek Mission in 1977.

For all his honoring of Navajo tradition, Liebler's rigid Anglo-
Catholic perspective inhibited his raising up Navajos to replace him
in the work of St. Christopher's. He found a promising young man,
Frank Benally, and though the Navajo's educational background was
limited to Chemawa Indian School, in Oregon, Liebler dispatched him
to an eastern boarding school, St. Peter's in Peekskill, New York. By
Liebler's own admission, Benally "found it frightfully hard to keep

abreast of lads who had been in first-rate preparatory schools." After one year Benally joined the Marine Corps and was later killed in an explosion.

His heir-apparent became Wayne Pontious, a Kansas native, who after visiting Liebler and St. Christopher's at Thanksgiving of 1954 decided to pursue ordination. Pontious entered Nashotah House and graduated in 1962. Immediately after being ordained to the diaconate by the Bishop of Chicago, Pontious and his family came to St. Christopher's. By the end of the year, the Utah bishop, Richard S. Watson, had ordained Pontious to the priesthood. He served St. Christopher's Mission for a full decade.

Bishop Watson ordained another Nashotah House graduate, Canadian-born Ian D. Mitchell, and assigned him to serve as assistant vicar (1964-67) at St. Christopher's. Records show there was a third clergyman on the St. Christopher's staff during 1967—Robert Dean Campbell, from Colorado. Utah elected Otis Charles bishop in 1971. When Pontious left in 1972, the St. Christopher's post was vacant for the first time in almost 30 years. In 1974 Bishop Charles appointed W. Herbert Scott Jr. as St. Christopher's vicar. Born in Oklahoma and a graduate of Union Theological Seminary of New York, Scott served St. Christopher's Mission for four years. Then came, briefly, the first Native American, Luke Titus of Alaska, and his Navajo wife. Dan Treece of Colorado came for a couple of years and he was followed by Richard Southworth. When Wesley Frensdorff was appointed Navajoland's bishop in 1983 he moved Plummer from St. John the Baptizer and assigned him the new post of regional vicar with responsibilities for the three Utah Region churches founded by Liebler—St. John the Baptizer, St. Christopher's and St. Mary's-of-the-Moonlight. The latter, where the late Mary Charles long served as lay pastor, was closed in 1995.

Many of the buildings in the St. Christopher's compound were erected physically by the hands of Liebler and his volunteers. When he departed he left behind a church and mission house, a vicarage, an eight-bed clinic, a schoolhouse and several work buildings and dormitories. Later an architecturally remarkable chapel was erected—a tall wooden cone which prompts an impression of a plains Indian tepee more than of any habitation in the southwest. For lack of funds the building was never completed; the congregation meets in a remodeled school building. Also remaining nearby is a swinging bridge which Navajo children used to cross the sometimes turbulent San Juan River to attend Liebler's school.

Liebler's lasting legacy is not the aging red arched stone cloisters or buildings and grounds between the red cliffs and the San Juan River. Instead, he left a vision and a prophecy—that one can be Indian and Christian, too! Half a century ago, when neither white nor Indian clergy were acknowledging the spiritual gifts of American Indians, Liebler, in spite of his Anglo-Catholic elitism, took the trouble to try to talk and understand the Navajo language; he made no effort to destroy the Navajo's ceremonies. In fact, on occasion he participated in the ceremonies. He wrote:

> In establishing St. Christopher's Mission, I had some preconceived ideas that at that time received but little sympathy from official headquarters. These ideas had to do chiefly with a respect for native culture that would indicate a method of presentation of the Gospel, not as a contradiction but as a fulfillment of what the Indians, by their own and their ancestors' meditations and reasoning, had found to be a satisfactory way of life; and furthermore, a presenting of the Catholic religion as being the fullness of the Christian revelation . . .

After almost 40 years the Liebler concept was dramatically showcased when 3,000 bishops, deputies and visitors witnessed and participated in the Native American Ceremonial Worship service, a highlight of the 70th General Convention of the Episcopal Church in July, 1991, in Phoenix, Arizona.

END NOTES

A single copy of a 1954 manuscript, *The Good Shepherd Mission to the Navajo,* written by Arizona retired Archdeacon J. Rockwood Jenkins, surfaced in late winter of 1992, coming into the hands of the former Good Shepherd vicar, Mark MacDonald, through a communicant of his former parish in Portland, Oregon.

It is from the archdeacon's exhaustive research that the early history of the 100-year-old mission at Good Shepherd is herein recorded. His material came from the voluminous correspondence between Eliza Thackara and the Westchester Branch of the Woman's Auxiliary as well as from archival materials of the Diocese of Arizona and the old Indian Rights Association of Philadelphia.

Born in Worcester, Massachusetts, in 1869, a graduate of Harvard in 1891 and Episcopal Theological Seminary in 1895, Jenkins came to Arizona in 1909 and served as archdeacon 1914-1943. First visiting Good Shepherd Mission in 1923, he served as its interim vicar in the summer of 1929. At age 85 he completed the manuscript, tediously typed in all capitals, elite face and single spaced. He died in 1963.

Written in prosaic 19th century language, the manuscript presents the author's dilemma about Navajo culture and traditional practice of the Christian religion. While the aging archdeacon, a product of European ethnocentric mindset, found merit in the Navajo values, he was unable to overcome some reservations:

> I found the Navajo to be a decidedly religious people and that their religion entered into every aspect of life. Now that sounds very well but the facts are that their religion is definitely pagan and has many decidedly demoralizing ideas and practices which are centered about their hopelessly superstitious dread of the *shin-dee,* or evil spirits . . . And yet it does have certain very fine expressions and customs that seemingly border on a Christian devotion, and almost puts us to shame in our habits of worship.

While Jenkins never resolved his own personal quandary, his writing does, in fact, sketch a dawning recognition that native traditional spirituality has value in the Christian world and that Christianity can be communicated in the Navajo's own cultural terms. The 70th General Convention of the Episcopal Church witnessed this connection when a Navajo *'Hataathlii'* (singer/healer/medicine man) chanted from the Beauty Way ceremony at opening services—and later appeared at the communion rail.

8

EPISCOPAL WORK IN THE
MOUNTAINS AND DESERT

Around 150 years ago in the Great Basin area of the inland west, white men were shooting diminutive desert dwelling Indians for sport. Few native peoples were treated more harshly than were the peoples who inhabited that vast inhospitable 200,000-square-mile region encircled by the Wasatch and Rocky Mountains on the east, the Mojave Desert on the south, the Sierra Nevada mountain range on the west, and the Snake River watershed on the north. For centuries prior to the ruthless white invasion, Paiute, Ute, Bannock and Shoshone peoples wrested a living from the harsh environment, moving with the changing seasons, scouring the land for anything edible.

At the end of the Civil War, U.S. expansionists headed west and embarked upon a new displacement of native peoples. Gold and silver were discovered in western Nevada and quite shortly the Indians' precarious dependence on nature's cycles was broken. The stands of piñon trees, from which pine nuts, a diet staple, came, were leveled for fuel. New treaties were forged and Indian tribes and nations apportioned to Christian denominations. By the end of the 19th century Episcopal missions sprouted up like dandelions all across the Great Basin and inland west.

However, a century later where once there had been many Indian congregations in the dioceses of Utah, Idaho, Nevada and Wyoming only five remained active. Only two of the five congregations had resident clergy; none had Indian clergy. With one exception every congregation had been established in the late 1800s; no new ministry had been begun in three quarters of a century. The existence of the Nevada congregation was tenuous; the Idaho church building was condemned, and on the Ute Reservation one congregation had been without a priest for 11 years and a second congregation's building had been home to pigeons for a decade.

A renaissance occurred when an Indian Episcopal gathering was called in the summer of 1987. The National Committee on Indian Work (NCIW) underwrote expenses for two dozen representatives of congregations in the dioceses of Idaho, Utah and Wyoming. A new coalition was born and the coalition was christened Mountains and Desert Regional Indian Ministries. Within a few years representatives from the dioceses of Nevada and Montana joined the coalition.

Faithful churchmen and churchwomen from the five scattered dioceses held in common a fear of abandonment and a sense of isolation from their own dioceses, from provincial structures, from the national church, and from other Indians. The Mountains and Desert coalition gathers twice annually. Meeting sites and conveners rotate and usually the host diocese's bishop attends and participates in the gatherings. Sometimes the meeting focuses on a work project. The once-isolated Indian congregations drew strength from each other, and concern about 'abandonment' was diminished.

WIND RIVER RESERVATION, WYOMING

It is seemly that the Mountains and Desert coalition was launched on the Wind River Reservation where Episcopal mission among the tribes of the region began. Two tribes occupy the Wind River Reservation and relationship between the Shoshone and Northern Arapaho has never been congenial. One of the first achievements of the fledgling coalition was to provide an arena for a step toward reconciliation. Representatives of the two reservations sat side by side in the gathering.

The coalition gathering was held at St. Michael's Mission to the Arapaho at Ethete. St. David's Mission at Fort Washakie is five miles away on the Shoshone side of Wind River Reservation. The reservation was teeming with activity; the gathering coincided with the annual July Wind River Reservation pow-wow. Tepees and campers dotted the mission ground. Among the visitors were 52 workers from Church of the Holy Spirit at Lake Forest, Illinois, which has a long-term companion relation with the Arapaho mission.

Participants in the gathering were impressed by evidence of a certain synthesizing of the traditional Indian religion and Christian beliefs. An example was the design of the chapel and the centrally placed altar in the shape of a ceremonial drum. Participants were

*Chief Washakie of the Shoshone
of Wind River Reservation.*

also impressed with ecumenical activity within the Christian faith as they participated in an open-air eucharistic celebration in which the Episcopal priest and the resident Roman Catholic priest were concelebrants.

Old missionary journals have told highly romanticized tales about the cast of characters instrumental in setting the Wind River Mission afloat—John Roberts, Sherman Coolidge and Chief Washakie. Elders on Wind River Reservation, however, say many of these stories are more legend than truth. Nonetheless, Episcopal work did begin on the Wind River in 1883 on the Shoshone Reservation and in 1913 on the Arapaho Reservation.

The Shoshone and Bannock on Wind River were parceled to the Episcopal Church in the 1872 Grant Peace Policy agreement. The following year George Randall, the first Missionary Bishop of Colorado, paid a visit to the reservation and conducted the first Episcopal services in a little log cabin. But due to the strain of the arduous journey and exposure to grim winter days, Randall contacted pneumonia from which he subsequently died.

A treaty had been made with the Shoshone and Bannock Indians in 1868 which reserved for these tribes a million-and-a-half-acre tract in a great valley along the Wind River of Wyoming. The venerable old Chief Washakie, around whom many stories are woven, signed the treaty on behalf of the Shoshone, who claimed to have occupied the lush valley since the 1700s. The Bannocks did not long remain on the Wind River Reservation but returned to their traditional homelands in Idaho and joined with the Idaho Shoshone band.

Meanwhile, the Arapaho Indians, of an entirely different linguistic stock from the Shoshone, after having been jostled from place to place by the federal government, appeared on Wind River in the cold winter of 1876. Federal authorities asked Washakie to quarter the Arapaho until spring. The old chief agreed; the Arapaho have been at Wind River ever since. Sixty years went by before the government made any cash settlement with the Shoshone for the eastern part of the reservation occupied by the Arapaho. From the very beginning, the two tribes remained aloof from each other and tension still surfaces between these neighbors on adjoining reservations. And, almost from the beginning, the Episcopal Church found it essential to maintain distinctly separate missions with the Shoshone and the Arapaho.

The Shoshone Mission

In 1883 a young Welshman, filled with missionary zeal, departed the green meadows of Britain to establish the mission on the Wind River Reservation. John Roberts remained on Wind River for 66 years. Roberts had been ordained in the beautiful Cathedral of Lichfield by the great apostle to New Zealand, Bishop Selwyn. The old Episcopal periodical, *The Spirit of Missions*, described young Roberts' arrival:

Wyoming at that time was virgin country; civilization had scarcely penetrated across the border, and the only means of travel beyond the terminus of the Union Pacific was the prairie schooner. It was February, 1883, and Wyoming was blanketed with the deepest snow in years, and Mr. Roberts was obliged to make the trip of 150 miles from Green River to Fort Washakie with the mail carrier. When they left Green River, it was 60-degrees below zero.

It took eight days to make the trip. At one place along the road, a young woman passenger was so badly frostbitten that Mr. Roberts stayed up all night chopping wood to keep a fire going so that she might be warm. In spite of that, she died the next day. Another day the stage driver was frozen to death, and Mr. Roberts drove the horses to the next station, trusting their instincts to find the way.

Roberts at first found growth of his mission very slow but gradually he earned respect of the tribesmen. During the first year he established a small school and enrolled 16, and by 1886 he had been engaged to superintend the government boarding school for 86 Indian children. Indian catechists and lay helpers, unnamed in literature, were trained by Roberts. With the help of the Shoshones, he translated parts of the Bible and the Book of Common Prayer. In 1899 Chief Washakie gave Roberts 160 acres to be used as the Shoshone Indian Mission School for Girls, which operated for many years.

There are fascinating stories in the old mission periodical about the late night conversion and baptism of the venerable old Chief Washakie. Wind River descendants of Washakie, however, say the stories simply are not factual. Furthermore, Washakie's baptismal records reveal that he was baptized at age 100, only three years before his death. Whether the Washakie baptismal story is fact or fiction, it is sketched herein because its frequent retelling in old publications has raised it to the level of legend:

One day Washakie's son went to the village, consumed too much alcohol, and in an ensuing fray with U.S. soldiers was killed. From his high mountain dwelling, Washakie sent word that in revenge he would come down the mountain the following day and kill every white man he met until he himself was killed. Then, Washakie went to bed.

Soon Washakie was awakened by someone seeking admittance to his lodge. It was the young priest, who said, "If you carry out this threat, the white men will kill you. You are the best chief your people have ever had, and they need you. You must not be killed. I am young and have few friends and will not be greatly missed. Therefore, take my life in exchange for that of your son."

Washakie, who reverently admired courage and bravery, could not take the life of the young missionary. What, he wanted to know, gave young Roberts such courage? The two men sat down to talk together, and at 3 a.m. Washakie was baptized. Chief Washakie, who governed his people for 70 years, lived to be 103. The Rev. Roberts officiated at the funeral of the old chief who was buried with full military honors.

Roberts also officiated a year after his arrival at the Wind River Reservation at the burial at the Shoshone cemetery of a woman legend says was Sacajawea, the woman who in 1806 led the Lewis and Clark expedition across the Rocky Mountains to the Pacific Ocean. Scholars disagree as to whether this aged woman was, in fact, Sacajawea, lost for 50 years and discovered at death to have been quietly living among her Shoshone people. Church records identify her as "Baptiste's mother." Baptiste was the name of the little boy called Pomp in the Lewis and Clark journals and it is Baptiste who is depicted straddling the back of the young Sacajawea in the many statues sprinkled across the country. Only God knows who actually lies buried at the Shoshone cemetery. However, in the great valley between the Shining Mountains, the Wind River Range and the Owl Creek Mountains, a substantial gray-granite column attests:

SACAJAWEA
DIED APRIL 9, 1884
A GUIDE WITH THE LEWIS AND CLARK EXPEDITION
1805-1806
IDENTIFIED, 1907 BY REV. J. ROBERTS
WHO OFFICIATED AT HER BURIAL

Arapaho Mission and the First Arapaho Priest

The first Arapaho ordained to the priesthood in the Episcopal Church was Sherman Coolidge who for 25 years served on the Wind River Reservation, home of the Northern Arapaho. Later he helped at intervals at the Southern Cheyenne-Arapaho mission of David Pendleton Oakerhater in Oklahoma, and as an old man was honorary Canon of St. John's Cathedral in Denver.

Conflicting accounts of the events which shaped the life of the Arapaho priest have appeared in old missionary journals, the disparities likely a result of perspective. Around 1869 *Desche-Wah-Ah*, a young Arapaho boy, was captured—whether by the Shoshone or the military remains a question—and brought to a military garrison near Lander, Wyoming. He was adopted by Captain and Mrs. Charles A. Coolidge, who named him Sherman.

Sherman wanted to be a minister. Old journals say that "at first the Coolidges opposed their foster son's choice of a profession on grounds that he was not suited to such a calling." In 1877, however, Sherman entered Shattuck Episcopal Military School in Faribault,

Minnesota. Bishop Whipple, in his autobiography, tells of the bright young Arapaho student. One day the young man came to the bishop and said, "Bishop, I suppose I am the only Arapaho who has become a Christian, and I should like to become a missionary to my people." Whipple entered Coolidge into Seabury Divinity School where he was an excellent student, and ordained him to the diaconate in 1884. He was ordained priest by John F. Spalding, Bishop of Colorado, in 1885 and sent to assist John Roberts, whose primary duty was to the Shoshone.

Work among the Northern Arapaho was begun in earnest with Coolidge's return to his home reservation, but it was not until 1914 that St. Michael's Mission was built. A brief reference to Michael Whitehawk in an undated Episcopal publication, *On the Trail to Tomorrow*, says Whitehawk translated St. Luke's Gospel into Arapaho and that St. Michael's Mission was named in his honor.

St. Michael's: the Noble Experiment

Nathaniel S. Thomas, Bishop of Wyoming 1909-1927, in establishing St. Michael's Mission set out to merge traditional Indian religion and Christian beliefs. From the outset the bishop pledged "not to try to make a white man out of the Indian but to try to help the Indian cope with the life dealt him." Patricia Duncombe in a 1981 publication, *Within the Circle*, wrote:

> Throughout the history of this mission there is ample evidence of the respect accorded to the values and practices of the Indian people. The design of St. Michael's emphasized Indian culture. The Old Men of the Tribe, the medicine men, prayed over the sites of the buildings. These buildings were arranged in a circle, like an Indian tipi village. Trees were planted in the center of the mission, in number like the poles of the Sundance Lodge, with prayer. Bishop Thomas followed the tribal custom of providing a feast for all when he visited, and of giving gifts to the leaders . . .
>
> Following this beginning, the policy continued through the years to build strong Arapahos, the work of St. Michael's won national acclaim as being very effective in meeting this goal. This work peaked in the 1930s . . . When the property was acquired in 1912 to establish an Arapaho mission, it is said that the Arapaho said *Hethadee,* meaning "good." The

word was eventually anglicized into "Ethete," and became the name for the mission's post office.

Despite its promising beginning, the Arapaho mission would eventually fall prey to standard paternalism. However, in the late 1960s, a reprieve seemed on the horizon when David S. Duncombe came to St. Michael's charged by the bishop to "give the mission back to the Indians." With his English-born wife, Patricia, a trained social worker and educator, the minister set out to restore the vision of the mission's founder. Mrs. Duncombe wrote:

> After consultation with local church people, new opportunities were opened up for the expression of worship and faith in traditional ways in the mission church . . . A new, centrally-placed altar was installed. The carpet around it was of the four sacred colors which represent Arapaho concepts of creation. The congregation approached the altar as though they were entering a ceremonial tipi, passing around it to the left to kneel in a circle to receive the communion . . . other traditional aspects of worship were incorporated, such as the use of cedar instead of incense, with the chief medicine man of the tribe blessing the church and congregation with it. He also blessed every child after baptism with an Arapaho prayer . . .
>
> In the early days of the mission, people often commented on the deep spirituality of the Arapaho people, and in our time this spirituality was very evident. This was not only expressed in church, but in the homes, and in such traditional observances as the sweat lodges, the feasts, the annual Sun Dances, and in the ceremonies of the Native American Church, in which many of our people were also active.

The Duncombes progressed toward rebuilding St. Michael's Mission to harmonize with Arapaho tradition. She directed the youth residential treatment center and had previous experience working among the Yaqui Indians near Tucson and among the Shoshone and Paiutes in Nevada. The St. Michael's circular compound, which offers space for a variety of community social and educational programs, was again teeming with activity. Together the couple slowly, over six and half years, gained trust of the community.

Tragically, the priest died of stab wounds inflicted by an intoxicated 16-year-old Arapaho youth, who a few years later died in an automobile accident while released on bail. The Wind River community was devastated with sorrow over their priest's death. At St. Michael's cemetery Duncombe was buried "in the Indian way," with the traditional wake, the give-away and the feast. His widow and their five children remained for a while at the mission where she continued to direct the Youth Residence Program. She subsequently joined the faculty at the University of Wyoming, Laramie, and later moved to Nevada.

After Duncombe's death several clergy—some far less sensitive to Indian cultural values—served St. Michael's. In 1979, Stan VerStraten came to St. David's on the Shoshone, and within two years he was assigned to serve also at St. Michael's and moved to Ethete. Eventually, the Shoshone mission was assigned to clergy from nearby Riverton.

Upon VerStraten's departure in 1989, the Arapahos were assigned their first Indian priest since Sherman Coolidge. But this man, a Chippewa, did not understand the Arapaho, and his new bride's discomfort about Indian ritual manifested itself in several ways, including letters to the editor of *The Living Church* following the 1991 General Convention, in which she labeled Native American ritual as "occult." The Chippewa priest eventually left the Episcopal Church and was deposed April 1, 1994. The ultimate irony lies in the fact that of all the Indian missions opened by the Episcopal Church, only St. Michael's was founded on a premise of honoring Indian values and culture.

For nearly five years Richard Mendez, a Shoshone from the Fort Hall Reservation in Idaho, served the Wind River congregations and doubled as a circuit rider trainer for Mountains and Desert Regional Ministries, funded in part by Episcopal Council of Indian Ministries.

When Bob Jones left Alaska to become Bishop of Wyoming in 1977, he held a serious goal to ordain an Indian leader on the Wind River Reservation. As one of the final acts of his tenure he ordained the first Shoshone of Wind River. On July 28, 1996, Patricia Bergie, who had studied in the diocesan ordination program, was ordained to the permanent diaconate. A former tribal official, Bergie works as a tour company guide on the reservation.

IDAHO: 100 YEARS AT FORT HALL

Among the native people of the Great Basin, women were valued and respected. Aside from their role as companion and mother, their foraging and gathering made them the principal providers and they were as capable as men of becoming a shaman, or holy person, or spiritual healer. When Christianity first came to the Fort Hall tribes, women

*Church of the Good Shepherd, 1921. A group from
Jamestown,Virginia Church there "for the laying of bricks."*
Courtesy, Archives of the Episcopal Church.

brought the word as they opened mission schools—Amelia J. Frost,
Ella Stiles, and Susan Garrett.

Therefore it was no radical transformation when the 100-year-
old Episcopal congregation at Fort Hall, Idaho—home of the
Shoshone-Bannock—accepted a woman in 1985 as its priest, ordained
a young woman deacon in 1994, and in Eastertide, 1995, ordained its
73-year-old matriarch as a perpetual deacon.

When the Mountains and Desert coalition organized in 1987, it
focused on self-help. Within the year, self-help and mutual support
became reality. The coalition's first effort had a gratifying outcome.
Indians restored an historic chapel at Fort Hall Reservation in Idaho.
In 1984 the 80-year-old Church of the Good Shepherd building, which
two years previously the Idaho Historical Society had designated an
historical site, was deemed structurally unsafe, condemned, padlocked,
and a rude beam nailed across the front door. An architect had estimated repairs would run $300,000, an insurmountable expense for
the diocese. Though the congregation could meet in the renovated

education building, the condemned chapel was a demoralizing symbol with a board nailed across the front door and made a negative statement to the reservation about the Episcopal Church.

The Wyoming, Montana and Utah Indian congregations put together a work crew which packed hammers and other construction tools and drove to Idaho to make repairs. The crew discovered that beneath the crumbling brick outside walls there was a structurally intact frame building. Suddenly restoration was possible! Condemnation proceedings halted. The historic building could be restored. No one remembered exactly when the chapel had been bricked in, but one member remembered that his family members had helped with the work.

A regional United Thank Offering request was submitted, jointly signed by all five dioceses of the coalition. The UTO awarded $22,000 for materials. The diocese was able to provide supplemental funding to cover costs for electrical technicians. With Indian volunteers providing the labor, the crumbling bricks were removed as were five layers of asphalt roofing. A new metal roof was installed and the church was painted. Within a year the Church of the Good Shepherd on the Fort Hall Reservation was reopened, its bright red door welcoming travelers from the interstate highway half a mile away.

The original chapel had been built at the fork of the Ross and Snake rivers in 1904 at a cost of $2,500 as a memorial to Mrs. Tazewell (Anna Robinson) Taylor of Norfolk, Virginia, by her family. In this church was a font given in memory of the work of the Connecticut Indian Association, which transferred its property to the Episcopal Church in 1899.

Under terms of the Grant Peace Policy, the Episcopal Church agreed to assume religious oversight for the Shoshone and Bannock tribes in Wyoming Territory, along with five Dakota agencies and a Ponca agency. Thus, technically, Bishop Hare of Niobrara had early jurisdiction over the Shoshone and Bannocks. His Dakota charges, however, consumed his total time and energy. Meanwhile, the Bannocks departed Wyoming and united with a separate band of Shoshone in present-day Idaho. In 1869 a half-million acre tract was reserved near Pocatello, Idaho, for various and scattered bands who had their homes on or near the old Oregon trail. The reservation was named Fort Hall and it became known as home to the Shoshone-Bannock.

Initially, operation of the agency was passed among various denominations. First it was Methodist, then Presbyterian, in 1871 Roman Catholic; in 1873 jurisdiction passed back to the Methodists. By 1883 the Mormons appeared. Then, in 1887 the interdenominational Connecticut Indian Association sent women to establish a mission school. The first teacher to appear was Amelia J. Frost. Shortly thereafter Ella Stiles arrived. She was teacher at the school for 10 years. A good many Indians were baptized, including the old chief, Billy George.

In 1899 the Connecticut Indian Association wanted to withdraw and offered to transfer to the Episcopal Church property which they held, consisting of a frame dormitory and mission rooms, and 160 acres of sagebrush land. The first Bishop of Idaho, James B. Funsten, wrote imperiously in a 1910 issue of *The Spirit of Missions*:

> These people were at that time [1899] mainly living in tepees, doing very little cultivating of land; very indifferent to all improvement, and slow intellectually. They keep up many of their wild, savage customs and costumes. They had advanced little in the knowledge of the Christian religion, and seemed very suspicious of any strangers, and of any effort by our missionaries. We opened our school under some earnest missionaries.

In March, 1900, the Episcopal missionary Susan Garrett offered to go to Ross Fork to take charge. A number of Indians were confirmed from time to time and much good work accomplished. Miss Garrett continued work for 10 years until she married and departed. Her successor was the Rev. S.W. Creasey who reported in 1912 that he had 24 children in his school and also ministered to the 200 Indian children in the government school. In 1913 the bishop wrote of the Fort Hall mission in *The Spirit of Missions*:

> I do not know of any more attractive bit of scenery than to stand out on the sage-bush plain, not far from our mission house (where we have our school for Indians), look away across the Snake River Valley, and see the tepees of the Indians, and, far off, the tall Saw-Tooth Mountains with their rugged outline and their snowy peaks. It is just the scenery that one might have looked upon years ago. Around these tepees are the Indians in their variegated costumes, their spotted ponies, and their little children, still playing with bow and arrow. Our church work with them has largely yet to be done. Last year, however, our clergyman baptized 100 Indians and presented *80 for confirmation*. Our hope for doing anything for the Indians lies chiefly with the young people, and so the school ought to be sustained and scholarships provided for these Indian children . . .

The government is now allotting to each Indian 20 acres of irrigated land and a much larger area of dry land for grazing. They will have the privilege of renting their land to the white families, which means that the isolation of the old reservation will be gone . . .

Some years ago we established a mission at Lemhi among a branch of the Shoshonis located there. Old Tendoy was the chief. There was a certain eloquence about the old fellow, a mingling of the grand and the comic. When the government wanted them to give up their reservation and move the 200 who composed their tribe to Fort Hall, the old man refused. He stood up among his people and, pointing to the craggy rocks where so many Shoshone had been buried, made a wonderfully eloquent speech about being compelled to leave the tombs of their ancestors. Finally the others went, and the government abandoned the reservation, but Tendoy refused to go. He was a brother of Chief Washakie.

The school's program was standard for the era—agriculture studies for the boys, housekeeping training for the girls—with a fourth "R" in the curricula for religious education. The school continued until the 1930s when the government began to operate reservation day schools.

At some point—no one recalls quite when—the mission was moved from the Snake River Valley to a gentle hill near the Shoshone-Bannock Agency. Forty years after the mission school closed the Diocese of Idaho in 1970 returned 150 acres of land to the Shoshone-Bannock tribes in accord with an 1890 agreement. The diocese retained 10 acres on which the buildings, church and cemetery are located.

Two Women Ordained

The Fort Hall mission has survived, often without resident clergy. Church Army clergy served the mission from time to time. Among them was the Rev. Clyde Estes, a South Dakota Sioux, who worked at Fort Hall in the 1960s. There were long periods in which laity were wholly responsible for keeping the doors open. Among these lay leaders was Lillian Vallely warden, witness, worker.

The first seminary-educated ordained woman priest to serve an Indian congregation came in 1985 as resident clergy for the Church of the Good Shepherd. She was the Rev. Joan LaLiberté, a Metís woman with forebears from Canada, who graduated from the Church Divinity

School of the Pacific in 1981 after a notable career in journalism stretching back over a decade. Joan LaLiberté came to Fort Hall looking to be there no more than three years, but found herself happily present for more than a decade. One of the advances she noted over the decade was a more cordial relationship between Christians and people who practiced the traditional religion. What she had hoped to see most was Good Shepherd communicants choosing an ordained vocation, and in the early 1990s two women from Fort Hall stepped forward to study through the three-year diocesan training program. They were Janice Nacke Atcitty and Lillian Vallely, the perennial senior warden. "Both these women have long been doing the ministry of the diaconate; their ministry and gifts have just not been appropriately recognized," said LaLiberté. "Janice brings able skills in youth ministry and Lillian is the best grief counselor I've ever seen. She's also a good preacher."

Atcitty was ordained deacon on January 29, 1994, at the Cathedral in Boise, becoming the first Shoshone-Bannock woman to enter holy orders. Her family members have long been members of the Fort Hall congregation. Married to a Navajo, the deacon has a daughter and a son and works for the tribal government in mental health social services.

When Mrs. Vallely reached retirement age after 30-plus years as an employee in the property and supply section of the Bureau of Indian Affairs on her home reservation, she decided to study for ordination as well as do volunteer work at the tribal museum. "Janice and I studied together to support each other," said Vallely, who has a history dating back to the 1970s in provincial and national leadership posts. She served as chairperson of the Province VIII Indian Commission and of the National Committee on Indian Work.

On May 14, 1995, Lillian Vallely, age 73, was ordained deacon before an overflow crowd at Holy Trinity Church in Pocatello. Associates from the Mountains and Desert Regional Ministries coalition and friends were present from many distant places, including Utah, Nevada, Wyoming, Georgia, New York and Washington, D.C.

"They're just giving me a title for doing the things I've been doing all along," said the new deacon.

"I've lived through a lot of bad racism here in Idaho," said Vallely. "What I wanted most, was to be a real part of my diocese—not separated or looked down upon, but to be a real part; to be recognized as a contributing individual not as a 'token' Indian." She said she believes she has reached that aim.

Vallely expanded on her views of life in the reservation setting:

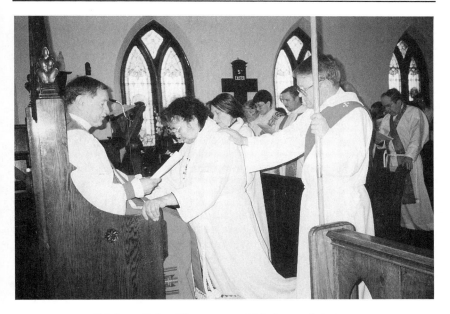

*Bishop John Thornton of Idaho ordaining
Lillian Vallely to the diaconate.*

Photo by Owanah Anderson.

The word "survival" is always with us. To retain our members, our culture and our tradition. To fight poverty, unemployment, alcoholism, drugs, satanism, school drop outs, racism in schools and jobs. It is more important because of the fast changing times we need to hang on to our ancestral customs which sustains our spirituality that is taught to each of us from birth.

High unemployment rates on the Fort Hall Reservation, as is the case of most of Indian reservations, contributes to the mission's inability to be fiscally self-sufficient. The diocese has had to rely on national church funding to support the work among the Sho-Bans. However, at his first diocesan convention after consecration, Idaho's new bishop, John Thornton, challenged the diocese to develop an endowment for the Indian work of the diocese, stating an intent to become unconstrained by the ebb and flow of national subsidy. Identifying the venture as the David Pendleton Oakerhater endowment, the bishop launched an appeal to raise $500,000. By mid-1994, $58,510 had been raised.

PYRAMID LAKE RESERVATION, NEVADA

Green grass carpeted the rectangle between St. Mary's church building and St. Joseph's hall. In most of America a green church yard is not unexpected. But this carefully tended garden of green grass, bright yellow marigolds and pale pink petunias grew in the high Nevada desert, symbolizing not only dogged perseverance but also rebirth of a community of the faithful.

The garden in the late summer of 1992 welcomed hundreds of visitors from across Nevada and distant dioceses to the centennial celebration of St. Mary the Virgin on the Pyramid Lake Paiute Reservation, Nixon, Nevada. A scant half dozen years ago there was every reason to believe that the St. Mary's Mission would not survive. With the recently consecrated bishop, Stewart Zabriskie, the author visited St. Mary's in 1986 and heard it said that "the people just aren't coming to church and just aren't interested anymore." I left the old-fashioned little chapel with the feeling I'd never be there again. The 92-year-old mission would surely be abandoned.

However, instead of withering, the congregation rose from the ashes of apathy and not only tediously transformed a desert plot into an English garden but also, during its centennial summer, communicants and community installed a new vicar, sent hundreds of invitations, and painted the church building and parish hall, inside and out. A children's choir rehearsed the offertory and bright-eyed acolytes drilled for the procession. The whole congregation practiced a special Sanctus adapted from a Zuni chant. They baked pies and cakes and cooked great quantities of other food. The whole reservation helped out; Pyramid Lake Cattlemen's Association provided many pounds of beef for the feast that followed Sunday services.

The concrete block building of St. Mary's, consecrated in 1912, is a beautiful little structure seating approximately 150. Copperish-brown hues highlight the faces of the figures in the stations of the cross. These American primitives are thought to have been created in the first quarter of the present century by the father of one of the deaconesses. An olive skinned madonna was made by Faithcraft Works in England and presented by Thomas Jenkins, Bishop of Nevada 1919-42. There is also a peace pipe hanging in St. Mary's church; it was made by the Ute Indians of Whiterocks, Utah, and is at least 60 years old.

A bell tower is located at the right of the chapel entrance and the bell is engraved: "Given by the Pah-Ute Indians and friends of the Mission to the Glory of God. November 4, 1927." A white picket fence encloses a few graves; other graves are at the top of a nearby hill. The altar and baptismal font are made from Pyramid Lake tufa rocks.

In 1917 a frame clergy and mission house was constructed. A spacious parish hall, funded through a $5,000 bequest through the Executive Council, was completed and used first for festivities of Christmas 1931. High on the hill above the church is a cemetery where more than 1,000 Indians are buried, many in unmarked graves.

There is a mystery about early efforts at bringing Episcopal presence to the Paiute. A cryptic clipping was recently uncovered from a 1923 publication of the Executive Council, *The Church at Work*, which said that a young Paiute from Nevada, Avery Winnemucca, was studying for Holy Orders in South Dakota. The Winnemucca family name is legendary among the Paiute. The article further disclosed:

> It was in 1862 that the Rev. Joseph H. Smeathman, the first missionary sent out by the Church to the Pahutes [sic], was murdered at Petaluma by Chief Winnemucca. Avery Winnemucca is the old chief's great grand-son . . .

There was no report on the murder of a missionary in the 1862 or 1863 editions of *The Spirit of Missions* nor was there a record of Avery Winnemucca ever being ordained.

Again, Women Launch the Mission

Early written records of St. Mary's Mission at Nixon show that women have always been in the role of leaders. Marian Taylor came as the first missionary after the Pyramid Lake Paiute tribe invited the Episcopal Church to open a mission among them. Supported by the Woman's Auxiliary of the Diocese of Western New York, Miss Taylor remained until her death in 1910. Her leadership and the leadership of women who followed her, including Deaconess Lucy N. Carter, earned early and broad response from the Paiutes and within a quarter of a century after arrival of the Episcopal mission almost all of the Pyramid Lake Paiutes had been baptized in the Episcopal Church.

Initially, the Episcopal Church had been assigned two other Nevada reservations, far removed from each other—Moapa and Fort McDermitt. Work was begun at Moapa in 1917 and at Fort McDermitt in 1932. The work long ago ceased.

The first services at Nixon were conducted in a small house loaned by the government, but by 1896 a chapel had been erected on a quarter of an acre of land provided by the Department of Interior. The chapel burned in 1912. Notable among the 48 lay and clergy leaders who have served at historic St. Mary's was Joseph Hogben, called the "buckaroo priest" because he visited his parishioners on horseback. Assigned to St. Mary's in 1937, he served until World War II.

Gareth Hughes, a lay worker and Shakespearean actor from Hollywood, was much loved by the people. Other well remembered vicars were Karl Tiedemann, Order of the Holy Cross, and William Hannafin, who served the congregation through 1990. During an 18-month vacancy in the early 1990s, Bishop Zabriskie drove the 50 miles from Reno at least once a month to conduct services at St. Mary's and "came to think of it as my spiritual home."

The Rev. Jean Rogers of Washington, D.C. was installed as vicar for St. Mary's and St. Michael's in early summer of 1992. Her unexpected resignation in less than two years resulted in disappointment across the reservation. By mid-summer of 1994, the Rev. Stan VerStraten, more recently a priest in Oklahoma but also formerly at Wind River Reservation in Wyoming, was called to serve the Pyramid Lake Paiute congregations.

Reynelda James who was "raised in St. Mary's" returned to Pyramid Lake with her husband Robert upon his retirement from federal employment in the mid-1980s. In the last decade this serene and soft spoken Paiute lay leader has not only helped the Pyramid Lake community to forge ahead but she has also brought an elder's wisdom and grace to national and regional Episcopal networks and boards. Among her many contributions has been organizing annual women's gatherings on her home reservation, attracting women from all over the land.

At the 1995 Winter Talk gathering in Oklahoma Mrs. James led a worship service for the 50-plus participants. Drawing from the traditional sense of sacredness of water and sage she gathered from the desert, she moved among participants gently sprinkling water she had brought from Pyramid Lake. She said:

> ... *Nu-nee Cui-ui-Ticutta Numu* (We People of the *Cui-ui Eaters*) believe our lake to be a sacred place, therefore the water within it. Sage grows plentiful around the desert lake. The sage and the lake water are used in prayers for blessings, thanksgiving, healing and cleansing.
>
> From the early times the elder women took their grandchildren and blessed them in the Sacred lake, offering prayers of thanksgiving for them. This tradition is carried on today.
>
> The lake water is used for baptisms in our churches, St. Michael's and All Angels' Church in Wadsworth and St. Mary the Virgin in Nixon on the Pyramid Lake Reservation.

The day of the baptism elders go out to the lake to get the water. A prayer is said over the water before it is taken from the lake. After the baptismal ceremony an elder takes sprigs of sage and the water and sprinkles each and every one. Saying a prayer and blessings for all.

Struggle for Survival

Until congressional legislation was enacted in 1990, the Pyramid Lake Paiutes had been forced to fight for nearly a century for survival of their lake, their subsistence and their life style. The turquoise blue, fan-shaped Pyramid Lake, 30 miles long and 11 miles at its widest, has been described as the most beautiful of all the desert lakes. It gained its name from the cone-shaped island which rises almost 300 feet from the surface of the water near the lake's eastern shore.

On the lake's shores since ancient times have lived the *Cui-ui-Ticutta*, now officially known as the Pyramid Lake Paiute. These people subsisted primarily on the lake's fine fish, including the giant Lahontan cutthroat trout, a species found in no other part of the world. Their diet was supplemented by small game, pine nuts and wild foods of the desert, including vegetation roots for which they dug with sticks. (In the early days these Indians were disparagingly labeled "digger Indians" by white invaders.) In the era of westward expansion these shy people were shot on sight for sport. Throughout most of the 20th century they have been pushed to struggle to protect the flow of water into their lake, their basic source of existence.

In 1859 the U.S. government agreed to establish for this Paiute band a reservation consisting of the lake, a narrow strip of barren and mountainous country surrounding the lake, and a 17-mile panhandle along the Truckee River which feeds the lake. The Truckee River starts at Lake Tahoe in the High Sierras on the Nevada-California border and flows almost 100 miles, past Reno, into Pyramid Lake. Scarcely was the ink dry on documents establishing the reservation before white squatters were encroaching on the lower Truckee River, the reservation's only irrigable land. A century-long struggle in courts and Congress to ban encroachment and secure water rights has ensued.

Though one of the landmark cases in Indian law, *Winters v. United States*, handed down in 1908, held that Indians had the right to water sufficient for the reservation's purposes from any stream running through or bordering any reservation, the U.S. Department of Interior, trustee for the Pyramid Lake Paiutes, wantonly failed to apply provisions to relieve the tribe of unlawful diversion of the Truckee River. In 1905 Derby Dam diverted half the flow of the Truckee to a giant irrigation system to benefit white settlers of the Nevada desert; fish could no longer get up the river to spawn; by 1938 the last of the great Lahontan trout had vanished.

By the 1960s Pyramid Lake had shrunk by 60 square miles; the pyramid was no longer an island. Anaho Island, home of the last great colony of white pelicans in North America, was accessible to coyotes and other predators who crossed the now-dry land to the rookeries. Most endangered, however, was the Pyramid Lake Paiute Tribe which depends upon on the lake for subsistence.

Litigation and lobbying had been devastatingly costly, sorely draining resources of the small tribe. The Episcopal Church's Coalition for Human Needs grant assisted somewhat with litigation costs. Though the Ninth Circuit Court of Appeals in 1981 upheld the right of the tribe to sufficient water, it would be another decade before the matter was finally resolved with passage of Fallon Paiute Shoshone Tribal Settlement Act authorizing $43-million and certain guarantees and concessions to the tribe in connection with its long-sought water rights.

THE UTAH UPSWING

The structure of the Episcopal Church is essentially one of a coalition of autonomous dioceses, and the degree to which the Episcopal Church has honored its commitment to bring the Gospel to Native peoples and the level to which Native values and cultural integrity have been honored historically depended, basically, on the perspectives of diocesan bishops. A case in point is that at almost precisely the same time in the 1920s that Edward Ashley, Archdeacon of Niobrara, was chairing an ecumenical committee to outlaw Indian dances, in Utah the Episcopal bishop wrote sensitively of the Ute people honoring the church with their turkey dance. It was 1924 when the Bishop of the Missionary District of Utah, Arthur W. Moulton, wrote in *The Spirit of Missions* about his profound impression at Convocation on the Uintah Indian Reservation where Episcopal mission had begun in 1897:

> All day they kept driving or riding in—hay racks, buckboards, buggies of ancient vintage, Fords, horses, ponies. They came out of the desert; they came over the mountains; they came from hamlets 50 miles away and from near by.

In the middle of the day the medicine man appeared with tents and blankets. A year ago this medicine man would not have a thing to do with us; he refused even to shake hands, but kept his face covered and used his influence against us. But this year he joined us. He joined the crowd; he took part in all the activities; he says we are all right.

At one end of the clearing we built an altar. It was a wonderful altar, with Navajo rugs for the foot pace and the altar steps and the fragrant sage brush massed about the reredos and the wings. On the retable stood the Cross and the candlesticks, and over the Cross hung a large picture of the Redeemer of all mankind. There was never an altar more beautiful, with all its rugged simplicity; no shrine ever more fitted into its surroundings as did this shrine of the sagebrush.

One morning as I was walking across the field I noticed an Indian man standing alone in front of the altar. His hat was in his hand and his head lifted toward the cross. He was a picture indeed—black braided hair, brilliant red shirt, bright blue overalls, yellow moccasins. All alone, he stood there motionless for 20 minutes . . . I hope and I think that he realized that in the new religion which we were presenting to him was to be found all that was best of his old life and ever so much new inspiration for the days to come.

The new religion, presented according to the rites and doctrines of the Episcopal Church—and perhaps the mode in which it was presented—had a remarkably strong appeal to the Ute people. Tradition has it that the Utes themselves asked the Episcopal Church to come to them, and high in the middle of Mormon country, 90 percent of the people of the Uintah Reservation were at one time Episcopalian.

Old records show that there had been 800 baptized and 600 presented for confirmation in a 12-year period between 1920 and 1932. The total population of the reservation in 1932 stood at a mere 1,250. Utes had numbered around 6,000 in 1880. *Indian Tribes and Missions,* published in 1934 by Church Missions Publishing Company, credits the awesome population decrease with "lack of necessities of life in a barren country, plagues of disease, and acts of lawlessness by renegade white men."

In 1925 there were four Episcopal mission centers on the Uintah Reservation: the Church of the Holy Spirit for Indians at Randlett, St. Elizabeth's Mission at Whiterocks, a chapel for Indians at Fort Duchesne, which had a hospital and agency office, and at Ouray.

Moulton was a "circuit rider" and visited the Uintah Reservation frequently. While bishop-in-charge of Nevada, he was president of the Nevada Indian Association which induced Congress to buy land for homes for Indians and persuaded the state legislature to place Indian children in public schools.

In 1895 the building was erected for Holy Spirit at Randlett. It stood originally about one mile from its present location. It was moved in 1962 to be more accessible to electricity and the tribal water line. The first service in the new location was in 1963, a week after Easter Day.

In the 1920s and 1930s Holy Spirit rendered a unique and badly needed service to the Utes through a farm school. An English couple, Mr. and Mrs. H. O. K. Richards, managed the school and were the first to teach the Utes the art of deep irrigation. Holy Spirit congregation has continued in unbroken continuity.

St. Elizabeth's at Whiterocks, built in 1905, provided religious education for 200 children who attended the nearby government boarding school. Long after the school closed, St. Elizabeth's chapel served the Ute people until it, too, closed in 1978. In the renaissance of the late 1980s, a fresh blue-trimmed St. Elizabeth's was reopened and rededicated January 28, 1989. The Rev. Quentin Kolb, a seminary-trained priest and member of the Uintah-Ouray (Ute) tribe, described the event for *IKHANA*, the Indian Ministries periodical:

> When St. Elizabeth's was built in 1905, there was no projection as to how long it would remain in use . . . as it was built as a place of worship for the Ute Indians and the students at the Whiterocks Indian School . . . When the school was phased out in 1952, the attendance suffered and the church began to deteriorate. This was not due to neglect on the part of devout Ute Episcopalians, but largely due to drastic cut in funds after many staff of the school transferred or moved elsewhere. The church continued to function [some 20 years] as a spiritual center with an occasional visit from one of the priests working in the Uintah basin. It mainly continued because of the strong lay leadership afforded by Henry Wopsock and the late Harriet Taveaport.

> Flocks of pigeons took up residence in the steeple . . . ravages of time [eventually] rendered the old building unfit for church services. In 1986, with sponsorship of the new Utah Bishop, the Right Rev. George Bates, a UTO grant was awarded for restoration of St. Elizabeth's. This grant was supplemented by a substantial amount from the diocese

and work began with the Ute Tribal Council providing support, such as police surveillance during construction. Then, help came from Mountains and Deserts Regional Ministry Coalition. From Fort Hall, Idaho, Wind River, Wyoming, and St. Patrick's in Washington, D.C. came volunteers for ground work. Even a local Boy Scout troop volunteered as did many local people . . .

St. Elizabeth's now has new bright white siding, a shiny new blue metal roof, new carpeting, newly painted and refurbished interior with storm windows, electric lights with ceiling fans, and a forced air furnace. The resurrected St. Elizabeth's was rededicated as a spiritual center for the community of Whiterocks and for all Episcopalians of the north benchlands of the Uintah basin by the Bishop Bates, whose kind and gentle support made it possible.

During the decade when St. Elizabeth's was closed Irene Gardner and her sister Geneva Chimburas kept the church alive by having services in their home. During this same time, the Church of the Holy Spirit—often without clergy—remained viable because of the faithful commitment of Nancy Pawwinnee and her sisters, Mary, Ruth and Clarice.

As a result of the renewed interest in these reservation churches their congregations have shown a great potential for growth. New native clergy have come to the Uintah and Ouray Reservation. In 1993 the Rev. Robert Two Bulls, a Lakota from Rapid City, South Dakota, was called to serve St. Elizabeth's. A second Native priest was added in late 1994 when the Rev. Richard Mendez (Shoshone) moved from Wind River Reservation of Wyoming to serve Holy Spirit.

Singers and dancers in full tribal regalia from St. Elizabeth's and Holy Spirit led the procession in the summer of 1996 when Carolyn Tanner Irish was consecrated as Bishop Coadjutor of Utah.

Utah's Urban Ministry

The first new Indian ministry in 75 years in the region of the Mountains and Desert was inaugurated in Salt Lake City in September of 1989. This work began as a social ministry among the urban people. The Rev. Quentin Kolb (Ute), the founder and director of the program, wrote:

We moved into a storefront/warehouse in January of 1990 and focused our work on urban Indians who are comprised of almost every tribe that has survived. We have concentrated on building community at the local level; working together, serving each other in negotiating a way of life that is strange to many of us.

Kolb, who was born in the 1920s, delayed retirement to continue the urban ministry which drew Salt Lake City commendations for community activities. The ministry moved from its storefront location to St. Mark's Cathedral in 1996.

THE MONTANA INCEPTION

In the early 1990s, the Church of the Incarnation, Great Falls, became heart and hub of a proposed new mission among Indians in Montana. The Episcopal Church had established no Indian mission in the giant diocese; the Roman Catholic Church began work early with the seven Montana Reservations—Crow, Fort Peck, Flat Head, Rocky Boy, Northern Cheyenne, Fort Belknap and Blackfeet.

It was among the Blackfeet that the Episcopal Church, under aegis of the Incarnation congregation, initiated an outreach in 1990 by beginning a preaching station. Located 140 miles to the northwest of Great Falls, the isolated Blackfeet Reservation is wedged between Glacier National Park, the Canadian border and the frigid town of Cutbank, frequently mentioned on the morning news as the nation's cold spot.

Working with the Blackfeet Tribal government and the United Methodist Church, the Episcopal group sought and received a substantial United Thank Offering grant ($27,196) for the program of Yellow Wolf Sanctuary youth project. The community spiritual center was designed to promote young Indian leadership in the church through Blackfeet language classes, recreation activities and tutoring as well as spiritual direction. A thousand people came to the opening day event for the Yellow Wolf youth project on May 1, 1994, in Browning.

Bishop C.I. Jones, ever since his 1986 consecration, had examined various outreach models to fulfill his pledge to establish mission among Montana tribes. First explored was a educational project on racism, but the idea failed to gain support. Next, the bishop appointed an Indian outreach committee and the diocese affiliated with Mountains and Desert Regional Ministry Coalition, sending Sarah Schmasow (Rocky Boy Cree) as the Montana spokesperson. Eventually, the diocese with substantial support from the Presiding Bishop's

Fund for World Relief and the Episcopal Council of Indian Ministry, focused on Thunder Child Adolescent Project, an innovative residential chemical abuse treatment program for Indian teenagers. This was the first Indian program to be an "initiative" project of the Presiding Bishop's Fund for World Relief. The fund in 1995 set about raising $200,000 within two years to underwrite the work of Thunder Child Youth Home in Great Falls. The initiative drew exceptional response, netting half its goal in less than six months.

Montana signals a potential 21st century approach to Indian mission. The chemical dependency program is built on the premise that Indian spirituality and cultural values are essential components in the healing process.

Indian mission has seen growth in the 1990s in the Great Basin and the region of the mountains and desert. It has been because Indians have at last been empowered by Episcopal Council of Indian Ministries and diocesan bishops to devise and design programs which will fit basic needs.

9

THE EPISCOPAL CHURCH'S FIRST
100 YEARS IN ALASKA

At the little seaport city of Sitka, described as "the fairest scene on the coast of North America," the diocese of Alaska gathered for its annual convention in autumn of 1995 to celebrate the 100th anniversary of the election of its first bishop, Canadian-born Peter Trimble Rowe, and to say goodbye to its sixth bishop, Steven Charleston, an Oklahoma-born Choctaw Indian.

There were only three mission congregations—all native—when Rowe was elected by the House of Bishops to serve Alaska. There were 52 parishes, missions and preaching stations—one-half native—when Charleston was elected in 1990 as the diocese's first Native bishop.

Alaska had been voted a missionary district in 1888 but the matter of a bishop for the district had been argued in the highest echelons of the Church four times previous to the Minneapolis convention of 1895. By the mid-1890s the Episcopal Church was caught up in a highly energized global evangelistic mode, supporting mission and bishops in Japan, China, Liberia, Haiti and several Latin American countries. At question, then, was whether the hierarchy chose to share the Gospel, in the words of Bishop Hare of Niobrara, "with heathens lying not far off but heathens lying cold on the church's bosom." The white population of Alaska Territory was nominal; the great gold rush was yet to come.

Though the Woman's Auxiliary delegates had pledged to give their United Thank Offering toward the support of a bishop for Alaska, the house debated intensely for two full days. The older bishops were adamantly opposed, resorting in fact, to leveling criticism toward Secretary of State Seward for having ever purchased the "ice chest" for $7,200,000 a quarter of a century earlier. The negative vote prevailed. Then an unlikely proponent, the powerful J. Pierpont Morgan, called aside his own New York bishop, Henry C. Potter, and urged him to negotiate a quick reconsideration. This was done, and Alaska had a bishop who would serve for 47 years.

Russian Orthodox Influence

A century before the first Episcopal missionary set foot in Alaska, the Russian Orthodox were ministering among the native peoples. Catherine, empress of all the Russias, in 1788 signed an imperial order sending missionaries to her American colony. Archimandrite Josaph led a group of 10 monks from the Valaam Monastery in Russia to Alaska in 1794 and they built their first church on Kodiak. Five years later Josaph was consecrated Bishop to Alaska, but drowned in a shipwreck on his way back from Russia to his see.

Among the first wave of Orthodox missionaries was Father Herman who dedicated his life to the Aleuts on Spruce Island in Kodiak. He was a humble monk who taught school, ministered to the sick, and got himself arrested in the 1800s while fighting for better treatment of Alaska Natives. The Aleuts called him *Apa*, or grandfather. Father Herman was canonized as a saint of the Orthodox Church in 1970, the first saint of the Orthodox Church whose work was in America. Another of the original group of monks was Father Juvenal who became the first Russian Orthodox martyr when he was killed by hostile Natives.

The Orthodox Church also canonized the first Native American saint, Peter, the Aleut. In the early 19th century, when the Russian Church was establishing missions in California, 14 Orthodox Aleuts were imprisoned by the Spanish Jesuits, who demanded that the Aleuts accept Roman Catholicism. The Aleuts refused and Peter is said to have bled to death following torture.

The Russians chose Sitka as the capital and built the imposing Baranoff Castle as home for the governor on top of the rocks that guarded the entrance to the harbor. It was at Sitka that the Russian Church built St. Michael's Cathedral, and Ivan Venianimof became the first bishop to serve in Alaska. In 1858 he was recalled to Russia where he eventually became the Patriarch of Moscow, the highest office of the Russian Church.

The Orthodox priests are said to have baptized 12,000 Native people by the end of the 18th century. Notwithstanding the fact that an estimated 48,000 Aleuts perished in the first 50 years of Russian rule, Russian Orthodox influence among Alaskan Natives was momentous. As recently as the 1970s the Orthodox Church was referred to as the "national church" among the Aleuts. After Russia sold the colony to the United States in 1867, support continued from the Russian Orthodox Church for Alaska Native mission until the 1917 revolution. Many Native people bear Russian surnames.

Orthodox dictum did not require the Native to become a Russian in order to become a Christian. By the middle 1800s, the Russian Orthodox mission had established bilingualism as its norm; Alaska Native languages were used liturgically and in the schools. However Dr. Sheldon Jackson, a Presbyterian who eventually became superintendent of education for Alaska, insisted that Alaska Natives could not become Christian until they had been acculturated or "civilized," and that the first step toward "civilizing" was eradication of the Native languages. Radically divergent Christian philosophy was imposed on Native Alaskans with the arrival of western Christianity, and primal religious traditions, present in the Americas for 30,000 years, have only within recent decades been re-examined by Christian theologians in quest of reconciliation.

The difference between Eastern Orthodox and western protestant practice stems from basic theological views; the Orthodox believe that all things were fulfilled in Christ, not replaced by Christ. Some groups of western protestant Christianity, led by Dr. Jackson, held irreconcilably opposed interpretations of the Gospel. Thus, during the first hundred years of Russian missionizing the traditional cultures were baptized into a newness of life, not discarded and replaced by alien cultures. When western Christianity arrived following the Alaska purchase, the Alaskan Native was victim of the deep separation between eastern and western theology.

Church of England Mission

In 1856 a highly individualistic Englishman, William Duncan, answered an ad placed by the Church Missionary Society of England for a missionary to the warring Tsimshian Indians along the west coast of Canada. A former dry goods clerk in Victoria, British Columbia, Duncan possessed no theological training but had deep religious convictions. He was hired and arrived at Fort Simpson and set about establishing a "Christian village" at old Metlakatla, which eventually grew to a population of 1,000 Indians and flourished for 30 years.

His English Church benefactors became uneasy about Duncan's informality in worship, and his position on the sacraments of Baptism and Holy Eucharist. It seems that Duncan was reluctant to represent the sacrament of Holy Communion as the Body and Blood of Jesus Christ because he was wary of potential misinterpretation by a people recently converted from cannibalistic ways. The Church Missionary Society and the Anglican Church of Canada voiced concern over his informality, whereupon Duncan, with the help of Episcopal Bishop Phillips Brooks of Massachusetts and Dr. Henry Ward Beecher, gained audience with U.S. President Grover Cleveland and congressional leaders. They granted Duncan and the Metlakatla colony refuge on any Alaskan island they chose. Over 800 Tsimshian Indians, led by Duncan, departed Canada and moved in 1887 to the "new Metlakatla" on Annette Island near Ketchikan.

An informal relationship existed between Duncan's mission and the Episcopal Church—Bishop Rowe baptized the Metlakatla children—but eventually, in 1941, the Metlakatla Christian Mission affiliated with the Methodists. Many of the Tsimshian people moved to Ketchikan and became active with St. Elizabeth's Indian congregation and it was St. Elizabeth's which nurtured a young Paul Mather, descendent of the Tsimshians who departed Canada with Duncan. Mather become the first Native Alaskan priest in 1930.

Anglican Influence

Far distant from old Metlakatla, the Canadian Anglicans entered Alaska when it was still Russian territory to bring the Gospel to the Athabascan Indians along the Yukon River and its tributaries. It was in the early 1860s when the Episcopal Church was endeavoring to survive the Civil War without rupture. The Rev. William W. Kirkby, later archdeacon, came down the Porcupine River to its confluence with the Yukon River in 1861 and there found about 500 Indians at Fort Yukon. Hudson's Bay Company, clearly violating Russian territory, had established Fort Yukon in 1847.

Images of that first service in Fort Yukon long existed in some of the older stories of the area. The Rev. David Salmon, commented, "I've heard that when Kirkby held that first service, he stood on a piece of caribou hide, and all the people gathered. When he pulled out the Prayer Book, people were fascinated. They'd never seen a book, you know? They didn't know what this was that he had, that was so white . . . and they were fascinated by the noise that the pages made when he turned them."

Kirkby was followed by the Rev. Robert McDonald, a Scotsman who later was named the first Archdeacon of the Yukon and spent

50 years in Canada working among Yukon Indians. He and Bishop William C. Bompas of the Canadian Diocese of Selkirk made regular visits to Fort Yukon, located eight miles north of the Arctic Circle, and paddled as far down the Yukon as the village of Tanana, 500 miles from Canadian territory. McDonald rapidly learned the native language and composed a system for transposing it into written form. He developed a dictionary and translated the entire Bible, the Book of Common Prayer of the Church of England and the Hymnal into the native language. The Rev. David Salmon, the first Athabascan priest, used the same transposition symbols and McDonald's translation of the New Testament to teach the people of Chalkyitsik to read their language in the late 1950s.

From 1881 until his death in 1885, a young English priest, Vincent C. Sim, served Archdeacon McDonald. Native clergy along the Yukon held the clergyman in memory a full century after his early death. Born in Windsor, England, he was assigned to the mission at Fort Chipewyan in northern Canada, and subsequently appointed assistant to Archdeacon McDonald, who sent him to the distant outpost, Old Rampart House, the Hudson's Bay Company trading post on the Upper Porcupine River.

From Old Rampart House Sim set off on two historic journeys, traveling by birch bark canoe and skin boat to bring the Gospel to the Athabascan peoples along the Yukon and Tanana Rivers. His 1883 and 1884 journeys covered 2,300 miles, taking him to preach and teach at places where no missionary had ever been. In his letters, he reported how eager the people were for the Gospel, sometimes keeping him up all night. His letters also recorded a great epidemic sweeping through the Native fishing camps along the rivers. Possibly diphtheria, the epidemic took a dreadful toll. Sim sometimes found only two or three survivors in a whole village. Of one village, he wrote: "We here found a man with two women and a child, the sole survivors of a small band of Indians who were carried off by the sickness in the summer of 1882."

During the winter of 1884-85 Fr. Sim's letters from Rampart House told that hunting was poor and the sickness continued in the land. Sim kept busy teaching and caring for the sick and building a church at the post. He pleaded for more help:

> The Upper Yookon [sic] taxes all my energies & with the still greater field of work on the Lower Yookon laying upon me, I feel the burden is greater than I can bear. Do Christian people at home really realize the state of things here?

The *Alaskan Epiphany* in its summer 1985 issue memorializes the young English missionary in an article entitled: "Vincent C. Sim . . . One of the First."

It was springtime now . . . and the young priest was dying. Weakened to the point of exhaustion by his travels and caring for the sick around him, he now would share in their way of dying as he had shared in their way of living. Through the window of the rough cabin he lay in, the newly built mission church could been seen. Spring had come to the land, bringing along warm days of blue sky and sunshine, ducks and geese landing on some of the thawed lakes, and the promise of summer—but by now he was oblivious to it all . . . He would die here, among those with whom he had worked and taught. They had taught him too, of course, how to survive and how to live in this land. They had accompanied him on his travels and now, for this last journey, they would care for him too. Perhaps one of those caring for him, there in the little cluster of cabins in the high canyons of the Porcupine River, was a tall young man, noted among his people for his wrestling ability. The tall young man would remember the priest from faraway England.

As the ice on the river broke, and the water began to run once more on the Porcupine . . . the young priest died. He was laid to rest in the Indian graveyard—a quiet, secluded spot on the top of a high hill. A neat rail and headboard were made and placed by an Indian around the grave. The name carved on the headboard read: "The Rev. Vincent C. Sim." He was barely 30 years old. He was one of the first.

The "tall young man" would tell his son stories on long Alaskan winter nights about this English priest. The son would listen and learn about the ministry among the Athabascan peoples, and in 1962 he would become the first Athabascan ordained to the priesthood—David Salmon of Chalkyitsik.

At the time of Sim's death, another Englishman was journeying to the United States, beginning an odyssey that would ultimately lead him to Alaska. His name was Hudson Stuck, and he would become the acclaimed Archdeacon of the Yukon, author and explorer. Many years later Stuck landed the Episcopal launch *The Pelican* at the deserted site of Old Rampart House. He climbed the hill and pushed through the grass to the graveyard. Stuck wrote:

Let it be remembered to the honour of the Church of England that she had sons and sent them into the wilder-

Archdeacon Hudson Stuck [1863-1920]
aboard The Pelican, *1911.*
Courtesy, Archives of the Episcopal Church.

ness long ago; upon whose labours we of the American
Church have tardily entered in these more comfortable
times, to reap, in some measure, the fruit.

The Comity Agreement

The Presbyterians had arrived in the southeast in 1877 and under
the dynamic Dr. Jackson, who would eventually occupy the highest
position of his denomination, major education programs for the native people were begun. Jackson soon realized that his denomination
could not singularly educate all Alaskan Natives. The U.S. government had assumed scant responsibility, so he sought out other
denominations to provide teachers in different areas. While historians disagree on whether such a meeting ever happened, it is said that
in the early 1880s an interdenominational meeting was held in Philadelphia out of which came an ecclesiastical "non-aggression pact." The

Episcopalians agreed to take on work begun by the Anglicans along the upper Yukon and the interior, and to help the Presbyterians along the Arctic Coast. Generally speaking, the rest of the enormous territory was apportioned thusly: the Methodists got Unalaska and the Aleutian Islands; the Baptists got Kodiak; the Congregationalists got Cape Prince of Wales region; the Moravians got the Kuskokwin region; the Roman Catholics received the mid and lower Yukon. And the Presbyterians, by the Comity Agreement, would continue their work in the southeast and extend work to the Arctic coast.

For reasons unknown, the Lutheran Church, which had maintained mission at Sitka in Russian America, was not a party to the agreement. Also conspicuously absent from the agreement were the Orthodox, who had been evangelizing Natives for most of a century and had 11 priests and 16 deacons at work in Alaska at the time of the U.S. purchase in 1867.

Each of the denominations of the Comity Agreement transported to Alaska the standard model of mission school education that they had rehearsed among the nations and tribes of the contiguous states. The bilingual schools of Russian America had attempted to build on indigenous talent and potential; the Americans built schools with intent to destroy Native languages and cultures.

Anvik, Where Episcopal Work Began in Alaska

Responding to vague instructions to go to Alaska and begin mission among the Athabascan Indians at some point on the Yukon River, a young missionary, the Rev. Octavius Parker, in June, 1886, arrived with his family at the coastal trading center of St. Michael, the principal supply depot of the great district extending up the Yukon River for 2,000 miles. Recently from the Willamette Valley of Oregon, the young missionary neither spoke any of the Athabascan languages nor did he have guides. Parker soon experienced overt hostility from St. Michael traders, who abominably exploited the Indians and opposed education for the Native peoples. After lingering in St. Michael for nine disheartening months, Parker welcomed an invitation from a large party of Indians from Anvik to establish a mission at their village, 450 miles upriver from the mouth of the Yukon.

Meanwhile, a young deacon from New York, John Wight Chapman, had come to St. Michael and together the young men arrived in Anvik in July to establish the mother church of Alaska. The missionaries found that the Anvik villagers knew no English and spoke only Athabascan plus a bit of Russian. For most of the year the villagers lived in underground houses and had only recently given up their stone knives and axes for ones of steel acquired from traders. The elder Chapman in 1912 wrote in *The Spirit of Missions*:

> I suppose that when we began work here in 1887 there was hardly any portion of our country which had been so little affected by civilization. Half a dozen traders and missionaries were scattered along the course of a river two thousand miles long. Our first task, as we saw it, was to become sufficiently acquainted with their language, and at the same time to acquaint them with sufficient English so to establish a means of mutual understanding.
>
> Rude buildings for a mission house and a schoolhouse were erected. Later a beginning was made upon a church building, and in 1894 the present Christ Church was completed.

Parker left the mission after only two years, and Chapman continued the work alone. In 1893 he took furlough and when he returned the following year he brought with him three women—a teacher, Deaconess Bertha Sabine; a medical doctor identified only as Dr. Glanton; and May, his bride. Anvik was home for the Chapman family for the next 61 years, a record in Alaskan mission history. Henry, the son of the Chapmans, became a priest and succeeded his father at the Anvik mission, serving there until 1948 and at other Alaska missions until 1963. Henry Chapman returned to Anvik from his retirement home in North Carolina for the centennial celebration at Anvik in July, 1987. He died at age 98 in 1994.

First United Thank Offering

The Woman's Auxiliary in 1889 designated $1,000, one-half of the first United Thank Offering, to build Christ Church at Anvik. May Seely Chapman, the bride Chapman brought back with him from his "outside" furlough, described both her first view of the mission which would be her home for the rest of her life and the first Sunday worship in the new church building in August of 1894:

> This eventful day had been misty in a fine rain. Anvik landmarks came into sight, idyllic, with white tents and little brown huts set in the green grass, smoke rising from the fires, the scarlet salmon hanging to dry upon the racks, against the silvery green of the willows and the dark spruces. To our left, rose the high rocky bluffs of the Yukon,

crowned with thickets of spruce and the feathery birch and alder. Slowly our little steamer rounded the last rocky point. Young natives had come out in their canoes and paddled swiftly all about the boat in welcome.

The mission premises came into sight, the new little log church with its white belfry and surmounting the cross. Within, hung the bell, the gift of a devoted churchwoman in New York, probably the first church bell to send its sound across those rivers. There were the storehouses, and the sawmill, more useful than a gold mine to the mission, and the gambrel roofed log building where school was held. Our own log cabin home, set high upon the hill.

Just then, as the boat came to the landing, the clouds parted, the sun shone out, and a rainbow, a rare sight in that latitude, stood above our new home welcoming us at the end of our 6,000 mile journey. We went up the paths, through the groups of waiting people, into the cabin, and knelt to give thanks and to ask a blessing upon the new life upon which we were entering.

We went into the church. The logs had been cut, and the foundation tiers laid, before Mr. Chapman had left in the summer previous. The native men had given one day at cutting logs without pay, and when the foundation was completed, the Doxology had been sung. The walls were raised by the native men voluntarily . . . the building was completed by Maurice Johnson, a Swede, and he had done careful and substantial work. The room was 25 feet square, and there was no furniture excepting the handsome stone font, given by our faithful friends of the Woman's Auxiliary in Newark, and the small Estey organ from Vermont.

Sister Bertha found an empty packing box, covered it with turkey red calico and draped it in white, and it was set between the two eastern windows to serve as altar. Its only furniture was a small wooden cross. We found glasses and filled them with the brilliant red spires of the deerweed and the feathery tipped grasses gathered from God's own garden along the river bank in front of the mission, and set them on each side of the cross upon the altar. A large sheet was hung across one corner of the room to serve as a "vestry". Benches had been brought in from the school room, and the church was as nearly ready for the service the next day as we could make it.

The people came to the church, 85 persons crowding into the room. The men sat on benches, the women crouched on the floor, abject figures with their hair falling over their downcast faces. The babies were snug in the parki hoods on the backs of the mothers. The toddlers ran about in bright calico shirts, vests like those of their fathers, and blue denim trousers buttoned on with large white agate buttons, a much admired decoration.

Familiar hymns were sung. The men looked up, listening to the service and the words of the interpreter. When the service was ended, the people still sitting quietly in their places, the minister came from the vestry and said: "Come, my children". One by one those boys and girls of that first school came and stood in a semi-circle before him, to be catechized.

Although Chapman never ceased to spread the gospel and build up the church, he also became a dedicated teacher and served as postmaster, radio operator, dentist, doctor and doer of everything that needed to be done. He was also a scholar, recording much of the local culture and language, and contributing papers to anthropological journals for many years.

The UTO funds were well invested. Christ Church at Anvik on the Yukon continues, after 100-plus years, to bring the gospel.

Point Hope on the Arctic:
Site of the Second Mission

Point Hope, to the far north on the Bering Sea, was the site for the second Episcopal mission in Alaska. It was begun by a layman, Dr. John B. Driggs, a physician from Wilmington, Delaware.

Whalers had long plied the Bering Sea and their impact at the coastal town of Point Hope had been devastating to the Eskimo inhabitants. A common practice of traders had been to trade the Native people liquor for whale bone, a highly marketable commodity a century ago; fashionable wasp-waisted women required baleen—long flexible strips from the mouth of the bowhead whale—for corset stays. In addition to the moral and spiritual devastation resulting from alcohol introduced by the whalers' trade, the Eskimos were physically devastated by the white men's diseases. Measles swept away whole villages. U.S. Navy officials informed Episcopal authorities of the condition of the Natives at Point Hope and urged that a medical missionary be sent. Driggs offered his services and reached Point Hope in July, 1890.

As the doctor stepped ashore, he helplessly watched as the Arctic waves swept away most of his belongings including his supply of coal. Once settled in a two-room house which would serve as school, dispensary and living quarters, the doctor's next challenge was to persuade the children to come to classes. There is a story that he lured his first pupil with a piece of molasses cake. Popular history has it that Driggs' first pupil was named *Kinneeveeuk*. Before the year was out, however, 50 children were in his school.

In addition to teaching, Driggs toiled endlessly to care for the ill and he often traveled many miles to outlying hunting camps to tend those too ill to be brought to him. One of his frequent stops, just south of Point Hope, was the village of Kivalina, home decades later of the first Eskimo priest, the Rev. Milton Swan, who was ordained in 1964.

Driggs, the layman, ministered at Point Hope for 18 long and lonely years. He weathered countless hardships. Winter came early one year and the supply ship failed to arrive. Adequate fuel and food became a very serious problem. At one time the only food left in the village was a dead walrus which washed ashore during a storm.

A further hardship for the doctor was the total lack of companionship from anyone outside Alaska. It was not until he had spent four unbroken years at the mission that the Episcopal Church sent him an assistant, the Rev. E. H. Edson. By 1908, though the doctor was only 54, his health failed and he was obliged to turn over his mission work to others. The legacy he left lives on. The liquor problem diminished; polygamy disappeared; the status of women and primitive health conditions improved. The school founded by Driggs had equipped Eskimos to protect themselves against unscrupulous whalers and traders. Driggs' goal had been to help people of Point Hope become educated Christian Eskimos, not imitations of the incoming caucasian Christians.

Episcopal mission on the northern Alaskan coast, begun by a lonely lay physician, today fans downward from Barrow, Point Lay, Point Hope, Kivalina, Noatak, Kotzebue and Nome.

St. James' Mission at Tanana

The third Episcopal mission in Alaska was at the trading post of *Nuchalawaya*, near Fort Adams, 800 miles upstream from the mouth of the Yukon. The Canadians had initiated the mission work and already translated the prayer book into the local dialect. In 1891 the Episcopal Church sent the Rev. Jules Prevost who upon the arrival of Bishop Rowe would be named the first Archdeacon of the Yukon. When a shoal formed in the Yukon River, denying accessibility to Fort Adams, the mission was moved down river to a point near Tanana and the newly established military post, Fort Gibbon.

Prevost moved rapidly toward extending work, plying up and down the river in his little missionary launch. During his 15-year stay as both priest and physician, he traveled to 32 Native villages and set up a school. Eventually, he acquired a small printing press, a gift of Episcopalians in the United States, and began publishing the first newspaper in the Alaskan interior, the *Yukon Press*. The village of Tanana did not depend on an adjacent mining camp but owed its existence to the military post, Fort Gibbon. Hudson Stuck, a frequent visitor to the area, wrote of the animosity between the town and the military post:

> . . . regardless of the animosity between them, the town was necessary to the post for two reasons: whiskey and wood. Most of the buildings in Tanana were saloons and civilian employees of the military post chopped approximately 3,000 cords of wood a year.
>
> The evil influence which the town and the army post have exerted upon the Indians finds its ultimate expression in the growth of the graveyard and the dwindling of the village.

Alaska's First Episcopal Bishop

Few men had training in their early ministry which so thoroughly fitted them for their life work as did the man chosen as the first bishop of Alaska, Peter Trimble Rowe. His first ministry had been on a Canadian Indian reserve on the shores of Lake Huron where traveling was done by small boats in summer and by snowshoes in winter. Later, working 13 years in northern Michigan, he experienced additional frigid weather and hardship. In Alaska he would travel by boat, snowshoes and dog-sled, spending many wintry days "mushing" with a dog-team, usually alone. He once made a 350-mile solo journey from Fairbanks to Valdez, camping out at night in minus 60-degree temperature. The trip took 18 days.

Rowe's consecration was held on St. Andrew's Day, November 30, 1895, at St. George's Church, New York City. He returned to Michigan, collected his family, settled his wife and two sons in Tacoma, Washington, and shortly departed for Juneau and Sitka, the old Russian capital. It was here that he would make his home and years later build St. Peter's-by-the Sea.

*Bishop Peter Trimble Rowe [1856-1942] arriving by
dogsled at St. John's in the Wilderness in 1912.*
Courtesy, Archives of the Episcopal Church.

When he reached Alaska in 1896, he found three Native mission stations. At the close of his work in 1942, there were 24 established centers of work, 12 of which were Indian missions. During Rowe's incredibly long tenure he saw standard transportation come from "mushing" by dog-team to river transportation aboard *The Pelican*, and finally to air travel across his giant jurisdiction. He flew with the daring bush pilots in the 1920s, and in 1927 made his first commercial plane flight from Nome to Point Hope in one day; it had once taken him three weeks to make the trip by dog-sled.

When the bishop made his first exploratory journey into the interior of his jurisdiction there were few white people and no one knew the size of the Native population. Though gold had been discovered—in fact, the Russians had taken out small quantities—it would be two years before the famous Klondike gold stampede. The bishop's first task was to explore the country, to learn what there was to be done, how best to do it, and then how to maintain the work once it was begun.

On his first trip into the interior he reckoned to cross the steep and perilous Chilkoot Pass descending into Canada and thence upon reaching the upper Yukon to float downstream. Departing from Juneau and traveling as far as possible by boat, he then acquired a train of 13 pack horses and headed north. Some 600 men were taking the same route to reach the gold fields at Forty Mile and Circle City. After crossing the summit, he hauled his own sled with a load of 450 pounds. Unable to gain passage by boat upon reaching the Yukon, he was compelled to build his own boat which he described as "20 feet long, 25 inches wide at the bottom . . . built from a log by an instrument of torture—the whipsaw."

On arriving at Circle City, near the Canadian border, the bishop found the rush and din of a booming camp of quickly erected saloons and loudly ringing dance halls. The young bishop, casting about for a place to hold a service, went to a saloon owner, George Baldwin, and was granted permission for the loan of the saloon. "Clean up this place," shouted Baldwin from behind the long bar, "We're going to have church. Down your drinks and get the liquor out of sight."

To his surprise, the bishop found that the Indians in Circle City "had Bibles, Prayer Books and Hymnals, which they could use too! They were eager for religious instruction." Within the next two years, the bishop would establish a hospital in Circle City and find a dauntless deaconess willing to come to this distant outpost to run the little log facility. She was Sister Elizabeth Deane, a nurse and graduate of a church training school. Later Dr. James L. Watt with his family served Circle City's Grace Hospital as lay missionary.

Rowe described his first journey into the interior in a letter dated July 21, 1896, to Mrs. A.M. Lawver, president of the Woman's Auxiliary in California:

> I left Juneau on April 22nd and after nearly two months of constant going reached Circle City on June 11th—1,000 miles . . . We had to travel all night, as a rule, when the ice and snow were hard . . . Circle City is 18 months old and the largest village of log cabins in our land. I found about 800 of the population white and over 300 Indian. There were about 500 "mines" in addition to the "diggings" or "washings". I held services for both Indians and whites. The only building I could use for the purpose was a saloon.

He made a second trip to the upper Yukon in 1898, going first to Dawson City in Canada where he visited Bishop Bompas—and noted in his diary that whisky sold for $75 a gallon. He then set out on the Yukon River and stopped at the little village of Eagle, where a survey had fixed the boundary between the United States and Canada. It was from this rustic little village that an Episcopal Indian evangelism team set out in the summer of 1990 in a 24-foot cruiser to retrace the bishop's journey.

The bishop in 1898 proceeded down river to a quieter Circle City—the gold seekers had moved on to Canada. The evangelism team, which visited many villages on the Yukon in 1990, found a very, very quiet Circle City—almost everyone in the village had been airlifted out to fight forest fires.

Subsequent Missions in the Yukon Basin

As with the Canadians before him, Bishop Rowe recognized Fort Yukon, lying north of the Arctic Circle at a point near where the Porcupine and Chandalar Rivers join the Yukon, to be the most important location along the great waterway. Here, furs were brought from a thousand miles distant to the Hudson's Bay Trading Post. When Rowe first visited Fort Yukon he found 300 Indians living there and Mrs. Bompas, the Canadian bishop's wife, conducting a school for 60 children. His correspondence tells that he immediately arranged for "the building of a small cabin for services, to cost $150 and appointed a good Indian as lay reader—I will pay him $100 a year."

Thus was established the fourth Episcopal mission of Alaska, St. Stephen's, at Fort Yukon. The small log church, built in 1898, was not replaced until 1942 and moved to its present location a dozen years later.

The man to be paid $100 a year was William Loola, trained by Archdeacon McDonald as catechist and layreader. In 1904 Loola became the first Athabascan ordained to the diaconate. Beginning with Loola, the bishop would continue this pattern in developing indigenous leadership which has long served the scattered Native villages.

A street named in Loola's honor meanders from the river up into the village, and his portrait hangs in the vestibule of St. Stephen's Church. He appears to be about 50 when the portrait was made, a handsome man with broad brow, and full thick black hair and mustache. In today's St. Stephen's there are three magnificent altar cloths of beaded moose skin, made by the women of the area to celebrate the end of World War I. St. Stephen's Mission for many years operated Hudson Stuck Memorial Hospital to which Alaska Natives were brought from incredible distances by dog-team for treatment.

In 1898 two missions were established at Eagle after gold was found on the banks of nearby creeks and the little river settlement became an overnight boomtown. St. Paul's was built in the town and

*William Loola [? - 1918], the first Athabascan
deacon of the Episcopal Church.*

St. John's in the Native village, three miles upstream. Within the
decade, the gold-hungry hordes moved on, and the walls of the old
military barracks for Fort Egbert collapsed with time, but today—
almost a century later—there are still two Episcopal churches in tiny
Eagle, Alaska. The 1990 evangelism team, welcomed by Athabascan
elder Louise Paul and her great grandson, held services in the tiny
log church which was built in 1900 in the Native village. Because it
was mid-summer, with an Alaskan twilight lasting until 2 a.m., it did
not matter that the dank and musty little building had no electricity.
The dozen or so faithful communicants reported that the last service
of Holy Eucharist had been some eight months previously when a
Canadian Anglican priest had visited.

Other Episcopal Indian missions founded along the Yukon River
and its tributaries included St. Andrew's at Stephen's Village, where
Deaconess Harriett Bedell long served; St. John's-in-the-Wilderness
at Allakaket, the only mission to serve the two distinct races, Indians
and Eskimos; Bishop Rowe Chapel at Arctic Village, where *Vine-ee-
khaak'aa* and later Albert Tritt founded the indigenous church; St.
Mark's at Nenana, which would become a center for schooling; and
St. Timothy's at Tanana Crossing, where within only a few years after
its founding there was scarcely a person who had not turned to the

church. The Episcopal Church became the center of community life up and down the Yukon, Porcupine and Chandalar rivers.

It was during the era of the great gold rush that work was begun at Fairbanks, today's diocesan headquarters. It is interesting to note that while the great Alaska gold rush came and went, the Episcopal missions founded around the turn of the century have, for the most part, remained.

Hudson Stuck: Archdeacon of the Yukon

When Rowe came to Alaska he expected that his work would be almost entirely among the Native peoples. However, the great Alaska gold rush forever changed the face of Alaska and the bishop shortly realized that his ministry would also include the horde of new transient caucasians—the stampeders—who flooded into the area seeking instant riches. So, at the turn of the century, after having established 13 churches, eight schools and three hospitals, the bishop cast about for capable assistance.

He recruited a most capable individual, Hudson Stuck, and in 1904 named him Archdeacon of the Yukon. Compared to Rowe and several other Alaska clerics, Stuck served a relatively short time. He died of pneumonia on October 10, 1920, at age 57. But during those 16 years his boundless energy and devotion to native peoples built so strong a foundation that even today one finds villages of his old jurisdiction still 100 percent Episcopalian. His message to the Native peoples was awesomely simple: over and over he preached " . . . the cardinal facts of religion: the Incarnation, the Crucifixion, the Ascension; the cardinal laws of morality: the prohibition of murder, adultery, theft and falsehood. In one of his several books, *The Alaska Missions,* completed shortly before his death, he wrote:

> As regards the native work, there are today, speaking broadly, no unbaptized natives left in Alaska . . . the writer knows of none in the Interior.

Born in London on November 11, 1863, Stuck was educated in English public schools and King's College, London. At age 22, he booked passage for Australia but disembarked at New Orleans, and wandered westward until finally settling in the small rural hamlet of Junction City, Texas. There he worked as an itinerant cowboy for $10 a month. Soon he was hired as a part-time school teacher at nearby Cuero. He became a layreader, Sunday school superintendent and volunteer in the small Cuero Episcopal church where he "lighted the fires and swept the floors." The young Englishman soon came to the attention of the Bishop of West Texas, James Steptoe Johnston, who procured a scholarship and sent him to study at the University of the South, Sewanee, Tennessee. Stuck compiled an outstanding academic record, graduated in 1892, and shortly after his twenty-ninth birthday he was ordained priest. After serving small churches in Goliad and Cuero, he was elected dean of St. Matthew's Cathedral in Dallas, where be became well known for his eloquence as a preacher and writer and for aggressive leadership in the diocese.

Rowe first met Stuck during the height of the Klondike gold rush at the church's 1898 General Convention. Six years later the bishop offered the 40-year-old dean the challenging post of "Archdeacon of the Yukon and Tanana Valleys and the Arctic Regions to the North of the Same." The district encompassed approximately 300,000 square miles, an area far bigger than the state of Texas.

Stuck was the only man other than the bishop to visit every Episcopal church, mission, or outpost of Alaska. The archdeacon's pattern of operation was to visit mission stations by boat, *The Pelican*, in summer and by dog-sled in winter. In fact, he traveled by dog-team some 2,000 miles annually, supervising 30 churches and missions. He actually served or supervised Allakaket, Anvik, Chena, Circle City, Eagle, Fairbanks, Fort Yukon, Nenana, Rampart and Tanana with as many as two dozen lesser missions along the routes between the principal points. Some places thrived between 1905-10 but had disappeared by 1920. Circle City had dropped from a population of 3,000 to 30 in three years.

When Stuck made his historic ascent up the 20,269-foot Mount Denali, he chose two Athabascan protégés, Johnnie Fredson and Walter Harper, for the team which set out in 1913 to conquer "the Great One." It was Harper, in fact, who had to assist Stuck the last few yards to reach the summit and become the first white man to reach the top.

A highly versatile man, Stuck wrote five books on Alaska which are still standards for the study of Alaska mission. *Ten Thousand Miles with a Dog Sled*, originally published in 1914, was reissued in 1988. Also published in 1914 was *The Ascent of Denali*. Ever the defender of Native Alaskans, he eloquently pleaded for restoration of the Indian name, Denali (the "Great One") for Mount McKinley. With publication of his first two books, he made an extensive eastern lecture tour raising money to build a hospital at Fort Yukon which was renamed the Hudson Stuck Memorial Hospital and which continued to serve the Native peoples until 1957.

In all his writing and on his extensive lecture circuits, he consistently insisted on preserving or modifying (rather than erasing) Native folkways. He expounded on how the sale of bright cotton clothing brought gain to the merchants but pneumonia to the Natives. He thought it vital to preserve Native skills, Native clothing, Native foods. He saw starvation wipe out whole families whose male hunter sought furs to sell instead of meat to eat, and spent their pathetic dollars ($5 for a $1,000 fur) on hundred-proof "rot-gut" whiskey.

Tay Thomas in her history of Alaska mission work, *Cry in the Wilderness,* published by the Alaska Council of Churches in 1967, describes the perspectives of the archdeacon:

> While Bishop Rowe developed a special kinship with the Alaskan newcomers, Hudson Stuck grew to know and love the Indians in a way almost unmatched by any other missionary. He knew well the problems they faced, he insisted in preserving native customs, skills, clothing and food.

Archdeacon Stuck brought to the mission in Alaska the talents of a first-rate mind. He lived an exemplary life of dedication and sacrifice. He defended the underprivileged and extended the concept of the missionary function far beyond the confines of holding services. In the best sense he was a social gospeler, willing to use economics, science and politics in God's work. Stuck built churches, schools, hospitals. He had a share in making Alaska the best known of the world's frontiers at a time when such an effort in public relations was incalculably valuable.

Winter came early on the Yukon in 1920. Sub-zero temperatures hit by October. Word had come that Archdeacon Stuck was critically ill at the home of Dr. and Mrs. Grafton Burke at Fort Yukon. The operator of a radio station at Eagle sent an inquiry to the Burkes. The answer came back in the frigid darkness: "He is on the long trail now." Alaska wept.

Even more eloquent was the brief statement in a 1920 church annual. It said: "Among missionaries alive in that year, Stuck was the most outstanding. He had traveled farther, accomplished more. Whereas the credit for such a statement must be divided among many, there probably was not a single one of his own contemporaries to deprive him of a large share of the honor due for such an extraordinary accomplishment."

In the old village of Fort Yukon there are two cemeteries—one for white people and a separate one for Indians. Hudson Stuck, Archdeacon of the Yukon, as he wished, is buried in the Indian cemetery.

Natives' Roles in Evangelization

A significant mass of literature has been preserved to tell of the white people who came into the vast land of Alaska to bring the Gospel message, but little has been written about the Native peoples' acceptance of the message and their roles in sharing the Gospel in the interior of Alaska. Oral history provides certain glimpses:

> In the long winter nights there is a story told about a man named *Vine-ee-khaak'aa* who long long ago journeyed by dog-team from his home at Arctic Village to Old Rampart House, the Hudson's Bay Company post on the Porcupine River in the vast interior of Alaska. Here he traded furs and caribou hides to an Anglican missionary for Bibles, Prayer Books and hymn books. Back in his village, surrounded by high mountains of the Brooks Range, an isolated and indigenous church was begun.
>
> The stories say that there were six leaders among the people; *Vine-ee-khaak'aa* was the first. The seventh leader, so it is said, was Albert Tritt, a visionary who encountered God and spent three years in retreat and prayer with only the Bible and Prayer Book. When he emerged from the retreat, he became a leader, first in his community, then moving in the manner of St. Paul, from village to village along the Upper Yukon River to build churches. When he began work on the first church building at Arctic Village, the community gathered around and expressed much curiosity about the steeple. He explained to the puzzled villagers that the steeple on the building was a spear or arrow aimed to heaven to carry their prayers.
>
> Eventually, this Athabascan apostle built churches in the neighboring villages of Chalkyitsik and Venetie. In the 1920s a prophecy by a man named *Dich'i'zyaa* was fulfilled when Albert Tritt was ordained to the diaconate.

Almost from the beginning of the Alaskan mission, the Episcopal Church, recognizing the centrality of the Holy Eucharist in the life of the church, sought means to assure presence of ordained clergy to celebrate this sacrament. Formidable climate and distance meant that presence of conventionally trained and ordained white mission priests among the scattered Native villages would be sporadic.

Rowe's decision to ordain Loola to the diaconate came in response to a petition from the Indians themselves. They appealed to the bishop for someone who would be on hand in the Fort Yukon community to baptize their children and marry their adults. Rowe also directed Loola to travel along the rivers giving Christian instructions at villages and fish camps. Rowe wrote:

> What a faithful servant the first native deacon proved himself to be. When he grew old and was no longer able to walk to the church he was drawn on a sled; when he could no longer stand, he sat in the chancel; when he was too weak even for this he had a little old abandoned school bell mounted above the gable of his cabin. Upon the ringing of this, his flock gathered about his bedside for a baptism, and with trembling emaciated hands he poured the water of regeneration.

Native people who served as lay readers or catechists were instrumental to the work of the church in many of the villages. Two who were active in Tanana, along the Yukon River, and in Nenana, along the Tanana River, were blind—David and Paul. "Blind David" would canoe or pole his canoe from village to village to hold services. Arriving in the village, carrying his great stick and a sheep's horn, he would blow the horn when it came time for the service. Grandmothers today still remember how everybody would come running at the sound of the horn and how the children would fight for the privilege of holding his stick.

Another early layreader, William Pitgu (or Pitka) of Rampart, on the Yukon River, moved to Tanana from Rampart when the church closed in Rampart as the gold rush died and the population declined. His granddaughter, Sally Hudson of Fairbanks, recently commented, "I have always wondered why our native people accepted the Gospel so readily . . . Why they welcomed it with such devotion and faith. I asked my grandfather that once, when I was a little girl, and he said, in our language, 'we have always known there was a Creator, someone above us, but now, through the Gospel, we know WHO that is . . . our Father, who loves us.'"

Stuck made repeated attempts, some fairly successful, to educate Native peoples for ordination. Johnnie Fredson took eight years to graduate from Sewanee and then lived out his short life teaching his people at Fort Yukon but was not ordained. Walter Harper, Stuck's prize student and half-Indian athlete, was drowned in 1917 with his bride as he set sail to enter military training on the U.S. mainland. It is ironic that Stuck's consuming desire to see a Native priest ordained was never realized.

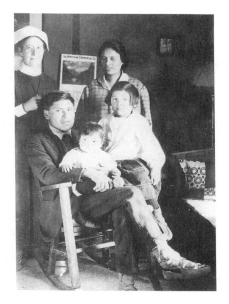

Harriet M. Bedell [1875-1969] at St. Andrew's Mission, Stevens Village on the Yukon, in September, 1928, with Henry Moses, lay reader and interpreter and family.
Courtesy, Archives of the Episcopal Church.

Harriet Bedell: A Woman Set Apart

In the same year that the first UTO Grant went to help build the church at Anvik, the Episcopal Church authorized the office of deaconess. The canon passed in 1889 specified: A woman of devout character and proved fitness, unmarried or widowed, could be appointed Deaconess by any Bishop. The appointment shall be vacated by marriage. Her chief functions were to care for the sick, give instruction in the Christian faith (under supervision of a clergyman), and—with approval—read Morning and Evening Prayer, and to "carry on social work and have a responsible part in the education of women and children."

Dauntless deaconesses made haste to brave the frost of the Arctic, and even before Bishop Rowe arrived there were women at work in the lonely outpost missions. None served more diligently than Deaconess Bedell who was first assigned in 1917 to teach at St. Mark's Mission in Nenana. While her work at the boarding school was exceedingly fulfilling, she found the non-Natives of Nenana irritating.

She recalled that she had been taken to task by a white woman once for taking communion at the same time as the Indians instead of ahead of them. When she approached Bishop Rowe about a transfer to a post which would bring her more directly in contact with the Native people, he sent her to Stevens Village on the Yukon, just 40 miles south of the Arctic Circle. There she opened a day school and mastered the art of dog-sled transportation. When a child was stricken with polio she bravely set off with the child for medical help at Fort Yukon, 160 miles upriver, in a temperature of 32 degrees below zero. Accompanied by two Native drivers and eleven dogs, she made the journey over an unbroken trail in less than a week and the little girl recovered.

Her last years in Alaska found her opening a boarding school in Tanana but the great depression struck and funds dwindled to the point that the school had to close. The deaconess served next in Florida among the Seminoles. She won the respect of the Mikosuki medicine men by respecting their faith in the Great Spirit. She was given the name of *Incoshopie*. The Diocese of Southwest Florida celebrates Harriet Bedell Day on January 8, the anniversary of her "birthday in eternity."

A Native's First Hand View

Moses Cruikshank at age eight was put on a boat at Fort Yukon and sent to St. Mark's Episcopal Mission, steaming first down the great Yukon River to Tanana, then up the Tanana River to distant Nenana. In his autobiography, *The Life I've Been Living*, published in 1986 by the University of Alaska, the Athabascan elder springs open a door to allow a glimpse of life in the Episcopal mission schools and Alaskan life as seen from a Native's view in the early part of the 20th century. His stories bring a human dimension to larger-than-life figures such as Hudson Stuck, who once fished Moses out of the Yukon River with a pike pole. Young Moses had fallen overboard from *The Pelican,* the famed Episcopal craft which plied the Yukon and its tributaries 5,200 miles each summer for many years carrying the missionaries to sprouting towns, widely-flung villages, and countless Native summer fishing camps. Among its passengers from time to time were Bishop Rowe and Stuck.

When young Moses arrived at St. Mark's Mission in 1913, the archdeacon had just made the world's first climb of Mount Denali (McKinley), the tallest mountain on the North American continent. At the school Moses was made "dog boy," cooking for and feeding the sled-dogs, as well as gathering fresh straw for the dogs' bedding. Later, through hard study and good marks, he vied for a summer job as cleaning boy aboard *The Pelican* and journeyed with the archdeacon all the way from Fairbanks to the mouth of the Yukon at St. Michael. Later young Moses "mushed" the winter trails with the missionaries, and in his autobiography he provides a fleeting glimpse of the esteemed Deaconess Bedell at St. Andrew's Mission, Stephen's Village.

Cruikshank's stories describe the archdeacon's invaluable lead dog, Muk, and of the near-panic brought on when Muk's tail froze to the ground one night in Nenana. He tells of Gunga Din, another choice sled-dog who got into a fight in Minto with government dogs and killed two. He tells of going to work as a water boy, at age 12, with the crew building the Alaska Railroad, a venture to provide overland access to the Alaskan interior. The elder retells the stories of his grandfather about the Hudson's Bay Company traders and the gold rush stampeders and the traditional Athabascan ways.

Most significant to an understanding of the Episcopal Church's early mission among Alaskan Natives, Cruikshank, a retired Bureau of Indian Affairs employee, recounts experiences of going to school at the Episcopal missions in Alaska and receiving further education at Mt. Hermon in Massachusetts. He tells of panning for gold, trapping, and driving the nails that built the Episcopal schools and village churches along the Yukon and Tanana rivers. The Bureau of Indian Affairs broke a precedent in the 1970s and named a school in Beaver for him, the first time a BIA school had been named for a living individual. Moses Cruikshank died in late 1996.

Southeast Coast

In the Comity Agreement Southeast Alaska, with its more moderate coastal climate, had been "drawn" by the Presbyterians for purposes of missionizing. However, since the 1850s there had been Anglican presence among the Tsimshian Indians of British Columbia, and they moved in 1887 with the lay missionary William Duncan from Canada to an island just across the international boundary in U.S. territory. The Duncan followers on leaving Canada had separated themselves from the Anglican church, but Bishop Rowe consistently attempted to minister to this defected group in his jurisdiction. In one of his reports, Rowe wrote:

> Last March, I visited Metlakatla and Ketchikan. At the former place, we spent five days with Mr. Duncan, who received us most kindly. The Indians made a feast, to which I was invited . . . I attended services in their wonderful

church, and preached. Time would fail me to describe the good work which has been done among these Tsimshians, the well-built houses, prosperous industries, the neat orderly condition of the people, and everything else. What a Christian civilization can accomplish among such a people is demonstrated here. Mr. Duncan and his work are independent of the Church or any denomination; but the order, simplicity, tone of the services, as well as form, point to Mr. Duncan's early familiarity with the prayers of the Mother Church . . . It is hoped that he may see his way to accept reconciliation with the Church.

In the council chamber, around a blazing fire of logs, we discussed with the elder Indians and Mr. Duncan the subject of a mission among the other Indians in this section of Alaska. He [Duncan] strongly recommended this among the Haidas on Prince of Wales Island. He knows them well; he pledged his aid and that of his people. These Haidas are scattered, desire a teacher and missionary. They number 500 or so, and were once hostile to white people but are not so now; they were the most warlike on the coast, and have a good reputation for industry.

We set out in a small boat [for Ketchikan] in the midst of rain—it rains nearly all the time here. Traveling in a small boat in the winter season is always dangerous and unpleasant. The ground is covered with a thick moss always water-soaked, and were it not for the resinous green cedar, one could not make a fire. Hence the *oolakan*, or candlefish, of these parts, which is so oily that they will burn like a candle, is such a boon.

At Ketchikan we were offered five acres of land if we would only open work there. It is a fishing place of about 100 inhabitants, a third of them native.

Eventually two missions were established in Ketchikan—St. John's for the white people and St. Elizabeth's for Indians. The Indian congregation included Tlingit and Haida Indians as well as Tsimshians who traced their Anglican heritage back to the polemic William Duncan and old Metlakatla. The bishop recruited as missionary to Ketchikan Thomas Jenkins, who in 1919 became Bishop of Nevada. Rowe described the school for Native children in Ketchikan, conducted by Jenkins' sister, as "the best in all Alaska."

A student in this school was a member of the Mather family,

A dinner honoring Bishop Rowe and Paul Mather
[? - 1942] (Tsimshian) at St. Elizabeth's in Ketchikan at
ordination of the latter to the diaconate.

Tsimshian Indians who moved from Annette Island to Ketchikan to seek employment in the several fish canneries. The father's name was Casper, and one of his sons was Paul. The lad excelled in his studies and attracted the interest of Rowe. Within a few years, the bishop sent Paul "outside," to the eastern United States for schooling. Paul Mather was ordained by Bishop Rowe to the diaconate in 1927.

In 1930 Mather became the first Native Alaskan to be ordained a priest of the Episcopal Church. *The Alaskan Churchman* reported:

> The Rev. Paul James Mather was advanced to the Priest-hood in St. John's Church, Ketchikan, on the morning of November 2, 1930, by the Right Rev. Peter Trimble Rowe . . . The service took place before a congregation that filled the church. Morning Prayer was read by Dean Rice of Juneau . . . The procession was formed in the Parish House . . .
>
> The Indian choir had complete charge of the music . . . At the conclusion of the service about one hundred and fifty

persons came forward to receive the new priest's blessing . . . In the afternoon a reception was held for Father Mather in the basement of St. Elizabeth's, about two hundred persons being present . . . Father Mather is the first native Alaskan Indian to become a priest of the church.

St. Elizabeth's in Ketchikan discovered a remarkable musical talent among its members. A fine brass band was formed, a choir was trained to sing the works of Mozart. Rowe described the little church as "attractive . . . with a fine basement which serves as parish house . . . they have a Woman's Guild, Young People's Fellowship . . . all in all it can hold its own with any congregation in the U.S."

As the St. Elizabeth's congregation grew spiritually, it began quietly working toward reconciliation with the mother tribe in Canada. In 1932 Mather and four of his congregation, all native Tsimshians and all descendants of those who left old Metlakatla with Duncan, visited their Canadian kin. A series of resolutions were all very formally presented, signed and agreed upon. And so it was that after 50 years the U.S. and the Canadian Tsimshians were reconciled.

When Bishop Charleston made his first visit to Ketchikan in 1991, he discovered that the Native people were still grieving that St. Elizabeth's, which they had built with their own hands, had been closed generations previously. He was shown the old building which was being used as a funeral home. Though a significant number of the Ketchikan Native population is nominally Episcopalian, there is little Native visibility at St. John's. Conrad, a son of the Rev. Paul Mather, accepted the invitation of St. John's rector to a reception for the author in the summer of 1996 during visit to the colorful old seaport village.

The Era of William Gordon

The third bishop of Alaska was William Jones Gordon Jr., who served more than a quarter of a century (1948-1974). At the time of his election, Gordon had not yet reached the canonical age of 30 to be consecrated bishop, and was the youngest to have been elected to the episcopate of the American Church. Born in rural North Carolina, Gordon went upon graduation from Virginia Theological Seminary in 1943 directly to Alaska, then a territory and a missionary district. He served the remote Point Hope mission, St. Thomas, until his election to the episcopate five years later. The Point Hope mission, in fact, was his sole congregation prior to becoming bishop. Point Hope, which one writer described as the loneliest spot on earth, was the place Gordon chose to be buried. In a cemetery fenced with the bleached rib bones of whales, Gordon was interred on June 18, 1994.

The astounding impact of this highly energetic leader has been splendidly summarized in Tay Thomas's biography, *An Angel On His Wing*. Following his retirement, Bishop Gordon continued activity as an Assisting Bishop of Michigan until 1986. His death came January 4, 1994.

Gordon was able to recruit an intrepid band of young white clergy to come to work in the Alaska bush country. Three of the Gordon-era clergy became bishops—of Hawaii, North Dakota and Wyoming. Gordon became an airplane pilot. The churchwomen's blue United Thank Offering boxes funded purchase of the bishop's planes, and he became familiar with every bush landing strip of the far north. The Rev. Titus Peter recently said, "One thing about traveling with Bishop Gordon, it was never dull!"

Gordon's lasting impact on ministry among Native peoples of his diocese was his creative and innovative approaches to ordination of indigenous clergy. He set out to build upon Rowe's design to serve the Alaskan Native population through ordination of indigenous clergy, and he master-minded an enabling canon—known initially as "Canon Eight"—through General Convention. It allowed the Alaskan church to ordain native clergy who trained and remained in home areas. His dream was to have an ordained person in every village who would celebrate the Eucharist weekly but who would be financially self-supporting.

By 1964 Gordon had ordained five native priests—Titus Peter, David Salmon, Isaac Tritt and Paul Tritt all of the Yukon Valley area, and Milton Swan of the Arctic Coast. In 1996, Titus Peter was still serving St. James at Birch Creek and David Salmon was retired but still assigned to St. Timothy's at Chalkyitsik. Paul Tritt was retired. Milton Swan and Isaac Tritt had died. In fact, Isaac Tritt died in 1993 just a few months before Bishop Gordon succumbed to cancer.

Other Native clergy, ordained by Gordon and still active in 1996, included Gilbert Trimble of Arctic Village, Raymond Hawley of Kivalina, Berkman Silas of Minto, Clinton Swan of Kivalina and Luke Titus of Minto. Patrick Attungana lived in retirement at Point Hope until his death in early 1993. Deacons ordained by Gordon who were still active in 1996 included Jerry Norton of Kivalina and Helen Peters of Fairbanks and Tanana.

Another deacon ordained by Gordon, Anna Frank, in 1983 became the first Alaskan Native woman priest. For seven years, Frank was the only American Indian woman priest, since Navajo Eloise Martinez (ordained in 1979) had renounced her vows. Carol Gallagher, a Cherokee of Maryland, was ordained in 1990. In 1992 Frank became the first Indian woman canon and in 1996 she became archdeacon for the Interior deanery.

All three Alaskan bishops who followed Gordon had previously held the post of director of Dakota Leadership Program of South Dakota, which trained leaders with extension courses. The first two came directly to the Alaska bishopric from the Dakota program. They were David R. Cochran (1974-1981) and George C. Harris (1981-1991), both native New Yorkers. Cochran and Harris looked to the model raised up by the English priest, Roland Allen, who advanced a fundamentally different strategy for both mission and ministry among indigenous people when he served 10 years as an Anglican missionary to China at the end of the 19th century, Allen's convictions on indigenous mission were considered quite radical, so radical that he was prompted to resign from parish ministry and spent the last part of his life in Kenya where he wrote extensively and argued to the end that the responsibility for leadership in the mission church be given to indigenous people.

Allen proposed that lay people should exercise serious responsibilities, that the church, wherever it is, should be "self-governing, self-supporting, and self-propagating," that responsibilities for mission churches be given to the Native peoples, that the Eucharist is central to the life of the church, and, therefore, clergy must be present to celebrate the Eucharist. The latter point opened new approaches for ordination training.

Bishop Gordon's Canon Eight clergy, coupled with the Roland Allen concept, was hailed as a viable model for providing low-cost clergy, and Alaska was looked to as the proving ground.

Gordon's Successors

Bishop Cochran, who had earlier served as vicar for the Standing Rock Mission in North Dakota, ordained five Native priests during his seven-year stint as Alaska's fourth bishop. They included three Inupiat (Eskimo) priests—Seymour Tuzroyluck Sr. of Point Hope, Wilfred Lane of Kotzabue and James Hawley of Kivalina; a Tlingit, Norman Nauska of Anchorage, and an Athabascan, James Gilbert of Arctic Village.

The initial wave of Canon Eight clergy grew old; few replacements came forward. From the onset, some of the Native Alaskan laity, while honoring the commitment of the non-stipendiary Native clergy, expressed serious concern about the need for ordained leaders to serve in a far broader capacity than that of "sacramentalist." Full time pastoral care was keenly needed in dysfunctional communities plagued by chemical abuse. In communities of high unemployment, the non-stipendiary clergy could seldom become self-supporting.

During the Harris decade, emphasis was on the ministry of the laity, encouraging continuing education for clergy and laity alike. Only two Native people stepped forward to be ordained priests—Anna Frank in 1983 and Elijah Attunaga in 1989. One Native person was ordained to the diaconate, Mary Nathaniel (Athabascan) of Chalkyitsik in 1990.

Further development of Native leadership, both ordained and lay, continues to be a major concern in the gigantic Diocese of Alaska. When the new bishop, Steven Charleston, came to the diocese in 1991, 16 of the 28 predominantly Native churches and preaching stations had no assigned resident priest.

Charleston had directed the now-defunct Dakota Leadership Program for two years in the early 1980s, after which for seven years he directed cross-cultural studies at Luther Northwestern Theological Seminary in St. Paul, Minnesota, and was a tenured professor in systemic theology. His sermons, lectures, and writing are widely acclaimed. Charleston's early professional experience included a two-year stint, 1980-1982, as executive director for the National Committee on Indian Work at church headquarters in New York. A graduate of the Episcopal Divinity School, he did his undergraduate work at Trinity College, Hartford, Connecticut, a campus to which he returned as chaplain in 1996 following resignation, for family reasons, as Bishop of Alaska.

A Light in Every Window

Mary Parsons, the communications officer for the diocese of Alaska, summed up the five-year Charleston tenure as follows:

> When Steven Charleston was consecrated Alaska's sixth bishop in March 1991, he asked of people who had no clergy presence in their villages and towns to "have at least one person open the church on Sunday morning, turn on the lights, start the fire and say a prayer."
>
> Out of his desire to see each congregation healthy and whole, he developed the "mission wheel." The four areas he believed to be critical for a healthy church community were evangelism, stewardship, Christian learning, and leadership development . . .
>
> To increase stewardship in the villages and towns where there was no clergy, he designed yellow offering cans, similar

in concept to the UTO "Blue Box," resulting in a noticeable increase in the funds contributed to the diocese from small churches.

He developed the initial body of work for the "Paths to Service Program" which simplified the steps involved in being ordained a "local" or "Canon Nine" deacon or priest. During his tenure the highly successful "Faith Into Tomorrow" program built up the fiscal resources of the diocese for the future . . .

Bishop Charleston himself carried the strong message of evangelism through his eloquent preaching and teaching. His ability to touch the hearts and souls of those he spoke to was one of his greatest gifts to the diocese of Alaska. He preached passionately about the love of God, not dwelling as much on theological theories as on life situations and the day-to-day burdens of his congregations. He transformed words into images which people never forgot, such as the vision of a single light burning in each church in Alaska.

Charleston viewed his role as that of a bridge-builder among the many cultures and communities of Alaska. One of his unfulfilled concepts was the Episcopal Video Network. Using video cassettes for local training and study materials, the network was to bring Christian learning to even the most remote areas of the enormous state.

The Native perspective was evident in the creation of a community of elders in the diocese, the Episcopal Society of St. Simeon and St. Anna. Each year, the four deaneries designate individuals past age 60 who have served in Alaska for at least 15 years. These persons are formally inducted into the society, receiving the gold diocesan cross to symbolize the honor in which they are held by the people of Alaska. In 1991 Bishop Charleston welcomed the first of these charter members and asked Bishop Gordon to serve as chaplain. As in Native tradition, this is a community of elders who support the whole diocese through their prayer life, their wisdom, and their living witness to Christian values.

Oakerhater Evangelism Team

The reality of a scarcity of clergy was made clear to the Oakerhater Evangelism Team which in the summer of 1990 traveled down the Yukon in a river cruiser christened *The Pelican III* to memorialize Hudson Stuck's river launch which plied the Yukon generations previously. The team, which took its name from the only American Indian saint in the Episcopal calendar of saints, visited nine villages without resident clergy. The 1,100 mile journey began at the ghost town of Eagle, a stone's throw from the Canadian border. With guitars and a repertoire of Native American songs, the 10-member team filled the church at Eagle with a spirit that would carry them on their journey and be repeated in village after village.

The services at Eagle ended with local communicants offering prayers of thanksgiving: "Thank you, Lord, for bringing these people here. Let their journey down river go well, and let lives be touched and changed." As the team departed, a youngster offered his piggy bank to a member of the Church Army, "to help the poor."

At the team's next stop, Circle City, it had been many months since a priest had come to celebrate Holy Eucharist. In this sleepy rain-soaked village, once a bustling boom town surrounded by "500 gold mines," Bishop Rowe had borrowed a saloon to hold the first Episcopal service. Now it was in the newest chapel along the Yukon that the evangelism team held services. The little frame Trinity Chapel, with window boxes of bright flowers, was built a half-mile south of the river to replace the old Episcopal church damaged in the Yukon's spring "breakup" several years ago. The team gathered magenta fireweed blossoms for the altar and rang the old bell which hung high in its outside belfry, to call the faithful to worship. They came—walking. Gone were the dance halls and saloons of Bishop Rowe's era and gone was Grace Hospital which the bishop built and to which he sent Deaconess Elizabeth Deane to serve Circle City's 3,000-plus population.

When the 1990 evangelism team reached Fort Yukon, anchored and laboriously climbed the steep muddy river bank, a delegation of Gwich'in Athabascans awaited. The delegation had come many miles from Arctic Village to elicit the national church's support for protection from oil exploration in the Arctic National Wildlife Refuge, home to the caribou on which 7,000 Gwich'in Native people of northeast Alaska and northwest Canada rely for subsistence. The delegation brought greetings of Trimble Gilbert, chief of Arctic Village. He is an Episcopal priest as was his father. In months to come, after the Alaska diocesan convention passed a resolution in support of the Gwich'in position, as did the 1991 General Convention, strong national Episcopal advocacy was built which helped halt a pending proposal in the U.S. Senate to open the refuge for oil exploration.

The "floating revival" river evangelists held services at St. Matthew's in Beaver, a fascinating community founded by a Japanese adventurer who brought his Eskimo family from the distant Arctic coast across the Brooks mountain range to start a trading post on the Yukon river. The team next stopped at Stevens Village, which had scarcely had Episcopal resident presence since Deaconess Bedell departed two generations previously. Though the visit was in the middle of the salmon fishing season, when villagers heard there would be services at St. Andrew's, they left their fishing camps to travel 30 miles upriver for the Eucharist. The team found a ghost town dreariness at Rampart, once a major gold mining center. The team was welcomed to Tanana by strong lay leaders, to Minto by resident Native clergy, to Nenana's beautiful St. Mark's Church—the best maintained perhaps in all Alaska—by laity.

The evangelism team observed spiritual renewal among Native Alaskans; joyful singing filling the air at Episcopal gatherings in the brief summer season of the midnight sun. The team was told that during the long winter nights, stories are yet told of *Vine-ee-khak'aa* and the others who long, long ago traded caribou hides for copies of the Holy Bible and Anglican prayer book and set about independently in the shadows of the high mountains of the Brooks Range at Arctic Village to build an indigenous church.

A second evangelism team traveled the Yukon in the summer of 1991, traveling to distant Anvik, the "mother mission of Alaska." The new bishop, making his first visit to various river villages, baptized and confirmed. Wherever *The Pelican III* docked the bishop preached hope and offered prayers for healing. At the village of Anvik, where Episcopal mission began in Alaska, the young Choctaw bishop stood before the altar of Christ Church, the chapel built with UTO's first grant, and pledged that new leadership will be trained as layreaders, catechists, deacons and priests.

"You Gave Us Hope"

To Native people, long dwelling in isolation, the prophetic young bishop instilled a new spirit of life in Christ that is sure to abide beyond the brief interval of his episcopacy. With trembling voice, Polly Simmonds, a lay deputy to the diocesan convention in the autumn of 1995, summed up the consensus of Native Alaskans when she addressed the bishop saying, "You gave us hope that we as Native people can be leaders; that we can deal with our own issues; that we can raise our voices to be heard." Tears stained brown faces, and those sitting near the window pointed to a stunning double rainbow that had suddenly appeared over the quaint old Sitka harbor.

10

INDIANS IN THE CITIES

The sight of your cities pains the eyes of the red man . . . There is no quiet place in white man's cities . . . The clatter only seems to insult the ears. —Chief Seattle, 1854

Nonetheless, two out of every three American Indians alive today endure the clatter and reside away from their reservation or ancestral homeland. Beginning with World War II, most moved—on their own volition or with a resolute push from the federal government—into the cities to search for jobs. In addition to the sadness of separation, the early migrants experienced snubs and stereotyping, cultural disorientation and identity crisis.

Many of the early urban migrants were third and fourth generation Episcopalians who, back home, looked to the Church as the center of community life. Once in the strange city the Indians quickly discovered that "The Episcopal Church Welcomes You" sign did not consistently apply. Caught between worlds, many lonely Indians who timidly stepped into the neat stone Episcopal structures of the city seeking a caring sanctuary, found instead a heartless bigotry from their new white neighbors.

Often, too, they found the city parishes lacking in that all-important spirit of community which was the backbone of church life on the reservations back home.

Once the Episcopal Church discerned that reservation Indians were disinclined to attend the white churches of the cities—seldom was it admitted that their white neighbors were equally disinclined to welcome them—a hesitant outreach was begun.

An early blueprint was drawn in 1948 by South Dakota Bishop W. Blair Roberts who reported that 3,000 Indians had moved to Rapid

City. "It is not easy," wrote the bishop, "for our Dakota people to take their place in the life of their white brethren. They tend to become a separated group."

He added, "Comparatively few of these people attend Emmanuel Church."

St. Matthew's, Rapid City

A man from Rosebud Reservation knew well why the Indians did not attend Emmanuel. He had moved his young family to Rapid City to find work. A lifelong Episcopalian, he went to Christmas Eve services in 1951 at Emmanuel and was told that he could not sit in the pews. The Sioux man—known today as the Venerable Noah Brokenleg, a revered elder among Native peoples of all tribes—came in and sat down in a back pew. The usher quickly appeared and said, "You're supposed to sit in the back," and gestured toward a separate backless bench against the wall. Father Noah just got up and left.

By the next Christmas, the Lakota had a church of their own in Rapid City. St. Matthew's was unfinished but midnight services, entirely in the Lakota language, were held all the same. "Planks were set on nail kegs for benches and even the floor was unfinished, recalled the Rev. Canon Martin Brokenleg, who was then seven years old. "My father was one of the layreaders [he was ordained a decade later] and I remember going with my parents to lay tile on the floor and to help paint the church. I remember sitting on the floor wrapped in blankets because it was so cold in there," he added.

Father Noah and another layreader, Albert Wright, borrowed a pump organ from All Angels in Sturgis for that Christmas Eve service. The two of them loaded it onto a pickup and got it into St. Matthew's. When it was time to return the organ, it took six men to move it. They said it took only two of them to bring it in because they were so excited to have their own church.

As the Rapid City Indian population grew, the Jesuit Father Zimmerman cared for all the Lakotas regardless of their denomination. The first Indian Episcopal priest to minister to the Lakotas in Rapid City was the Rev. Levi M. Rouillard. He made pastoral visits to their tents and shacks along Rapid Creek, conducting services in their homes. Mrs. Rouillard later said, "We *tiole*-ed all around. We never have to eat at home. We just go visit in time for meals." (*Tiole* means to visit, specifically to be invited to eat.)

Every fifth Sunday, Father Rouillard would travel by train— he had somehow acquired a railroad pass—to visit his former communicants in Minneapolis and Chicago.

St. Matthew's has remained the "Indian" church of Rapid City and by the mid-1990s had a communicant strength of 350. A year-long vacancy befell St. Matthew's when the Rev. Robert Two Bulls left in 1993 after serving for six years. The Rev. George Benson of Arkansas was subsequently called as St. Matthew's new rector.

Twin Cities

One of the major relocation centers, Minneapolis became a domicile of pan-Indian groups which begat new cultural forms blending the characteristics of many tribes. In 1968 the American Indian Movement (AIM) was born in reaction to accusations that Minneapolis police routinely brutalized Indian people. Today, Minneapolis has almost 25,000 Indians, the eighth largest urban Indian population in the nation.

The Rev. David W. Clark, a long-time priest among the Sioux people of South Dakota, in the 1950s established the first ministry to urban Indians in the Minneapolis-St. Paul area. Father Rouillard later regularly rode the train in from Rapid City to baptize the Lakota babies who would grow up to become the first generation of urbanized Indians.

From the 1950s the diocese of Minnesota maintained some sort of mission in the Twin Cities—sometimes minimal, sometimes more. The senior mission is Mazakute Memorial in St. Paul, named for the first Dakota priest in the Episcopal Church. Established in 1976 to serve spiritual and social needs of the growing urban Indian population, Mazakute was a congregation even before it found an old church which members restored to house its many programs.

A United Thank Offering grant enabled the congregation to move into its own building, a unique structure of Native traditional motif. Mazakute is one of the few Indian urban congregations which has its own church building. Its founding vicar was the Rev. Leslie Bobtail Bear (Dakota) who left the Episcopal Church for another communion and returned to his native South Dakota.

Another South Dakota native, the Rev. Virgil Foote (Lakota), became vicar of the congregation in 1981. The congregation—a mixture of Ojibwa, Sioux, Winnebago and other Indian tribes, black, white and hispanic people—held a healing service monthly in which the ceremonial pipe and the drum a were used. Hymns were often sung in languages of Native people.

Across the Mississippi River in Minneapolis is All Saints', also begun in the 1970s. For 15 years it shared space with other organizations. All Saints' vicar, the Rev. Marvin Red Elk, began a creative outreach in prison chaplaincy and chemical dependency for the expanding Indian population. After Red Elk suffered a fatal heart attack, the All Saints' congregation called the Rev. Philip Allen, an Oglala Sioux whose recent ministry had been with a Navajo congregation. Within 18 months, the average Sunday attendance tripled. The diocese was able to acquire a larger facility when a Nazarene congregation closed down. When Allen retired in 1995, care for All Saints' passed to the Rev. Melanie Spears, the first Lakota woman and the fifth American Indian woman ordained to the priesthood.

Chicago: St. Augustine's

Inspired by the example of the Rev. David Clark, who brought Sioux services to Minneapolis, the Rev. Peter J. Powell founded the first urban Indian social outreach program in the nation—St. Augustine's Indian Center in Chicago. Begun in 1962, this center continues to serve the more than 18,000 Indians in that city. For three decades it has remained the largest Native American casework agency in the nation. St. Augustine Center's program has given invaluable service in assisting with the transition from rural and reservation environment.

A scholar and adopted Cheyenne, Father Powell holds fast to the theological position championed by St. Augustine of Hippo, the center's patron saint, who taught that the Church must be the preserver of the cultures of the peoples served. His published works are: *Sweet Medicine: The Continuing Role of the Sacred Arrows, the Sun Dance and the Sacred Buffalo Hat in Northern Cheyenne Life* (1969); *The Cheyennes, Ma'heo'o's People: A Critical Biography* (1980); and *People of the Sacred Mountain: A History of the Northern Cheyenne Chiefs and Warrior Societies* (1981). The latter won both the National Book Award and the Anisfield-Wolf Award in Race Relations. All royalties are distributed among the Cheyenne people.

From the outset it was the founder's intent that St. Augustine's not seek funding assistance from the national church nor the diocese and that the center would be placed in Indian hands. This was accomplished in 1972. Since that time all key board and staff positions have been held by Native Americans. Seventeen persons, representing eight tribes, are on staff. Each month they serve an average of 250 to 300 families, whose membership totals more than 2,000 persons. They represent 35 tribes.

St. Augustine's in Chicago.

Denver Cathedral

It was Whitsunday, 1994. First, the sound of a Sioux drum reverberated through the great cathedral and Lakota singers chanted an exhortation as old as time. A short silence followed. Then the majestic pipe organ and full chorus burst forth joyously with "Hail Thee, Festival Day." The Cathedral of St. John's in the Wilderness, Denver, actualized "Hark! for in myriad tongues . . . ," from the Pentecost hymn, in liturgy, in procession, in presence and, after the service, with an afternoon picnic and pow-wow celebrating *Pejo Toh-Wi Wachipi* (the Season of the Grass Turning Green) to mark the first anniversary of the return of Native American ministry to St. John's.

The procession down the center aisle of the crowded cathedral was, in itself, strikingly multi-ethnic. A host of Native people, many in tribal dress, was followed by a large group of godparents, grandparents and parents carrying toddlers and babies to be baptized. In the midst of the mostly white families was an Indian family with a bright-eyed baby to be baptized. At the end of the procession was the first American Indian bishop, Harold S. Jones, still straight and stately, showing only slight signs of his 85 years. The Gospel was read in both Lakota and English; Bill Center, a Sioux lay pastor, led the vast congregation in the Four Directions Ceremony; the Native American melody, *Lacquiparle* (Hymn 385) was sung.

In his homily, Bishop Jones spoke of prior bonds between the Denver cathedral and the South Dakota Indian. "Today is a great event for both Native people and for St. John's," said the Lakota elder and bishop, "as our people worship together."

Throughout a cloudless May afternoon, drumbeat and song echoed across the cathedral grounds. A teepee stood at the edge of the green lawn and under the lofty old trees Native crafts were offered for sale, a "fast-food" stand offered frybread, a clown entertained happy children of various races. Participating in honoring dances were many of the Indian leaders of the Denver metroplex. Little by little, whites joined in the dancing. The blending of cultures was a reminder of the ancient gathering of nations.

Even before the ill-advised federal Indian relocation policy of the Eisenhower administration, there had been intermittent Episcopal Indian ministry in Denver. The work was generally under aegis of the cathedral. The Rev. Sherman Coolidge (Arapaho) was an honorary canon at St. John's in the 1920s, and during the Great Depression the national church assigned the Rev. Vine Deloria Sr. to St. John's as a missionary. He and his successors visited the cathedral every Advent for 18 years and returned to the South Dakota missions laden with toys and donations of clothing and other items. In 1951, when Father Deloria left South Dakota to take a parish in Iowa, his replacement was Harold Jones. Later, John Artichoker, principal of Hare School on the Rosebud Reservation, became liaison with the cathedral. In 1958, Russell Nakata, newly appointed canon of the cathedral, began a ministry that would last for 20 years. During the 1960s many activities of the White Buffalo Council took place at the cathedral.

By 1968 there were monthly services in the Lakota language. A prime mover of the active and viable Indian congregation was Helen L. Peterson, a Sioux who had been born on the Pine Ridge Reservation. Ten years later the diocese took over the Episcopal Community Services Agency administered by the cathedral, ending direct involvement of St. John's with the Indian work for a time. In fact, Indian work in the diocese disappeared for several years until the mid-1980s when the Rev. George Pierce, a Church Army captain, transferred to Colorado from South Dakota, where he had extensive experience in the reservation communities. Assisted by Judy Maurer, Captain Pierce was instrumental in establishing *Mni Wiconi* (Living Waters) which by mid-1984 began meeting at the cathedral.

A year later the congregation moved to St. Barnabas on Vine Street in Denver. There was great promise; 200 came to the Indian service at Christmas of 1985. A Ventures in Mission grant from the national church assisted the diocese to bring a Native clergyman aboard. An ecumenical worshiping community jointly funded by Lutherans was envisioned, but discord over Native traditional theology and Christian theology surfaced within the congregation, and disappointment at the demise of promise was felt by many.

In spring of 1993, a reconciled community was invited back to St. John's Cathedral, and the Season of the Grass Turning Green pow-wow in 1994 celebrated the first anniversary of the return. The pow-wow became an annual event on Pentecost Sunday.

In addition to the St. John's worshiping community, the Denver metroplex, with an estimated 29,000 Indian population, looked to an ecumenical hospital chaplaincy program called Caring Association for Native Americans (CANA). In the Native tradition, family members of the ill accompany the patient to the city for treatment and through the CANA program trained Native volunteers provide a multiple support system to Native patients who are referred to Denver medical facilities from distant reservations. Episcopal support to CANA flowed from the diocese and national church.

Diocese of Milwaukee

No single Episcopal worshiping center serves the estimated 12,000 tribal people in Milwaukee, which includes large numbers of Oneida with whom the Episcopal Church has maintained mission for almost 200 uninterrupted years. It has been estimated that 10 percent of the Indians in Milwaukee are Episcopalians, but they are spread through three congregations—St. John's, St. Luke's and All Saints' Cathedral.

In 1992 Bishop Roger White established an Episcopal Native American committee and challenged members to gather a Native community. Appointed to head the committee was Dewey Silas, an Oneida who left his reservation in 1960 to work in a Milwaukee foundry. In early 1994 Silas, a communicant at St. Luke's, was ordained to the diaconate and began study in autumn of 1996 through the new alternative study program launched in the Diocese of Minnesota. Expectations are that he will become the first Oneida priest since Cornelius Hill died in 1907.

State of California

Though the state of California has the nation's second largest American Indian/Alaska Native population—242,165 according to the 1990 census—only two of the six Episcopal dioceses in the state have ministry directed specifically to Indians. In a third diocese, San Joaquin, in the hispanic Santa Margharita Church in Fresno, a sizeable number of communicants are Yaqui, Spanish-speaking indigenous people.

Over all, more mission has expired in the state in the last decade than has been begun. Work in Los Angeles began with great promise in 1984 when a young priest with Oneida blood emerged out of the maze of the sprawling city with a vision of gathering an Indian worshiping community. Michael Griffith, with help from a Ventures in Mission grant, organized Eagle Wings Mission station. Discouraged by bureaucracy, Griffith departed and a Chippewa priest, Gary Turner, came in 1988. A promising ecumenical community developed with an annual "Gathering Table" convocation. However, by 1989 the diocese discontinued support to Eagle Wings, citing the mission station's scant likelihood of attaining parish status.

For almost 30 years, up until the early 1980s, the Diocese of California supported Good Samaritan Mission in San Francisco, a storefront ministry which was a major success in aiding transition from reservation and rural life to urban existence. Good Samaritan was directed 1975-81 by the Rev. Robin Merrell (Nez Perce) a highly respected individual in the mission district of the city. Assisting with the vital legal and social outreach work in the bay area was another Indian priest, Harvard-educated Randolf Rice (Assiniboin), who served on the National Committee on Indian Work in the mid-1970s. When Merrell left, the work continued fitfully for a few years, then faded away.

Also doomed was an ecumenical Indian program in San Diego, ranked tenth in urban Indian population. Episcopal participation in the interdenominational social outreach program peaked and faded by the end of the 1980s.

Sixty years ago there was a vital and visible ministry among the Karuk people in the Diocese of Northern California. The Church of the Holy Spirit, in the hamlet of Orleans, had, according to *The Spirit of Missions,* been given land in 1914 by "Indian Fannie, a medicine woman of eighty-odd years." Though old records are mute on what happened to the mission, in 1933 an article said:

> Twelve adults and some 40 to 50 children are regular attendants at the mission church . . . A well-to-do Englishman with a fine Indian wife (he being the layman in charge

of the church when the rector is absent, and she being guild president) . . .

The Karuk work ended. However, in recent years, a lay leader in the diocese, Tim Cantrell (Piegan-Blackfoot), a law enforcement officer, was key to rekindling a ministry among Indians in the diocese with the Church of the Four Winds at St. John's in Roseville, a suburb of Sacramento. Four Winds Native American Worship Center has been described as "a ministry, in part, of reconciliation . . . of acknowledgment . . . a ministry which hopes to bring the fullness of God and the strength of God's love to those who have so often been shown a wrathful, avenging God." Cantrell was admitted to the postulancy program of the diocese in 1995.

The second site for urban ministry in California is in the Silicon Valley at St. Philip's, located just five blocks from the Indian Center in San Jose. Persons most responsible for the development of the singular St. Philip's Indian work were Sherry LeBeau, originally from Pine Ridge Reservation and a resource instructor for a high school district; Hank LeBeau, her husband and a mental health officer for San Jose Indian Health Center; and the rector, the Rev. Jerry Drino, whose experience included work among Utes, the Blackfeet of Montana, the Gwich'in of Alaska, and linkage with Cheyenne River in South Dakota, the reservation from which Hank had come as a teenager in 1961.

Until he found St. Philip's, LeBeau had scarcely entered a church in 30 years, though he was a fifth generation Episcopalian. His grandfather, Jobe White, had served 51 years as layreader at Messiah, Iron Nation, Lower Brulé Reservation in South Dakota. At St. Philip's Hank LeBeau found what he was looking for.

At Winter Talk in Oklahoma in 1994, Sherry LeBeau and Tim White Weasel, another South Dakota native who found his way to St. Philip's, were received into the Episcopal Church. The Lebeaus have since enrolled in the Master of Divinity program of the Vancouver School of Theology. Their study is conducted on-site at St. Philip's by tutors.

Phoenix

Phoenix, with the sixth largest American Indian urban population, held forth stirring promise for Episcopal urban Indian ministry in the early 1980s when Wesley Frensdorff, interim Bishop of Navajoland, became an assistant bishop in Arizona. Before his vision could be realized, however, he was killed in a plane crash in 1988, and with exception of the modest-sized congregation, Good Samaritan, which meets in the chapel of the historic Cook College and Theological School in Tempe, there has been little visibility of Episcopal commitment with Indians in Arizona's urban areas.

Good Samaritan, led primarily by the Lakota laywoman Vivian Winter Chaser, has been served from time to time by diocesan appointed clergy. An outreach to nearby White Mountain Apache and Pima reservations has been ongoing and ministry to the homeless has flowed out of Trinity Cathedral.

St. Stephen's, Phoenix, is a congregation with involvement in ministry to Native Americans dating back for 20 years. Through its rector, David Bailey, St. Stephen's has proposed offering its 85-bed, on-site retreat center as transitional housing for young adult Native Americans coming into the Phoenix area from the state's 19 reservations and elsewhere to attend community colleges and the state university.

Seattle

The Native American Task Force of the Diocese of Olympia arranged a festive welcome when the Episcopal Council of Indian Ministry (ECIM) met in Seattle in the summer of 1994. On the program were a clambake on the Suquamish Reservation, across Puget Sound from the Emerald City; a talking circle at St. Mark's Cathedral in Seattle with a variety of local participants—both Indian and non-Indian; and a picnic feast under the trees on the cathedral grounds.

But the highlight was the worship service at St. Mark's attended by several hundred persons, including clergy who had driven great distances on a mid-week August afternoon to join the diocese's Native American Task Force for the occasion. Bishop Steve Charleston delivered a stirring homily and concelebrated with Bishop William Wantland. Several other Native Americans were participants in the liturgy.

The Church Council of Greater Seattle, often spearheaded by Lutherans, has long been in the vanguard in the struggle for Indian treaty rights. Episcopal involvement in the Church Council has fluctuated from time to time, especially over the highly charged issue of fishing rights in the 1970s. The Boldt Decision of 1974 affirmed the Indian fishing rights and created a backlash of conflict and controversy within the diocese. Bishop Ivol I. Curtis whose tenure spanned the era of unrest, 1964-1976, was subjected to the white fishing industry's disapproval for his position on Indian issues and eventually withdrew his open support. His successor, Robert H. Cochrane, was a member of a group made up of the major heads of judicatories and kept up an interest in Native Americans.

In 1987 Bishop Cochrane publicly read "The Apology to the Tribal Councils and Traditional Leaders of the Indian and Eskimo Peoples of the Pacific Northwest." This formal apology, made on behalf of nine Christian denominations, expressed repentance for "longstanding participation in the destruction of traditional Native American spiritual practices."

The Seattle Church Council expanded its concerns beyond fishing rights to include Natives' rights to worship, designation of Snoqualmie Falls as a sacred site, and Native American higher education initiatives.

When Vincent W. Warner Jr. became the diocesan bishop in 1990 he formed a Native American Task Force which began with 60 members and later reduced that number to a more realistic dozen. Ted George, a member of the Suquamish tribe and descendent of Chief Seattle, has been a leader of the group.

Salt Lake City

When the Ute priest, the Rev. Quentin Kolb, became the urban missioner for the Diocese of Utah in 1989, instead of establishing an office at the diocesan headquarters, he looked for the center of the Indian community in Salt Lake City, and reckoned it to be in the near neighborhood of the Indian Health Services clinic.

The center became a drop-in spot for 65-75 people each day. Morning Prayer was said daily in Kolb's office and about 25, mostly men, joined for the Eucharist each Wednesday. Eucharist was celebrated mid-week to accommodate individuals who rely on public transportation, which is drastically curtailed on weekends. The Salt Lake urban program offered a range of support services, including regular AA meetings, hospital chaplaincy, potluck Wednesday lunches and a basketball team. The site for the center was necessarily moved in 1996 to the diocesan cathedral.

Kolb, who continued to postpone retirement, was active for the past decade in a number of regional and national boards including the Jubilee board and the Witness board, and was a founding member of the Episcopal Council of Indian Ministry and the Mountains and Desert Regional Ministry.

Although the Episcopal Church had maintained mission on the Uintah Ouray Reservation on the eastern edge of Utah since 1897, introducing the urban program was a leap in faith on the part of the diocesan bishop, George Bates, who was sensitive to the fact that Salt Lake City was one of the 25 cities of the nation with the largest Native American populations. The new Utah coadjutor, Carolyn Tanner Irish, has indicated a like interest in Indian ministry.

Tiospaye Wakan

John Jacob Astor of New York City gave money to Bishop William Hobart Hare to build South Dakota's Calvary Cathedral as a memorial to Mrs. Astor who had been principal benefactor for several Indian boarding schools in South Dakota.

There was, however, little Lakota/Dakota presence at the cathedral until 1990 when Bishop Craig Anderson appointed the Rev. Martin Brokenleg as canon at the cathedral and assigned him to develop an Indian worshiping community. Brokenleg, a professor at Augustana College in Sioux Falls, introduced native forms of liturgy to an enthusiastic congregation which identified itself as *Tiospaye Wakan* (Holy or Sacred or Extended Family). Soon it had a regular attendance of 80 to 100, with occasional attendance as high as 250.

An indisputable high point of *Tiospaye Wakan* was a commemorative service on the 100th anniversary of the massacre of Wounded Knee when names of 376 known victims were read in the pre-dawn hours of December 29, 1990. Throughout the century history books had acknowledged only 149 Sioux casualties, but careful scholarly research identified more than twice the number that the U.S. government had acknowledged.

Nebraska

Eight denominations cooperate to minister to American Indians in the cities of Omaha and Lincoln, both of which have, in the past two decades, seen a major influx of Native peoples. The first minister was Episcopalian. When he departed the ministry in 1990, an American Baptist replaced him. The goal of the ecumenical program is "to establish worshiping communities that respect, affirm and integrate the spiritual and cultural values of Indian people with the essentials of the Christian faith."

St. Mark's in Gordon, Nebraska, located only 18 miles south of the Pine Ridge Reservation, was designated in 1986 as a Jubilee Center, and during its first year as such nourished both spiritually and physically a Native American community which moved from the reservation to the sandhill farm and ranch community of 2,100.

Bismarck, North Dakota

When General Convention of 1991 voted a fund for new ministries among Native Americans it enabled the Episcopal Council of Indian Ministry (ECIM) to respond to unfilled needs in urban communities. For instance, ECIM helped to launch the Native American Ministries program at St. George's parish in Bismarck with a new ministries seed grant in 1993. Directed by Carol DeWall, a laywoman originally from Pine Ridge Reservation in South Dakota, the program was initiated as an outreach and grew toward a self-directed worshiping community with weekly Eucharist at United Tribes. In addition to new ministry in Bismarck, the hub city of south central North Dakota, ecumenical urban Indian programs continue in the twin border cities of Fargo, North Dakota, and Moorhead, Minnesota.

Montana

The Church of the Incarnation in Great Falls in the early 1990s activated Native American work in the huge Diocese of Montana which has seven Indian reservations. First it loaned its assistant rector, the Rev. Kerry Holder, to begin a preaching station at Browning on the Blackfeet Reservation. Next, Incarnation entered into a co-sponsorship of Thunder Child Adolescent Project, an innovative residential chemical abuse treatment program for Indian teenagers in Great Falls. There was also Incarnation's involvement with a youth center on the Blackfeet Reservation.

Montana ranked 13th in Indian population among states in the 1990 census count. Historically, the Roman Catholic Church was assigned mission oversight but early in his tenure, Bishop C.I. Jones pledged to introduce native work. With Incarnation's leading, the new work was nurtured generously by the diocese and various agencies of the national church, including ECIM's new ministry fund. The project captured the interest of the Presiding Bishop's Fund for World Relief which designated it as an initiative project and set about raising $200,000 toward its support. Some 1,500 young people gathered in Indiana for the Episcopal Youth Event of 1996 dedicated offerings to the project.

Licensed through the highly successful Thunder Child Treatment Center of Sheridan, Wyoming, the Great Falls project provides a 45-day, live-in treatment program in a homelike setting for Indian youth suffering from chemical dependency.

Working with the Blackfeet Tribal government and the United Methodist Church, an Episcopal group sought and received a substantial United Thank Offering grant for Yellow Wolf Sanctuary youth project. The community spiritual center was designed to promote young Indian leadership in the Church through Blackfeet language classes, recreation activities and tutoring, as well as spiritual direction. A thousand people came to the opening day event for the project on May 1, 1994, in Browning.

Diocese of Iowa

With roots extending back more than 30 years, St. Paul's in Sioux City, Iowa, has maintained an inclusive program for the Native American community. It began in 1954 when the parish started to hold services for Indian people and invited Lakota/Dakota priests and layreaders from the neighboring South Dakota reservations to conduct the worship services.

St. Paul's was established a century ago as a white mission and experienced many financial set-backs through the years. Finally, in 1964 the congregation merged with other Sioux City churches. The Indian congregation, however, continued at St. Paul's. In 1968 the Rev. Philip Allen, a Lakota seminary-trained priest, took charge of the growing congregation and organized the American Indian Center. Several clergy followed Allen, and St. Paul's has been served since 1988 by the Rev. David Titus.

Portland, Oregon

The Church of the Four Winds in Portland is a testimonial to the perseverance of Dr. Helen L. Peterson, an indomitable cradle Episcopalian who was born on the Pine Ridge Reservation and spent her long and varied professional career in advocacy of Indians. On her retirement as a regional officer of the Bureau of Indian Affairs, Peterson for seven years dedicated her energy to building an ecumenical worshiping community and served as chairperson for Four Winds as well as the Province VIII Indian Commission. In 1993 an ecumenical trio succeeded her at the helm of Four Winds—Anne Scissons (Sioux), Episcopal; Ramona Soto Rank (Klamath), Lutheran; and Chris Smith (Makah), Presbyterian.

Four Winds resulted from a commitment to Peterson by former Oregon Bishop Matthew P. Bigliardi in 1983. The late Rev. Paul Cheek, who had served the large congregation on the Oneida Reservation in Wisconsin for seven years, had original oversight of the Indian ministry, and Four Winds services were held monthly at St. Aidan's.

Church of the Four Winds, Portland, Oregon.
Dr. Helen Peterson (Oglala) with John Scannell, the rector
of St. Michael's and All Angels and Mark MacDonald,
former priest-in-charge.

For three formative, happy and vital years the Church of the Four Winds was served by the Rev. Mark MacDonald, rector of St. Stephen's, the city's cathedral in earlier years. In November of 1989 the Indian ministry gave itself the name Church of the Four Winds. In addition to conducting the customary services, MacDonald worked closely with the Indian children, training them to serve as acolytes and crucifers and to serve the church in other capacities, often performing the Lord's Prayer in Indian sign language. One of MacDonald's gifts to the congregation of Four Winds was an icon of David Pendleton Oakerhater, done by the renowned iconographer, Paul Mihailescu.

Throughout its history, Four Winds involved clergy of other faiths and Native American religious leaders who have brought a rich diversity to the spiritual life of the urban Indian community. When MacDonald was called to serve in Navajoland he was replaced by the Rev. Constance Hammond.

In 1992 the Four Winds moved across town to St. Michael and All Angels after its board and the vestry of St. Michael's thoroughly discussed expectations of both groups and the need for coordination.

Many joint services and celebrations have taken place at St. Michael's and the success has been due in large part to the sensitivity and wisdom of the longtime rector, the Rev. John S. Scannell. A large residential building next door to the church serves as home to Four Winds.

The Church of the Four Winds in Portland began as an experiment and thrived to celebrate its tenth anniversary in August, 1994. Among participants in the joyful celebration Eucharist and potluck in Laurelhurst Park were Episcopal Bishop Robert Ladehoff, the Rev. Darryl Lundby, an assistant to the Lutheran bishop of the Oregon synod, and several members of the Episcopal Council of Indian Ministry.

A Gathering Together

EICM has annually sponsored an Urban Coalition, holding meetings in Minneapolis, Denver, Rapid City, Sioux Falls and Phoenix. Participants are invited to come, two-by-two, from a dozen urban communities, to share experiences, goals, road-blocks and high points of growing urban ministry. The gatherings usually have been sparked by the Rev. Canon Martin Brokenleg of South Dakota and the Rev. Mark MacDonald of Minnesota.

The coalition has generated interest in developing urban Indian worshiping communities in such places as Fresno, California, among Yaqui people. There has surfaced, as well, interest in the Diocese of Dallas, which has a large Indian population.

URBAN INDIAN POPULATION, 1990 CENSUS

Rank	City	Episcopal Activity
1	Los Angeles-Anaheim-Riverside, CA	Efforts died
2	Tulsa, OK	No separate Indian church
3	New York-Northern New Jersey-Long Island	None
4	Oklahoma City, OK	No separate Indian church
5	San Francisco-Oakland-San Jose	Congregation in San Jose
6	Phoenix, AZ	Minimal
7	Seattle-Tacoma	Minor Activity
8	Minneapolis-St. Paul	Two mature congregations
9	Tucson, AZ	Minor Outreach
10	San Diego, CA	None
11	Dallas-Fort Worth	New outreach
12	Detroit-Ann Arbor	None
13	Sacramento, CA	Suburban "Four Winds"
14	Albuquerque	Effort died in 1991
15	Chicago-Gary-Lake County	St. Augustine's in Chicago
16	Anchorage, AK	None
17	Denver-Boulder, CO	Congregation at Cathedral
18	Portland, Vancouver, WA	Church of the Four Winds
19	Philadelphia-Wilmington-Trenton	No
20	Washington, DC	Outreach activity
21	Houston-Galveston	Never
22	Fort Smith, AR-OK	None
23	Milwaukee-Racine	Committee in Milwaukee
24	Yakima, WA	None
25	Salt Lake City	Sound worshiping and social outreach

11

TWENTIETH CENTURY
SOUTHERN REVIVAL

Today, across the whole of the south, where the Episcopal Church enjoys major communicant strength, there have been only two sustained missions among Native Americans—St. Paul's, among the near-forgotten Monacans in Amherst County, Virginia, and St. Anna's, among the Poarch Band of Creek Indians in Escambia County, Alabama. However, there is a growing mixed congregation at St. Francis of Assisi at Cherokee, North Carolina, and a Washington, D.C. parish, St. Patrick's, supports an outreach.

England's Queen Elizabeth I, upon sending out the first settlers to her colony of Virginia, proclaimed that "God hath reserved" the poor infidels of the New World to be "introduced into Christian civility by the English nation." Her Virginia colony, after baptizing Pocahontas, did little to introduce the Christian religion to the "savages" along the shore. Neither did the early American Church. Between 1724 and 1907, the most ignoble era of Indian subjugation in the southland, one finds no evidence of Anglican/Episcopal activity among the region's indigenous population. Neglect prevailed following retirement in 1724 of the colonial governor, Spottswood, who had advanced certain education initiatives including special Indian study at William and Mary College.

At the end of the Revolutionary War the Anglican Church in the Americas was, of course, in shambles. For a full generation after separation from England, the fledgling Episcopal Church struggled to deal with its independence. It was either unable or unwilling to focus on western expansion or on justice issues concerning Indian affairs. Thus the Episcopal Church was unconscionably mute while missionaries of the American Board of Commissioners for Foreign Missions (ABCFM) were standing in solidarity with the Cherokees against the state of Georgia. Founded in 1810 by the Presbyterians and Congregationalists the ABCFM interdenominational organization, funded in part by the U.S. government, became the primary missionizing outreach among the tribes of the southeast.

The Forgotten Monacans of Virginia

Not until early in the 20th century did the Episcopal Church begin work among southern Indians. The new work was among a band long fragmented, near decimated and virtually forgotten in the foothills of the Blue Ridge Mountains of Virginia. The Monacans are of Siouan stock, left behind it is believed, when the nomadic Sioux wandered for generations across the south and east. First European contact was made by Captain John Smith, who in 1608 sent a company of 120 men up the James River into the ancestral homeland of the Monacans. Anthropologists believe that there were more than 10,000 Monacans in a large territory stretching from the Rappahannock River to the Roanoke River when Jamestown was settled. In the mid-1700s the Monacans gathered on Bear Mountain in Amherst County.

Through the centuries the Monacans were viewed as different than their neighbors—Cherokee, Algonquin, and other coastal Indians. It has been suggested that the Monacans mixed with Tuscaroras who remained behind when the main body moved in the 1700s from the Carolinas to join their kindred of the Iroquois Confederacy in New York state.

There was early Caucasian mixture among the Monacans, who late in the last century were "discovered" living in isolation on Bear Mountain near the locale described by the Smith expedition almost 300 years before. There likely had been mixing with a settlement of freed black slaves long established on the opposite side of Bear Mountain. Considerable tension, however, was noted between the people who "looked like Indians" and their neighbors who were descendants of freed slaves. The term "free issue," initially applied to slaves given freedom before the Civil War, became all inclusive, and the Indian mountain people despised identification as "issues." Furthermore, the Indians refused to attend black schools. They were not allowed in white schools. The Indians refused black medical facilities, nor would they worship at black churches.

Episcopal mission arrived among the Monacans in 1907 and has remained ever since as the heart of community life. A seminarian, Arthur Gray Jr., dreamed of going to Japan as a missionary. His father, rector of Ascension Church in nearby Amherst, encouraged his son to look closer to home for mission work. A descendant of Virginia gentry, young Gray, during the summer between graduation from the University of Virginia and entry into Alexandria Theological Seminary, was able to acquire land and raise $1,500 to build the mission church and school for the Monacans on Bear Mountain.

For the next half-century, the Monacan mission was run by a series of devoted deaconesses. First to come was Cornelia Packard, daughter of the dean of Alexandria Theological Seminary. Almost from the time the mission was established, the faculty and students of Sweet Briar College, an elite girls school located in Amherst County, provided financial support to the deaconesses. In 1916 Sweet Briar friends funded a mission home for the deaconesses, and in 1922 they added another schoolhouse and parish house.

The indomitable deaconesses taught generations of the Monacan children; the children would have had no education otherwise. The last of the deaconesses was the courageous and stalwart Florence Cowan, who in the 1950s led the challenge on school integration on behalf of Monacan children. Her seven-year desegregation battle to give Indian children access to white schools was finally won in 1963.

In 1965 the Church Army came to Bear Mountain mission and for three years Captain Robert Hicks served the Monacan congregation. He was followed by Captain John Haraughty, a native of Western Oklahoma, who knew well insidious racism as it relates to American Indians. When Captain Haraughty arrived at St. Paul's most of the families were landless, struggling to subsist as tenant farmers, having long ago lost their own small farms for non-payment of county taxes. With the social change of the 1960s and the proliferation of federal programs, Monacan leaders such as Phyllis Hicks, assisted by Captain Haraughty, succeeded in obtaining federal funding for job training and housing.

Captain Haraughty continued the battle for many years to break down old barriers that kept a racially, socially, and culturally isolated group of American Indians from medical, educational, and housing opportunities available in the mainstream of 20th century American life.

Captain Haraughty retired in 1991. The Rev. Susan Lehman, chaplain at Sweet Briar College, served as part-time interim for St. Paul's. The companion relation between St. Paul's and Sweet Briar went all the way back to the founding of the mission. In fact, the Rev. Arthur Gray, father of the mission's founder, was an original trustee and teacher at Sweet Briar.

In the last few years the Monacans have sought to gain an understanding of their identity. Being informed by anthropologists of their Siouan heritage, the Monacans made contact with the Lakota/Dakota people of the northern plains. George White Wolf Branham lived among the Lakota and learned their language and spiritual traditions, and certain practices were transported to Bear Mountain.

In 1988 at the encouragement of Captain Haraughty, Peter Houck, a Lynchburg pediatrician, wrote *Indian Island in Amherst County,* from which the Monacan Tribal Association identified 700 persons with genealogical ties to Monacan surnames over the past two centuries. A year later the association had established a tribal government and was recognized by the state of Virginia. It was a momentous occasion when the governor of Virginia officially recognized Bear Mountain Monacans as one of the eight indigenous Virginia tribes, reversing 60 years of official efforts to deny their existence.

When the Rev. B. Lloyd retired in 1991 as executive director of the Appalachian Peoples' Service Organization (APSO), a position he had held for some 20 years, he was assigned sacramental work at St. Paul's. It was agreed that Lloyd would travel monthly to St. Paul's, located 130 miles from his home in Blacksburg, Virginia.

Citizens of the Monacan Tribe have started to reclaim their ancestral land on Bear Mountain, purchasing 100 acres which includes their old burial ground. Proceeds from their first annual pow-wow provided the down payment. Upon repossessing the land, the tribe looked toward the second phase of a cherished dream: to establish a Monacan museum in an Episcopal school building adjacent to St. Paul's church, where the present generation's parents and grandparents were educated. The museum will stand as witness to a new spirit of pride among a people often forgotten and wholly isolated from other Indian people.

The Rt. Rev. A. Heath Light, Bishop of Southwestern Virginia, recently reported a community effort of the Monacan people whose lives have revolved around the St. Paul's mission:

> The mission site has a church, once occupied school rooms, a fellowship hall and grounds used for recreation. The church attendance dropped off after 1960 when the children were integrated into local public schools. In the past five years there has been a resurgence of activity at the site including ceremonies, programs, bazaars and fund raising activities. The site has also received attention from historians and archaeologists who recognize the cultural value of the site. There is an effort to convert many of the

old mission buildings into a museum. The role the Episcopal Church has played in their lives will be highlighted in the museum among other things.

Bishop Light in 1995 deeded to the Monacan Indian Nation a 13-acre tract of land which contains the old log cabin used by the deaconesses of old as a schoolhouse. A United Thank Offering grant in 1994 enabled conversion of the schoolhouse into a tribal museum.

St. Anna's Among the Eastern Creeks

In 1929 Edgar Van W. Edwards, priest-in-charge of Trinity Mission, Atmore, Alabama, reported to Bishop William G. McDowell that there were many in the Poarch Indian community centered in the Perdido Hills area that he believed were "unchurched." The bishop replied, "Then, see if you can round them up and we will try to start a mission." Edwards made house-to-house calls among the Creek Indians who had long lived in near obscurity in rural Escambia County, remaining behind when the main body of the nation had been removed a century earlier, in the 1830s, to Oklahoma. The priest told the Indians that he would preach in the little one-room school house on a specified night. The night came; Edwards came; no one else came. This happened several times.

Finally, Edwards was informed that before any of the tribesmen would respond the minister would have to see Acting Chief Fred Walker. (The real Chief, Aleck Rolin, was around 100 years of age and very feeble.) Edwards called on Chief Walker and was given permission to preach and the first service saw the little school house packed, with many standing outside.

Encouraged by the response, the bishop sent a medical missionary and his wife, a United Thank Offering volunteer, to minister to the Alabama Creeks. Dr. and Mrs. R. C. Macy, who had served as missionaries in Mexico, offered health care and treatment to all the Indians in Escambia County, who then made a living as sharecroppers, small farmers, migrant farm laborers and unskilled laborers in timber and turpentine industries.

The first Episcopal baptism was that of the beloved Chief Aleck Rolin, a few days before he died. By the end of the first year of the mission, 50 were enrolled in Sunday school and eight people were ready for baptism.

Baptism was by immersion; it was the only way the Indians knew, and thus, accepted. Bishop McDowell promptly appeared for confirmation. Another first of that year was an Episcopal wedding, that of the new Chief's daughter, Ruby Walker, and Alfred Jackson.

In less than three years there were two church buildings, built in the middle of the depression by the Creeks themselves. The first was St. John's-in-the-Wilderness. Three miles away was the second chapel, St. Anna's, named by the Indians to honor Mrs. Macy who had been widowed during the previous year but chose to stay on to assist with the mission. Both church buildings doubled as schools.

For 18 years the Episcopal churches provided virtually all the education available to about 600 Creek Indians. Since the turn of the century, Indians had been excluded from the rural county's white schools, and no schools were provided for the Indians. The Episcopal schools offered elementary education, but the Indian children were not permitted to ride the white school buses into Atmore for junior and high school.

In the mid-1940s St.-John's-in-the-Wilderness closed. St. Anna's has continued for more than a half-century. On two occasions, St. Anna's was visited by the Sioux priest Vine Deloria Sr., and through the years various Episcopal Church workers provided the Poarch band of Creek Indians with many social and education services as well as spiritual guidance.

The Poarch Creeks initiated a quest to link with other Episcopal Indians in the late 1980s, appearing at national Indian Church gatherings such as Winter Talk. A delegation journeyed to Alaska to the consecration of the Choctaw bishop in the early 1990s. A major step was taken in 1994 when the Poarch band with the cooperation of the Diocese of the Central Gulf Coast issued an invitation to host the 1995 Paths Crossing conference, a showcase for partnership ministry between Native and non-Native congregations.

When 89 Paths Crossing participants reached the Poarch Creek Reservation in the piney woods and palm marshes of southern-most rural Alabama they heard a resounding affirmation of the role of the Episcopal Church in the fate and fortune of a band of Indians who moved in one generation from isolated obscurity to self-sufficiency as the federally recognized Poarch Creek Tribe.

Buford Rolin, former officer of both the National Committee on Indian Work and the National Congress of American Indians, is an Eastern Creek. "The Episcopal Church provided us the spark to reclaim our heritage," said Rolin, who is an officer in his tribe and lay leader in the Diocese of the Central Gulf Coast. He said that St. Anna's has been the center of community life since the early 1930s. "It was the 20 acres of land that had originally been acquired in 1929 by the Episcopal Church that became the nucleus, the core, the heart of our reservation," Rolin said. "In 1964 the church provided 17.2 acres to the tribe and this tract became the first parcel of our reservation which has now grown to 2,400 acres."

Escambia County ran a school on property conveyed by the church in the 1950s until the segregation ended in the 1964. But "segregation did not conclude automatically," said Rolin. "Robbie McGhee's grandfather had to stand in the middle of the road in the path of the county school bus in 1964 with a shotgun to get it to stop to pick up Creek students to take them into Atmore for a high school education."

Robert McGhee, 24, who serves on several national Episcopal Church bodies, was appointed in spring 1995 to the Episcopal Council of Indian Ministries. He pointed out that records maintained by the missionaries served as documentation required in the federal recognition process. "Though it took from 1964 to 1984 to gain the tribal status we now have, we might never have gotten federally recognized except for those scrupulously maintained rolls and records of births, baptisms, marriages and funerals kept by the missionaries."

Florida: the Indomitable Deaconess

In 1903 the Diocese of South Florida made a tenuous try at mission among the Seminoles, a disparate lot clustered in isolated villages of open-sided palmetto-thatched huts or *chickees* across the Everglades, a sea of grass, water and jungle hummocks. Victims of a series of Seminole Wars, the Indians escaped deportation by hiding out in the Everglades. Tricked, betrayed and defrauded by whites for generations, these skeptical survivors were scarcely open to accepting the white man's religion when William C. Gray, first Bishop of the Missionary Jurisdiction of Southern Florida, opened Glade Cross Mission. After a decade and no converts the work was abandoned.

Then in 1933 during the Great Depression a deaconess, Harriett M. Bedell, came into southern Florida fund-raising for her impoverished mission in Alaska. The 57-year-old deaconess had spent 16 years working with the Athabascan Indians in Alaska and prior to that 10 years with the Cheyenne in Oklahoma. She ended up spending the rest of her long life—36 more years—in Florida in a mission among the Miccosukee, the most aloof, detached and unapproachable of all the Seminole bands. Slowly gaining a modicum of acceptance in the villages and swamps, the deaconess devised plans for marketing authentic Seminole handiwork such as skirts and jackets pieced together in distinctive patterned patchwork style.

Eventually, the tribal council gave her permission to teach the Christian religion, but she soon discovered that while they listened

*Harriet Bedell with Miccosukee Seminoles
in Florida in the 1930s.*
Courtesy, Archives of the Episcopal Church.

politely and examined the pictures of the life of Jesus, the Seminoles had by no means accepted Christianity. The determined deaconess did not falter, and though she supposedly retired at age 68 she doggedly continued her life's mission, locating new markets for crafts, helping to cure the ill, teaching Seminole children to read, and withstanding hurricanes. The Miccosukee came to trust the deaconess to such an extent that they named her *In-co-shopie* (Woman of God).

Hurricane Donna in 1960 destroyed the Glade Cross Mission and in effect ended the ministry of the Episcopal Church with the Seminole Indians of Florida. Harriet Bedell died at age 94 in 1969. The Diocese of Southwest Florida memorializes her ministry each January 8.

Washington Metropolitan

A group of Episcopal Indians residing in the Washington, D.C., area came together around a project: designing an appropriate observance of the 500th anniversary of the 1492 voyage of Christopher Columbus. Led by the late Rose Robinson (Hopi), the group organized the Washington Metropolitan Episcopal Urban Indian Caucus.

Looking to the outreach committee of St. Patrick's church, the urban caucus approached the Washington National Cathedral in 1989 seeking cooperation to hold a unique kind of observance of the Columbus quincentennary—an ecumenical religious service with the litany focused on a celebration of the passage of 500 years during which unrelenting and systematic change failed to destroy the Native spirit of the Americas.

The new dean of the cathedral, Nathan D. Baxter, agreed to participate. The Bishop of Washington, Ronald Haines, endorsed the proposal and agreed to take part personally in the celebration. The National Committee on Indian Work and its successor, the Episcopal Council of Indian Ministries, endorsed the project. Presiding Bishop Edmond L. Browning, arranged his schedule to be present as chief celebrant. General Convention of 1991 passed a resolution designating the Washington service as the Episcopal Church's official event for commemoration of the 500th anniversary.

So it was. Approximately 150 miles from the first permanent English settlement on the shores of America—a settlement whose purpose was claimed to be that of sharing the Gospel, according to rites and doctrines of the Church of England, with "savages along the shore"—3,000 people in the National Cathedral on October 12, 1992, heard a Choctaw bishop, Steven Charleston, say:

> We are gathered for a purpose, a reason. We are gathered to form a new community of God's people, to start afresh and anew for another 500 years in America . . . The new community begins with remembering. The power to remember and pass on the story of the people is at the heart of what it means to be a tribe or the people of God . . . I do not need to tell you how much my people loved this sacred land . . . They loved it with such passion that they called it "the mother."

12

FROM SURVIVAL TO
SELF-DETERMINATION:
THE LAST HALF OF THE 20TH CENTURY

A stately tall Ojibwa priest rises to speak before the House of Deputies of General Convention. He waits for the din and commotion to quieten. It is mid-afternoon of the sixth day of the historic Special Convention on the campus of Notre Dame University in South Bend, Indiana, in late summer of 1967. Fervent and impassioned debate has earlier ensued on the "Black Manifesto," on the Vietnam war and the draft, on trial liturgy and on seating women in the House of Deputies.

When at last he has the full attention of the House, George A. Smith of Minnesota reminds the deputies that "Indians have a natural genius for the symbolic in religion . . ." The grandson of Enmegahbowh, the first Indian priest in the Episcopal Church, Father Smith then speaks on self-determination. He says:

> . . . there is increasing evidence that Indians want greater self-determination. Now is not the time to withhold your support.

Self-determination, articulated by Indians for half a century, was scarcely heard by the church hierarchy until 1995 when participants of the annual Winter Talk gathering ratified a Statement of Self-Determination, which asserted "native people's intent to affirm our rightful place within the Episcopal Church and the Anglican Communion." The following winter, participants stirred considerable furor by announcing the birth of a new Native Episcopal Church which would "incorporate spiritual traditions and customs of our many peoples as we celebrate the Gospel of Jesus Christ."

The chronological journey had been long from missionaries of Queen Anne's Society for the Propagation of the Gospel in Foreign Parts to "self-determining," and the Indian had often been a victim in church polity. Once the Episcopal Church timidly tested the water of western expansion in the 1870s, it plunged in alongside evangelical sister churches, making a mighty missionary splash across the northern high plains, embarking not only in a spiritual endeavor but also a cultural conquest. Twelve present-day dioceses had active Episcopal Indian ministry by 1900.

Tribal Religions Banned

"Civilization" had taken such a toll that there were less than 250,000 Indians listed in the 1890 census. The buffalo was gone, the land base was gone and economic conquest was considered *fait accompli*. The mere quarter million survivors of America's holocaust faced yet another blow when the federal government outlawed tribal religions. By 1904 comprehensive government regulations banned the practice of all tribal religions, and traditional Native persons who wished to worship in the manner of their ancestors became outlaws in their own land. Though Episcopal missionaries were a bit more lenient that some of their puritanical brethren—they looked the other way when certain Sioux placed food at graves of departed relatives—nonetheless, South Dakota's Archdeacon Edward Ashley chaired an ecumenical committee to outlaw Indian dances.

The 20th century had scarcely dawned before churches began a systematic withdrawal from its commitments in mission among the native peoples, losing interest in its earlier undertaking, and thus abandoning a people whose own religions it had sought to eradicate. The Episcopal Church paid more heed to its missions in distant Japan, Greece and Cuba than, as Bishop Hare was wont to say, "to heathens not far off but lying cold on the church's bosom."

At the time of the Episcopal Church's withdrawal Indians were reeling from the final maneuver of conquest—enactment of the Dawes Severalty Act, commonly called the Allotment Act, which broke up Indian reservation life and decreased Indian holdings by almost 100-million acres between 1887 and 1934. With the division of tribal lands, severe problems developed almost immediately from which Indian nations required generations to recover.

The devastating Dawes Act was promulgated by the spate of

Indian political advocacy organizations which sprang up in the last decades of the 19th century. The well-meaning wealthy, convinced they knew what was best, put on white-tie benefit banquets in New York's hotel ballrooms and showcased a few token Indians in their midst. Old photographs provide a glimpse of the opulence of the events, and feature the Arapaho priest, Sherman Coolidge, seated among the benefactors. Lake Mohonk Conference of the Friends of Indians assembled annually from 1883 until 1917 at the sumptuous Hudson Valley resort, and humanitarian reformers, academics, and government officials, along with influential persons only tangentially concerned with Indian rights, pondered the fate and questionable future of the "redman."

Cure to the Indian Problem

The Indian Reorganization Act was passed in 1934, lifting certain oppression, including the near 40-year ban on all forms of traditional worship. The Indian was at the bottom rung of all socio-economic indicators with the lowest income, poorest health and shortest lifespan. In the early years following World War II Congress sought a permanent cure for the "Indian problem" by termination and relocation. Termination was a scheme designed to conclude treaty/trust relationships and obligations to tribal governments; relocation was designed to accomplish the ultimate Indian assimilation by providing reservation Indians with a one-way ticket to urban ghettos where the Bureau of Indian Affairs (BIA) set up offices to assist in resettlement. The first offices of the new relocation program were in Chicago and Los Angeles. Later there were BIA offices in 10 other cities, including Denver, Dallas, Cleveland, Detroit and the San Francisco Bay area. The Episcopal Church feebly followed.

Up until the mid-point of the 20th century dioceses decided, for the most part, the extent of Indian work within their boundaries and how—and if—the mission would be executed. At the national level, certain people were helpful, such as United Thank Offering workers, but bishops of the missionary districts had to supplement their meager purses through journeying about the country, wheedling cash from the affluent to carry on Indian work. Bishop William D. Walker journeyed to New York to call upon the Vanderbilts, who helped purchase a railroad "cathedral" car for his North Dakota domain. Bishop William Hobart Hare had to come east to petition for help from the Astors, who paid for Indian schools and church buildings in South Dakota. Hudson Stuck, the Archdeacon of the Yukon, had to set out on

*The Venerable Vine Deloria Sr. [1901-1990) ca. 1954
when he arrived at church headquarters in New York City
to serve as secretary for Indian work.*

exhausting speaking engagements to raise funds to support medical
facilities along the Yukon River.

1954: Indian Office Established

A milestone decision was made in the tenure of Presiding Bishop Henry
Knox Sherrill, in the 1950s, the great growth period of the Protestant
Episcopal Church. Instead of relying entirely on missionary district
or diocesan decisions on the nature of Indian ministry, the church
established an Indian office at Church headquarters.

In 1954, for the first time in almost 350 years of Anglican-Indian
relations, an Indian was placed in a national executive post at Church
headquarters. The Rev. Vine Deloria Sr. became the assistant secretary for Indian Work. Though the South Dakotan Yankton Sioux served
at the national church headquarters but four years, he sparked a fire
that would alternately flame and smolder for the next four decades.

No Indian successor was appointed to replace Deloria when he departed the New York position in 1958. Indian work was subsumed by the Home Department and the Rev. Clifford Samuelson became executive officer for special field ministries.

Betty Clark Rosenthal, a member of the Clark missionary family which labored long in both South Dakota and among the Navajo, became scribe for the emerging redesign of Indian work in the Episcopal Church. Born and reared on the Crow Creek Reservation, Rosenthal remained in the east after attending Mt. Holyoke College and doing graduate work at the University of Wisconsin and Harvard. In addition to Episcopal provincial activities, she sat on the board of directors of various national Indian advocacy organizations. By 1960 she had married, had three children and was expecting the fourth when she was asked to develop the report on the Church's Indian work policy, mandated by the 1958 convention. It was at Roanridge, Missouri, the Church's Rural Work Center, that Rosenthal somewhat reluctantly agreed to prepare the report for the 1961 General Convention. She recalled that a good number of Indian clergy, catechists and lay workers were present at the Roanridge gathering. "At least three Delorias were there: Vine Sr., Ella and Susie. Susie was always the quiet one."

The flame blazed high in 1961 when the winds of change begin the stir that would reshape the national consciousness, and the Detroit General Convention passed nine resolutions on Indian work calling for a halt to the Church's "receding ministry." Paramount in the findings of the special study was recognition that each jurisdiction could not be viewed in isolation. It could not be "business as usual," without a centralized effort in place. Diocesan autonomy had created an awful isolation for Indian communicants, an isolation that was scarcely addressed until late in the 20th century.

Rosenthal is credited with generating heretofore unheard of momentum around Indian issues in the 1961 convention. She said, "We brought Indian people and Indian work into the midst of the 1961 General Convention. They've been on the scene ever since."

Samuelson and Rosenthal introduced "the Great Society" to Indian mission in 1964, and brought 400 Indians and an equal number of non-Indians to a conference on Indian poverty in Washington, D.C. Resentment of non-Indian domination was made plain, and for the first time in history, a channel for national Indian leadership opened up. *The Episcopalian* said:

> [At] the American Indian Capital Conference on Poverty
> at Washington Cathedral . . . Samuelson was chairman of
> the steering committee and earned an Indian name as "the

man who is not afraid." The conference was planned for 50 people, 500 came including every Episcopal [Indian] clergyman.

The result was a breakthrough in giving tribal governments a say in decision-making on the Johnson administration's war on poverty. With the Episcopal Church's entry into the arena to attain social justice for the nation's downtrodden, the Native American had a new advocate in shaping public policy.

General Convention Special Program

In September 1967 Presiding Bishop John E. Hines called on the Episcopal Church to "take its place humbly and boldly alongside of, and in support of, the dispossessed and oppressed people of this country for the healing of our national life." Likely it was not the "dispossessed" Indian that deputies to the 62nd General Convention in Seattle had in mind when voting, but the American Indian and Eskimo were partners with the National Committee of Black Churchmen (NCBC) as recipients from the General Convention Special Program (GCSP) $9-million fund established to respond to the Primate's charge.

In 1968 Vine Deloria Jr., author, attorney and advocate, stormed onto the scene in the unlikely role of a member of the Church's Executive Council. The son and grandson of Episcopal priests, Deloria had not yet published his iconoclastic treatise, *God is Red*. The document he wrote that laid groundwork for the present-day structure of Native American ministry within the Episcopal Church was called MRI—More Real Involvement, which underscored self-determination and demanded more involvement of Indian people in Indian ministry decision-making. Deloria, after conferring with Indian clergy and laity across the country, wrote:

> We seek the right to devise and direct programs which will fit our basic needs and communities in the life and program of the Episcopal Church.

In response to Deloria's arresting appearance at the February 1969 Executive Council meeting with a concise plan for implementation, the council voted to establish a National Committee on Indian Work (NCIW) and agreed in principal to 10 other articles speaking to mutual accountability.

In August a special convention was convened at Notre Dame University. George Alvin Smith stood before the House of Deputies

Vine V. Deloria Jr. in 1968
when he served on Executive Council.

and spoke on self-determination, and asked for support to the motion on the floor, made by Dr. John Ellison from the Diocese of New Mexico and Southwest Texas, that $100,000 in the General Convention Special Fund be earmarked for the newly established (NCIW). The motion further proclaimed ". . . mission to Indians and Eskimos as a top priority for the next triennium."

On that tense Thursday afternoon in South Bend, a 40-year old Dakota priest from Standing Rock Reservation, Wilbur Bear's Heart, politely asked for education funds for Indian children, and Kent Fitzgerald (Ojibwa), the newly appointed staff person for Indian Work, was introduced.

(The Church's memory of these actions concerning Indians has been overshadowed by the memory of a convention erupting in chaos when Mohammed Kenyatta of Black Economic Development seized the microphone and demanded reparations "in the amount of $200,000 for past offenses against Black Americans.")

Fitzgerald had formerly served as U.S. Indian Service

superintendent in Crown Point, New Mexico. His appointment was the result of the organizational adeptness of Betty Rosenthal and the language and energy of Vine Deloria Jr.

Rosenthal master-minded the design of the first advisory committee on Indian work, a response to the 1961 General Convention, and its membership included editors and historians, physicians and attorneys, anthropologists and Indian "experts." Luminaries sitting on the committee included: the Commissioner on Indian Affairs, Robert Bennett; Congressman Ben Reifel; Alvin Josephy, author and historian; and Ella Deloria, distinguished author and sister of Vine Deloria Sr., who served as an officer of the advisory group 1965-67. "Largely, they were members of the Episcopal Church, and they were the best informed people on Indian affairs in the country," said Rosenthal.

Vine Deloria Jr., the draftsman for the dream of present-day Native ministry, resigned from the General Committee Special Program after the South Bend gathering. He departed in a literary flurry, writing:

> The Episcopal Church has embraced the shades of Rudyard Kipling and the styles of imperialistic England for too long to make a sudden, sophisticated, and substantial move into America of the sixties. When it did move the Episcopal Church chose the most tangible but least sophisticated weapon in its institutional arsenal, Money. Unless the church moves substantially into the support of theological education of considerable content, it will probably remain vulnerable to the ebb and flow of popular social issues and become a pale version of a private foundation . . .

He published *God is Red* in 1973. In this work he held that "Christianity has failed both in its theology and its application to social issues."

NCIW Emerges

The National Committee on Indian Work lasted for 20 years. By and large the 10 Indians on NCIW, hand-picked by regional caucuses, were far from flamboyant; the five bishops by present-day yardsticks would measure conventional. The members could have been characterized as anything but militants, radicals, activists or protesters. Yet, the first grant the new Indian committee made was to the Alcatraz Island Occupation, the first Indian protest movement of this century to capture the national spotlight.

In early November of 1969, Indians had invaded and reclaimed the land known as Alcatraz Island "in the name of all American Indians by right of discovery." Six weeks later, the new, predominantly-Indian NCIW, voted to grant $5,000 to the occupation band on Alcatraz. Of the five bishops—mainly from missionary districts—four Indian clergymen, three Indian laymen and the solitary laywoman serving on first NCIW, not a single one has ever been identified with the protest movement of the 1960s. Yet the NCIW made their first grant to "Indians of All Nations" which took over the deserted federal prison. The February, 1970, issue of *The Episcopalian* said:

> Mr. Kent Fitzgerald, Executive Officer for Indian Affairs of the Episcopal Church and NCIW Executive Secretary, said Indians who have been occupying Alcatraz Island are seeking legal title to it and funds to convert it into an American Indian Educational Center. The Indians claim the land under provisions of a still-existing 1887 federal law which gives Indians the right to make application for an allotment of federal land not in use.
>
> The NCIW at an early November meeting, set guidelines for the allocation of a $100,000 fund for community development among Indian and Eskimo communities established by Special General Convention II last fall.
>
> Chairman of the National Committee is the Rev. George Smith, Cass Lake, Minn., a member of the Ojibway [sic] tribe. Vice-chairman is the Rev. Webster Two Hawk, Mission, S.D., a Rosebud Sioux and chairman-elect of the Rosebud Tribal Council.
>
> Members of the committee are: Bishops Conrad H. Gesner, South Dakota; Charles J. Kinsolving, III, New Mexico and Southwest Texas; George T. Masuda, North Dakota; Philip F. McNairy, Co-adjuter of Minnesota; and Chilton Powell, Oklahoma.

Members elected by five regional conferences of Indian and Eskimo Episcopalians were as follows: Alaska—the Rev. Titus Peter (Athabascan), Alfred Grant (Athabascan); Great Lakes—the Rev. George A. Smith (Ojibwa), Joycelyn Ninham (Oneida-Stockbridge); Great Plains—the Rev. Webster Two Hawk (Sioux), the Rev. Innocent Goodhouse (Sioux); and Southwest—Oscar Lee House (Navajo/Oneida), Francis Riggs (Cheyenne). William J. Gordon Jr. of Alaska succeeded Bishop Gesner upon Bishop Gesner's retirement in 1970.

A training initiative which would long be in Episcopal Indian ministry's budget received its first grant out of the General Convention Special Programs (GCSP) funds. It was Cook Christian Training School, Tempe, Arizona, which was awarded $10,000 for an internship program for Indian students. It was reported that enrollees included 20 Episcopalians from Alaska and the upper midwest. Episcopal subsidies to the Presbyterian school would sporadically flow for many years.

In addition to the school project, other projects funded by GCSP would have a lasting and positive impact on the lives of Native peoples. A grant of $5,000 was made to the Tanana Chiefs' Conference for a project related to construction work on the pipeline "which will carry recently discovered North Slope oil to a year-round open seaport." An Alaska grant helped to forge major change in the lives of Alaskan Natives. In July, 1970, the NCIW awarded $10,000 to the Alaska Federation of Natives. Organized in 1966 to represent Natives' land claims, AFN consistently had support of Bishop William J. Gordon Jr. Eventually, AFN would make major changes in federal law to benefit Alaskan Natives.

The $100,000 in GCSP funds were expended with final awards including: Reactivation of Old Community Well, Dresslerville Indian Colony, Nevada, $940; Red Scaffold Community Enterprize, Eagle Butte, South Dakota, $9,000; National Council on Alcohol and Drugs, Minneapolis, Minnesota, $2,289; Indian Ecumenical Conference, Crow Reservation, Montana, $3,000.

Fishing Rights

Hank Adams, a member of the GCSP Screening and Review Committee, was an advocate of fishing rights for Indians of the Pacific Northwest. In a foreshadowing to the danger and unrest to come, the Tacoma Indian leader was shot in January, 1971. Episcopal advocacy of fishing rights, which would remain a major issue throughout the 1970s, was evidenced by a $25,000 GCSP grant to Survival of American Indians Association, directed by Adams, in February, 1969. On learning of the attack on Adams' life, Presiding Bishop John Hines sent a telegram to the governor and attorney general of the state of Washington asking for "maximum effort to apprehend and bring to trial those responsible for the assault." Efforts of Adams and other Pacific Northwest Indians eventually resulted in the Boldt Decision which affirmed Indians' fishing rights in the northwest.

The Lutheran Church was highly visible in support of the 1972

Trail of Broken Treaties, in which 2,000 Indians coming from regions all over the United States, arrived in Washington, D.C., completing a month-long trip. The Episcopal Church, through NCIW, gave $10,000 in a special grant at the request of Olympia's Bishop Ivol Curtis. The funds were used for such expenses as travel, food, housing and communication. Local churches and diocesan organizations responded with help along the way. One of the leaders was Hank Adams. The nation took note of other 20th century warriors who would later be seen in the role of militants. They included Dennis Banks, Russell Means and the Bellecourt brothers. *The Episcopalian*, in its January, 1973, edition, said:

> The press gave little notice to the gathering until November 3 when 500 Indians, angry at the government's seeming indifference to their requests, occupied the Bureau of Indian Affairs' offices, which they held until the November 7 election. The press reported considerable damage to the building . . . The NCIW cannot condone deliberate destruction of property, public or private. At the same time, responsible Indian leadership cannot condone the Indian community's having the highest infant mortality rate, the highest unemployment rate, and the lowest life expectancy (44 years) in the United States. American Indian people must expect the United States to live up to its treaty obligations, made in good faith.

The GCSP did not have popular support from people in the pews and by 1973 it had been discontinued. Never to disappear, however, was the Indian demand to have a voice in programmatic policy-making within the Episcopal Church.

New Configurations

An ordination initiative championed by Alaska's Bishop Gordon would change forever the Episcopal Church's ordination requirements. A United Thank Offering grant awarded at the Houston General Convention (1970) was to be used to

> . . . help train Indian and Eskimo priests to serve in the more than 20 native communities, now served by the Episcopal Church in Alaska. The men will support themselves or be supported by the church to the extent that the local church can support them, resulting in fully self-supporting congregations in bush Alaska and giving to these churches

a dignity and responsibility not possible when their ministry and support came from the outside . . .

In the early 1970s a survey among seven major Christian denominations with 499 Indian congregations revealed that there were only 68 ordained Indians in the field to serve the Indian congregations. To respond to the clergy shortage, the Native American Theological Association was organized in 1978. Headed by Dr. Howard Anderson, the NATA consortium of five denominations developed special education programs and seminary affiliates.

Clearly hearing an imperative from the grass roots constituency on the need for trained Christian leaders, NCIW sought alternatives in models for education of Indian people for ordained and lay leadership and looked to ecumenical models for assistance. While NCIW's budget was modest, a large percentage of it was allocated to the Minneapolis-based NATA and Cook Christian Training School in Tempe, Arizona.

The Venture in Mission program of Presiding Bishop John Allin's administration provided substantial funding for NATA, and out of the innovative training model came a half dozen Indian clergy. However, when the Rev. Virgil Foote of St. Paul, Minnesota, resigned as Mazakute vicar in 1995, not one of the group was still serving full-time as a priest.

Another new configuration emerged in 1970 with the formation of a coalition of 14 aided western dioceses. Coalition 14 would affect Native American mission to a major degree for the next two decades. Vested with responsibility to apportion block grants from the national church to aided former missionary dioceses, the principally non-Indian C-14 body annually allocated more than $1 million from coffers of the national church. Around 80-90 percent of the allocation was earmarked for Indian work. Few Indians sat at the table to determine allocations. In later years several efforts were made to ensure Indian involvement in the allocation process. It would be 20 years before Indians were placed at the helm in allocating the primary funding of the Church for Indian work.

Other Ethnic Desks Established

Following the model of NCIW, the National Commission on Hispanic Affairs was authorized by the 1970 Houston General Convention; the Asian Commission and Episcopal Commission of Black Ministries emerged in 1973.

The first officer for Black Ministries, Frank Turner, became a bishop; the first officer for Asian ministry, Winston Ching, remained in the position for more than 20 years and was promoted in 1994 to program director for all ethnic ministries and other offices in a cluster called Congregational Ministries. The first Hispanic officer, George Rivera, was soon succeeded by Maria Cuerto who was jailed for refusal to cooperate in the investigation of Puerto Rican terrorist activities.

Since Fitzgerald's tenure eight Indians have held the Church Center position which has changed in character with each Primate. Dr. Howard Meredith (Cherokee) of Oklahoma replaced Fitzgerald in 1973. While Meredith was NCIW executive director the Pine Ridge Reservation became for 71 days a lead story on the nightly news. The Episcopal Church's position in the 1973 Wounded Knee occupation necessitated a special NCIW newsletter which said:

> As representatives of the militant American Indian Movement (AIM) continued to occupy the tiny town of Wounded Knee on the Pine Ridge Reservation in South Dakota, NCIW clarified the Committee's involvement and attitude toward the Indian demands.
>
> The Rev. Ronald A. Campbell, a Sioux from the Sisseton Reservation, tells of his own growing up on a reservation; his excitement and raising hopes for his people on first hearing about AIM; and his subsequent disillusionment when the organization's activities shifted to violence.
>
> The Rev. Innocent Goodhouse, Standing Rock Sioux, Fort Yates, North Dakota, writes not to condemn AIM but to attempt to help us understand AIM . . . "most of the Indian movements are made up of young people. AIM is the most visible at the moment but not the only one. In this first taste of successfully getting the ear of the public we have some of them become extreme . . . But we must be patient with the Indian."

Another voice to be heard on the Wounded Knee confrontation was that of Vine Deloria Sr., who had by then retired as Archdeacon of Niobrara. He preached to 4,000 persons in March 1973 at the Cathedral of St. John the Divine in New York City. He said, "The stand made at Wounded Knee took place because Indians can no longer contain anger resulting from their treatment by the white majority." Five hundred Indians were bussed from reservations in the New York area for the cathedral's special service. A story in the May, 1973, edition of *The Episcopalian* said:

The Indian contingent was met on the Cathedral steps by Dean James Morton who celebrated the Mass. The great golden center doors, used only on special occasions, swung open. The liturgy included Dakota Indian songs; the Gospel was translated into the native Dakota tongue by President White Hawk of the Inter-district Indian Council in South Dakota; Matthew King, an Indian, read the Epistle.

The archdeacon's son, Vine Deloria Jr., in a speech at the University of Minnesota, urged Indians to put aside confrontational tactics and seek to win their treaty rights through Congress. Another voice heard was that of South Dakota Bishop Walter H. Jones, who said:

Ours is a stand beside the young person caught in the whirlwind of events he does not understand. It is a stand beside the forgotten person who tries to have a grievance heard . . . Nearly 100 years ago the Episcopal Church of the Holy Cross was used to house the victims of Wounded Knee. Today it is again being used to house the homeless and the stranger who heard something was going on in Wounded Knee and drifted in.

At church headquarters there was a quiet interval during the brief tenure of Fayetta McKnight (Seneca-Cayuga), also from Oklahoma, who replaced Meredith in 1974 as NCIW executive director. During the same year, Father George Smith was replaced as NCIW chair by Philip Allen (Sioux), then working as student advisor at St. Olaf College in Northfield, Minnesota. A New York native, Marcia Steele (Oneida) succeeded Allen as NCIW chair.

In 1975 Dr. Cris Cavender (Dakota) served a three-month stint as NCIW executive. He was fired following a confrontation and confusion over his job description. Cavender said he thought the executive director should be responsible to the thousands of Episcopal Indians represented by NCIW, but "815 (the Episcopal Church Center) expects the director to interpret the Episcopal Church to the Indians."

In 1976 a concept for a separate Navajo diocese was offered at General Convention, which modified the concept and created the Navajo Area Mission. In 1977 Clyde Red Shirt (Oglala Sioux) from the Pine Ridge Reservation in South Dakota was named NCIW executive director. A reorganization of NCIW occurred in late November, 1977, when a team of 15 American Indians headed by Dr. Helen Peterson (Oglala Sioux) met in Denver. The following spring a new National Committee on Indian Work was appointed and included:

George Abrams (Seneca) of New York; Owanah Anderson

(Choctaw) of Texas; Father Wilbur Bear's Heart (Sioux) of South Dakota; Belle Beaven of California; Father Ron Campbell (Sioux) of South Dakota; Father Innocent Goodhouse (Sioux) of North Dakota; Thomas Jackson (Navajo) of Navajoland; the Rt. Rev. Walter Jones of South Dakota; Norman Nauska (Tlingit) of Alaska; Kenneth Owen (Sioux) of South Dakota; Helen Peterson (Sioux) of Colorado; the Rt. Rev. Frederick Putnam of Navajoland; Ross Swimmer (Cherokee) of Oklahoma; and Father Webster Two Hawk (Sioux) of South Dakota.

The new NCIW reviewed the "More Real Involvement" document drafted by Deloria almost a decade previously, and determined that most points raised were still valid and not yet fully met. Training of ordained leadership was again established as the number one and over-arching priority. Communication was labeled as essential; legislative advocacy was identified as a critical need. The NCIW elected Owanah Anderson chairperson; she served until 1982 and was succeeded by Lois Antoine (Sioux) of Mission, South Dakota.

Steven Charleston (Choctaw), not yet 30, succeeded Red Shirt as executive director in 1979. A graduate of Episcopal Divinity School, Charleston was at that time weighing ordination. A man who would later electrify audiences globally, Charleston was characterized by colleagues at the Episcopal Church Center as a quiet and thoughtful young man who was "perhaps yet in the process of defining himself."

Charleston's major contribution to the "Indian desk" was seeking new approaches to Native leadership development. He resigned the post in 1982 to become director of the Dakota Leadership Program in South Dakota and was subsequently ordained to the priesthood. A decade after leaving the New York position, he was elected Bishop of Alaska.

Charleston was succeeded at Church Center by Alan Sanborn (Penobscot). Owanah Anderson (Choctaw), after serving as field consultant for a year, became staff officer for Native American Ministries in 1984. Bishop William Wantland (Seminole) was elected NCIW chair and served from 1984 until 1987. After several years' effort, spearheaded by Province VI, a field staff position for Native ministries was approved in 1983. Two Sioux men briefly served in the position—the Rev. Virgil Foote (Dakota) of Minnesota and Sherman Wright (Rosebud Sioux) of South Dakota. In the autumn of 1986 Dr. Carol Hampton (Caddo) was appointed to the post and established the Indian Ministries Field Office in Oklahoma City. She served in that position until 1994 when the position fell victim to Church Center downsizing. Dr.

*National Committee on Indian Work, 1981.
Lois Antoine, chairperson (left), leads other
members of NCIW in a worship service.*

Hampton remained on staff but in a position as field officer for the Congregational Ministries Cluster.

Winds of Change

Two major consultations on Native American ministry, jointly sponsored by C-14 and NCIW, were held in Oklahoma City in 1984 and 1986. Echoing the "More Real Involvement" statement of the 1960s, both consultations called for greater empowerment of Indian peoples in decision-making levels of the Episcopal Church. Among the recommendations from the first consultation was for NCIW members to be designated for appointment by constituency, and for all dioceses which have a significant Native American population to establish diocesan Indian committees. By 1987 all NCIW members were representatives of, and accountable to, a diocesan Indian committee or urban congregation. Four new diocesan Indian committees have either emerged or been re-activated.

A significant outgrowth of the revitalized Indian ministry which surfaced in the mid-1980s was the Province VIII Indian Commission. Led by Helen Peterson, the provincial commission broadened its outreach and program with a primary focus on development of new urban Indian ministry in western cities. The persistent Dr. Peterson worked tirelessly for nearly a decade to raise the consciousness of the power structure of the Province of the Pacific, appearing at provincial synods and representing Indian interests with the province's Cross-Cultural Ministry Development organization and its successors.

Her efforts helped to shape Indian congregations and committees in several cities of the west. For a brief period urban ministry surfaced in San Francisco, Albuquerque, Los Angeles and Denver. Only the Denver ministry survived. During 1987 she chaired NCIW while continuing her provincial activities. It was through Dr. Peterson's leadership that the model congregation, Church of the Four Winds, was founded in her home city of Portland, Oregon. In 1994 the church celebrated its 10th anniversary as a thriving, viable urban congregation. Due to failing health, Dr. Peterson resigned both the provincial and congregation work in the summer of 1994.

Meanwhile, NCIW's leadership changed and Phillip Allen served again as chair. He was succeeded in 1989 by Cecelia Kitto of South Dakota, a Santee Sioux medical doctor.

In the mid-1980s, after having almost exclusively looked to NATA and Cook Christian Training School as primary resources for development of Indian ordained and lay leadership, NCIW reassessed direction. In the spring of 1986, not one Episcopal Indian was in a seminary. Upon the invitation of Seabury-Western Theological Seminary, a group of Native and non-Native leaders met and developed the Evanston Covenant, envisioning a center of Native American theological study at the Illinois seminary. NCIW pledged substantial funding to the Seabury program and seven Indian postulants were on the Seabury campus in autumn of 1986.

From 1986 through 1993 substantial scholarships were awarded to 16 Indians to study at Seabury-Western, but due to a variety of obstacles, what started out with great expectations sputtered to a dreary conclusion. Half of the seminarians stayed for the three full years and graduated. Of those, only four were serving Indian congregations by Epiphany of 1996. The Seabury experiment was given up, the dearth of Indian clergy was still distressing.

Birth of ECIM

Presiding Bishop Browning entered office with a theme of inclusivity. "There shall be no outcasts," he said. From the beginning he gave extraordinary attention to Native American ministry. During his first 18 months in office Bishop Browning visited Navajoland, attended an Oklahoma Consultation, participated in two convocations—Minnesota and Niobrara (South Dakota)—met with the NCIW, and visited Living Waters, the Denver urban Native American congregation.

A turning point in governance came in the spring of 1988 when the Executive Council met in South Dakota and focused on Native American ministry. The 40-member body visited the Pine Ridge Reservation, stopped to pay tribute to the fallen at the site of the Wounded Knee massacre, and heard a powerful meditation by the Rev. Steven Charleston, then a professor at Luther Northwestern Seminary, St. Paul. The bearded Choctaw priest, looking like a prophet of the past, drew special attention as he spoke of the ministry of carpentry:

> . . . whose purpose is to build something functional that is sturdy, that lasts, that is beautiful, that is aligned, that works for the sake of the Church. Jesus was a carpenter. He shaped, weighed, balanced. The Episcopal Church has an extraordinary opportunity. You must trust native leadership. Let it go. Let it go.

The outcome was a charge from Bishop Browning to his Blue Ribbon Task Force on Indian Affairs to develop a design for a comprehensive, coordinated Native American ministries model. The task force met several times over the next year and after consultation with Indian communities presented recommendations for a completely new configuration which brought a "confluence of NCIW and that part of C-14 which responds to funding needs for Native American Ministry." The Executive Council at its November, 1989, meeting approved recommendations.

Thus was born the Episcopal Council of Indian Ministry (ECIM).

At the next General Convention in Phoenix ECIM was affirmed with Resolution B002a:

> *Resolved,* the House of Deputies concurring, That the 70th General Convention of the Episcopal Church,
>
> a. Supports the Episcopal Council of Indian Ministries (ECIM), urging the Council to continue to develop and strengthen Indian ministries;
>
> b. Commends the Presiding Bishop's Blue Ribbon Task

Sister Margaret Hawk [1913-1993] escorting the Presiding Bishop Edmond L. Browning across her home reservation, Pine Ridge. The site of the Wounded Knee massacre of 1890.

Force for Indian Affairs for its work in developing the concept of the Episcopal Council of Indian Ministries;

c. Acknowledges the twenty-one year contribution of the National Committee on Indian Work (NCIW) to the vital support of American Indian/Alaska Native ministry, recognizing that NCIW has now been subsumed into ECIM.

d. Thanks Coalition-14 for its partnership with Indian ministry, and its role in the development of a new expression of Indian outreach.

Resolved, That the Secretary of General Convention be instructed to send copies of this resolution to the Chairs of the Episcopal Council on Indian Ministry, the Presiding Bishop's Blue Ribbon Task Force on Indian Affairs, the National Committee on Indian Work, and Coalition 14.

The founding chair of ECIM was the Venerable Philip Allen (Oglala Sioux), then Archdeacon for Indian work in the Diocese of

Minnesota. Also appointed by the Presiding Bishop were Dr. Blue Clark (Creek), Ginny Doctor (Mohawk), the Rev. Anna Frank (Athabascan), Carmine Goodhouse (Sioux), the Rev. Quentin Kolb (Ute), Linda Napai-Dudley (Navajo), Beulah Turgeon (Sioux) and four bishops: Craig Anderson of South Dakota, Robert Anderson of Minnesota, Steven Plummer of Navajoland and George Harris of Alaska. Upon retirement of the latter, the new Alaska bishop, Steven Charleston, was appointed to ECIM.

In addition to developing a responsible internal/external process for apportioning base budget support to aided dioceses, ECIM immediately set about designing and implementing new programmatic activities. Culturally appropriate evangelism models were launched; a new curriculum resource, *In the Spirit of the Circle*, was shared all across the church and in ecumenical settings, where half a dozen years after release it was still receiving accolades.

Cornerstone to ECIM's emerging character has been hewn at Winter Talk where some 69-75 native people come together each January to vision and share, discern and dream, strategize and craft, and draw strength from each other. From the Arctic Coast to the Gulf Coast, from Maine to Hawaii, Native people from 20-25 tribes and nations and an equal number of dioceses convene in rural wooded Oklahoma at St. Crispin's Conference Center. Led by Bishop Charleston, Winter Talk's themes have ranged from building new models for evangelism, lay and youth ministry, to planning new structures for indigenous ministry.

Maori Model

In 1990 ECIM made the first of several visits between the Maori Anglicans of Aotearoa (New Zealand) and Native Anglicans of the Americas. U.S. Indians went to New Zealand seeking information on structure and effectiveness of the non-geographic indigenous Maori diocese. The 12-person U.S. team found that the structure of the Church of New Zealand allows the Maori full and equal stature with their own episcopal oversight. The team was awed by the phenomenal growth of the Maori Church, which by the mid-1990s required five bishops to serve an area scarcely larger than Colorado. There are some 300 clergy, mostly non-stipendiary.

These visits provided stimulus for forming a vital new network, the Anglican Indigenous Network, which by 1993 included not only Maori and U.S. Indians, but also Canadian Indians, Native Hawaiians and aboriginal peoples of Australia. The network expanded into the

General Convention 1991. The group meeting the Archbishop of Canterbury Robert Runcie include Carol Hampton (Caddo), Margaret Hardy (Navajo), Owanah Anderson (Choctaw) and Steven Charleston (Choctaw).

southern hemisphere when a sizeable delegation of Anglican Indians from the U.S. participated in the Anglican Encounter in Brazil in the spring of 1992. Anglican Indigenous Network was hosted by Alaska in 1995 and Canada was designated host for the 1997 gathering.

The Phoenix Convention

In addition to the resolution affirming creation of ECIM, several other resolutions passed at the 70th General Convention were of special significance to Native Americans. The resolutions called on the Church to:

Celebrate Survival of Native Americans with an appropriate observance of the 500th anniversary of the voyage of Christopher Columbus, and designate the Eucharistic celebration on October 12, 1992, at the National Cathedral, Washington, D.C., as the Episcopal Church official celebration.

Be advocate for fair and just settlement of Indian claims and to call on Congress to create a Special Presidential Commission on treaty and civil rights of American Indians.

Support efforts at local, state and national levels to ensure American Indian religious freedom, "identifying the practice of religion as a fundamental human and civil right."

Oppose the opening of the Arctic National Wildlife Refuge for oil development, affirming positions of both the Alaska Diocesan Convention and the Executive Council.

Consent to election of a suffragan bishop for the Diocese of South Dakota.

Open the process for a change of canons to permit Navajo Area Mission deputies voice and vote in General Convention.

The Diocese of Arizona had several years previously invited the Navajo Area Mission to join with them as "host" for the 1991 General Convention and a Navajo *Hataathlii* (holy person) stood beside the Navajo bishop at the opening ceremonies. A headline of the *Episcopal News Service* proclaimed, "Native Americans Shed 'Best Kept Secret' Role at General Convention." The news story, written by David Skidmore, stated:

PHOENIX—They are often omitted and forgotten members of the church, overshadowed by larger minority groups. America's first dispossessed—Native Americans—have also often been the least vocal piece of the church's racial mosaic. But Saturday, at the General Convention's second major worship service, they let their voice be heard.

"One of the best kept secrets of our church," said Alaska's Bishop Steven Charleston to more than 3,000 delegates and visitors present, "is its Native American ministry." Charleston, a Choctaw, was one of four Native American bishops participating in the service. Joining them at the altar platform were Bishop Te Whakahuihui Vercoe of New Zealand, a Maori; Presiding Bishop Edmond L. Browning; and Dr. Owanah Anderson and Dr. Carol Hampton of the Native American Ministries Office.

The service was both a witness to the pain of Native America's 500-year-old encounter with European culture and a prayer for reconciliation. Following the traditional Native American invocation which addresses the four compass points, 15 Native American speakers gave reflections on their culture's experience with white people since

Columbus landed on a Caribbean island in 1492. Representing Dakota, Choctaw, Mohawk, Navajo, Arikara, Caddo, Cherokee, Tlingit, Oneida and Lakota peoples, the speakers recited a sobering litany of massacre, slavery, eviction, and assimilation.

The Rev. Kenneth Armstrong, a Cherokee from the Diocese of Oklahoma, told about the final subjugation of the Plains Indians. Whereas estimates put Indian numbers at 25 million in 1492, he said, by 1890 they numbered less than 250,000. "There was an assumption that Indians had vanished," he concluded.

Reviewing this century's experience, several speakers recounted the submergence of Native Americans into mainstream society and consequent drop from the national consciousness. "The dominant society is unable to relate to us as contemporary beings and sees us only as relics of the past, museum pieces, stereotypes," said the Rev. Duane Fox, an Arikara from the Diocese of North Dakota. "Racism is too often defined as black and white."

. . . a message of forgiveness and union was echoed by other presenters: Martin Brokenleg, Rosebud Sioux from South Dakota; Ginny Doctor, a Mohawk from Central New York; Bessie Titus, an Alaskan Athabascan; Ron Campbell, a South Dakota Sioux; as well as Bishops William Wantland of Eau Claire and Charleston, and retired Bishop Harold Jones of South Dakota, the church's first Native American bishop . . .

Celebration of Our Survival

The primary event of 1992 was the ECIM observance of the 500th anniversary of the voyage of Christopher Columbus. More than 3,000 people journeyed to Washington National Cathedral and jubilantly joined to celebrate survival of Native Americans. The event was a dream-made-real initiated by Washington Metropolitan Episcopal Urban Caucus, headed by the late Rose Robinson (Hopi). The caucus which met at St. Patrick's church sought ECIM's sponsorship; in turn ECIM promoted a resolution through the 1991 General Convention designating the event a church-wide observance.

A 12-hour dusk-to-dawn prayer vigil proceeded the service. Participants included Indians from 35 tribes from all over the United States, plus representation from Canada and Latin America as well

*Indian bishops at Eucharist celebrating 500 years of
survival, Columbus Day 1992. Pictured left to right are
the Rev. Martin Brokenleg (Sioux), Bishop Harold Jones
(Sioux), Bishop Steven Plummer (Navajo), Presiding
Bishop Browning, the Ven. Philip Allen (Sioux), Bishop
Steven Charleston (Choctaw), Bishop William Wantland
(Seminole) and host Bishop Ronald Haines.*

Photo by James Solheim, Episcopal News Service.

as Native Hawaiians and a Maori bishop. The liturgy was well-planned
and authentic—from the cedar incense gathered from a special tree
in the Cheyenne Nation to the thunderous drums reverberating in
the great cathedral. Jeffrey Penn, writing for *Episcopal News Service,*
stated:

> Amid a fierce debate in recent years over Christopher
> Columbus's role in the obliteration of Native American cul-
> tures, more than 3,000 people journeyed to the Washington
> National Cathedral on Columbus Day and jubilantly cel-
> ebrated 500 years of survival by Native Americans.
> The October 11 and 12 celebration in the nation's capi-
> tal, itself named in honor of Columbus, did not laud the

Italian explorer, nor his so-called "discovery of the New World." Instead, in prayer, music, and preaching, worshippers from throughout the Western Hemisphere paid tribute to the memory of Native Americans in a dramatic service that was both a testimony to their struggle and a defiantly forward-looking and conciliatory event . . .

In what one Native American Episcopal priest described as "the proudest day of my life as an Indian person," the three-hour cathedral service was a tapestry of emotion and drama that wove together strands of sorrow and hope present in the collective memory of Native Americans . . .

The thunderous beating of drum . . . joined the cadence of a Native American chant in a two-part harmony that pierced the silence of the cathedral, calling the congregation to "worship God in the beauty of holiness." At the Eucharist, four Native American bishops joined Presiding Bishop Edmond L. Browning in consecration of the gifts, including William Wantland (Seminole) of Eau Claire, Charleston (Choctaw) of Alaska, Steven Plummer (Navajo) of the Navajo Area Mission, and Harold Jones (Sioux) retired suffragan bishop of South Dakota . . .

The Choctaw bishop of Alaska, Steven Charleston, delivered a sermon that will be long remembered. Without note, wholly extemporaneously, he spoke and was interrupted by applause as he said:

Our people, like sheep to the slaughter have survived peril, famine, disease, distress, racism, oppression, exploitation, and even death itself. We have survived. We are more than just survivors. We are those victorious, those brought to life again, those who know the truth, those who hear the truth, those who speak the truth, and hear the words of St. Paul. "For I am convinced that neither death nor life, nor angels nor rulers, nor things present, nor things to come, nor powers, nor height nor depth, nor anything else, in all creation, will be able to separate us from the love of God in Christ Jesus our Lord." Brothers and sisters, we are more than conquerors. I stand to proclaim a new beginning. I stand to proclaim a new community. I stand with my ancestors. I stand with my people. I stand with God. Who stands with me? Amen.

ECIM: Poised to Soar

The Cathedral celebration was hailed, in some quarters, as a highpoint in church history. ECIM stood poised to deal with future challenges. It elected a strong Mohawk laywoman as its next chair, and serving with Ginny Doctor as vice-chair and secretary were two academics, the Rev. Canon Martin Brokenleg (Lakota), a professor at a Lutheran college in Sioux Falls, South Dakota, and Dr. C.B. Clark (Creek), a vice-president of a Methodist university in Oklahoma City. Departures, through rotation or resignation, from ECIM roster were Carmine Goodhouse (Sioux), the Rev. Quentin Kolb (Ute), Linda Napai Dudley (Navajo), Beulah Turgeon (Sioux), Bishop Robert Anderson and Bishop Craig Anderson. New members were Bishop Steven Charleston of Alaska, Bishop Creighton Robertson of South Dakota, Bishop Stewart Zabriskie of Nevada, the Rev. Carol Gallagher (Cherokee) of Pennsylvania, Reynelda James (Paiute) of Nevada, and Brokenleg of South Dakota.

Future doctors, lawyers and—likely—Indian chiefs were aided with ECIM scholarships to the tune of $75,095 from 1992 to the spring of 1995. An ECIM committee made recommendations for Martin Luther King Jr. Legacy Fund scholarships for 46 Native students whose fields ranged from doctoral level theology to kinesociology, in addition to pre-law, pre-med and political science. Not only did Native people receive through the scholarship fund, but contributions to the fund came out of Native communities as well. For instance at Pyramid Lake, Nevada, women held fry bread dinners to help raise more than $1,500. The Oakerhater Merit Award became an established prize for seminarians. Of significant consequence was solid endorsement, after review, of a Canadian seminary—Vancouver School of Theology—which developed a Native ministries program. Through extension study under a mentor and campus study for two-weeks each summer the program can lead to a masters of divinity degree. ECIM was able to assist financially a dozen VTS students.

The ECIM-sponsored annual Paths Crossing event became a perennial showcase for cross-cultural understanding and exchange of ideas. Settings varied widely, from the affluent suburban parish of Holy Spirit, Lake Forest, Illinois (1989), to Pine Ridge Reservation, located in Shannon County, South Dakota, the poorest county in America (1994). By custom the event is held on the weekend following Easter Day. Other sites for the "bridge building between white and Native American Episcopalians" have been St. Patrick's, Washington, D.C., 1990; Christ Church, Cincinnati, 1991; Diocese of Arkansas in Little Rock, 1992; All Saints' urban Indian congregation, Minneapolis,

1993; the Diocese of Central Gulf Coast with its single Native congregation, St. Anna's, Atmore, Alabama, 1995; and the Oneidas of Holy Apostles in Wisconsin, 1996. The Navajos at the Church of the Good Shepherd and Standing Rock missions in North Dakota have invited future gatherings.

Each triennial, ECIM sponsored a National Native Youth Festival. Designed by Native youth, the festivals have drawn young Native people from all across America—Maine to Hawaii, Alaska to Alabama. "Dreams of Long Ago, Tomorrow" was held at Roman Nose State Park, Oklahoma, in 1989; "Soaring Young Spirits" was held at Thunder Head Episcopal Camp, South Dakota, in 1992. The third, "Time to Awake, Hope, Act," was attended by 100 at Bemidji State University, Minnesota, in 1995.

A loose-knit coalition of urban congregations began gathering annually in 1989 coming two-by-two (usually a clergy person and lay person) to re-energize through affirmation of the work of each, sharing experiences, goals, roadblocks, and high points of growing urban ministry. The first gathering was in St. Paul and subsequently have included Phoenix, Rapid City, Denver and Sioux Falls.

Legislative Advocacy Activities

ECIM entered boldly into the arena of advocacy on treaty rights and justice issues. Strong support was given to Wisconsin Chippewa treaty rights. Global compassion surfaced with support for indigenous peoples of Brazil and of Chiapas, Mexico. Another resolution launched by ECIM which gained Executive Council endorsement in 1992 concerned the Canadian Cree Indians. Affirming the position of the Anglican Church of Canada, ECIM supported the Grand Council of the Cree Indians and the Inuit of Kuutjuaraapic in their opposition to the James Bay II Hydro-Quebec Project, which would inundate a vast portion of the Cree Reserve.

For a full decade both ECIM and its predecessor, NCIW, supported redress on the wrongful taking of the Black Hills from the Great Sioux Nation of South Dakota. The Supreme Court ruled in 1980 that 7,300,000 acres were illegally confiscated in 1877, a year after the Battle of the Little Bighorn and in violation of the 1868 Fort Laramie Treaty. The court, in affirming a financial award of $105 million, commented "that a more ripe and rank case of dishonorable dealing will never, in all probability be found in our history." The Sioux, asserting that they wanted the Black Hills back, declined monetary settlement. The ill-fated Bradley Bill, seeking to redress the theft, received support from the Episcopal Church and the Niobrara Council. There was subsequent support for creating a Presidential Commission to recommend equitable redress. The issue remains unresolved.

After the diocesan convention in Alaska passed a resolution opposing opening the Arctic National Wildlife Refuge for oil exploration, major efforts in conjunction with the Washington Office of the Episcopal Church, netted support strong enough to hold back potent special interest groups, such as oil companies. Episcopal leaders in opposition to opening the reserve included the Rev. Trimble Gilbert, then Chief of Arctic Village, which was almost 100 percent Episcopalian.

Another legislative advocacy issue into which significant energy was poured was American Indian Religious Freedom Act amendments. In 1979 a report was made to Congress detailing over 500 instances where federal policy infringed upon Native American religious practices. In 1988, in the *Lyng v. Northwest Indian Cemetery* case, protection for Native American religious sites on federal land was negated. In 1990 in the Unemployment Division of *Oregon v. Smith* case, protection was discarded for the ceremonial use of the peyote cactus, an essential ingredient in the rituals of the 250,000 member Native American Church. This last case brought great movement within the religious community to re-establish First Amendment rights of religious freedom by enacting new legislation through Congress. ECIM joined with some 20 other organizations in support of religious freedom for Indians. Congress in 1994 enacted legislation which guaranteed American Indians the right to use the sacrament of peyote in traditional religious ceremonies. This landmark religious freedom legislation ended over a century of persecution and prosecution of members of the Native America Church (NAC). President William Clinton in 1996 signed an executive order that provided redress on sacred sites protection, ensuring an aspect of religious freedom.

ECIM addressed other resolutions enacted at the Phoenix General Convention: a suffragan bishop for the Diocese of South Dakota was no longer pursued after election of an Indian as diocesan; the Indianapolis Convention in 1994 ratified canons to give Navajo Area Mission voice and vote in General Convention; Indians have been active leaders in the interdisciplinary, multicultural Environmental Stewardship Team.

"Dreams Give Wings to a Fool's Fantasy"

ECIM entered 1993 "feeling their oats." By the end of February ECIM had convened a consultation on education and training in Minneapolis, bringing together Native people to blueprint an image of Native criteria on credentialing and certification of training for ordination. Indian-specific special canons, national competencies, discernment, and the General Ordination Examination (GOE) were topics the body discussed with candor that comes with confident optimism. ECIM folded the design into a 12-point strategy to transform training into a model self-determined by Native peoples.

Mid-way through 1993 there were ominous signals of program and personnel down-sizing at Church Center, and "restructuring." Virtually every diocese of the Church was visited to gain insight into what people in the pew saw as priorities for the future. Evidently few saw ECIM as a viable piece of the next triennium's priorities; in fact, one diocese was quite critical.

Meanwhile, ECIM plunged ahead addressing issues such as religious freedom, youth ministry and theological education by extension through the Vancouver School of Theology. Responding to the eight-year-old behest of the Presiding Bishop and to a current request of the Commission on Native Hawaiian Ministry, ECIM voted to open its circle and invited Native Hawaiians to enter.

After five years of existence, ECIM appeared doomed. *Episcopal Life* (March, 1994) carried a bold headline stating:

COUNCIL BACKS RADICAL CHANGES
IN STRUCTURE

Executive Council at its Norfolk, Virginia, meeting in late February had unanimously voted to combine racial/ethnic commissions into a single multi-ethnic advisory committee with each of the four ethnic groups having three representatives.

Within a week, ECIM convened in San Jose, California, for its previously scheduled semi-annual meeting. Members "hurled a lance into the sand," and sent copies of a document it adopted to Executive Council members. Titled the "San Jose Declaration," the document cited current work of ECIM and drew attention to the recommendation of the 1993 Partners in Mission (PIM) Consultation of global partners which called for "an action plan which endows the Native Americans with the freedom and authority to organize and manage their own affairs, including training, within the life of the church." [Full text of the document is included in Appendix C.] The San Jose statement concluded:

> It does not seem wise to throw away a quarter of century
> of effort to develop ECIM after only four years of operation,

especially in view of the fact that ECIM is already accomplishing the kind of operations the current re-structuring proposals are hoping to do in the future. ECIM has built networks across cultural and language barriers, brought people together to work and train side by side, led the celebration of our common life together, and has made partnerships a living reality. We are now modeling and living the goals that the Church has set for the next triennium . . .

Indian people learn from the past and honor the gifts we have been given by those who have gone before. These gifts and skills include the ability to move from survivors to advocates, the creativity to develop mentor relationships and team ministries, and the gift of listening and sharing with others that makes networks and partnerships thrive. These gifts and skills can only enhance the whole life of the Episcopal Church. Therefore, it is the unanimous recommendation of ECIM, representing the American Indian/Alaskan Native members of the Episcopal Church, that this organization be continued as an essential part of any restructuring as a model for the whole Church.

Indian Ministry Future?

At the San Jose meeting the Choctaw Bishop of Alaska was charged with taking the ECIM termination proposal to the Program Budget and Finance Committee at the General Convention meeting in Indianapolis in August. The rationale stressed that ECIM, a primarily Indian council appointed by the Presiding Bishop, had been charged by the Executive Council in 1989 with allocating subsidies of more than a million dollars annually to dioceses with major Indian work, and that a body was necessary to accomplish the charge.

In one of its last actions before adjournment, the 71st General Convention approved the 1995-97 triennial budget. Included in the motion for approval was a recommendation from the Standing Committee on Program, Budget and Finance calling for "maintenance of discrete identity of ECIM."

Mid-way through Eastertide of 1995, seven months after General Convention, the new ECIM, down-sized from 13 members to five, was appointed to steer the course of Indian ministry for the balance of the 1995-97 triennium.

The Presiding Bishop appointed a Cherokee, Creek, Lakota,

Ojibwa and an Osage-Comanche from the dioceses of Pennsylvania, Central Gulf Coast, El Camino Real, Minnesota and Oklahoma. The Rev. Carol Gallagher (Cherokee) was the only one of the newly appointed group to have served previously on ECIM and was the only ordained person. A resident of the Diocese of Pennsylvania, she began pursuit of a doctorate at Princeton in 1994. Robert McGhee (Creek), age 24, was employed by his tribe's social services office. He had plans to enter graduate school to pursue a master's degree in social work. Sherrie LeBeau (Lakota) was serving as junior warden of a major urban Indian congregation at St. Philip's in San Jose, California, and taught in local schools. Frank Oberly (Osage-Comanche) of Oklahoma was chair of the diocesan Committee on Indian Work and a certified public accountant. Eli Hunt (Ojibwa) was head of the Minnesota Committee on Indian Work. Hunt was elected chair of the Leech Lake tribe and resigned ECIM in 1996; his successor was the Rev. John Robertson (Dakota), also of Minnesota.

Gallagher, Oberly and McGhee were tapped for additional service on the Multi-Cultural Committee, the successor group to the individual racial/ethnic commissions previously chartered by the Executive Council. Also named to the Multi-Cultural Committee was Pua Hopkins, Native Hawaiian, along with Hispanics, Asians, African-Americans and an at-large representative.

Statement of Self-Determination

The seventh annual Winter Talk in January 1995 issued a statement signed by 53 participants from 22 dioceses and 26 tribes and nations pledging the fortitude and boldness to move out of the missionary model and claim a rightful place within the Episcopal Church and the Anglican communion—"equal partners in the full life of the Body of Christ as we accept the obligations of leadership in this new vision of the Church."

"We respect the spiritual traditions, values and customs of our many peoples, and we incorporate them as we celebrate the Gospel of Jesus Christ," the statement said. A variety of daily worship services at the gathering blended Christian liturgy with tribal worship rituals, many of them unlawful as recently as 1934. Plains tribes used smoke in a cleansing ritual, while Paiute and Native Hawaiians used water ceremonies, and Navajo used corn pollen for their blessing.

In the "Statement of Self Determination" which Winter Talk participants signed, the covenant read, "We proclaim our God-given right to determine our own destiny as we accept full responsibility for

Six bishops at the Anglican Indigenous Network (1995).
Arthur Malcolm (Australian Aboriginal),
Ben Te Haara (Maori), Gordon Beardy (Cree),
Steven Charleston (Choctaw), Muru Walters (Maori)
and Whakahuihui Vercoe (Maori).

shaping our future under the guidance of the Holy Spirit." [Full text of the statement is included in Appendix D.]

"We do not leave our own dioceses or the Episcopal Church," stressed the Rev. Dr. Martin Brokenleg (Rosebud Sioux), a facilitator for the event. "What we are doing is deliberately taking a bold step toward shouldering responsibilities for our own vision of ministry." Recognizing the necessity of skilled, trained leaders, an initial step was taken toward establishing an alternative training institute in the Diocese of Minnesota. Partnership with the diocese was assured by Bishop James Jelinek.

The unforeseen American Indian renaissance which burst forth in the 1970s and 1980s clearly illustrated that the North American Native peoples were determined to remain distinct societies and to maintain their identity while creating their own expressions of Christianity and preserving their traditional value systems. Many peoples have become victims of long occupations by foreign powers; many have disappeared from the surface of the earth. The American Indian has survived.

"The time is long past when others will make decisions for us," said Charleston. "We can't go backward—the only way is forward into our future. It's still a fight for survival. And we will survive," concluded Charleston, seen as one of the principal Church leaders of the coming century.

Appendix A

CHRONOLOGY OF ANGLICAN/ EPISCOPAL MISSION TO NATIVE AMERICANS IN THE UNITED STATES

1579 Gospel first preached by clergy of Church of England to an assembly of American Indians by chaplain to Sir Francis Drake on coast of Northern California.

1587 Manteo, first American Indian convert to Church of England, baptized at Roanoke, the lost colony.

1606 James I issued Charter for Jamestown Colony, first permanent English settlement; ordinance deemed a purpose of colony "to preach and plant true word of God among savages according to rites and doctrines of Church of England."

1613 Pocahontas baptized while being held hostage in Jamestown harbor.

1622 English abandoned missionizing in Virginia, entered into an extermination policy following Indian uprising protesting further encroachment.

1644 John Eliot began Indian work in Massachusetts; continued until his death in 1695; translated Bible into Algonquin language; established 14 "Praying Towns."

1696 Trinity Church in New York City organized; one of its early rectors translated Book of Common Prayer into Mohawk language.

1704 Society for Propagation of the Gospel in Foreign Parts sent its first missionary, Thoroughgood Moore, to Iroquois Nations of New York state.

1712 First chapel for Mohawks erected at Fort Hunter; Queen Anne sent altar silver. Church of England mission spread to all six Iroquois Nations.

1743 The Rev. Henry Barclay reported that only a few Mohawk remained unbaptized.

1746 Sir William Johnson named the Crown's Indian Commissioner in New York and exercised tremendous influence on his Mohawk brother-in-law, Joseph Brant, who remained loyal to Church and Crown during Revolutionary War, moving to Ontario following war; responsible for founding St. Paul's of the Mohawks, first protestant chapel of province. Brant translated English prayer book in Mohawk language.

1816 John Henry Hobart, Bishop of New York, founded first American Indian mission of Episcopal Church. For mission among Oneida, then in New York, Hobart later ordained Eleazar Williams who was likely Mohawk but claimed to be the lost Dauphin of France.

1823 Oneidas exiled to Wisconsin; Episcopal Church went with them. Hobart Church was first consecrated building of Territory of Wisconsin.

1834 First Episcopal services held in present Diocese of Idaho at Fort Hall, agency offices for Shoshone-Bannock Reservation.

1852 Enmegahbowh, with Dr. James Lloyd Breck, established St. Columba's at Gull Lake, Minnesota. This mission to the Ojibwa became the mother mission of Indian work west of the Mississippi River.

1857 First Anglican mission in today's Alaska at Metlakatla in Canada; mission moved in 1887 to U.S. territory.

1859   Bishop Jackson Kemper ordained Enmegahbowh to diaconate.

Henry Benjamin Whipple consecrated first Bishop of Minnesota; served in that capacity for 42 years; known as "Apostle to the Indians."

1860   First mission among Santee Sioux founded at Redwood, Minnesota.

1862   U.S. government failed to forward treaty-obligated rations and annuities to Santee; uprising followed. First Indian prison ministry when Bishop Whipple confirmed 100 Santee in Fort Snelling prison.

Anglican missionaries arrived at Fort Yukon; when Episcopal missionaries arrived in 1896 they found groundwork laid with translations of Bible and prayer book.

1863   Episcopal Church accompanied exiled Santee to Dakota Territory.

1867   In Minnesota, Enmegahbowh ordained as first American Indian priest of the Episcopal Church.

1868   First Sioux, Paul Mazakute, ordained to diaconate; next year to priesthood.

Good Shepherd on the Onondaga Reservation in New York organized.

1869   Rising Sun, an Ojibwa, began his long quest for an Episcopal missionary on Turtle Mountain Chippewa Reservation in present-day North Dakota.

1870   First Niobrara Convocation held at Church of our Most Merciful Savior on the Santee Reservation; by 1872 Episcopal mission among Sioux extended to Yankton, Crow Creek, Cheyenne River and Lower Brule Reservations, along with work at Flandreau and mission among the Ponca.

1871   U.S. government ended treaty-making era after negotiating 650 treaties with 350 Indian Nations.

After a decade of high visibility in Indian advocacy, Bishop Whipple whipped the Episcopal Church into action; Episcopal standing committee on Indian Affairs established. By 1882, the Episcopal Church sent 80 missionaries to Indian Country and ordained 20 Indians to the diaconate and two to the priesthood.

1872   William Hobart Hare consecrated Bishop of Niobrara, with non-geographic jurisdiction over the Great Sioux Nation. When he died in 1909, there were 100 Indian congregations where there had been nine; 26 Indian clergy where there had been three.

1874   George Armstrong Custer led 1,200 cavalrymen into Black Hills in violation of terms of 1868 Treaty of Fort Laramie. Expedition confirmed presence of gold.

1875   Mission extended to Rosebud Reservation in South Dakota.

1876   June 25: Battle of Little Bighorn, Sioux Victory Day.

1877   U.S. government illegally confiscated Black Hills. In 1980, U.S. Supreme Court ruled the taking of the Black Hills unlawful.

1877   Mission extended to Pine Ridge Reservation.

1881   David Pendleton Oakerhater, Cheyenne, ordained to diaconate at Grace Church, Syracuse, New York; returned to Indian Territory and for 12 years was the only Episcopal presence in the land which became Oklahoma. Served 50 years as deacon among Cheyenne-Arapaho.

1882   Episcopal mission begun at Sisseton-Wahpeton Reservation in South Dakota.

1883 Mission started at Wind River Reservation with arrival of John Roberts, a Welshman, who would remain at the Wyoming reservation for 60 years.

Episcopal mission extended to the last of the South Dakota Reservations with work begun on the Standing Rock.

1884 Sherman Coolidge graduated from Seabury and became first Arapaho ordained; returned to Wind River to work among his own people and establish St. Michael's at Ethete, Wyoming.

1885 Rising Sun's long quest realized for mission to Turtle Mountain Chippewa.

1885 First Oneida, Cornelius Hill, ordained to diaconate; in 1903 he was ordained to priesthood.

1887 Dakota students returned from eastern study and initiated mission on North Dakota side of Standing Rock Reservation, leading to founding of St. Luke's at Fort Yates and St. James' at Cannon Ball.

Mother mission of Episcopal Church in Alaska established at Anvik; first United Thank Offering helped to build Christ Church in 1889.

1889 Episcopal Church assumed work begun interdenominationally among Shoshone-Bannocks at Fort Hall, Idaho; established Church of the Good Shepherd.

1890 Second Alaska mission founded: Point Hope on the Arctic among the Eskimo. It was not until 1964 that the first Eskimo was ordained to priesthood—Milton Swan.

Wounded Knee Creek, S.D., December 29—376 hungry and disarmed Indians slain and buried in common grave. Seventh Cavalry sustained 25 fatalities. Action motivated, in part, to suppress further spread of Ghost Dance religion based on teachings of a Paiute medicine man named Wovoka.

1891 Fort Totten mission established in North Dakota.

1892 First Episcopal presence among Navajos when lay teacher appeared at Fort Defiance.

1895 Peter Trimble Rowe arrived in Alaska as first bishop; served 47 years.

1896 Work began in Nevada among Pyramid Lake Paiutes; almost all of the tribe converted to Christianity.

1897 Hospital opened at Fort Defiance, Arizona; funded originally by Westchester, N.Y., branch of Woman's Auxiliary.

Work began in Utah on the Uintah Reservation; in early years of 20th century 90 percent of Utes were confirmed Episcopalians.

1899 Standing Rock Sioux Episcopalians journeyed to Fort Berthold to evangelize Arikara, leading to founding of St. Paul's mission.

1901 Good Shepherd on the New York Seneca Cattaraugus Reservation established.

1907 Mission to Monacans of Bear Mountain, Virginia, organized by a priest's son who aspired to be a missionary to Japan.

1917 Second Navajo hospital opened at San Juan Mission, New Mexico.

1923 Initial Navajo work in Utah started; re-activated in 1942 with arrival of Fr. Liebler at Bluff.

1929 Mission began among Eastern Creek near Atmore, Alabama.

1930-1954 More mission work ceased than began.

In the "relocation" area, distant dioceses such as California and Chicago organized urban outreach. One of the few worshiping communities was at Good Samaritan in San Francisco, which was served by a Native American priest, Fr. Robin Merrill. When he departed, the congregation slowly dissolved. St. Augustine's in Chicago, under Fr. Peter Powell, continues to the present day.

1954 The Rev. Vine Deloria Sr. named to head Indian Office at Episcopal Church Center in New York City.

1958 General Convention ordered a special study of the Church's Indian work policy.

1961 General Convention passed nine resolutions on Indian work.

1965 National Advisory Committee on Indian Work appointed; produced "The American Indian in the Mission and Ministry of the Episcopal Church."

1968 "More Real Involvement" document, by Vine Deloria Jr., issued; established framework for future Indian mission.

1969 National Committee on Indian Work established; the Rev. George Smith (Ojibwa), Chairman; Kent Fitzgerald (Ojibwa), Executive Director.

1970 First American Indian bishop: Harold S. Jones (Santee Sioux), Suffragan Bishop of South Dakota. Coalition 14 formed to receive block grants from national church through dioceses; served 20 years as primary source for allocating funds for most all Indian mission work of the Church until 1990.

1977 First sustained diocesan Committee on Indian Work organized in Oklahoma; during the decade 10 other provincial, diocesan or congregational committees were eventually formed.

1980 Second American Indian bishop: William C. Wantland (Seminole), of Eau Claire.

1984 Oklahoma I Consultation, jointly sponsored by NCIW and Coalition 14 in Oklahoma City.

In addition to work earlier established in Minnesota, the mid-1980s saw new urban Indian mission organized in Denver, Portland, Albuquerque; Denver's congregation sputtered and reincarnated; Albuquerque's perished; Portland's remained strong and vital.

1985   18 Bishops and Indian leaders issue Evanston Covenant, a new model in Native American seminary study at Seabury-Western Theological Seminary; seven enrolled autumn 1986; program continued until 1993.

1986   Covenant of Oklahoma II issued at the second joint consultation in Oklahoma City when 85 Church leaders, including 50 Native Americans and the Presiding Bishop, set guidelines for Native American mission and ministry for the future. The Presiding Bishop established a Blue Ribbon Task Force for Indian Affairs.

1987   New networks formed including Mountains and Desert Regional Ministry, Urban Indian Caucus and Clergy Coalition; only the latter collapsed.

Province VIII Indian Commission re-vitalized; Province VII Indian Commission authorized but never thrived.

1988   The Executive Council met at Rapid City, South Dakota, and surveyed conditions at Pine Ridge Reservation; the Presiding Bishop announced expansion of his Blue Ribbon Task Force on Indian Affairs and charged it with developing a design for a comprehensive, coordinated Native American ministries model.

1989   Blue Ribbon Task Force's recommendations adopted by Executive Council. Established Episcopal Council of Indian Ministry (ECIM) and assigned it responsibilities for allocating $1-million-plus to aided dioceses with major Indian work.

First Annual Winter Talk, a national gathering of Episcopal Indians to vision and share, discern and dream, strategize and craft, and draw strength from each other. Held annually in January. First national Native Youth Festival, held each triennial since. First annual gathering of a loose-knit coalition of urban congregations, first annual meeting of Paths Crossing.

1990 Third American Indian bishop: Steven T. Plummer (Navajo), of Navajoland Area Mission. First of a series of visits between the Maori Anglicans of Aotearoa (New Zealand) and Native Anglicans of the Americas; led to founding Anglican Indigenous Network which meets every 18 months or so.

1991 Fourth American Indian bishop: Steven Charleston (Choctaw), of Alaska.

Highly visible Indian presence at 70th General Convention in Phoenix.

1992 "Celebration of our Survival" at Washington National Cathedral attended by 3,000; hailed in some quarters as a highpoint in Church history.

1993 Unparalleled strides made by ECIM in creating new designs in education, global networking, legislative advocacy, youth ministry and empowerment.

1994 ECIM fell victim to national church down-sizing and "restructuring" when Executive Council voted in February to combine racial/ethnic commissions into a single multi-ethnic advisory commission. ECIM boldly challenged with a document entitled "San Jose Declaration." General Convention, meeting in Indianapolis, voted recommendation to Standing Commission on Program, Budget and Finance calling for "maintenance of discrete identity of ECIM."

Fifth American Indian bishop: Creighton Robertson (Sioux) of South Dakota

1995 Winter Talk VII issued a statement signed by 53 participants from 22 dioceses and 26 tribes entitled, "Statement of Self-Determination," proclaiming a rightful place within the Episcopal Church and the Anglican Communion "as equal partners in the full life of the Body of Christ."

1996 Winter Talk VIII called for a transformed Native Episcopal Church; bold new training for leadership in covenant with the Diocese of Minnesota: strong focus on launching a new Indigenous Theological Training Institute in partnership with the Diocese of Minnesota.

1997 Mark MacDonald elected seventh Bishop of Alaska.

The
Community
of the
PARACLETE

P.O. BOX 61399
SEATTLE, WA 98121

Appendix B

A SURVEY OF NATIVE AMERICAN EPISCOPAL MINISTRY: 1997

1	ALASKA	Twenty-five predominately American Indian/Alaska Native congregations and six "mixed" congregations for a total of 3,465 baptized members and 2,024 communicants.
2	ARIZONA	Urban worshiping community at Cook Theological College in Tempe; congregation in Phoenix, and outreach through St. Stephen's with Navajoland.
3	ARKANSAS	Companion relationship with Diocese of South Dakota since 1991; significant partnership with Niobrara Deanery.
4	CENTRAL GULF COAST	St. Anna's near Atmore, Alabama, has served Eastern Creek congregation since early 20th century.
5	CENTRAL NEW YORK	Church of the Good Shepherd on the Onondaga Reservation, founded 1868; continues as an active witness of the Gospel in the Onondaga Nation.
6	CHICAGO	St. Augustine's Indian Center since the relocation period of the 1950s; continues social outreach and "community" for urban Indians.
7	COLORADO	A growing urban congregation regularly worships at St. John's Cathedral.

8	DALLAS	With the nation's 11th largest urban Indian population in Dallas/Fort Worth metroplex, tentative move made in summer of 1996 to minister to Indians at St. Martin's, Lancaster. Long association between Annunciation in Lewisville and St. Christopher's in Navajoland.
9	EAU CLAIRE	Advocacy on treaty rights through its Seminole bishop. Diocese has aided reservation substance abuse programs. Mixed congregations at Cathedral and Ashland.
10	EL CAMINO COAST	Strong Indian worshiping community at St. Philip's, San Jose, with new leadership emerging and new training programs.
11	FOND DU LAC	Holy Apostles on the Oneida reservation is the largest and oldest Indian congregation in the U.S. with 1,054 baptized and 870 communicants. There are also two mixed congregations (Christ Church, Green Bay, and All Saints, Appleton).
12	HAWAII	New strength evidenced in leadership development areas after Native Hawaiian Episcopalian Commission linked with mainland native peoples and Anglican Indigenous Network.
13	IDAHO	Century old Church of the Good Shepherd Mission on Shoshone-Bannock Reservation at Fort Hall.
14	IOWA	The Indian long-standing congregation at St. Paul's, Sioux City, operates health and social outreach programs.
15	KANSAS	Developing community for Episcopal Indians on campus of Haskell Indian Nations University, Lawrence.
16	MAINE	Motivated by 1992 Celebration of Survival, Diocese of Maine launched a Native American advocacy committee.

17	MILWAUKEE	Indian families active in All Saints Cathedral and St. John's, Milwaukee; new leadership emerging.
18	MINNESOTA	Strong and vital diocesan Committee on Indian Work. There are 11 reservation congregations; two urban congregations in the Twin Cities. New training initiative.
19	MONTANA	Thunder Child youth treatment program and Blackfeet youth program jointly created by Incarnation in Great Falls, diocese and national church, primarily through PB Fund.
20	NAVAJO-LAND	Three regions: New Mexico, Utah and Southeast with 1,500 baptized members at 13 chapels and house churches.
21	NEBRASKA	Diocese participates in ecumenical urban Indian ministry in Lincoln-Omaha communities and continues outreach to Winneabago Reservation.
22	NEVADA	St. Mary's, Nixon, and St. Michael and All Angels, Wadsworth, on the Pyramid Lake Reservation, serve the century-old Paiute congregation.
23	NORTH DAKOTA	Five predominately Indian congregations on four reservations; joint diocesan urban programs. Urban worshiping community in Bismarck.
24	NORTHERN CALIFORNIA	Native American ministry is through St. John's in Roseville, begun in 1993; a subsequent Church of the Four Winds begun at Foresthill.
25	OKLAHOMA	Full time missioner to the Cheyenne Arapaho in Western Oklahoma; ecumenical worshiping community among the Potawatomi at Shawnee. Strong vital Oklahoma Committee on Indian Work dates back to 1977.

26	OLYMPIA	The diocese is a partner in the ecumenical Native American Task Force in Seattle.
27	OREGON	The stabilized interdenominational Church of the Four Winds meets regularly at St. Michael and All Angels parish in Portland and maintains strong linkages with Ecumenical Ministries of Oregon. A diocesan Indian committee is active.
28	SAN JOAQUIN	Newly emerging outreach with Yaqui people in Fresno; initiated in Hispanic congregation of San Marghrita.
29	SOUTH DAKOTA	Historical center of Native Ministry. There are 67 reservation congregations and many mixed congregations; urban ministry at Rapid City and Sioux Falls. New training program through Vancouver School of Theology has produced a new wave of potential Lakota/Dakota clergy.
30	SOUTHEAST FLORIDA	New outreach through Holy Comforter Hispanic congregation among indigenous people who have immigrated to diocese from Nicaragua.
31	SOUTHWEST VIRGINIA	St. Paul's, near Amherst, has a Monacan congregation which has 200 baptized and 78 communicant members.
32	UTAH	New vitality in Uintah Reservation with two full time Indian clergy. Two congregations: St. Elizabeth's at Whiterocks and Holy Spirit at Randlett. Urban ministry in Salt Lake City.
33	WESTERN NEW YORK	The Church of the Good Shepherd on the Seneca Cattaraugus has continued since 1901. There are also eight mixed congregations. The diocese estimates 200 baptized and 100 communicant members.

| 34 | WESTERN NORTH CAROLINA | Cherokee families from the reservation of the Eastern Cherokee worship with St. Francis of Assisi at the town of Cherokee; leaders, encouraged by new bishop, have indicated interest in the broader Episcopal Church's American Indian community. |
| 35 | WYOMING | Estimated 1,614 Episcopal baptized Indians in diocese. Arapaho congregation at Ethete and Shoshone congregation at Fort Washakie, both on Wind River Reservation. A mixed congregation at Crowheart. |

Appendix C

EPISCOPAL COUNCIL OF
INDIAN MINISTRIES

SAN JOSE DECLARATION

"Those who cannot remember the past are condemned to repeat it." —George Santayana

A new day is at hand for the structure and life of the Episcopal Church. A drastic restructuring has been proposed that will change the way many of our Indian Ministries are conducted. The current consideration of proposals which would effectively dissolve the Episcopal Council of Indian Ministries do not reflect the history or the visionary leadership which have brought us to the present point.

Since James the First occupied the throne of England and sealed the Jamestown Charter, there has been a continuous Anglican commitment to mission and ministry among American Indians. After many generations of missionary effort, the Episcopal Church began to recognize the need to include American Indians and Alaskan Natives in the structure of the Church. The movement in the Episcopal Church for Indian self-determination began in 1968 with a call for "more real involvement" from Vine Deloria, Jr. who was then a member of Executive Council.

In response, the Executive Council adopted a resolution in February of 1969 which paved the way for a National Committee on Indian Work (NCIW). General Convention in 1976 adopted a re-structuring, as our people have survived so many other attempts to eliminate us. By 1977, NCIW was back in full operation.

In 1984, a Consultation of Indian Church leaders was held in Oklahoma which called for long term commitment to Indian leadership for Indian concerns. A second consultation in Oklahoma in 1986, with the concurrence of NCIW and Coalition 14 called for fuller Indian responsibility and involvement in decision-making.

As a result, the whole matter was referred to the Presiding Bishop's Blue Ribbon Task Force on Indian Affairs, which hammered out a proposal to create the Episcopal Council of Indian Ministries, which was adopted by the Executive Council by resolution calling for implementation in November of 1989. This decision was ratified by both NCIW and C-14. ECIM came into being in 1990.

In the four years that ECIM has existed, it has:

- implemented youth programs at local, diocesan and national levels
- established an effective mechanism to allocate funds
- provided assistance to Indian theological students and leadership development projects
- affirmed Winter Talk, a yearly gathering of lay and ordained Indians who share issues and ideas
- nurtured Paths Crossing, a network of companion parishes and dioceses
- hosted the 500 Years of Survival Celebration
- designed and implemented Evangelism programs
- improved communications through *IKHANA* and video cassettes

By 1993, ECIM was a founding partner in International Anglican Indigenous Network of Australian Aboriginal People, Maoris of New Zealand, Native Hawaiians, as well as Canadian and American Indians. The network is presently being expanded to include native people in Mexico, South and Central America.

The current work of ECIM reflects the recommendation of the 1993 Partners in Mission Consultation calling for "an action plan which endows the Native Americans with the freedom and authority to organize and manage their own affairs, including training, within the life of the church."

It does not seem wise to throw away a quarter of century of effort to develop ECIM after only four years of operation, especially in view of the fact that ECIM is already accomplishing the kind of operations the current re-structuring proposals are hoping to do in the future. ECIM has built networks across cultural and language barriers, brought people together to work and train side by side, led the celebration of our common life together, and has made partnerships a living reality. We are now modeling and living the goals that the Church has set for the next triennium.

When we consider that the net savings in the national budget which would be realized by the dissolution of ECIM would amount to less than $20,000 a year, can we say that such action is justified, even in times of budget shortfalls?

Indian people learn from the past and honor the gifts we have been given by those who have gone before. These gifts and skills include the ability to move from survivors to advocates, the creativity to develop mentor relationships and team ministries, and the gift of listening and sharing with others that makes networks and partnerships thrive. These gifts and skills can only enhance the whole life of the Episcopal Church. Therefore, it is the unanimous recommendation of ECIM, representing the American Indian/Alaskan Native members of the Episcopal Church, that this organization be continued as an essential part of any restructuring as a model for the whole Church.

Adopted unanimously on the Feast of St. Joseph,
1994, San Jose, CA

Appendix D

STATEMENT OF SELF-DETERMINATION

Winter Talk 1995

We, the indigenous peoples of the Episcopal Church, gathered at the National Indigenous Peoples Congress, Seminole Nation, January 28 through February 2, 1995, as brothers and sisters in Christ, affix our names to this document as a joyful declaration of our identity as free and equal members of The Episcopal Church and the Anglican Communion.

We publish this statement to proclaim the Good News of our freedom in Christ and to announce a new hope for Christians throughout the world.

We are the sons and daughters of many proud and independent sovereign peoples.

We are the heirs of ancient heritages who honor the memory and courage of our ancestors.

We are the stewards of a great tradition.

We are the survivors of a tragic history.

We are the keepers of a bright future for our children.

Therefore, we proclaim our God-given right to determine our own destiny as we accept full responsibility for shaping our future under the guidance of the Holy Spirit.

To this end, we extend the hand of forgiveness and reconciliation to all who will journey with us in justice, faith, and compassion.

We respect the spiritual traditions, values and customs of our many peoples, and we incorporate them as we celebrate the Gospel of Jesus Christ.

We affirm our rightful place within The Episcopal Church and the Anglican Communion.

Therefore, we proclaim our spiritual role as equal partners in the full life of the Body of Christ as we accept the obligations of leadership in this new vision of the Church.

In this new relationship, we extend the hand of friendship to all people of faith who will journey with us in equality, dignity, and devotion.

We embrace the wisdom of our elders who are caregivers of God's creation.

We take up the cross of Christ as we stand as one people united for peace, mercy, and justice.

We speak for the poor, the hungry, the dispossessed, and the forgotten.

Therefore, we proclaim our vision of a renewed Church healing a broken world as we lift our share of the burden in order to build a new community.

To this end, we extend the hand of love to all who will journey with us in commitment, sacrifice, and humility.

In support of this statement, we pledge ourselves in love, faith, and hope.

We call upon our generations both past and present to bear witness to our pledge, and to add their strength to ours in fulfilling these declarations.

We call upon the Church to acknowledge the sovereignty of indigenous peoples and to support us as equal partners in the recreation of a new community.

Most of all, we call upon God through the grace of our Lord Jesus Christ and the Holy Spirit to bless and sanctify all that we now undertake for the sake of God's people and for the glory of God's holy Name.

AMEN.

Proclaimed and signed at Winter Talk VII,
National Indigenous Peoples Congress,
Seminole Nation, January 28-February 2, 1995.

[Signatures of all present: 55 persons]

SELECTED BIBLIOGRAPHY

Addison, James Thayer. *The Episcopal Church in the United States: 1789-1931.* New York: Scribners, 1951.

Agnew, Brad. *Fort Gibson: Terminal on the Trail of Tears.* Norman, OK: University of Oklahoma Press, 1980.

Anderson, Gary Clayton and Woolworth, Alan R. *Through Dakota Eyes: Narrative Accounts of the Minnesota Indian War of 1862.* St. Paul, MN: Minnesota Historical Society Press, 1988.

Anderson, John A. *The Sioux of the Rosebud: A History in Pictures.* Norman, OK: University of Oklahoma Press, 1971. Second Printing, 1980.

Bacon, Ron. *Maori Legends: The Creation Stories.* Auckland, NZ: Shortland Educational Publications, 1984.

Bailey, M. T homas. *Reconstruction in Indian Territory.* Port Washington, NY: Kennicat Press, 1972.

Barker, Rodney. *The Broken Circle: A Story of Murder and Magic in Indian Country.* New York: Simon and Schuster, 1992.

Beaver, R. Pierce. *Church State and the American Indian: Two and a Half Centuries of Partnership in Mission between Protestant Churches and Government.* St. Louis: Concordia Publishing House, 1966.

Beck, Peggy V. and Walters, Anna L. *The Sacred: Ways of Knowledge, Sources of Life.* Tsaile, AZ: Navajo Community College, 1977. Fifth printing, 1988.

Bell, Martin. *The Way of the Wolf: The Gospel in New Images.* San Francisco, CA: Harper and Row, Publishers, 1968. Third printing, 1970.

Bendek, Emily. *The Wind Won't Know Me: A History of the Navajo-Hopi Land Dispute.* New York: Alfred A. Knopf, 1992.

Berger, Thomas R. *Village Journey.* New York: Hill & Wang, 1985.

Berkhofer, Robert F. Jr. *The White Man's Indian: Images of the American Indian from Columbus to the Present.* New York: Alfred A. Knopf, 1978.

_____. *Salvation and the Savage: An Analysis of Protest Missions and American Indian Responses, 1787-1862.* New York: Atheneum, 1972.

Bonvillain, Nancy. *The Mohawk: Indians of America Series.* New York: Chelsea House Publishers, 1992.

Bordwich, Fergus M. *Killing the White Man's Indian: Reinventing Native Americans at the End of the Twentieth Century.* New York: Doubleday, 1995.

Bowden, Henry Warner. *American Indians and Christian Missions: Studies in Cultural Conflict.* Chicago: University of Chicago Press, 1981.

Brophy, William A. and Sophie D. Aberle. *The Indian: America's Unfinished Business: Report of The Commission on the Rights, Liberties, and Responsibilities of the American Indian.* Norman, OK: University of Oklahoma Press, 1966.

Brown, Dee. *Bury My Heart at Wounded Knee.* New York: Bantam Press, 1972.

Brown, Joseph Epes. *The Sacred Pipe: Black Elk's Account of the Seven Rites of the Oglala Sioux.* Norman, OK: University of Oklahoma Press, 1953.

_____. *The Spiritual Legacy of the American Indian.* New York: Crossroad, 1982.

Canfield, Gae Whitney. *Sarah Winnemucca of the Northern Paiutes.* Norman, OK: Univerity of Oklahoma Press, 1931.

Capps, Walter Holden, ed. *Seeing With a Native Eye.* New York: Harper and Row, 1976.

Champagne, Duane. *Native America: Portrait of the Peoples.* Detroit: Visible Ink Press, 1994.

Churchill, Ward. *Struggle for the Land: Indigenous Resistance to Genocide, Ecocide, and Expropriation in Contemporary North America.* Monroe, ME: Common Courage Press, 1993.

Clark, Ann and Helen Post. *Brave Against the Enemy: A Story of Three Generations of the Day Before Yesterday, of Yesterday, and of Tomorrow.* Lawrence, KS: Haskell Institute Printing Department, Education Division of United States Indian Service, 1944.

Collier, John. *On the Gleaming Way: Navajos, Eastern Pueblos, Zunis, Hopis, Apaches, and Their Land; and Their Meanings to the World.* Chicago: Sage Books, 1949, 1962.

Crosby, Alfred W. Jr. *The Columbian Exchange: Biological and Cultural Consequences of 1492.* Westport, CT: Greenwood Press, 1972.

Davis, Robert Yarborough. *The Pilgrimage.* Albuquerque, NM: CEC Publishers, 1980.

Dawley, Powel Mills. *The Episcopal Church and its Work.* Greenwich, CT: The Seabury Press, 1955.

de Tocqueville, Alexander. *Democracy in America.* New York: Schocken Books. (Reprint of 1840 work.)

Debo, Angie. *The Rise and Fall of the Choctaw Republic.* Norman, OK: University of Oklahoma Press, 1934.

_____. *And Still the Waters Run: The Betrayal of the Five Civilized Tribes.* Princeton, NJ: Princeton University Press, 1940. Fourth Paperback Printing, 1991.

_____. *A History of the American Indians of the United States.* Norman, OK: University of Oklahoma Press, 1970. Sixth printing, 1979.

_____. *The Road to Disappearance: A History of the Creek Indians.* Norman, OK: University of Oklahoma Press, 1941. Sixth printing, 1989.

Deloria, Ella. *Speaking of Indians.* Vermillion, SD: University of South Dakota. 1979 (Reprint.)

Deloria, Vine Jr. *God Is Red.* New York: Gosset & Dunlap, 1973.

_____. *God is Red: A Native View of Religion.* (The Classic Work Updated). Golden, CO: Fulcrum Publishing, 1994.

_____. "A Native Perspective on Liberation." Gerald Anderson and Thomas Stransky, eds. *Mission Trends No. 4. Liberation Theologies in North America and Europe.* New York: Paulist Press, 1982.

_____. *Behind the Trail of Broken Treaties*. New York: Delta Books, 1974.

_____. *Red Earth, White Lies*. New York: Simon & Schuster, 1995.

DeMallie, Raymond and Douglas R Parks, eds. *Sioux Indian Religion*. Norman, OK: University of Oklahoma Press, 1987. Second printing, 1988.

Demos, John. *A Family Story From Early America*. New York: Alfred A. Knopf, 1994.

Diedrich, Mark. *Dakota Oratory: Great Moments in the Recorded Speech of the Eastern Sioux, 1695-1874*. Rochester, MN: Coyote Books, 1989.

Dooling, D.M. and Paul Jordan-Smith, eds. *I Became Part of It: Sacred Dimensions in Native American Life*. New York: Harper Collins paperback edition, 1992.

Dudley, Joseph Iron Eyes. *Choteau Creek: A Sioux Remembrance*. Lincoln, NE: University of Nebraska Press, 1992.

Eastman, Charles A. *The Soul of the Indian*. Boston: Houghton Mifflin, 1911.

Edmunds, R. David, ed. *American Indian Leaders: Studies in Diversity*. Lincoln, NE: University of Nebraska Press, Bison Books, 1980.

Egan, Ferol. *Sand in a Whirlwind: the Paiute Indian War of 1860*. New York: Doubleday & Company, 1972.

Erodes, Richard. *Native Americans: The Sioux*. New York: Sterling Publishing Co., Inc., 1982.

Erodes, Richard. *Crying for a Dream: The World Through Native American Eyes*. Santa Fe, NM: Bear and Company, 1990.

Fejes, Claire. *People of Noatak*. New York: Alfred A. Knopf, Inc., 1966.

Foreman, Grant. *The Five Civilized Tribes: Cherokee, Chickasaw, Choctaw, Creek, Seminole*. Norman, OK: University of Oklahoma Press, 1934.

Foreman, Grant. *Indian Removal: The Emigration of the Five Civilized Tribes of Indians*. Norman, OK: University of Oklahoma Press, 1932. Eleventh printing, 1989.

Gill, Sam D. *Native American Religions: An Introduction.* Belmont, CA: Eadsworth, 1982.

Glasrud, Bruce A. and Alan M. Smith, eds. *Race Relations in British North America, 1607-1783.* Chicago: Nelson-Hall, 1982.

Grant, John Webster. *Moon of Wintertime: Missionaries and the Indians of Canada in Encounter Since 1543.* Toronto: University of Toronto Press, 1984.

Gregory, Jack and Rennard Strickland. *Sam Houston with the Cherokees: 1829-1833.* Austin: University of Texas Press, 1976.

Gridley, Marion E., ed. *Indians of Today.* Chicago, IL: Indian Council Fire, Third Edition, 1960.

Grinnell, George Bird. *When Buffalo Ran.* Norman, OK: University of Oklahoma Press, 1966.

_____. *By Cheyenne Campfires.* Lincoln, NE: University of Nebraska Press, 1971. (Reprint of 1926 work.)

Grinde, Donald A. Jr. *The Iroquois and the Founding of the American Nation.* The Indian Historian Press, Inc., 1977.

Harrod, Howard L. *Renewing the World: Plains Indian Religion and Morality.* Tucson, AZ: University of Arizona Press, 1987.

Hartley, William and Ellen. *A Woman Set Apart.* New York: Dodd Mead & Co., 1963.

Hausman, Gerald. *Meditations With Animals: A Native American Bestiary.* Santa Fe, NM: Bear and Company, 1986.

Hayes, Charles Wells. *The Diocese of Western New York: History and Recollections.* Rochester, NY, 1904.

Hacked, Robert A. *Oliver La Farge and the American Indian: A Biography.* London: The Scarecrow Press, Inc. 1991.

Hillerman, Tony. "Sacred Ground." National Geographic Traveler 6, no. 3 (May-June 1989): 44-59.

Hirschfelder, Arlene and Molin, Paulette. *The Encyclopedia of Native American Religions.* New York: Facts-on-File, Inc, 1992.

Hoebel, E. Adamson. *The Cheyennes: Indians of the Great Plains.* New York: Holt, Reinhart, and Winston, 1960. Second edition, 1978.

Hoig, Stan. *The Peace Chiefs of the Cheyennes.* Norman, OK: University of Oklahoma Press, 1980. First paperback printing, 1990.

Holmes, David L. *A Brief History of the Episcopal Church*. Valley Forge, PA: Trinity Press, International, 1993.

Houck, Peter W. and Mintcy D. Maxham. *Indian Island In Amherst County*. Lynchburg, VA: Warwick House Publishing, 1993.

Howe, M.A. DeWolfe. *The Life and Labors of Bishop Hare, Apostle to the Sioux*. New York: Sturgis & Walton Company, 1912.

Hultkrantz, Ake. Christopher Vecsey, ed. *The Study of American Indian Religions*. New York: Crossroad, 1983.

Huyghe, Patrick. *Columbus Was Last*. New York: Hyperion, 1992.

Jackson, Helen Hunt. *A Century of Dishonor*. New York: Harper, 1881.

Jacobs, Wilbur R. *Dispossessing the American Indian: Indians and Whites on the Colonial Frontier*. Norman, OK: University of Oklahoma Press, 1985.

Jahoda, Gloria. *The Trail of Tears: The Story of the American Indian Removals 1813-1855*. New York: Wings Books, 1975.

Jenkins, J. Rockwood. *The Good Shepherd Mission to the Navajo*. Monograph, 1954.

Jenkins, Thomas. *The Man of Alaska*. New York: Morehouse-Gorham Co., 1943.

Jennings, Francis. *The Invasion of America: Indians, Colonialism, and the Cant of Conquest*. New York: W.W. Norton and Company, 1976.

Jennewein, J. Leonard and Jane Boorman, eds. *Dakota Panorama*. Freeman, SD: Pine Hill Press, Dakota Territory Centennial Commission, 1962. Third Printing, 1973, Brevet Press.

Jorgensen, Joseph G., ed. *Native Americans and Energy Development II*. Boston: Anthropology Resource Center and Seventh Generation Fund, 1984.

Josephy, Alvin M. Jr. *Now that the Buffalo's Gone: A Study of Today's American Indians*. New York: Alfred A. Knopf, 1982.

_____. *The Patriot Chiefs: A Chronicle of American Indian Leadership*. New York: The Viking Press, 1961. Third Printing 1963.

_____. *500 Nations*. New York: Alfred A. Knopf, 1995.

Kater, John L., ed. *The Challenge of the Past; The Challenge of the Future.* Cincinnati: Forward Movement, 1994.

Kelsay, Isabel Thompson. *Joseph Brant, 1743-1807: Man of Two Worlds.* Syracuse, NY: Syracuse University Press, 1984.

Kidwell, Clara Sue. *Choctaws and Missionaries in Mississippi: 1818-1918.* Norman, OK: University of Oklahoma Press, 1995.

Killoren, John J., sj. *"Come Blackrobe": De Smet and the Indian Tragedy.* Norman, OK: University of Oklahoma Press, 1995.

Koning, Hans. *Columbus: His Enterprise.* New York: Monthly Review Press, 1976.

_____. *The Conquest of America: How the Indians Lost Their Continent.* New York: Monthly Review Press, 1993.

Kopper, Philip. *The Smithsonian Book of North American Indians: Before the Coming of Europeans.* Washington, D.C.: Smithsonian Books, 1986.

Lafferty, R.A. *Okla Hannali.* Norman, OK: University of Oklahoma Press, 1972.

Lazarus, Edward. *Black Hills, White Justice: The Sioux Nation Versus the United States 1775 to the Present.* New York: Harper Collins, 1991.

Lewis, Norman. *The Missionaries: God Against the Indians.* London: Arrow Books, Limited, 1989.

Liebler, H. Baxter. *Boil My Heart For Me.* Jericho, NY: Exposition Press Inc., 1969.

Lincoln, Kenneth, and Al Logan Slagle. *The Good Red Road: Passages into Native America.* San Francisco: Harper and Row, 1987.

Lurie, Nancy Oestreich. *North American Indian Lives.* Milwaukee: Milwaukee Public Museum, 1985.

Lyons, Oren and John Mohawk, eds. *Exiled In the Land of the Free.* Santa Fe: Clear Light Publishers, 1992.

Manross, William N. *History of the American Episcopal Church.* New York: Morehouse-Gorham Co., 1950.

Marriott, Alice. *The Ten Grandmothers: Epic of the Kiowas.* Norman, OK: University of Oklahoma Press, 1945.

Mattiessen, Peter. *In the Spirit of Crazy Horse.* New York: Viking Press, 1975.

_____. *Indian Country.* New York: Viking Press, 1984.

Maxwell, James A., ed. *America's Fascinating Indian Heritage: The First Americans: Their customs, Art, History, and How They Lived.* Pleasantville, NY: Reader's Digest Association, Inc. 1978.

McGregor, James H. *The Wounded Knee Massacre.* Rapid City, SD: Fenwyn Press Books, 1940.

McLuhan, T. C. *Touch the Earth: A Self-Portrait of Indian Existence.* New York: Promontory Press, 1971.

McNickle, D'Arcy. *Native American Tribalism: Indian Survivals and Renewals.* New York: Oxford University Press, 1973. Reprint, 1979.

Meredith, Howard L. *The Native American Factor.* New York: The Seabury Press, 1973.

Meyer, William. *Native Americans: The New Indian Resistance.* New York: International Publishers, 1971.

Milanich, Jerald T. and Susan Milbrath, eds. *First Encounters: Spanish Explorations in the Caribbean and the United States, 1492-1570.* Gainesville, FL: University of Florida Press, 1989.

Milner, Clyde A., II and O'Neil, Floyd A. *Churchmen and the Western Indians: 1820-1920.* Norman, OK: University of Oklahoma Press, 1985.

Mooney, James. *The Ghost Dance Religion and Wounded Knee.* New York: Dover, 1973. (Reprint from 1896 publication.)

_____. *The Ghost Dance Religion and the Sioux Outbreak of 1890.* Chicago: University of Chicago Press, 1965.

Morey, Sylvester M., Editor. *Can the Red Man Help the White Man?: A Denver Conference With the Indian Elders.* New York: The Myrin Institute, Inc., 1970.

Nabokov, Peter, ed. *Native American Testimony: A Chronicle of Indian-White Relations from Prophecy to the Present, 1492-1992.* New York: Penguin, 1991.

National Council of the Episcopal Church. *The Spirit of Missions, Volumes 1-124.* New York: 1836-1959.

_____. *Builders for Christ.* Dawley, Powel Mills, ed. Greenwich, CT: The Seabury Press, 1955.

_____. *This Land is Our Land: The American Indian in American Society 1970.* New York: The National Council on Indian Work, 1970.

Neihardt, John G. *Black Elk Speaks.* Lincoln, NE: University of Nebraska Press, 1961. (Reprint from 1932.)

Nye, Colonel W.S. *Carbine and Lance: The Story of Old Fort Sill.* Norman, OK: University of Oklahoma Press, 1937. Third Printing, 1969.

Osgood, Phillips Endecott. *Straight Tongue: A Story of Henry Benjamin Whipple, First Episcopal Bishop of Minnesota.* Minneapolis: T.S. Denison & Company, 1958.

Parlow, Anita, ed. *A Song from Sacred Mountain.* Baltimore: Port City Press, Oglala Lakota Legal Rights Fund, 1983.

Pattel-Gray, Anne. *Through Aboriginal Eyes: The Cry from the Wilderness.* Geneva, Switzerland: WCC Publications, 1991.

Peelman, Achiel. *Christ is a Native American.* Maryknoll, NY: Orbis Books, 1995.

Perry, Richard J. *Apache Reservation: Indigenous Peoples & the American State.* Austin: University of Texas Press, 1993.

Perry, William Stevens. *The History of the American Episcopal Church: 1587-1783.* Boston: James R. Osgood and Company, 1885.

Perdue, Theda. *Nations Remembered: An Oral History of the Cherokees, Chickasaws, Choctaws, Creeks, and Seminoles in Oklahoma, 1865-1907.* Norman, OK: University of Oklahoma Press, 1993.

Phillips, Carol, ed. *A Century of Faith: 1895-1995, Episcopal Diocese of Alaska.* Fairbanks, AK: Centennial Press, 1995.

Pierce, George Preble. *Leadership in Crisis: The Lakota Religious Response to Wounded Knee, 1973.* Ann Arbor, MI: U.M.I., 1992.

Pitezel, John H. *Life of Rev. Peter Marksman, An Ojibwa Missionary: Illustrating the Triumphs of the Gospel Among the Ojibwa Indians.* Cincinnati: Western Methodist Book Concern, 1901.

Powell, Father Peter John. *People of the Sacred Mountain.* Two vols. San Francisco: Harper and Rowe, 1981.

_____. *Sweet Medicine: The Continuing Role of the Sacred Arrows, the Sun Dance, and the Sacred Buffalo Hat in Northern Cheyenne History.* Two vols. Norman, OK: University of Oklahoma Press, 1969.

_____. *The Cheyennes, Máheóo's People: A Critical Bibliography.* Bloomington, IN: Indiana University Press, 1980.

Prevar, Stephen L. *The Rights of Indians and Tribes.* New York: Bantam Books, Inc., 1983.

Prichard, Robert. *A History of the Episcopal Church.* Harrisburg, PA: Morehouse Publishing, 1991.

Prucha, Francis Paul. *American Indian Policy In Crisis: Christian Reformers and the Indian, 1865-1900.* Norman, OK: University of Oklahoma Press, 1976.

_____. *Indian-White Relations in the United States: A Bibliography of Works Published 1975-1980.* Lincoln, NE: University of Nebraska Press, 1982.

_____. *The Indians in American Society: From the Revolutionary War to the Present.* Los Angeles: University of California Press, 1985.

_____. *The Great Father: The United States Government and the American Indians.* Lincoln, NE: University of Nebraska Press, 1984. Second printing, 1986.

Quinn, David Beers. *Set Fair for Roanoke: Voyages and Colonies, 1584-1606.* Chapel Hill: University of North Carolina Press, 1985.

Roberts, David. *Once They Moved Like the Wind: Cochise, Geronimo, and the Apache Wars.* New York: Simon & Schuster, 1993.

Ronda, James P. and Axtell, James. *Indian Missions: A Critical Bibliography.* Bloomington, IN: Indiana University Press, 1978.

Rosensteil, Agnate. *Red and White: Indian Views of the White Man, 1492-1982.* New York: Universe Books, 1983.

Rountree, Helen C. *The Powhatan Indians of Virginia: Their Traditional Culture.* Norman, OK: University of Oklahoma Press, 1989.

_____. *Pocahontas's People: The Powhatan Indians of Virginia Through Four Centuries.* Norman, OK: University of Oklahoma Press, 1990.

St. Clair, Robert and William Leap, eds. *Language Renewal Among American Indian Tribes: Issues, Problems, and Prospects.* Roslyn, VA: National Clearinghouse for Bilingual Education, 1982.

Sandoz, Mari. *Crazy Horse.* Lincoln, NE: University of Nebraska Press, 1961. (Reprint from 1942.)

_____. *The Battle of the Little Bighorn.* Lincoln, NE: University of Nebraska Press, 1978.

Shaw, Anna Moore. *A Pima Past.* Tucson, AZ: The University of Arizona Press, 1974.

Small, Deborah with Maggie Jaffe. *1492: What Is It Like to Be Discovered?* New York: Monthly Review Press, 1991.

Sneve, Virginia Driving Hawk. *That They May Have Life: The Episcopal Church in South Dakota, 1859-1976.* New York: The Seabury Press, 1977.

_____. *They Led a Nation: The Sioux Chiefs.* Sioux Falls, South Dakota: Brevet Press, Inc., Fifth Printing, 1992.

_____. *Completing the Circle.* Lincoln: University of Nebraska Press, 1995.

Society for the Propagation of the Gospel. *Encyclopedia of Missions.* London: 1891.

Standing Bear, Luther. *My People the Sioux.* Lincoln: University of Nebraska Press, Bison Book Edition, 1975.

Stein, Howard F. and Robert F. Hill, eds. *The Culture of Oklahoma.* Norman, OK: University of Oklahoma Press, 1993.

Steiner, Stan. *The New Indians.* New York: Harper and Row, 1967.

Steinmetz, Paul B., J.S. *Meditations with Native Americans: Lakota Spirituality.* Santa Fe, NM: Bear and Company, 1984.

_____. *Bible and Peyote Among the Oglala Lakota: A study in Religious Identity.* Knoxville, TN: The University of Tennessee Press, 1990.

Steltenkamp, Michael F. *The Sacred Vision: Native American Religion and Its Practice Today.* New York: Paulist Press, 1982.

Stolzman, William. *The Pipe and Christ: A Christian-Sioux Dialogue.* Chamberlain, SD: Tipi Press, 1986.

Stuck, Hudson. *The Alaskan Missions of the Episcopal Church.* New York: Domestic and Foreign Missionary Society, 1920.

_____. *Ten Thousand Miles with a Dog Sled: A Narrative of Winter Travel in Interior Alaska.* Lincoln, NE: University of Nebraska Press, 1988. (Reprint from 1914 work.)

Szasz, Margaret Connell. *Education and the American Indian: The Road to Self-Determination Since 1928.* Albuquerque, NM: University of New Mexico Press, 1974. Second edition and Second printing, 1979.

Talbot, Steve. *Roots of Oppression: The American Indian Question.* New York: International Publishers, 1981.

Tax, Sol. *Indian Tribes of Aboriginal America.* Chicago: University of Chicago Press, 1952.

Thomas, Davis and Karin Ronnefeldt, eds. *People of the First Man: Life Among the Plains Indians in Their Final Days of Glory: The Firsthand account of Prince Maximillian's Expedition up the Missouri River, 1833-34.* New York: E.P. Dutton, Inc., 1976.

Thomas, Tay. *An Angel on His Wing: The Story of Bill Gordon, Alaska's Flying Bishop.* Wilton, CT: Morehouse Publishing, 1989.

_____. *Cry in the Wilderness.* Anchorage: Color Art Printing Co., Inc. 1967.

Thornton, Russell. *American Indian Holocaust and Survival: A Population History Since 1492.* Norman, OK: University of Oklahoma Press, 1987.

Time-Life Books. *The American Indians: The First Americans, The Spirit World, The European Challenge, People of the Desert, The Way of the Warrior, The Buffalo Hunters, Realm of the Iroquois, The Mighty Chieftains, Keepers of the Totem, Cycles of Life, War for the Plains, Tribes of the Southern Woodlands, The Indians of California, People of the Ice and Snow, People of the Lakes.* Alexandria, VA: Time-Life Books, 1994-1995.

Tinker, George. *Missionary Conquest: The Gospel and Native American Cultural Genocide.* Minneapolis: Augsburg Fortress Press, 1993.

Title IV Indian Education Curriculum Development Project. *Arapaho Memories.* Ethete, WY: Wyoming Indian High School, 1985.

Tooker, Elizabeth. *Native American Spirituality of the Eastern Woodlands: Sacred Myths, Dreams, Visions, Speeches, Healing Formulas, Rituals, and Ceremonials.* Mahwah, NJ: Paulist Press, 1979.

Treat, James, ed. *Native & Christian: Indigenous Voices on Religious Identity in the United States and Canada.* New York: Routedge, 1995.

Uintah-Ouray Ute Tribe. *A Brief History of the People.* Fort Duchesne, Utah: Uintah-Ouray Ute Tribe, 1977.

Underhill, Ruth M. *The Navajos.* Norman, OK: University of Oklahoma Press, 1956. Seventh printing 1983.

_____. *Red Man's Religion: Beliefs and Practices of the Indians North of Mexico.* Chicago: University of Chicago Press, 1965.

U.S. Commission on Civil Rights. *Indian Tribes: A Continuing Quest for Survival.* Washington, DC: United States Commission on Civil Rights, 1981.

_____. *The Navajo Nation: An American Colony.* A Report of The U.S. Commission on Civil Rights, September, 1975.

Viola, Herman J. *After Columbus: The Smithsonian Chronicle of the North American Indians.* Washington, DC: Smithsonian Books, 1990.

Van Every, Dale. *Disinherited: The Lost Birthright of the American Indian.* New York: Avon Books, 1967.

Vecsey, Christopher. *Traditional Ojibwa Religion and Its Historical Changes.* Philadelphia: American Philosophical Society, 1983.

_____. ed. *Handbook of American Indian Religious Freedom.* New York: The Crossroad Publishing Company, 1991

Vizenor, Gerald. *Wordarrows: Indians and Whites in the New Fur Trade.* Minneapolis: University of Minnesota Press, 1978.

_____. *The People Named the Chippewa.* Minneapolis: University of Minnesota Press, 1984.

Wadsworth, Lorraine, ed. *St. Mary's the Virgin Centennial Celebration: 1892-1992.* University of Nevada, Reno, 1992.

Wallace, Anthony F.C. *The Death and Rebirth of the Seneca.* New York: Vantage Books, 1972.

Wallace, Anthony. *The Long Bitter Trail: Andrew Jackson and the Indians.* New York: Hill and Wang Farrar, Straus and Giroux, 1993.

Walters, Anna Lee. *The Sun Is Not Merciful.* Ithaca, NY: Firebrand Books, 1985.

Weatherford, Jack. *Indian Givers: How the Indians of the Americas Transformed the World.* New York: Fawcett Columbine Books, 1988.

Welch, James. *Fools Crow.* New York: Penguin Books, 1986.

Wheat, Margaret M. *Survival Arts of the Primitive Paiutes.* Reno, NV: University of Nevada Press, 1967.

Whipple, The Rt. Rev. Henry B. *Light and Shadows of a Long Episcopate.* New York: The Macmillan Company, 1899. Second printing, 1900.

White, Greenough. *An Apostle of the Western Church: Memoir of the Right Reverend Jackson Kemper, First Missionary Bishop of the American Church.* New York: Thomas Whittaker, 1911.

Wilkins, Robert P. and Wyona H. Wilkins. *God Giveth the Increase: The History of the Episcopal Church in North Dakota.* Minneapolis: Lund Press, Inc., 1959.

Wright, Muriel H. *A Guide to the Indian Tribes of Oklahoma.* Norman, OK: University of Oklahoma, 1951. Second printing, 1979.

ABOUT THE AUTHOR

Owanah Anderson, born in rural Choctaw County, Oklahoma, was profoundly influenced by her grandmother, "who told us—my many cousins, my brother and me—wonderful stories on sultry summer nights, sitting on the back porch of her modest farm home with whip-poor-wills and screech owls sounding off in the distance on Pontie Creek." "My mother's mother was a small woman, I doubt she ever weighed 100 pounds," Anderson said. "But my grandmother was the almighty matriarch of the big Choctaw family of near and distant kin. Rigidly Presbyterian, she shepherded us all to a rural mission church each Sunday where we sat on backless benches under a brush arbor while a Choctaw preacher held forth interminably—all Sunday morning and, after a potluck mid-day meal, far into the hot afternoons. We cousins scarcely understood a word the preacher said; he spoke entirely in Choctaw and my grandmother adamantly refused to teach us our language. A victim of the era (pre-World War II), she had been so long oppressed by her societal surroundings that she had come to discount relevance of the Choctaw. So when I implored her to teach me Choctaw, she admonished me to 'learn English good . . . maybe so you grow up and be school teacher.' I do wish she might have lived to see the renaissance of Indian pride."

As was the case with many Indians of Anderson's generation, she learned to survive in two worlds, honing marketable skills of the non-Indian world and holding onto insights and values of the Indian world. She married a *no hollo* (white man), a North Texas attorney who was a steadfast Episcopalian. It was his influence "and strong jury argument" which led her to confirmation and beyond.

She was active in many of the reform movements of the 1970s on state and local, national and international levels. "Eventually, I focused primarily on Indian issues," she said. "It became apparent there were many other articulate people who could and would address world peace, social reform and women's issues, but as my friend, Ada Deer, pointed out, there were so few of us to impact Indian issues."

In 1983 her husband died. It was also the year that the Reagan Administration terminated an Indian women's leadership program Anderson had founded and directed. She was recruited as a consultant for the Episcopal Church's Office of Indian Ministry to survey and help develop a national ministry with urban Indian communities. In 1984 Anderson was asked to move to New York to head up the "Indian desk." She agreed to come for three years and ended up staying more than a dozen.

INDEX

Adams, Hank 320–321
Adams, John 117
Adams, The Rev. William 31, 33
Alaska Federation of Natives 320
Alcatraz Island Occupation 318–319
All Saints' (MN) 285
Allen, Roland 278
Allen, The Rev. Philip 79, 197, 286, 296, 324, 327, 329
    —photo 334
Allin, The Most Rev. John 174, 322
Allotment Act. *See* Dawes Allotment Act
American Board of Commissioners...Foreign Mission 67, 301
American Indian Movement (AIM) 116–117, 285, 323
American Indian Religious Freedom Act 338
Anderson, The Rev. Howard 79, 143
Anderson, Owanah 124, 167, 324–325, 332
    —photo 331, back cover
Anderson, The Rt. Rev. Craig B. 122, 123, 125–126, 294, 330
Anderson, The Rt. Rev. Robert M. 60, 78–79, 330
Anglican Church of Canada 47, 49, 130, 133, 252, 256, 265,
    269, 273, 337
Anglican Indigenous Network
    —photo 342
Queen Anne 16, 19, 21, 26, 39
Antoine, Lois 325
    —photo 326
Anvik, AK 256–259, 267, 282
Arapaho Indians 153, 162, 224, 225, 226, 228–231
Arctic National Wildlife Refuge 281, 332, 338
Arikara Indians 86, 130, 131, 141–142
Arthur, The Rev. Buddy 174, 209
Ashley, The Rev. Edward 99, 103, 106–107, 121, 312
    —photo 115
Ashley, The Rev. Thomas P., deacon 139, 140, 141
Astor, Mrs. John Jacob 104, 106, 117, 294
Atcitty, The Rev. Janice Nacke, deacon 236
Athabascan Indians 171, 252, 253–254, 256, 264, 267, 273, 278, 281
Attunaga, The Rev. Elijah 279
Attungana, The Rev. Patrick 277

Bannock Indians 223, 225–226, 233
Baptists 145, 149, 256, 294
Barclay, Henry 20
Barclay, Thomas 19
Bates, The Rt. Rev. George 244, 294
Battle of Adobe Walls 153
Baxter, The Very Rev. Nathan D. 309
Bay of Quinte 25–26
Bazille Creek 84, 90
Bear's Heart, The Rev. Sidney 140
Bear's Heart, The Rev. Wilbur 118, 124, 317, 325
Beaven, Belle 325
Bedell, Deaconess Harriett M. 42, 160–163, 271–272, 307–308
　　—photo 271, 308
Beede, The Rev. Aaron McGaffey 136, 138–140
Benally, Benjamin 206–207
Bergie, The Rev. Patricia, deacon 231
Berkeley Divinity School 92, 93
Bexley Hall 140
Bigliardi, The Rt. Rev. Matthew P. 296
Biller, The Rt. Rev. George, Jr. 114, 158
Birch Coulee 57, 71, 72–73, 74
Bird, The Rev. Henry L. 207
Black Hills 68, 106–109, 121, 122, 126, 337
Black Kettle 100, 152–153, 156
Blackfeet Indians 246
Blue Ribbon Task Force on Indian Affairs 122, 126, 328
Boldt Decision 292, 320
Bompas, The Rt. Rev. William C. 263
Bosomworth, Thomas 11
Botelho, The Rev. Eugene 206–207
Brant, Joseph 19, 20, 21–26, 29
　　—photo 23
Brant, Molly 21–22, 23, 26
Breck, The Rev. James Lloyd 31, 33, 45, 46, 48–50, 51, 69
Brokenleg, The Rev. Martin 110, 118, 125, 284, 294, 333, 336, 342
　　—photo 334
Brokenleg, The Rev. Noah 118, 123, 124, 284
Brooke, The Rt. Rev. Francis Key 157, 160, 161
Brother Juniper 211, 212–213, 219
Brown, John S. 137, 139, 140, 141
Browning, The Most Rev. Edmond L. 9, 78, 108, 122–123, 126,
　　176–177, 209, 309, 328, 332, 335
　　—photo 329, 334
Brulé (Sioux) Band 52
Bureau of Indian Affairs (BIA) 12, 51, 66, 67, 137, 236, 273,
　　313, 317, 321

Burleson, The Rt. Rev. Hugh Latimer 113, 114–115, 120
Burnham, Deaconess Mary D. 154, 156
Burt, The Rev. Heckaliah 93, 98, 99

Caddo Indians 157, 165
Cady, Anne E. 188–191, 192, 193
    —photo 188
Calvary Cathedral (SD) 110
Campbell, The Rev. Ronald A. 323, 325, 333
Canajoharie 21, 22, 24
Carson, Kit 178
Carter, Deaconess Lucy N. 239
Carter, Deaconess Sybil 37, 69–70
Casady, The Rt. Rev. Thomas 158
Cass Lake 69, 75–76, 77
Cavender, Dr. Cris 324
Cavender, The Rev. Gary 79
Center, Bill 288
Chapel of the Blessed Redeemer (Santee) 90
Chapel of the Messiah (Minnesota) 74, 78
Chapman, May Seely 257
Chapman, The Rev. Henry 257
Chapman, The Rev. John 256–259
Charles, The Rt. Rev. Otis 173, 208, 220
Charleston, The Rt. Rev. Steven 125, 176, 249, 276, 279–280,
    282, 292, 309, 325–326, 328, 330, 332, 335, 336, 340, 343
    —photo 331, 334, 342
Cherokee Indians 145, 148, 149–150, 167, 168, 302
Cheyenne Indians 152–153, 156–157, 159–163, 167
Cheyenne River Reservation (Sioux) 83, 92, 93, 99, 113, 118, 120, 124
Chickasaw Indians 12, 145, 151–152
Chief Gall 83, 104, 107
Chief Turkey Legs 163–164
    —photo 164
Chief Washakie 225, 226, 227
    —photo 225
Chief Whirlwind 159
Chilocco Indian School 161
Chivington, Col. John 152
Choctaw Indians 114, 145, 146, 148–149, 157–158, 282
Chokecherry Canyon Murders 207–208
Christ Church (Anvik, AK) 257
    —photo back cover
Christ Church (Crow Creek Reservation) 98
Christ Church (Red Shirt Table, Pine Ridge) 118
Church Army 86, 116, 117, 136, 288, 303

Church Council of Greater Seattle 292
Church Divinity School of the Pacific (CDSP) 174
Church of Our Most Merciful Savior (Niobrora) 85
Church of Our Most Merciful Savior (Santee) 119, 121
Church of the Four Winds (Portland) 296–298
    —photo 297
Church of the Good Shepherd (Idaho) 232–233, 235
    —photo 232
Church of the Good Shepherd (Navajoland) 118, 173, 174, 175,
    177–179, 186–187, 189–198, 209, 222
Church of the Good Shepherd on the Onondaga 38–40
Church of the Good Shepherd on the Seneca 41–42
Church of the Holy Apostles (Oneida Reservation) 17, 30, 34, 38
Church of the Holy Comforter (Lower Brulé) 99
Church of the Holy Cross (Pine Ridge Reservation) 106, 109, 116
Church of the Holy Fellowship (Yankton Sioux) 88
Church of the Holy Name (Choteau Creek, Yankton) 88, 126
Church of the Holy Spirit (IL) 224
Church of the Holy Spirit (Uintah Reservation) 243, 244, 245
Church of the Incarnation (Montana) 246, 295
Clark, Dr. Blue 330, 336
Clark, Lois 165–166
    —photo 166
Clark, The Rev. Aaron Baker 101
Clark, The Rev. David W. 101, 192–195, 285
Clark, The Rev. John B. 101, 115, 131, 143
Clark, The Rt. Rev. Stephen C. 215, 218
Clarkson, The Rt. Rev. Robert H. 85, 86, 88, 90, 96, 112
Cleveland, The Rev. William Joshua 88, 93, 99, 101, 105
Cloud, Vernon 124
Coalition 14 322, 326, 328
Coalition for Human Needs 242
Cochran, The Rt. Rev. David R. 278
Cochrane, The Rt. Rev. Robert H. 292–293
Columbus, Christopher 4, 308, 331, 333–335
Comanche Indians 153, 157, 162
Comity Agreement 255–256
Commission on Native Hawaiian Ministry 339
Congregationalists 27, 54, 59, 82, 87, 103, 141, 146, 256, 302
Cook Christian School 174, 292, 320, 322
Cook, The Rev. Charles S. 97, 106
Cook, The Rev. Joseph W. 87, 88–89, 93, 97, 106, 111
Coolidge, President Calvin 119
Coolidge, The Rev. Sherman 162, 225, 228–229, 288, 313
Cooper, The Rev. Roland 42
Crazy Horse 104, 105, 107

Creasey, The Rev. S.W. 234
Creek Indians 108, 145, 149, 165, 305–307
Creek, Mary 11–12
Cross, The Rev. William Skala 137, 140
Crow Creek Reservation 83, 89, 92, 93, 98, 315
Curtis, The Rt. Rev. Ivol I. 292, 321
Custer, General George Armstrong 66, 92, 106–107, 109, 120, 152

Dakota Conflict (Dakota and Minnesota Uprising) 54–58, 68, 70, 102, 103, 129
Dakota Leadership Program 140, 278, 279
Davis, Arthur Vining 195, 196
Davis, The Rev. Robert Yarborough 202, 204, 205–206
Davis, The Rev. Solomon 31, 32–33
Dawes Allotment Act 155, 157, 312–313
de las Casas, Bartholomew 4
de Tocqueville, Alexis 146
Deane, Deaconess Elizabeth 263
Delaware Indians 24
Deloria, Ella 114, 315, 318
Deloria, Francis 87, 89, 105, 113–114
Deloria, The Rev. Philip 89, 97, 104, 106, 112–114
—photo 115
Deloria, The Venerable Vine, Sr. 104, 111–114, 121, 124, 195, 288, 314, 315, 323
—photo 314
Deloria, Vine, Jr. 114, 124, 316, 318, 324, 325
—photo 317
DeSmet, Father Pierre Jean 86
Devils Lake Sioux Reservation 71, 81, 129–130, 131, 136–137
DeWall, Carol 144, 295
Dick, Pauline 198
Doctor, Virginia (Ginny) 40–41, 330, 333, 336
Dodge, Chee 180, 189
Dolan, The Rev. James H. 38
Dorsey, The Rev. J. Owen 93, 95
Drake, Sir Francis 2–3
Driggs, Dr. John B. 259–260
Driving Hawk Sneve, Virginia 82, 120, 128
Dudley, Captain Robert 136
Duluth, Missionary District (Diocese) of 70, 75
Duncan, William 251–252, 273–274
Duncombe, Patricia 229–231
Duncombe, The Rev. David S. 230–231

Edwards, The Rev. Edgar Van W. 305
Eliot, John 12, 13, 14, 15
Elizabeth I 1, 301
Elliott, The Venerable Norman x
Emmanuel Church (SD) 116, 284
Enmegahbowh xi, 28, 46–50, 51, 62–64, 76, 77, 133–135, 311
    —photo 49
Episcopal Council of Indian Ministry (ECIM) x, 40, 79, 126,
    176, 231, 247, 292, 295, 298, 307, 309, 328–343
Eskimos 259–260, 278
Estes, The Rev. Clyde 123, 235
Eymer, Sophie (Mrs. Luke C. Walker) 88

Fairfield, The Rev. Andrew H. 143–144
Ffennel, The Rev. R.A.B. 99
Fitzgerald, Kent 118, 317–318, 319
Flandreau Colony 95, 101–102, 105
Floberg, The Rev. John F. 140
Foote, The Rev. Virgil 79, 285, 322, 325
Fort Berthold (ND) 130, 131, 140–142
Fort Defiance (AZ) 173, 177–181, 188–191
Fort Gibson (OK) 147, 150
Fort Hall Mission 231–238
Fort Hunter (NY) 19, 20, 21
Fort Marion (FL) 153
Fort Randall 81
Fort Ridgley 56, 57, 71
Fort Ripley 55, 62
Fort Sill (OK) 153, 156
Fort Snelling 59, 61, 84, 112
Fort Stanwix 24
Fort Sully (ND) 99
Fort Totten (ND) 130, 131, 136–137
Fort Towson (OK) 148
Fort Yates (ND) 138–140
Fort Yukon (AK) 252–253, 264, 267, 268, 281
Four Winds Worship Center (Sacramento) 291
Fowler, The Rev. Jack 197, 209
Fox, The Rev. Duane 136, 142, 333
Frank, The Venerable Anna 277–278, 279, 330
Franklin, Benjamin 18
Fredson, Johnnie 267, 270
Freeman, The Rt. Rev. George W. 149–150, 151
Frensdorff, The Rt. Rev. Wesley 174, 197, 209, 220
Frost, Amelia J. 232, 234
Funsten, The Rt. Rev. James B. 234

Gallagher, The Rev. Carol 277, 336, 341
Garrett, Susan 232, 234
General Theological Seminary (New York City) 31, 125
General Convention, 1835–18th 30
General Convention, 1871–30th 66, 90
General Convention, 1883–34th 131
General Convention, 1892–37th 157
General Convention, 1895–38th 249
General Convention, 1958–59th 315–343
General Convention, 1961–60th 315
General Convention, 1967–62nd 316
General Convention, 1970–63rd 321, 322
General Convention, 1976–65th 173
General Convention, 1985–68th 165
General Convention, 1988–69th 108, 174
General Convention, 1991–70th 9, 108, 125, 175, 221, 231,
     281, 328, 331–333
     —photo 331
General Convention, 1994–71st 340
General Convention, 1997–72nd 71, 173
General Convention Special Program (GCSP) 316–320
George, Ted 293
Gesner, The Rt. Rev. Conrad H. 116, 319
Gilbert, The Rev. James 278
Gilbert, The Rev. Trimble 281, 338
Gilfillan, The Rev. Joseph Alexander 68–69, 74
Given, The Rev. Davis 195, 197
Good Samaritan Mission (CA) 290
Good Shepherd Hospital 182–186
Good Teacher, The Rev. 99
Good Thunder 53, 58, 59, 71–72
Good Thunder, Snana
     (also called Tinkling and Maggie Brass) 54, 59, 71–72
Goodhouse, Carmine 144, 330
Goodhouse, The Rev. Innocent 140, 319, 323, 325
Gordon, The Rt. Rev. William J., Jr. 276–278, 319, 320, 321
Grant Peace Plan 66–67, 84, 87, 102, 107, 136, 178, 225, 233
Gray, Dr. Richard 95–96
Gray, The Rev. Arthur, Jr. 302
Gray, The Rt. Rev. William C. 307
Gregory, The Rev. Henry 147–148
Gull Lake 47–48, 51–52

Haines, The Rt. Rev. Ronald 309
     —photo 334
Hampton, Dr. Carol 325, 332
     —photo 331

Hannafin, The Rev. William 240
Haraughty, Captain John 303–304
Hardy, Margaret 177, 197, 198
  —photo 331
Hare, The Rt. Rev. William Hobart xi, 27, 34–37, 72, 88, 91–96, 98,
  100–101, 102–103, 105, 107, 109, 111, 113, 114, 180, 233, 294
Harper, Walter 267, 270
Harris, The Rt. Rev. George C. 278, 330
Hart, Lawrence 166
Harte, The Rt. Rev. Joseph M. 174, 197
  —photo 175
Hatuay 4
Hawk, Sister Margaret
  —photo 329
Hawley, The Rev. James 278
Hawley, The Rev. Raymond 277
Heagerty, The Rev. W.B., M.D. 75
Hemans, The Rev. Daniel C. 85, 88, 92
Heriot, Thomas 2
Father Herman 250
Hicks, Phyllis 303
Hill, Cornelius 33–34, 38
Hines, The Most Rev. John E. 316, 320
Hinman, The Rev. Samuel Dutton 53–54, 55–56, 59, 61, 72–73,
  81, 83, 84, 85, 87, 95, 96–97, 109, 111
Hobart Church 29, 31, 34
Hobart, The Rt. Rev. John Henry 27, 28, 29, 35, 37, 91
Hogben, The Rev. Joseph 239
Hole-in-the-Day 47, 64
  —photo 63
Hopkins, Pua 341
Hopkins, The Rt. Rev. Harold A., Jr. 143
Howden, The Rt. Rev. Frederick B. 199, 202, 203, 205
Hughes, Gareth 240
Hunkpapa (Sioux) Band 52
Hunt, Eli 341
Huntington, The Rt. Rev. Frederic Dan 39

Indian Rights Association 180, 185, 222
Indian Territory 92, 145–169
Inglis, Charles 21, 23
Ireland, Emily 200–201
Irish, The Rt. Rev. Carolyn Tanner 245, 294
Iroquois 17–18, 19, 22, 23–25, 27, 28, 38–41, 145
Iroquois Confederacy 17, 302

Jackson, Dr. Sheldon 251, 255
Jackson, The Rev. Barnett 167
Jackson, Thomas 325
Jacobus, The Rt. Rev. Russell E. 38
James I 5, 7
James, Reynelda 240–241, 336
Jamestown 5–9
Jamestown Charter 5, 12
Jasmer, The Rev. David 197, 198
Jay, Cornelia 179, 191
Jelinek, The Rt. Rev. James L. 79, 342
Jenkins, Archdeacon J. Rockwood x, 179, 180, 222
Jenkins, The Rt. Rev. Thomas 238
Jim, Katherine 205
Johns, The Rev. Russell, deacon 38
Johnson, Sir William 20–22
Johnson, The Rt. Rev. Frederick Foote 114
Jones, The Rt. Rev. Bob 231
Jones, The Rt. Rev. C.I. 246–247, 295
Jones, The Rt. Rev. Harold S. 111, 118–119, 122, 123, 126, 174, 176, 197, 288, 333, 335
　—photo 334
Jones, The Rt. Rev. Walter H. 116, 118, 324, 325
Joyner, The Rev. Nevill 105, 118
Father Juvenal 250

Kah-O-Sed, The Rev. Edward 69, 76–77
Karuk Indians 290–291
Kemper, The Rt. Rev. Jackson 30–33, 38, 45, 50, 145–148
Kendrick, The Rt. Rev. John Mills 180, 181, 184
Ketchikan, AK 252, 273
Kiker, The Rev. Norman, deacon 168–169
Kinsolving, The Rt. Rev. Arthur Barksdale II 193, 195, 197
Kinsolving, The Rt. Rev. Charles J. III 319
Kiowa Indians 152, 153, 156, 157, 162
Kirkby, The Venerable William W. 252–253
Kirkland, Samuel 22, 27, 41
Knickerbacker, The Rt. Rev. David Buel 133–134
Knowles, The Rev. James, deacon 168
Kolb, The Rev. Quentin 244, 245–246, 293, 330

Ladehoff, The Rt. Rev. Robert 298
LaLiberté, The Rev. Joan 235–236
Le Jau, Francis 10, 11
LeBeau, Hank 291

LeBeau, Sherry 291, 341
Leech Lake (Pillager), Ojibwa Band 49, 65, 69, 77
Lieber, Joan Eskell 219
Liebler, The Rev. H. Baxter 206, 210–220
    —photo 215
Light, The Rt. Rev. A. Heath 304–305
Little Bighorn 104, 107, 152, 337
Little Crow 53, 55, 57, 61, 71, 129
Lloyd, The Rev. B. 304
Loola, The Rev. William, deacon 264, 269–270
    —photo 265
Loud, The Rev. Johnson, Jr. 78
Lower Brulé 89, 92, 93, 98–99, 101
Lower Sioux 51, 71–74, 84
Lower Sioux Agency (also Redwood and Lower Sioux) 52–58, 72
Lutheran Church 256, 289, 296, 298, 320, 336

MacDonald, The Rev. Mark x, 78, 79, 197–198, 222, 297
    —photo 297
Madison, The Rev. Samuel, deacon (Nabicu) 69
Madwaganonint 69
Mankato, MN 58–60, 82
Manteo 1–2
Maori of New Zealand 125, 330–331, 332, 334
Marshall, The Rev. Joseph 106
Martinez, Eloise 174, 208
Mason, The Rev. Yazzie, deacon 174, 208
Massasoit 13
Masuda, The Rt. Rev. George T. 319
Mather, The Rev. Paul 252, 274–275
    —photo 275
Mazakute Memorial Mission (MN) 90, 285
Mazakute, The Rev. Paul 58, 85–86, 87–88, 88–90, 92, 95, 113, 126
    "Bough Church"—photo 89
McAllister, The Rt. Rev. Gerald N. 164, 165
McDonald, Archdeacon Robert 252–253
McDowell, The Rt. Rev. William G. 305
McGhee, Robert 307, 341
McIntosh, Chief Roley 149
McKinley, Howard 192, 193
McKnight, Fayetta 324
McNairy, The Rt. Rev. Philip F. 319
Mdewakanton (Sioux) Band 52, 55, 71, 78, 129
Means, Russell 116, 321
Mendez, The Rev. Richard 231, 245
Meredith, Dr. Howard 323, 324

Merrell, The Rev. Robin 290
Metacom (also called "King Philip") 13–15
Methodist Church 47, 145, 233–234, 246, 252, 256, 295, 336
Metlakatla 251–252, 273
Midewiwin (Grand Medicine) 47, 64, 69, 70
Mille Lacs (Ojibwa) Band 62, 65
Minneconjou (Sioux) Band 52, 109
Minnesota Committee on Indian Work (MCIW) 69, 79
Mission Hill Indian Church (OK) 168
Mitchell, The Rt. Rev. Walter 189, 193
Mohawk Indians 17, 18–20, 21, 22, 24–26, 28, 40, 145, 147, 148, 336
Monacan Indians 301, 302–305
Montileaux, The Rev. Charles 122
Montileaux, The Rev. Cheryl, deacon 122
Moore, Thoroughgood 18
Moravian 148, 256
Mormons 234
Morrison, The Rt. Rev. James Dow 70
Moulton, The Rt. Rev. Arthur W. 206, 242, 244
Mount Denali 267
Mountain, The Rev. Moses 137, 140, 142
Mountains and Desert Regional Indian Ministries 224–225, 231,
        232, 245, 246
Myrick, Andrew 52, 57, 72

Nakata, The Very Rev. Russell 288
Napai-Dudley, Linda 330
Nashotah 31
Nashotah House 31, 33, 34, 210, 220
Nathaniel, The Rev. Mary, deacon 279
National Committee on Indian Work (NCIW) 77, 79, 224, 236, 279,
        309, 316, 318–320, 321, 322, 323, 324–325, 326, 328
        —photo 326
National Native Youth Festival 337
Native American Task Force (Seattle) 292–293
Native American Theological Association 322
Nauska, The Rev. Norman 278, 325
Navajo Culture 171–172
Navajoland Area Mission 173–179, 209, 332
Ninham, Joycelyn 319
Niobrara Convocation 88, 102, 103, 108, 119–127
        —photo 121
Niobrara Cross 119
Niobrara Jurisdiction 27, 48, 66, 81–128
Noisy Hawk, The Rev. Lyle 79
Norton, The Rev. Jerry, deacon 277

Oakerhater Evangelism Team 280–282
Oakerhater, The Rev. David Pendleton, deacon xi, 39, 68, 152–156, 159, 162–163, 165, 166–168, 237
—photo 153
Oberly, Frank 341
Ogilby, The Rt. Rev. Lyman C. 116
Oglala (Sioux) Band 52
Ojibwa Indians 45–50, 62–64, 68–71, 74, 81
Oklahoma Committee on Indian Work 164–166, 167
Oklahoma Consultations 326, 328
Oneida 30–38
Oneida brass band
—photo 36
Oneida Indians 17, 20, 22, 27–29, 92
Onondaga Indians 18, 22, 24, 38–40
Osage Indians 95, 167, 197
Otey, The Rt. Rev. James H. 148–149, 151
Owen, Kenneth 325

Paiute Indians 223, 238–242
Paiute Mission 238–242
Parker, The Rev. Octavius 256
Parsons, Mary 279
Partners in Mission, 1993 339
Paths Crossing Gathering 306, 336
Pawnee Indians 158, 162, 165
Pendleton, Mrs. George 154
Pendleton, Senator George 154
Peter, The Rev. Titus 277, 319
Peters, Mattie C. 199–201
Peters, The Rev. Helen, deacon 277
Peterson, Dr. Helen L. 123, 288, 296, 324, 325, 327
—photo 297
Pierce, The Rev. George P. 86, 117, 288
Pierce, The Rt. Rev. Henry Miles 156
Pine Ridge (Oglala Sioux) Reservation 83, 105–106, 109–110, 112, 118, 119, 122, 124, 323, 328
Pitchlynn, Peter 149
Plummer, The Rt. Rev. Steven T. 173–177, 197, 208, 219, 220, 330, 335
—photo 175, 334
Pocahontas 6–7, 301
Point Hope Mission (AK) 259–260, 262, 276
Polk, The Rt. Rev. Leonidas 148
Ponca Indians 67, 86, 92, 93, 95–96, 119
Pontious, The Rev. Wayne 220
Porter, The Rev. Boone 209

Potawatomi Indians 168–169
Potter, The Rt. Rev. Alonzo 91
Powell, The Rev. Peter J. 286
Powell, The Rt. Rev. Chilton 319
Powless, The Rev. Edmund, deacon 38
Prairie Island Sioux Community (Minnesota) 73–74, 78
    Chapel of the Messiah—photo 75
Pratt, Richard H. 153, 154
Presbyterian Church 53, 95, 102, 132, 145, 146, 149, 178–179,
    233, 251, 256, 296, 302
Presiding Bishop's Fund for World Relief 246, 295
Prettyfeather, Martin (renamed Martin See-Walker) 139, 140, 142
Prettyflute, Charles 140
Prevost, The Rev. Jules 260–261
Province VIII Indian Commission 236, 296, 327
Putnam, The Rt. Rev. Frederick W. 174, 208–209, 325

Quakers 67, 168–169
Queen Anne 25

Raleigh, Sir Walter 1–2
Randall, The Rt. Rev. George 225
Red Cloud 83, 93, 105–106
Red Elk, The Rev. Marvin 286
Red Hail 139
Red Lake (Ojibwa) Reservation 69, 77, 198
Red Shirt, Clyde 324
Reedy, The Rev. James J.W. 159
Rees, The Rev. William D. 137
Reifel, Dr. Ben 123, 318
religious freedom 332, 338
Renville, The Rev. Victor 103
Rice, The Rev. Randolf 290
Riggs, Francis 319
Riggs, Stephen Return 59
Rising Sun xi, 131, 132
    —photo 135
Roanoke 1, 2
Roberts, The Rev. John 225, 226–229
Roberts, The Rt. Rev. W. Blair 115, 283
Robertson, The Rev. John 79, 105, 341
Robertson, The Rt. Rev. Creighton Leland 126–127, 336
Robertson, Thomas A. 58
Robinson, Rose 309, 333
Rogers, The Rev. Jean 240
Rolin, Buford 306

Roman Catholic 4, 7, 18, 21, 28, 64, 87, 95, 103, 132, 137, 141, 157–158, 233, 246, 256

Rosebud Reservation (Sioux) 83, 93, 100–101, 122, 125

Rosenthal, Betty Clark 315–316, 318

Ross, The Rev. Amos 61, 106, 111–112

Ross, The Rev. George 78

Rouillard, The Rev. John 112

Roulliard, The Rev. Levi M. 116, 284–285

Roulliard, The Rev. Thomas 74

Rowe, The Rt. Rev. Peter Trimble 73, 114, 249, 252, 260, 261–264, 266, 267, 268, 273–274, 275, 281
  —photo 262, 275

Roy, Robert 79

Russian Orthodox 250–251, 256

Sabine, Deaconess Bertha 257, 258

Sacajawea 142, 228

Sagayeathquapiethtow 19

St. Andrew's (Pine Ridge Reservation) 106

St. Anna's (Alabama) 301, 305–307

St. Anne's (Navajoland) 189, 193

St. Antipas 69

St. Augustine's (Chicago) 286
  —photo 287

St. Christopher's (Navajoland) 173, 206, 210–213, 219, 220
  —photo 215

St. Clair, The Rev. George Whipple 72

St. Clair, The Rev. Henry Whipple 72, 73, 74

St. Columba's (White Earth Reservation) 48, 64, 68–69

St. Cornelia's (Lower Sioux, Minnesota) 72–73

St. David's (Wind River) 224, 231

St. Elizabeth's (Alaska) 252, 274, 276

St. Elizabeth's (Standing Rock) 104

St. Elizabeth's (Uintah Reservation, Utah) 243, 244–245

St. Francis of Assisi (NC) 301

St. Gabriel's (Standing Rock, ND) 139

St. James' (Sisseton-Wahpeton Reservation) 103

St. James' (Standing Rock, ND) 138, 140

St. James' (Tanana, AK) 260–261

St. John the Baptist (Sisseton-Whapeton) 103

St. John's (Minnesota) 53–54, 72

St. John's (Eagle, AK) 265

St. John's in the Wilderness Cathedral (Denver) 287–289

St. Luke's (Sisseton-Wapeton Reservation) 103, 127

St. Luke's (Standing Rock, ND) 138

St. Luke's-in-the-Desert (Navajoland) 203–204

St. Mark's (Navajoland) 173, 189, 194
St. Mark's Mission (AK) 265, 267, 271, 272–273, 282
St. Mary's (Pyramid Lake Paiutes) 238–242
St. Mary's (Sisseton-Wahpeton Reservation) 102–103
St. Mary's Chapel (Flandreau) 102
St. Mary's School for Girls 111
St. Mary's-of-the-Moonlight (Navajoland) 218, 219, 220
St. Matthew's (Beaver, AK) 281
St. Matthew's (Rapid City, SD) 284–285
St. Matthew's (White Swan, Yankton Reservation) 88
St. Michael and All Angels (Portland) 297
St. Michael's (Wind River) 224, 229–231
St. Patrick's (Washington, DC) 245, 301, 309, 333
St. Paul's (Fort Berthold, ND) 140–142
St. Paul's (IA) 296
St. Paul's (SW Virginia) 301
St. Paul's School (Yankton Reservation) 97
St. Peter, the Aleut 250
St. Philip's (CA) 291
St. Regis Reservation 25, 28, 30
St. Stephen's (AK) 264
St. Sylvan's (Turtle Mountain, ND) 136
St. Thomas' (Fort Totten, ND) 137
St. Thomas Church, New York City 102
Salisbury, Susan 53
Salmon, The Rev. David 252, 253, 277
Salt, The Rev. Wellington Jefferson, deacon 134–136
Samuelson, The Rev. Clifford 315–316
San Jose Declaration 339–340
San Juan Bautista (Navajoland) 206, 218–219, 220
San Juan Mission (Navajoland) 173, 174, 183, 199–209
Sanborn, Alan 325
Sand Creek Massacre 152
Sanford, The Rev. David 159
Santee (Sioux) Indians 52, 81, 82–84, 85–90, 101, 112, 129, 130
Santee Reservation 71, 83–85, 88, 89–90, 92, 95, 97, 100, 101,
    111, 118, 119
Schmasow, Sarah 246
Schuyler, Fanny 179
Seabury-Western Theological Seminary 49, 73, 76, 77, 106, 118,
    125, 169, 229, 327
Secker, The Most Rev. Thomas 20–21
self-determination 311–312, 316–318, 339, 341–343
Selwyn, The Rev. William T. 97, 106
Seminole Indians 145, 162
Seminole Mission (Florida) 307–308

Seneca Indians 9, 18, 22, 38–39, 41–42, 147–148
Shakopee 53, 55
Shawnee Indians 147, 168
Sherrill, The Most Rev. Henry Knox 314
shin-dee 182, 217, 222
Shoshone Indians 223, 224, 225–228, 231, 233
Shoshone-Bannock Indians 67, 93, 233, 235, 237
Sibley, General Henry 57–58, 61, 71, 129
Silas, The Rev. Berkman 277
Silas, The Rev. Dewey 289
Sim, The Rev. Vincent C. 253–254
Sioux Indians 45–46, 81
Sioux Land Cessions
     —map 94
Sioux social standards (traditional) 88
Sisseton-Wahpeton (Lake Traverse Sioux) Band 105, 126
Sisseton-Wahpeton Reservation 95, 102–103, 124, 125
Sitka, AK 249, 250, 256, 261
Sitting Bull 83, 95, 103, 104, 107, 132
Six Nations Reserve 26, 40
Smith, The Rev. Fred W. 64, 76
Smith, The Rev. Michael 78
Smith, The Rev. Frederick, deacon (Kadawabide) 69
Smith, The Rev. George A. 69, 76–77, 166, 311, 316, 319, 324
Smith, The Rev. Michael 168
Society for the Propagation of the Gospel (SPG) 8, 10, 11, 15,
     16, 18–19, 20, 21, 26, 39, 145, 312
Spears, The Rev. Melanie 79, 286
Spotted Tail 83, 100–101, 108, 109
Standing Bear, Luther 96
Standing Rock Reservation (Sioux) 83, 95, 103–104, 107, 114,
     125, 131, 132, 138–140
Stevens Village, AK 272, 282
Stiles, Ella 232, 234
Stiteler, Lizzie (Mrs. William Joshua Cleveland) 88, 101
Stuart, John 22, 23, 24
Stuck, Archdeacon Hudson 254, 261, 266–268, 270, 280, 313
     —photo 255
Sturges, Helen 211, 216, 219
Sumner, The Rev. George 197
Sun Dance 154, 162, 229
Suttcliffe, The Rev. David 198
Swan, The Rev. Clinton 277
Swan, The Rev. Milton 260, 277
Sweet Briar College 303
Swift, The Rev. Henry 93, 99
Swimmer, Ross 325

Talbot, The Rt. Rev. Joseph Cruikshank 85
Tanana, AK 253, 260–261, 267, 270, 272, 282
Taopi 53, 56–57, 71
Taopi, The Rev. Christian, deacon 85, 92
Taylor, Marian 239
Tekakwitha, Kateri 18
Termination Act 313
Thackara, Eliza 181–185, 188, 189, 222
Thayendanegea 19. *See* Brant, Joseph
Thomas, Tay 268, 277
Thomas, The Rt. Rev. Nathaniel S. 229
Thorne, Ethel 192
Thornton, The Rt. Rev. John 237
    —photo 237
Thunder Child Youth Home 247, 295
Thurston, The Rt. Rev. Theodore P.
    —photo front cover
Titus, Bessie 333
Titus, The Rev. David 296
Titus, The Rev. Luke 220, 277
Tlingit Indians 278
Trail of Tears 146
Treaty of Fort Laramie 83, 100, 105, 107, 108
Treaty of Fort Stanwix 24
Treaty of Medicine Lodge 159
Trelease, The Rt. Rev. Richard M., Jr. 207, 208
Trimble, The Rev. Gilbert 277
Trinity Church (New York City) 20, 21, 23
Tritt, The Rev. Albert, deacon 265, 269
Tritt, The Rev. Isaac 277
Tritt, The Rev. Paul 277
Tsimshian Indians 251–252, 273–276
Turgeon, Beulah 330
Turnbull, Jane 205
Turner, The Rev. Doyle 69, 78, 79
Turtle Mountain Chippewa 131, 132–136
Tuzroyluck, The Rev. Seymour, Sr. 278
Two Bulls, The Rev. Robert 245, 285
Two Hawk, The Rev. Webster 319, 325

United Thank Offering (UTO) 188, 196, 201, 202, 233, 244,
    246, 249, 257–259, 277, 285, 296, 305, 313, 321
United Theological Seminary 79
Urban Ministry 115–116, 144, 245–246, 283–299, 337
    —chart 299

Utah Mission 242–246
Ute Indians 223, 238, 242–247

Vallely, The Rev. Lillian, deacon 235, 236–237
     —photo 237
Vancouver School of Theology 126, 144, 291, 336
Venianimof, Bishop Ivan 250
Vercoe, The Rt. Rev. Whakahuihui 125, 332
VerStraten, The Rev. Stan 231, 240

Wabasha 51, 53, 55, 58, 71, 88
Wadleigh, George H. 177, 179–180, 198
Wahpehan, The Rev. Philip Johnson, deacon 85, 88, 92
Wahpeton and Sisseton (Lake Traverse Sioux) bands 52, 57, 61
Walker, The Rev. Luke C. 85, 88, 89, 92, 99, 105, 112
Walker, The Rt. Rev. John Thomas 166
Walker, The Rt. Rev. William D. 131–132, 134–135
Wanchese 1
Wantland, The Rt. Rev. William C. 124, 166, 167, 176, 292, 325, 333, 335
     —photo 334
Warner, The Rt. Rev. Vincent W., Jr. 293
Washita Village Massacre 152
Watson, The Rt. Rev. Richard S. 220
Wauneka, Rose 186–187, 190
Welsh, Herbert 66
Welsh, The Rev. Herbert H. 140, 142
Welsh, William 66, 67, 87, 88, 93, 95, 97, 98, 100, 178–179
West, Emily 53, 56, 84
Westchester County Woman's Auxiliary 179–181, 189, 222
Weston, Chief David 101–102
Wheelock, Eleazar 21, 22, 26
Whipple, The Rt. Rev. Henry Benjamin xi, 50–52, 59, 60–61, 62, 65–
     68, 77–78, 84, 91, 96, 102, 109, 129, 133, 153–154, 229
     —photo 60
Whirlwind 156
Whirlwind Mission
     —photo 161
Whirlwind Mission (OK) 160, 167
Whirlwind School 159, 162
White Earth Reservation 64, 77, 133
White Horse (Tsiithlagai) 216–217
White, The Rt. Rev. Roger 289
White Wolf Branham, George 304
Wicks, The Rev. John Barrett 152, 154, 155–156
Wilcox, Lena D. 203, 204

William and Mary College 8, 9, 10
Williams, The Rev. Eleazar 26–30
—photo 27
Williamson, John P. 59, 82, 87
Wilson, Dick 117
Wind River Reservation 197, 224–231
Winnebago Indians 54, 81
Winter Talk Gatherings 311, 330, 341–342
Wolfrum, The Rt. Rev. William 174
Worcester, The Rev. Samuel 146
Wounded Knee 106, 109–110, 294, 328
—photo 110
Wounded Knee Occupation 116–117, 323–324
Wright, Sherman 325
Wright, The Rev. Alfred 149

Yankton (Sioux) Band 52, 83, 90, 93, 105, 129
Yankton Reservation 85–90, 92, 97, 102, 111, 113, 114
Yanktonais (Sioux) Band 52, 83, 93, 98, 129
Yaqui Indians 290
Yellow Bear, Paul 141–142
Young, The Rev. H. St. George 97

Zabriskie, The Rt. Rev. Stewart 238, 240, 336
Zotom, The Rev. Paul, deacon 152, 155, 156